W9-CLW-169

Equity and Excellence in Education

Routledge Research in Education

For a full list of titles in this series please visit www.routledge.com

Equity and Excellence in Education

in Education

Towards Maximal Learning
Opportunities for All Students

**Edited by
Kris Van den Branden,
Piet Van Avermaet, and
Mieke Van Houtte**

Routledge
Taylor & Francis Group
New York   London

First published 2011
by Routledge
270 Madison Avenue, New York, NY 10016

Simultaneously published in the UK
by Routledge
2 Park Square, Milton Park, Abingdon, Oxon OX14 4RN

Routledge is an imprint of the Taylor & Francis Group, an informa business

© 2011 Taylor & Francis

The right of Kris Van den Branden, Piet Van Avermaet, and Mieke Van Houtte to be identified as the authors of the editorial material, and of the authors for their individual chapters, has been asserted by them in accordance with sections 77 and 78 of the Copyright, Designs and Patents Act 1988.

Typeset in Sabon by IBT Global.
Printed and bound in the United States of America on acid-free paper by IBT Global.

Library of Congress Cataloging-in-Publication Data

Equity and excellence in education : towards maximal learning opportunities for all
    students / edited by Kris Van den Branden, Piet Van Avermaet and Mieke Van Houtte.
       p. cm. — (Routledge research in education ; 50)
    Includes bibliographical references and index.
    1. Educational equalization—Cross-cultural studies.   I. Branden, Kris van den.
II. Avermaet, Piet van.   III. Houtte, Mieke van.
    LC213.E676 2011
    379.2'6—dc22
    2010030486

ISBN13: 978-0-415-88501-0 (hbk)
ISBN13: 978-0-203-83233-2 (ebk)

Contents

Figures

Tables

1 Promoting Equity and Excellence in Education

An Overview

Piet Van Avermaet, Mieke Van Houtte, and Kris Van den Branden

INTRODUCTION

In different parts of the world, equity and excellence in education is a major issue of concern. Spurred by national studies of school effectiveness and international comparative studies on young students' development of key skills (such as reading comprehension skills, mathematical and science competencies), educational policies in many countries have tried to combine a concern for equity in education (providing high-quality education and learning opportunities for students of different backgrounds) with a striving for excellence (stimulating outstanding performance and the development of specialist skills). This volume aims to compile a wide range of research-based contributions, providing a state of the art of what we know about this topic today. One of the key questions the various contributions in this volume aim to answer is whether the pursuit of educational excellence is fully compatible with the aim of organizing an equitable educational system.

In this introduction, we will set the scene, by providing the reader with historical background on research about equity and excellence in education and presenting an overview of the ways in which the key concepts related to this issue have been approached and made operational in policy documents and research studies. In doing so, we aim to give the reader a clear picture of the scope and contents of the various chapters in this volume: Rather than offering a summary of the different chapters in a separate section, we have chosen to integrate our references to the chapters of the book into our outline of the major theme of this book. We will conclude this chapter with a range of recommendations that aim to inspire educational policy makers who are dedicated to stimulating equity and excellence and researchers to carry out quantitative and qualitative studies into this intricate matter. Our recommendations will be based largely on the contributions of the different authors who wrote a chapter in this book.

SITUATING EQUITY AND EXCELLENCE IN EDUCATION

On December 10, 1948, the General Assembly of the United Nations adopted and proclaimed the Universal Declaration of Human Rights. Article 26 of this declaration focuses on individuals' right to education:

Article 26

1. Everyone has the right to education. Education shall be free, at least in the elementary and fundamental stages. Elementary education shall be compulsory. Technical and professional education shall be made generally available and higher education shall be equally accessible to all on the basis of merit.
2. Education shall be directed to the full development of the human personality and to the strengthening of respect for human rights and fundamental freedoms. It shall promote understanding, tolerance and friendship among all nations, racial or religious groups, and shall further the activities of the United Nations for the maintenance of peace.
3. Parents have a prior right to choose the kind of education that shall be given to their children.

The previously mentioned headings 1 and 3 refer to each individual's right to have free *access to education* in the elementary and fundamental stages and for parents to choose the kind of education that their children will follow. Around the time it was issued, the UN document gave expression to an unprecedented educational ambition that had been taken up in the preceding years by many countries in the world. For many centuries before, access to education had been the exclusive right of particular (privileged) groups of children, while other groups such as girls, minorities, and the children of laborers had been systematically excluded from the educational system. In numerous policy documents that have been issued at a national and international scale since then, universal access to education has been connected with the battle against poverty, discrimination, sickness, economic and social strife, discrimination, and racism. Access to education (at the very least to primary education) is now generally believed to raise an individual's chances to build a good life, find a suitable job, move upward on the social ladder, and be well-prepared for modern-day globalized information and communication society. By providing chances to everybody to learn to read and write, process information, and develop key skills in science, mathematics, and complex problem-solving, education is believed to function as a springboard for human beings, irrespective of how wealthy, educated, or powerful their parents are. By strengthening students' respect for human rights and fundamental freedoms, and by promoting understanding, tolerance, and friendship, education is believed to contribute to a better and more peaceful world.

But does education really work for all? Can education cater to the learning needs of all students, regardless of the mother tongue they speak and the socioeconomic environment in which they have grown up? Has the massification of education led to full democratization as far as the acquisition of knowledge and skills are concerned? What have been the consequences of opening up education to all individuals and all layers of society in terms of (a) the ultimate level of attainment that students reach, and (b) the differences between individual students and student groups in academic achievement? To what extent is the ambition to create powerful education for all and offering all students, irrespective of their background, maximal chances to develop a broad range of competencies truly compatible with the ambition to allow certain students (or student groups) the opportunity to acquire excellence in a limited range of competencies?

FROM EQUAL ACCESS TO EQUAL OUTPUT
AND EQUAL OPPORTUNITIES

The consolidation of equal access to education for all in the post-war period, which was accompanied by a public discourse emphasizing the emancipation of the whole population, has given rise to a rich vein of social and educational research. From the 1960s onward, research reports started showing that ensuring a mere right of access to education for all did not automatically result in the enhancement of social and racial equality. A long series of studies (e.g., Coleman et al., 1966, and Lucas, 2001, for the United States; Garnier & Hout, 1976, for France; Kerckhoff, 1975, and Willis, 1977, for the United Kingdom; Pelleriaux, 2001, and Tan, 1998, for Belgium) have persistently shown that socially disadvantaged groups of pupils, who had been denied access to education in earlier ages, are still granted access to the academic strands of secondary education, to higher education, and to highly achieving, prestigious schools to a far lesser extent than the children of highly educated parents.

This mechanism appears to be strongly linked with inequity at the level of educational output: Socially disadvantaged groups of pupils show systematically lower levels of performance in key disciplines in compulsory education, lower degrees of success in higher education, and lower results in terms of final degree. They have been shown to develop key skills of elementary education (such as a basic academic proficiency in the main medium of instruction and basic mathematical skills) to a considerably lesser extent than the children of parents who were highly successful in education themselves. Forty years after the publication of the Coleman report (Coleman et al., 1966), Gamoran and Long (2006) concluded that (a) schools in the United States are still highly segregated along racial and ethnic lines, and (b) that there are still major achievement gaps between Black and White pupils and between pupils of low and high socioeconomic status (SES). In many other countries alike, pupils coming from a socially advantaged background still have the best chances to be successful in education, whereas pupils from a socially disadvantaged background run a serious risk of not, or insufficiently, developing the competencies that are necessary to succeed in the academic strands of secondary education and in higher education and to succeed and further develop in life after compulsory schooling.

In the Coleman report (Coleman et al., 1966), the inequities in terms of access and academic output were linked with the notion of *equal opportunity*, which was defined in terms of the consequences of schooling for individuals with equal backgrounds and abilities.

> In this definition, equality of educational opportunity is equality of results, given the same individual input. (p. 14).

By controlling for family background, studies into equality of educational opportunity investigate which particular school and schooling conditions influence achievement. So, by controlling for individual inputs, these studies assess equality of results among students with similar backgrounds.

The notion of equality of educational opportunity may even be taken one step further, referring to the equality of results for pupils with differing backgrounds:

> In this definition, equality of educational opportunity is equality of results given *different* individual inputs. The most striking example of inequality here would be children from households in which a language other than English, such as Spanish or Navaho, is spoken. Other examples would be low-achieving children from homes in which there is a poverty of verbal expression or an absence of experiences which lead to conceptual facilities. (Coleman et al., 1966, p. 14)

According to some, this would correspond to the ideal of a truly meritocratic society: the idea that everyone, irrespective of class, race or gender, should have an equal chance to perform well in school and ultimately to obtain the higher rewarded positions in society (Gewirtz & Cribb, 2009). Whether they do or not then primarily depends upon the students' effort, persistence, and initiative (variables that the students themselves can influence) rather than on static background variables such as gender, the socioeconomic status of their parents, their mother tongue, or their cultural or religious background. At first sight, such an educational system would provide greater opportunities for able and hard-working children from lower-status families to move up, while at the same time requiring children from higher-status families to prove themselves in school if they want to maintain their benefits (and thus for education to break down the intergenerational reproduction of social divide) (Brint, 2006).

However, to ascertain whether an educational system lives up to this ideal (if, at least, this should be considered an ideal situation), researchers would need to define first what kind of output the system should produce: What competencies should these hard-working students develop, and what measures would be used to assess the degree of success and the quantity/quality of educational output?

DEFINING OUTPUT

The initial objectives of mass schooling mainly focused on the development of basic skills such as literacy and calculation skills, supporting morality, and creating loyal citizens (Brint, 2006). Today, in every industrialized society, schools assume a central position in the process of sorting and allocating people to appropriate jobs (Brint, 2006; Parsons, 1959). Obtaining high educational degrees has become a crucial condition for people to find good jobs in society; one of the major goals of mass education is to award credentials that will help people to find work and to increase the number of high-skilled workers modern-day economies appear to be in demand of. Educational credentials have come to play the stratifying role that family resources and family reputation once played: Educational attainment is regarded as a more important determinant of an individual's chances of building up a good life than family background (Brint, 2006). Conversely, the economic needs of today's society strongly dictate what attainment goals will be crucial in the educational curriculum. A fine example in this respect is provided by the Lisbon Strategy of the European Union, aiming to make the EU "the most competitive and dynamic knowledge-based economy in the world capable of sustainable economic growth with more and better jobs and greater social cohesion." Raising the quality of education is regarded as one of the essential strategies in this respect. The benchmarks to be achieved by 2020 are the following:

- At least 95% of children between the age of 4 and the age for starting compulsory primary education should participate in early childhood education.
- The share of 15-year-olds with insufficient abilities in reading, mathematics, and science should be less than 15%.
- The share of early leavers from education and training should be less than 10%.
- The share of 30- to 34-year-olds with tertiary educational attainment should be at least 40%.
- An average of at least 15 % of adults (age group 25–64) should participate in lifelong learning.

The example shows that educational systems, on the one hand, have to make sure that virtually every child participates in education from a very early age on and develops core abilities by the age of 15 ("reading, mathematics, and science"), while at the same time a high percentage of the population should acquire excellence in specialist areas (as denoted by the aspired high levels of participation in tertiary education). In this way, the almost mythic fear that governmental policies aiming to enhance equity in education threaten to undermine the overall quality level of the educational system, and the chances of the happy few to obtain levels of excellence in particular, has been countered during the past 15 years—at least in policy documents—with an aspiration to obtain excellence for the many, rather than for the happy few.

The Power of Tests

In quite a number of countries around the world, this ambition has given rise to educational policies that involve a tighter governmental grip on quality control, systematic procedures of standard setting, a range of measures allowing for (or stimulating) competition between schools, and the introduction of high-stakes testing. "Accountability" has become the new buzzword in educational policy making: Using the results of standardized tests as the ultimate benchmark and making school results public, governments aim to monitor the overall level of excellence of the public school system by rewarding well-performing schools and sanctioning failure in low-performing schools (Anagnostopoulos, 2005; Au, 2008; Linn, 2000). In a similar vein, governments (and the media) pay considerable attention to the results of international comparisons of students' achievement (e.g., the Programme for International Student Assessment [PISA] of the Organisation for Economic Co-operation and Development [OECD]). In higher education this evolution is accompanied by a process of international quality assurance and accreditation.

The Problem with Tests

Over the past decades, however, high-stakes, standardized tests (and the accountability logic they are embedded in) have met with fierce criticism. Among others, concerns have been raised about their potentially negative impact on equity in education. For one, because high-stakes tests typically involve the assessment of cognitive skills that are relatively easy to measure and score, they may privilege particular groups of students who are more talented or who have had better chances to develop these particular competencies, either at school or outside (for instance, by being intensively supported by their highly educated parents to score well on the tests) (Au, 2008; Linn, 2000). In addition, the use of standardized tests may give rise to a narrowing of the curriculum, as teachers will be tempted to teach to the test at the expense of their efforts to adapt lesson content to student learning needs and interests (Anagnostopoulos, 2005). Some competencies (that are easily tested) may gain greater importance, whereas others that are less suitable for standardized testing (such as high-level problem-solving or competencies related to the development of human personality as requested in the previously mentioned UN declaration) may lose ground. As a result, the limited range of key competencies that can easily be tested is likely to be acknowledged as the truly legitimate knowledge, urging teachers to explicitly focus on this knowledge in teacher-centered and lecture-based pedagogies (Au, 2008; Hilliard, 2000; Posner, 2004).

At the student level, centralized, standardized testing may have a profound impact on individual school careers. Test results may be used to decide which students will be allowed to enroll in higher education. On the basis of these tests, students may be ranked and classified, and segregated into different tracks, which may not be optimally adapted to the students' full potential, learning needs, and personal interests. As Zimmer, Ikeda, and Lüdemann show on the basis of their analysis of the PISA 2006 data (see Chapter 3, this volume), early institutional differentiation (tracking) often has a negative impact on the equity of educational systems. In many countries with early tracking systems, low-SES students and ethnic minority students are overrepresented in the technical and vocational strands of secondary education, which offer fewer perspectives to enrollment in higher education than the academic strands (Au, 2008; Hilliard, 2000). In these strands, low-SES students run a high risk of not developing crucial competencies related to societal participation and lifelong learning, to become demotivated, and to ultimately leave the school system without any qualifications. In Chapter 4, this volume, Van Houtte elaborates on why this would be the case. For one, in the "lower tracks" of early tracking systems, teacher expectations tend to be relatively low with regard to student development: The focus of educational activities is more likely to be concerned with behavior control rather than with academic skills and with mechanistic drilling of subskills and easy content rather than with stimulating complex problem-solving skills. In Chapter 6, this volume, Stevens adds that teachers' views on how to cope with ethnic minority students in lower tracks may be strongly influenced by the public discourse and educational policy of the nation-state the teachers belong to. Comparing teachers in the United Kingdom (with its public accountability system) and Flanders (with its early tracking system in secondary education but without centralized testing), Stevens found that Flemish teachers had more negative views and less knowledge of Turkish minority students and blamed these students for underachieving in education. Lowering their expectations with regard to the students' academic development, the teachers were inclined to allocate scarce educational resources (such as attention and interactional support) to those students they perceived as still being motivated to behave and do well in school. In contrast, teachers in the English case-study school appeared to have more knowledge and positive views of Turkish minority students and held the educational system responsible for their underachievement. They appeared to devise strategies of "educational triage" through which scarce educational resources were targeted to those students perceived as still likely to achieve the benchmark of success imposed by the educational system.

In sum, accountability systems, involving high-stakes testing and high-stakes decision-making with regard to students' educational careers, may, in the end, have a negative impact on the overall quality of the educational system and more particularly on the extent to which all students, irrespective of their background, are offered maximal learning opportunities. As illustrated earlier, there are clear indications that the evaluation by means of centrally administered, standardized tests tends to focus more on the ranking of schools on the one hand, and the selection and allocation of students, their grade level promotion, and graduation on the other hand (Au, 2008), rather than being optimally used to raise the quality of education in terms of excellence and equity.

In this respect, it is quite significant that the Finnish educational system, which appears to be very successful in reconciling excellence with equity (see Linnakylä, Välijärvi, & Arffman, Chapter 9, this volume), does not follow the international accountability trend (involving high-stakes, centralized testing), but rather prefers to give a large degree of autonomy to the local school level and the individual teacher. In a similar line of reasoning, Duru-Bellat and Mingat (in Chapter 2, this volume) emphasize that equity in education should not be automatically equated with the fact that all students, irrespective of their social background or gender, should develop the very same competencies in compulsory education or should obtain the same scores on the very same standardized measurement (equality of output). They write:

> Since the student body is heterogeneous from an academic point of view, each pupil should be stimulated to make the most of his or her capacities: Ultimately, the excellence of the whole system is assessed by evaluating its capacity to cope with this diversity.

In this perspective, educational output is not a fixed student-proof variable, but rather a variable that is sensitive to the obvious fact that different students have different talents, motivations, and ambitions. The output that should be strived for is to make every student excel according to his or her capacities and so to offer every student maximal chances to fully develop their personal potential. In this view, "equality of output" is replaced with "differential excellence." This is not to say, however, that the range of competencies that individual students should be able to develop cannot contain a *common core* that they share with all other, or certain other, groups of students. There might be, for instance, a set of competencies that each single student, irrespective of their personal ambitions and talents, should be able to develop (e.g., a certain level of literacy skills necessary to participate to modern-day information and communication society, or attitudes and competencies related to coping with diversity and living together in a peaceful world, as mentioned in the UN declaration, article 26 (2)). But besides this common core, a more *differentiated core* should also be identified, linking up with the ambitions of smaller groups of students after leaving compulsory education, whether geared toward participation in specific programs in higher education or participation in certain segments of the labor market or society. To establish the quality of educational systems, then, assessment programs would need to contain appropriate methods and techniques to measure whether students have reached the attainment targets connected to both the common core and the more differentiated core. In other words, assessing the "differential excellence" of educational systems requires assessment programs that allow for a certain degree of differentiation among different groups of students (at the level of output) and for an assessment of the extent to which the educational systems created optimal opportunities to students to follow a trajectory suited to their personal needs and capabilities (at the process level). In this line of reasoning, the excellence of educational systems becomes dependent on its actual level of equity: Educational systems that only cater for the learning needs of a minor proportion of the student population (the 10% most excellent students) can hardly be called excellent (see Chapter 2, this volume).

EXPLAINING UNDERACHIEVEMENT

Even if systems of early tracking and public accountability have been found to increase the inequity of educational systems, they do not provide a full explanation of why low-SES and language minority students are systematically underachieving in so many countries around the world (Hallinan, 2002) and why the "automatic redistribution" at the end of every generation promised by the meritocratic believers has not been realized so far. The empirical evidence feeds the nagging impression that static background variables that are, ultimately, beyond children's control have an almost deterministic impact on the extent to which children will be able to profit from the time they spend in the compulsory educational system. Various sociological theories and models have been proposed to explain this phenomenon. Social reproduction theorists, such as Bowles and Gintis (1976) or Willis (1977), contend that those already advantaged by the social order are precisely the ones who are most likely to be selected and privileged in the next generation under the guise of meritocracy (Brint, 2006). A wide range of factors other than academic merit appear to determine the final educational and occupational attainment to sustain a theory of meritocracy (Brint, 2006); many of these variables are linked with the fact that educational systems (in terms of the language that is used as a medium of instruction, the curriculum choices that are made, the teachers' expectations, the supportive role parents are expected to take up, etc.) are suited to the learning needs of privileged children, far more than to those of socially deprived children.

Ultimately, the situation of persistent underachievers in compulsory education appears to be characterized by a *mismatch* between their interests, ambitions, talents, background, and capacities on the one hand and various features of the educational environment (teachers' style and expectations, the curriculum, the school context and culture) on the other hand. In this respect, Bourdieu (1986) has claimed that individuals enter the educational system with different levels of cultural capital and cultural know-how, based on their social backgrounds. To Bourdieu, it is obvious that the attitudes, features, and behaviors of working-class students are incongruent with the middle-class attitudes, features, and behaviors characterizing educational institutions. As a consequence, students from more disadvantaged backgrounds have more difficulties in adjusting to the school context, increasing the risk of failure. For students from more advantaged backgrounds, on the other hand, sociocultural experiences at home and at school are quite similar. Already at home they become acquainted with general cultural values and knowledge, linguistic skills, and the norms that typify interaction within the educational context (Bourdieu, 1966; Bourdieu & Passeron, 1970). Moreover, educational institutions tend to ignore the existing differences between students from different backgrounds, as such perpetuating and even increasing these differences by not paying attention to students' cultural deprivation. Paradoxically, schools tend to ignore differences and diversity by treating the students as equals and by not adjusting their teaching methods or criteria of assessment to individual differences. Traditional teaching methods are typically based on the treatment of classes as homogeneous student groups who will learn the same subject matter in the same pace on the basis of a uniform, teacher-centered teaching approach. Students' actual level of prior knowledge is insufficiently taken into account. And if the students fail to behave as equals when they are being assessed or tested, schools react to test results by trying to "re-homogenize" the heterogeneous student group. These attempts to create same-level groups may have counterproductive effects for disadvantaged students. Either the students have to go through the same "treatment" again (the one that did not work in the first stage), or they run the risk of ending up in a vicious cycle in which lowered teacher expectations, curriculum, and input reduction (that characterizes many remedial programs) threatens the learning potential of the educational environment (Dar & Resh, 1994; De Fraine, Van Damme, & Onghena 2002; Thomas & Collier, 2002).

Describing these pupils' situation as a mismatch has the advantage that the responsibility for educational success (or the blame in cases of failure) does not necessarily fall entirely on the teacher and the school system. For instance, investigating boys' underachievement in the British school system, Francis and Skelton (Chapter 5, this volume) emphasize that students' own attitudes toward school and educational achievement have a strong impact on their performance at school. The authors bring together a substantial body of empirical work showing how constructions of masculinity centering around "laddishness" are likely to have a negative impact on boys' attainment. The notion of being "one of the lads" evokes a group of young males engaged in hedonistic practices (including "having a laugh," disruptive behavior, alcohol consumption, objectifying women, and an interest in pastimes and subjects constructed as masculine). For these lads, it is considered not cool to work hard or achieve at school. Conversely, in Chapter 11, this volume, Antrop-González, Vélez, Garrett, and Baldwin describe a number of case studies of highly successful ethnic minority pupils in the United States and Belgium: One of the main variables that determines their academic success is their strong sense of (ethnic and religious) identity and their overriding ambition to beat the minority stereotype and do well in education. Compelling as these personal accounts may be, they may raise the impression that only the headstrong and highly ambitious members of the group of potential underachievers, who are ready to put in an excessive amount of effort, will be capable of crossing the social divide. If this is the case, this would lead to the perverse mechanism that the educational system will cater for excellence, while it is up to individual students to raise the level of equity.

The various chapters in this volume show and illustrate in a convincing way that in order for educational systems to raise their levels of excellence and equity, the effort of all parties involved (students, parents, teachers, principals/headmasters, teacher trainers, the local community, policy makers) will be necessary. Sustained and concerted action is needed to raise the extent in which education can cater for the needs of all students. Even if students' personal effort and learning motivation are of paramount importance, school teams can do a lot to positively enhance the students' attitudes toward learning. Later in this chapter, we will draw inspiration from the various chapters in this volume to show the different agents in the educational system can take a lot of measures to support disadvantaged and advantaged children to perform well. The first preliminary step in this process is to recognize that the educational system is not some abstract, untouchable, unchangeable institution ruled by unbeatable, deterministic mechanisms; to improve its level of output, the educational system will need to be actively constructed by all parties involved in joint collaboration.

RECOMMENDATIONS

In this section, we will list a number of measures that may be taken at different levels of the educational structure (at the level of national or regional educational policy, at the local community level, at the school level, and at the level of the classroom) in order to raise equity in education while maintaining excellence.

High Challenges, High Support

In Chapter 10, this volume, Jaspaert and Van den Branden report a Flemish study showing that the literacy skills of adolescents in the vocational strand of secondary education does not significantly grow anymore between the ages of 14 (the onset of the vocational strand in Flanders) and 18 (the end of compulsory education). In this study, the scores of the 18-year-old students in Flemish vocational strands did not significantly differ from the scores of 14-year-old students (who were in the same track) on the same reading comprehension and writing test. One of the main explanations for this dramatic result that the authors propose is that the teachers and instructors in the vocational strand seem to have given up the ambition to further promote these students' literacy skills (in view of the primacy of practical and professional competencies) and provide the students with only minimal stimuli and support to further develop their reading and writing skills.

In this way, this study ties up with the many other chapters in this volume and the literature on school effectiveness and student achievement (e.g., Marzano, 2004; Teddlie & Reynolds, 2000) that emphasizes the crucial importance of high expectations and high challenges in education: Throughout the system and the curriculum, students need to be offered educational content that is above their current level of development and be invited to "stretch their muscles." Low expectations are all too often translated by teachers in the (over)simplification of tasks and texts, the reduction of the learning potential inherent in the educational activities that students are invited to participate in, and a narrowing down of the curriculum (cf. the emphasis on explicit teaching of subskills instead of a focus on higher-level, complex problem-solving and meaningful content).

When students are offered stimuli to participate in challenging, meaningful activity, they should be supported to perform these tasks and learn from the experience. Synthesizing the results of over 800 meta-analyses relating to student achievement, Hattie (2008) concluded that neither the students' social or cultural background nor variables related to teachers' working conditions (such as class size) are vital when it comes to raising the effect size of education on student achievement: The teacher is the crucial factor in optimizing the learning opportunities for all students. Teachers should actively guide their students through the performance of challenging tasks, by providing individualized feedback that is tuned to the students' level of prior ability, applying a variety of teaching strategies, and meanwhile attending to affective aspects of learning. One of the highly successful ethnic minority students in the previously mentioned study by Antrop-González et al. (see Chapter 11, this volume) puts it very clearly:

> A good teacher is one who knows you, cares about what you do, pushes students, and cares about the stuff going on in your life. A good teacher also wants you to absorb information and understand it.

In a similar vein, Jaspaert and Van den Branden emphasize that the basic principles of challenging tasks and active teacher guidance imply that some students may have to be interactionally supported more than others. In this respect, a number of scholars have supported the idea of a truly egalitarian view on education, in which socially deprived students are given *more* support at school in order to have the *same* chance of success. In this view, equity amounts to treating pupils in an unequal way precisely because they are unequal (notably because they face unequal starting conditions). In other words, a formal equality of treatment (at school) would be unfair as long as there are "objective" inequalities (between families) (see Duru-Bellat and Mingat, Chapter 2, this volume). In their analysis of why the Finnish educational system is so successful in reconciling equity with excellence, Lynnakylä, Välijärvi, and Arffman (Chapter 9, this volume) point out that especially in comprehensive educational systems where tracking is postponed until the age of 14 or 15, minority and low-SES students receive a lot of support not only from their teachers but also from their (more proficient) fellow students. In this sense, the heterogeneity of the group (whether in terms of proficiency, cultural background, language skills, or other learner variables) becomes an asset for high-quality education rather than an obstacle (also see Van den Branden, 1997, 2000). At the same time, the Finnish system is characterized by different levels and methods of student counseling and support; this implies that teachers and student counselors need to receive adequate training (whether preservice or inservice) to cope with diversity and differentiate their interactional support in order to cater to different students' learning needs. Similarly, Francis and Skelton (Chapter 5, this volume) emphasize that teachers have an important role to play in supporting and stimulating boys in the United Kingdom to perform well at school:

> [T]eachers need to be aware of gendered (and "raced" and classed) patterns in achievement and learning, but informed by an understanding of these trends as socially constructed and partial. As such, teachers should be encouraged to see their role as widening horizons and repertoires of behavior among pupils rather than exacerbating existing stereotypes through their teaching.

Bridging the Language Gap

The language used at schools to educate children and adolescents is different from the language spoken at home in many different aspects. The language of instruction is cognitively more complex than informal language at home and is typically used to refer to decontextualized, abstract phenomena, lines of reasoning, and mental procedures. Whereas it takes only 2 years to learn the informal variety of a new language, it may take 7 to 9 years to fully acquire the academic variety of a second or foreign language (Baker, 2004;

Cummins, 2009). Students who have had little opportunity at home or in the local environment to grow accustomed to this particular use of language, and/or were raised in another language than the school language, need to be given sufficient support at school to acquire the academic, standard variety of the main medium of instruction in order to be able to use this variety as a tool for learning across the curriculum. In the United States, the famous *Lau v. Nichols* civil rights case (Baker, 2004) asserted the right of students who were not raised in English to receive specific (linguistic) support in order to have a fair chance of educational success.

> [T]here is no equality of treatment merely by providing students with the same facilities, textbooks, teachers and curriculum; for students who do not understand English are effectively foreclosed from any meaningful education. . . .We know that those who do not understand English are certain to find their classroom experiences wholly incomprehensible and in no way meaningful. (*Lau v. Nichols*, 1974)

A strategy that is much preferred by schools in this respect is to organize pull-out classes for minority students and offer them an intensive or additional program of second language (L2) lessons. The impact of these lessons on the students' overall academic achievement has been shown to be relatively restricted considering the time, energy, and resources that the investment requires (Baker, 2004; García & Kleifgen, Chapter 8, this volume; Hattie, 2008): In many cases, the L2 lessons are not linked sufficiently with the regular curriculum, some L2 teachers tend to lower their expectations and tune the curriculum down, the benefits of heterogeneous grouping are lost, the language teaching is teacher-dominated and form-focused, rather than working toward the processing of meaningful language in motivating, challenging contexts. In other words, the L2 education fails to fully live up to the promise to act as a "scaffold" for the minority pupils' acquisition of academic content in the second language (or standard variety of the majority language).

In Chapter 8, this volume, García and Kleifgen make a strong case in favor of bilingual education: For emergent bilinguals, the use of their home language may be the key to providing them with excellence and equity in education. Minority language speakers should, in the first place, be seen as individuals who have built up a wide resource of language-related skills and practices, all of which they can exploit to build up valuable and rich learning experiences in a school context. Bringing together an impressive overview of relevant research, García and Kleifgen point out that the importance of bilingualism as a resource to provide an excellent education to emergent bilinguals is still widely misunderstood.

> Different ways of using the students' home language practices in education are thus crucial to address equity and excellence in the education

of *all* language minority students, but especially in the education of those who are in the process of developing the majority language and becoming bilingual.

Deconstructing the Prevailing Learning Paradigm

Not only language use but the learning experiences, in general, that students build up at school tend to differ from learning outside school in many ways (Marzano, 2004; Resnick, 1987). Outside school, people learn mainly "by doing": In highly contextualized situations, people acquire new knowledge, skills, and attitudes while trying to pursue goals that are relevant to their personal needs. Learning in real-life situations can be quite accidental and will be strongly determined by the social circumstances in which the learning experience is embedded, the learner's personal choices and decisions, and the interactional support that is offered by other people who are involved in a joint project (Clark, 1996). On the contrary, at school, learning goals are mostly determined beforehand by the teacher or another authority; the way the learning process is organized will often be preplanned by the teacher, which implies that different learners are supposed to go through the very same learning process at the same time, at the same pace, and taking the same intermediate steps. In this way, differences between students from different backgrounds tend to be ignored or leveled out. The diversity in students' social, cultural, and learning background is not exploited as an asset for learning but tends to be regarded as a potential obstacle that needs to be overcome in order to guide every student to the acquisition of the legitimate body of knowledge in the formal learning environment. Typically, if the school norms, interaction patterns, communication modes, language codes, and methods of knowledge acquisition are beyond discussion, and particular groups of students are found to persistently underachieve, the educational system tries to set up remedial interventions that give the underachieving student group a chance to better adapt to the expectations and requirements of the educational system. The proliferation of early intervention programs is a strong indication of this tendency: Educational experts and family counselors aim to intervene in the home context and "prepare" children for school life. From a very early age, children will need to learn how to learn.

As Dyson (Chapter 12, this volume) points out, much of this well-intended work is driven by a deficit approach, sending out the (implicit or even explicit) message that parents are not raising their children in the most appropriate or adequate way. Vandenbroeck (Chapter 7, this volume) adds that early childhood education and care (ECC) quite often fails to reach the families who need support the most; the impact of the early interventions would allegedly be greater if ECC staff members were better trained to take into account their clients' perspective and sociocultural knowledge, and fine-tune their interventions to the learning needs and personal perspectives of the parents and children involved. In this way, truly co-constructive learning experiences can be built up.

A number of authors in this volume (e.g., García & Kleifgen, Chapter 8, this volume; Jaspaert & Van den Branden, Chapter 10, this volume; Vandenbroeck, Chapter 7, this volume) acknowledge the strong potential of introducing characteristics of informal learning in the formal learning environment of the school. If education aims to prepare students to fully participate in societal life and higher education, then it should foster true participation itself. Education should be connected to students' lives; bridges between students' current knowledge and real-life experience on the one hand and academic content on the other should be constructed; students should be granted more initiative and responsibility in terms of negotiating content and designing learning routes (Cole, 1990). Turning classrooms into more powerful learning environments will require the empowerment of disadvantaged students, the provision of ample space for students' outside school experiences, the exploitation of competencies they have (already) acquired outside school, and the acknowledgment of diversity as an asset for education (Bransford, Brown, & Cocking, 1999). In this perspective, the norms, interaction patterns, communication modes, language codes, and methods of knowledge acquisition that are taken for granted at school will have to become negotiable. By acknowledging diversity and adapting teaching methods to it, schools may be better equipped to compensate for children's differences at the outset of their school career; the school then adapts to the students rather than the students to the school. As a consequence, schools will also need to reconsider their relationship with the parents, the neighborhood, the local community, and the society at large.

Extended Schooling

The existing research on equity and excellence in education, and the way educational policy has reacted to this, has given rise to a strange paradox: On the one hand, researchers and policy makers duly acknowledge that student's achievement is still strongly influenced by sociocultural and socioeconomic variables; on the other hand, many of the policy measures that are taken or proposed to cope with this problem fail to take the sociocultural and socioeconomic context in which schooling is situated into account. The majority of policy measures (e.g., providing schools in disadvantaged areas with extra financial means, introducing accountability systems aimed to monitor quality standards, etc.) seem to be starting from the idea that the educational system stands the best chance to solve its most urgent problems if the system functions autonomously, without interference from the world outside. But can schools really be expected to meet the challenge of providing maximal learning opportunities to all students on their own? Isn't there a reasonable chance that learning opportunities will maximize for many students if schools and the local community (of which schools are an integral part) work together, join hands and forces, and enrich each other's efforts?

In Chapter 12, this volume, Dyson analyzes the extent to which the concept of "extended schools" has been implemented and has produced promising results so far. In the United Kingdom, "extended schools" target the most disadvantaged children (and, in most cases, families), who are seen as those most at risk of suffering from social and economic change and least likely to be supported effectively by traditional public services. They reorient services around the needs of those children (offering a mixture of extracurricular activities, child care, child and family support, adult learning, and community use of school facilities) with a view to tackling the multiple problems by which children and their families are beset. In this way, they aim to remove the barriers that prevent children from learning, enabling them to realize better educational outcomes, and, in the fullness of time, to develop into "productive adults." Reviewing the experiences with extended schools in the United Kingdom so far, Dyson warns the reader against too much optimism: Because extended schools are local projects, their impact will be local (at best) and may even be temporary. On the other hand, the available research clearly shows that closely integrated networks of family and community support, focusing on strongly disadvantaged neighborhoods, may make a significant contribution to raising the children's chances of performing well at school and developing key competencies. In a similar vein, Antrop-González et al. (Chapter 11, this volume) strongly emphasize the crucial importance of social networks in their case studies of successful minority children. Their stories show that, for successful minority students, the moral and mental support they receive from their parents, friends, siblings, and people that surround them are of crucial importance. Obviously, parents and others will be more inclined to actively and positively support minority students if they themselves believe that (a) education can make a difference, and (b) their child stands a good chance of doing well in education. Moreover, parents may be more inclined to stress the importance of education and urge their child to do well if they are well informed about their children's school life and the educational system and are treated as valuable partners by teachers and principals. Rather than blaming parents for children's underachievement, schools should try to build on the resources that parents and children bring to the school, look for levers of change in community life, clear away obstacles (including financial ones) on the way to students' success in education, intensify cooperation and communication with parents and the rest of the neighborhood, and build up a better understanding of the impact (and potential) of the local context on young people's development.

CONCLUSION

Striving for excellence and equity will require actions at different levels of the educational system that interact with each other: At the level of national or regional educational policy, the school policy level, classroom level, and local community level, sustained and goal-directed actions will need to be taken, taking into account the inherent diversity that student populations bring to school today. The chapters in this volume provide no holy recipes or "one-size-fits-all" solutions that will work irrespective of the context in which they are implemented. On the contrary, promoting maximal learning opportunities for all students, irrespective of their cultural, linguistic, or socioeconomic background, will require a highly contextualized approach taking into account the perspectives of the many partners involved. Even if most people tend to associate "education" with the institutes we call schools, "learning" is not: Learning is what young people are bound to do, at every single moment they are positively stimulated to do so and in any situation in which learning is valuable and worthwhile for themselves. Ultimately, maximizing learning opportunities has to do with enriching young people's lives in many different ways, whether at school or outside; with taking serious (and valuing) the contributions of all the people who take up a role of facilitating and actively guiding learning; with valuing the competencies young people have already acquired and using these as a stepping-stone for further learning; and with acknowledging that ultimately young people themselves are the masters of their own development.

REFERENCES

Anagnostopoulos, D. (2005). Testing, tests, and classroom texts. *Journal of Curriculum Studies*, 37(1), 35–63.

Au, W. W. (2008). Devising inequality: A Bernsteinian analysis of high-stakes testing and social reproduction in education. *British Journal of Sociology of Education*, 29(6), 639–651.

Baker, C. (2004). *Foundations of bilingual education and bilingualism* (4th ed.). Clevedon: Multilingual Matters.

Bourdieu, P. (1966). L'école conservatrice. Les inégalités devant l'école et devant la culture. *Revue française de sociologie*, 7, 325–347.

Bourdieu, P. (1986). The forms of capital. In J. G. Richardson (Ed.), *Handbook of theory and research for the sociology of education* (pp. 241–258). London: Greenwich Press.

Bourdieu, P., & Passeron, J. C. (1970). *La réproduction. Eléments pour une théorie du système d'enseignement*. Paris: Les Éditions de Minuit.

Bowles, S., & Gintis, H. (1976). *Schooling in capitalist America. Educational reform and the contradictions of economic life*. London: Routledge & Kegan Paul.

Bransford, J., Brown, A., & Cocking, R. (Eds.). (1999). *How people learn: Brain, mind, experience, and school*. Washington, DC: National Academy Press.

Brint, S. (2006). *Schools and societies* (2nd ed.). Stanford, CA: Stanford University Press.

Carter, B., & Fenton, S. (2010). From re-thinking ethnicity to not thinking ethnicity. *Journal for the Theory of Social Behaviour*, 40(1), 1–18.

Clark, H. (1996). *Using language*. Cambridge: Cambridge University Press.

Cole, M. (1990). Cognitive development and formal schooling: The evidence from cross cultural research. In Luis C. Moll (Ed.), *Vygotsky and education: Instructional implications and applications of sociohistorical psychology* (pp. 89–110). Cambridge: Cambridge University Press.

Coleman, J., Campbell, E., Hobson, C., McPartland, J., Mood, A., Weinfeld, F., et al. (1966). *Equality of educational opportunity.* Washington, DC: U.S. Government Printing Office.

Cummins, J. (2009). Bilingual and immersion programmes. In M. Long & C. Doughty (Eds.), *The handbook of language teaching* (pp. 161–181). Chichester: Blackwell.

Dar, Y., & Resh, N. (1986). *Classroom composition and pupil achievement: A study of the effect of ability-based classes.* New York: Gordon & Breach Science.

Dar, Y., & Resh, N. (1994). Separating and mixing students for learning: Concepts and research. *Pedagogisch Tijdschrift, 19,* 109–126.

De Fraine, B., Van Damme, J., & Onghena, P. (2002). Accountability of schools and teachers: What should be taken into account? *European Educational Research Journal, 1,* 403–428.

Gamoran, A., & Long, D. A. (2006, December). *Equality of educational opportunity: A 40-year retrospective* (WCER Working Paper No. 2006–9). Madison: University of Wisconsin–Madison, Wisconsin Center for Education Research.

Garnier, M., & Ho;ut, M. (1976). Inequality of educational opportunity in France and the United States. *Social Science Research, 5,* 225–246.

Gewirtz, S., & Cribb, A. (2009). *Understanding education. A sociological perspective.* Cambridge: Polity Press.

Hallinan, M. T. (2002). Equality in education. In D. L. Levinson, P. W. Cookson, & A. R. Sadovnik (Eds.), *Education and sociology. An encyclopedia* (pp. 241–246). New York: RoutledgeFalmer.

Hattie, J. (2008). *Visible learning. A synthesis of over 800 meta-analyses relating to achievement.* New York: Routledge.

Hilliard, A. G. (2000). Excellence in education versus high-stakes standardized testing. *Journal of Teacher Education, 51*(4), 293–304.

Kerckhoff, A. C. (1975). Patterns of educational attainment in Great Britain. *American Journal of Sociology, 80,* 1428–1437.

Linn, R. (2000). Assessments and accountability. *Educational Researcher, 29*(2), 4–16.

Lucas, S. (2001). Effectively maintained inequality: Education transitions, track mobility, and social background effects. *American Journal of Sociology, 106*(6), 1642–1691.

Marzano, J. (2004). *Building background knowledge for academic achievement. Research on what works in schools.* Alexandria, VA: ASCD.

Parsons, T. (1959). The school class as a social system. *Harvard Educational Review, 29*(4), 297–318.

Pelleriaux, K. (2001). *Demotie en burgerschap. De culturele constructie van ongelijkheid in de kennismaatschappij.* Brussel: VUBPRESS.

Posner, D. (2004). What's wrong with teaching to the test? *Phi Delta Kappan, 85,* 749–751.

Tan, B. (1998). Blijvende sociale ongelijkheden in het Vlaamse onderwijs. *Tijdschrift voor Sociologie, 19*(2), 169–197.

Teddlie, C., & Reynolds, D. (2000). *The international handbook of school effectiveness research.* London: Falmer Press.

Thomas, W., & Collier, V. (2002). *A national study of school effectiveness for language minority students' long-term academic achievement.* Santa Cruz:

University of California at Santa Cruz, Center for Research on Education, Diversity, and Excellence.

Van den Branden, K. (1997). Effects of negotiation on language learners' output. *Language Learning, 47*, 589–636.

Van den Branden, K. (2000). Does negotiation of meaning promote reading comprehension? A study of primary school classes. *Reading Research Quarterly, 35*, 426–443.

Willis, P. E. (1977). *Learning to labour. How working class kids get working class jobs*. Aldershot: Gower.

2 Measuring Excellence and Equity in Education
Conceptual and Methodological Issues

Marie Duru-Bellat and Alain Mingat

INTRODUCTION

Policy makers who aim to promote equity and/or excellence in education need to make a clear diagnosis comparing the current level of equity/excellence with the target level. However, both "excellence" and "equity" are complex concepts that first must be made operational and translated into empirical measures. This chapter will focus on the typical problems that the measurement of both equity and excellence raises, and on the choices that need to be made when trying to solve these problems. Among others, these problems relate to the definition of the concepts themselves, the empirical parameters needed to describe them, the measurement techniques that are utilized, and the social significance of both equity and excellence. The debate around these choices, which are indistinctively of a conceptual, methodological, and moral nature, is not purely academic, and, far from being neutral, has many political consequences.

EXCELLENCE AND EQUITY AS JOINT ISSUES

In this section, we will first try to define the two central terms of this volume and chapter: "equity" and "excellence." We will start with the latter.

What Counts As Excellence?

At first sight, it seems relatively straightforward to define excellence in education. However, many different aspects need to be taken into consideration. For one, shall we focus on the length of the students' educational career or on the level of performance they achieve? And should students' level of performance be defined (a) at crucial moments in a school career (e.g., assessing reading comprehension skills at the end of primary education), so while individuals are still participating in compulsory education, or (b) toward the end of their schooling career, so with reference to the final attainment targets of compulsory education, or (c) rather focus on the period of adulthood, referring to skills needed for societal participation and lifelong learning? Especially if the latter perspective is taken, researchers should be aware that the operationalization of skills may differ from one country to another, and some of the crucial competencies that are studied may even have been acquired outside school (in everyday life, for instance), whereas others are far more dependent on the quality of the educational system.

Another important question is: excellence in what? What aspects of excellence will be assessed, knowing that students are different from one another in numerous ways? Should we select a limited number of core subjects, or calculate the average of a large number of different subjects? Should we assign greater importance to some competencies and no importance to others? In this respect, we should keep in mind that whereas education aims at transmitting knowledge on the one hand and values and behavioral skills on the other, the former are relatively easy to measure and compare, whereas this is obviously much more difficult for the latter. Finally, should we focus on the pupils' level of achievement at different stages of compulsory schooling or at later stages, when different educational strands are institutionalized, so that wide variance in performance can be considered as normal? An alternative would be to define excellence in terms of a common core curriculum, starting from the objective that all students of the same generation should achieve all the predetermined, minimal goals of that curriculum.

Whatever perspective they choose, researchers should compensate for highly individualized perspectives on excellence—focusing on individual pupils' outcomes—by taking into account a system-wide perspective. For instance, in some African countries, institutions for higher education may be pleased to send a small number of their students abroad to the most-prestigious French schools, while overlooking the fact that a large proportion of the students who enrolled in the same institutions failed. Another telling example is offered by the PISA data[1]: Whereas most of the countries included in the PISA study show relatively similar results as far as the performances of the top 10% of students are concerned, the performances of the entire student populations differ widely. Excellence must therefore be evaluated both in terms of the performance of the happy few and the capacity of the system to stimulate growth throughout the whole student population.

Excellence Without Equity?

As a matter of fact, it may prove impossible (or at least debatable) to define excellence without taking equity into consideration, first, because it is necessary to take into account not only the output that students produce but also the way in which the output was produced by the educational system. In this respect, we can raise the question whether we should consider the sheer volume of public resources allocated to education or rather the volume of resources that actually reach the students ("resources" referring to money but also to time, contents, pedagogical assistance, and so on). Another set of questions refers to whether excellence is more accurately defined when researchers take into account the distribution of those resources between different pupils and pupil groups (for instance their degree of concentration). From this perspective, excellence could be defined as a mix of average performance and equity. Educational systems then would not be defined as excellent if they receive rich resources but allocate them to only a restricted part of the student population. Similarly, systems would not be called excellent if they generate strong inequalities between pupils in terms of performance, or if they generate small inequalities combined with a very low level of average achievement. The assessment of the match between pupils and resources is highly important in that perspective, because attaining a high average level with limited inequalities would probably require allocating resources unevenly among the pupils, in view of the existing (academic, social) disparities.

All this implies that assessments of excellence should not be limited to blind measurements of pupils' attainment but rather should include system characteristics such as coverage, financing (public/private), and structures (early tracking/comprehensive, types of student grouping), which impinge on both the average level of performance and the distribution of pupils' outcomes (for a synthesis of the literature, see Wössmann, 2003). For instance, comparisons between countries based on the PISA data show that early tracking is generally associated with both increased inequality and lower mean level of achievement (Duru-Bellat & Suchaut, 2005; see also Danish Technological Institute, 2005). A focus on system characteristics is all the more obvious when a country is poor and its resources are limited, but this issue is worthy of attention in every country because resources are always limited and excellence never fully achieved.

Does this imply that there is a necessary trade-off between the excellence that an educational system can generate and the number of pupils that need to be catered for within the limits of a certain budget? If so, that would amount to ratifying the idea that there is a strong link between results and resources. As a consequence, providing excellent education is necessarily a costly matter, and high quality will probably lead to less quantity (if the budget remains the same). We should, however, beware of drawing simplistic conclusions. For one, the previously mentioned links can be observed when comparing the educational output of rich versus poor countries, but the relationship is much more moderate when countries that are more similar from an economic perspective are taken into account (see Mingat, 2006). This weaker relationship is also observed when comparing schools within a given country (Hanushek, 1997).

The issue of trade-off between the excellence and equity of education is also a matter of profound debate. Because the pursuit of equity often requires that educational systems focus on the weakest pupils, the highly achieving students may suffer and, what's more, the overall level of achievement may drop. Actually, research shows that things are highly complicated. PISA data, for instance, show that many of the countries with the highest share of very bright pupils also show the smallest gap between the weakest and the brightest students. This seems to indicate that educational policies aiming at improving average efficiency and those aiming at reducing social inequality are not entirely incompatible.

Research further shows (see, e.g., Duru-Bellat & Suchaut, 2005) that the size of social inequalities is weakly associated with the average performance level, but not in the direction that is expected (the relation is negative but weak, barely reaching significance). In other words, the countries with the largest social inequalities also tend to have a relatively larger proportion of weak students. Conversely, countries with a high degree of social equality have, on average, high proportions of highly performing students. As a matter of fact, with regard to equity, some structural characteristics of the system, such as its degree of openness, may crucially matter: The degree of "inclusion"—that is, the degree to which the system allows a large share of pupils to attend school in a unified structure—has an impact on the overall equity of the educational system (see, e.g., Mons, 2007).

Whose Equity and Excellence?

Moving now from a systemic to an individual perspective, a number of questions remain. First, whose excellence are we talking about? Should we take into account the average level of the student population or the level achieved by the best or the lowest 10%? In this respect, we should take into account the relative dimension of excellence. Because the measurement of excellence always involves some kind of comparison, the question is raised which group should be used as a comparison group to draw conclusions on the excellence of the student group at stake? In terms of ranking, the population or the sample taken as the basis for comparison is crucial. Researchers may define excellence within a classroom, a school, a country, a sample of countries, or even within the pupils themselves (taking into account the efforts they made, the use they made of their talents, etc.). In our opinion, such comparisons should not be too specific, nor geared to fit specific expectations (otherwise anybody or any group may be called excellent, depending on the basis of the comparison one prefers to make). An acceptable research strategy consists in relying on a wide array of competences, within the domain of interest. This entails taking a more heuristic perspective, and in this way raising the chances that the analyses produce balanced information, even though researchers should remain cautious about drawing normative conclusions from the exercise.

Obviously, international comparisons are confronted with all these challenges, because they are inherent to the construction of a complex comparative study. For one, in internationally comparative studies, researchers should try to assess skills that are general enough to allow for comparisons between countries, while within each of these countries, the pursuit of excellence may focus upon specific, and different, subjects. In a similar vein, internationally comparative studies face the challenge of how to deal with disparities among schools and social groups (that are typically larger in some countries than in others) while ranking the participating countries on the basis of pupils' mean scores.

Why Equity?

Today, equity, rather than equality, is on the agenda, and it is important to understand the meaning of this semantic slide. It is widely admitted that the Coleman report in 1968—referring to "Equality of Educational Opportunity"—announced a major shift in the prevailing view on equality in education (see, e.g., Gamoran & Long, 2007). Let us recall that the question addressed to Coleman by the U.S. Congress was whether the weak performance of poor and ethnic minority pupils could be explained by the insufficient amount of resources allocated to their schools. Formal equality was no longer judged as sufficient; the focus shifted to the equality of performance, with the joint notion of equality of opportunity, that is, the opportunity to attain the same results. This led researchers to examine whether, when controlling for pupils' background, schooling conditions offered different pupils equal chances to achieve similar levels of output. This "value-added" approach prompted researchers to observe whether schools discriminate between pupils, or whether certain schooling conditions—for instance, the available resources or the racial mix of the school population—led to specific inequalities.

However, decades of sociological research in education, from the work of the Swedish sociologist Husen in the 1960s onward, have confirmed that merely avoiding discrimination may not suffice to allow pupils who make an "unequal start" to achieve equal results (see Crahay, 2000). This is why equity differs from equality: Equity implies the distinction between fair and unfair inequalities. Equity amounts to treating pupils in an unequal way precisely because they are unequal (notably because they face unequal starting conditions). In other words, a formal equality of treatment (at school) would be unfair as long as there are "objective" inequalities (between families). Thus, at school, some degree of discrimination (notably allotting more resources to certain pupils) is justified to level the playground so that truly fair competition may take place. In other words, equity refers to the current concept of equality of opportunities, which is supposed to justify later inequalities of performance at school and of reward in adult life.

Ultimately, the previously mentioned unequal treatment should lead to equal results for students from different (and unequal) groups, without controlling for pupils' background. To achieve this purpose, schools should adapt to pupils, allowing the latter to compensate for inequalities spring-ing from unequal starting conditions. In an ideal world, the equality of results between the groups observed at the end would certify the equality of opportunities accomplished as a result of certain school policies. How-ever, in real life, pupils' performances will remain unequal, while it remains impossible to assess the degree to which chances have become truly equal. As Barry (2005) said: "Only a small proportion of the factors that make a difference to opportunities can be measured" (p. 42). As a result, the current common educational practice to consider all differences in achieve-ment between groups as inequalities (which amounts to postulating that at the start, every child was both able and willing to be excellent in school) appears to be questionable.

The data that are currently used in research (with regard to differences in outcomes) do not allow us to assess the distribution of opportunities (notably those offered by school itself). Whereas students cannot reach an outcome without having had the opportunity to achieve it, the reverse does not hold. One can perfectly well have the opportunity to achieve an out-come without achieving it *de facto*. A "chance" is something that a person might or might not take, and hence, one may raise the issue of "merit," merit being the willingness to make the best use of one's own capacity[2] (for a discussion, see Duru-Bellat, 2009). As long as it is impossible to assess the impact of unobserved variables that generate some degree of inequality or the impact of personal and true choices in the observed inequalities of outcomes, it becomes almost impossible to draw political conclusions. For instance, should we consider the underrepresentation of girls in scientific tracks as an instance of inequality (or inequity)?

Following this perspective, equality looks more like a utopian dream than a realistic aim. This should not lead us to drop any concern for the opportunities that schools offer to pupils. Social inequalities do exist, but schools should focus upon the inequalities that are produced by the educa-tional system itself. Consequently, it seems legitimate to adopt an incremen-tal perspective, assessing as precisely as possible the inequalities produced between two points in time. By doing so, researchers may at least have a chance to figure out what mechanisms are at work.

So, in the end, the notion of equity qualifies the notion of equality. It also creates a link with the issue of justice. Following political philosophers such as Rawls, we should not stick to a single notion of equality but rather focus on the question which inequalities we can consider as fair. Some inequalities of performance may be judged as fair, under some conditions (for instance, if the competition was fair, or if equality of opportunities was secured) and at some levels of schooling.

The question also arises, upon returning to the definition of excellence itself, whether the focus should be on differences between individuals or groups, or on the proportion of the population that is performing below some minimum threshold; the latter would be in accordance with the

Rawlsian perspective. As far as education is concerned, the content of a minimum package may be identified within a short-term perspective and in terms of academic achievement (for instance, every individual has to reach a minimal level of reading proficiency at the end of primary education). However, a longer-term perspective can also be adopted, defined as what is necessary in adulthood (for a "good life," as Rawls would suggest). For researchers adopting a Rawlsian philosophy (see, e.g., Benadusi, 2007), this calls for the use of threshold indicators describing the minimum level of formal academic achievement for every pupil (in PISA, for instance, the percentage of a country population performing below a predetermined threshold). This would constitute an equity criterion, warranting, in democratic societies, a certain degree of citizenship and basic human rights.

THE CHOICE OF INDICATORS AND METHODS

The previous considerations may inform researchers to make considerate choices with regard to which aspects of the educational system should be studied (e.g., which kind of performance, which percentage of pupils attaining a certain threshold of performance, etc.) and which groups should be compared. Depending on the choices that are made, social inequalities will differ. If one chooses to compare specific groups at the extreme ends of a continuum, inequalities are likely to be larger than when larger groups, which by definition are more heterogeneous, are taken into account. For example, if one compares the 5% top achievers with the 5% lowest achievers, the differences between these two groups are likely to be much larger than when making comparisons involving 20% of the students at both ends. In a similar vein, the way of assessing the size or the evolution of the inequalities poses additional challenges.

Tables versus Models

When studying the distribution of educational resources, researchers may start by examining how performance varies across individuals. Many simple indicators are available then. For instance, calculating standard deviations (in relation to the mean level of the students' scores) is a straightforward option; likewise, calculating the percentage of pupils whose performance drops below a certain threshold has become common practice. When researchers focus on the distribution of public resources between pupils, an indicator such as the Gini coefficient is widespread, especially when countries are compared.[3]

But the question most at stake has to do with the width of the inequality between groups. To calculate this, a first step would be to proceed to bivariate analyses on the basis of tables, comparing scores across different groups (e.g., according to gender, social background variables, etc.). These tables, which often corroborate the commonsense feeling of people in the street, are certainly useful at the start of the process of analysis: They suggest that it may be worthwhile to move on to more in-depth analyses in order to explore the scores of members of different groups.

But in spite of their seeming face validity, the gaps between different groups' level of performance that these tables reveal may be spurious. First of all, even if the gap between some groups' level of performance is significant, we cannot draw any straightforward conclusions about the relevance of the variable at stake. For instance, tables may reveal inequalities between boys and girls at certain points in their educational career; this, however, does not allow researchers to draw firm conclusions on gender-related discrimination, for instance if tracking is based on marks and if marks are unequal among boys and girls. Models taking into account both gender and marks may show that when the marks obtained are similar, there are no differences between boys' and girls' educational career. So, some differences that are observed may not result from some discrimination (between boys and girls) but only from the fact that girls get better marks and marks matter in decisions about schooling careers.

In the same way, we may wonder what conclusions could be drawn if native pupils' average scores are found to be much higher than those of immigrant pupils? Is it being nonnative which is at stake (implying underlying problems having to do with language, for example) or other factors that are linked to being an immigrant in a particular country (e.g., having a low-qualified or unemployed father)? In both cases, it should be obvious that tables may blend different variables or processes taking place in real life, at the level of the individual or at the contextual level (e.g., immigrant pupils' scores may be strongly related to characteristics of the schools they attend). To be able to draw more firm conclusions about the equity of educational systems, a more analytical approach is necessary.

In this respect, multivariate modelling has become the most common strategy for many researchers. Such models allow researchers to take into account a list of variables at the same time and assess their specific impact on the dependent variable, while controlling for other ones. As the previously mentioned example showed, this may lead to quite different conclusions about the gap between different groups' level of performance. Concerning the comparison between native versus immigrant pupils' performance, this approach may reveal that if, for instance, the impact of parents' characteristics (such as their level of education or occupation) is controlled for, the gap is strongly reduced. So, in all, the decision as to whether an observed inequality is large or significant is partly dependent on the tools that are used to measure it.

In the previously mentioned example, our conclusion would be the following: Everything else being equal, being immigrant versus native does not really matter. At this point, sociologists may start feeling a bit uneasy and question the models themselves. Quite similar to the method preferably used in experimental sciences (i.e., experimentation), modelling allows for estimations on the basis of simulations generated by mathematical models, resulting in observations that may be associated with very uncommon situations. For instance, what would be the difference in scores between native and immigrant pupils if "everything else was equal," that is, if their other personal characteristics (parents' occupation, family size, etc.) were the same? One does not need to be an experienced sociologist to realize that this is a quite unrealistic perspective; in real life, all the variables at play (e.g., the mere fact of being an immigrant pupil, parents' social position, etc.) are interconnected and cannot be combined at leisure, at the risk of creating true "sociological fiction." This is the kind of fiction researchers create when they claim (as Coleman did) that ethnic minority pupils make greater progress when they attend schools enrolling a substantial proportion of native pupils. However interesting this perspective may be (for instance, because it runs counter to fatalistic notions about inequalities fundamentally having to do with "cultural inheritance"), it remains a very uncommon situation in the context in which the study was undertaken.

So, whereas disentangling variables is a necessary step in statistical analyses, researchers should also take a more "historical" step, in which the global and present configuration of the variables in the context of the study is taken into consideration. Producing sound analyses should not only be done out of methodological considerations; the quality of analysis may also have strong political consequences. That would, for instance, be the case when researchers only retain the part of the variance explained by a variable without considering its weight in the population. For example, the specific negative impact of being handicapped may be very large in a statistical model, while covering only a limited share of variance at population level; this variable may prove to be only a marginal variable when accounting for inequalities at the system level.

Another case in which the educational context must be taken into account has to do with the kind of political conclusions that are typically drawn by the school effectiveness movement. This vein of research has uncovered certain characteristics of the "efficient school" (e.g., in terms of climate, teachers' expectations, etc.) when controlling for student characteristics, but in reality, those "efficient schools" are typically attended by pupils from a privileged background. We may wonder, then, to what extent these studies yield the kind of indicators that can be adopted in any school, irrespective of the students they are enrolling, and whether this would pay due homage to the kind of challenges that schools attended by the least-privileged pupils have to meet when trying to raise their level of efficiency (Thrupp, 1995). One possible coping strategy would be to compute models with an interactive structure (assessing the impact of a climate factor, for instance, combined with features of the student body). However, as mentioned before, modelling, being a statistical tool that is fit for analyzing certain processes, cannot make up for deep observations and thick descriptions of what is going on in true life.

To end this section on modelling, we would like to emphasize that this technique is very suitable for separating inequalities at the individual level from those at work at the contextual level. Coming back to the issue of immigrant pupils, modelling will help researchers to assess which part of the students' performance is generated by the context in which their schooling takes place. For instance, some part of the performance gap with native pupils may be explained by the fact that these pupils attend less-effective schools, whereas another part may be due to the social or ethnic mix of the student body (see Mickelson, 2007). So a restriction of analyses to the individualistic level would be spurious: Not taking into account the context (using multilevel models) may lead to an overestimation of the impact of pupils' cultural or ethnic origin.

Comparisons Across Time and Space

When researchers aim to compare educational processes across time and space, the issue of the relevance of disentangling variables arises again. The phenomena that are studied are necessarily embedded within a context that induces a number of problems for the comparative approach itself.

If one wants to describe how educational means are distributed in different countries or during different periods, indicators can be relatively simple. To compare different periods of time, for example, we can analyze the evolution of the Gini indicator, or compute the differences between certain percentages. But if one wants to characterize the evolution of social inequalities during a certain period, the choice of suitable indicators is not easy. As sociologists like Mare (1981) have shown, most indicators, even linear regressions, do not allow researchers to disentangle two distinct phenomena:

1. What aspects of the evolution that is observed result from the evolution of the distribution of educational means? For one, some global expansion of education may have resulted in weaker inequalities, because, as long as access to an educational level increases, its capacity to differentiate between groups decreases.
2. What aspects result from an evolution that Mare calls "pure inequality of opportunity," that is, the mechanisms through which children of a privileged background have access to higher levels of education or better marks, irrespective of the context they live in?

The only way to assess the second kind of phenomena would be to use multiplicative indicators, the most common of which is odds ratios coupled with logistic regressions.[4] These have become a norm in the methodology of social mobility and in comparative studies of social inequalities in general.

Using this methodology, the conclusion of the first large comparative study on social inequalities in education (led by Shavit & Blossfeld, 1993) was that, despite the marked expansion of all educational systems under study, in most countries there had been little change in socioeconomic inequality of educational opportunity.

This statement has led to fierce debate among sociologists, including discussions about the most proper way to accurately assess the evolution of social inequalities across time (see, e.g., Hellevik, 1997). Actually, it is now recognized (see Marshall & Swift, 1999) that the two previously mentioned kinds of measures—direct comparisons of percentages versus odds ratios—do not grasp the same kind of inequalities. Additive indicators and all sorts of measures integrating the evolution of the overall distribution of educational means are important to assess the evolution of access to education: Who gets what? How much does each group get? In other words, how did the "distributional outcome" evolve, and how did the inequality of academic results evolve? Here, education is considered as a "product" in itself; if the least-advantaged group gets more, that may be called "progress" in its own right.

With odds ratios and multiplicative indicators, what is at stake is the process of allocation of pupils to the different levels of education and the degree to which this process is biased by social inequalities. In this case, not so much inequalities in terms of outcomes are explored, but rather inequalities of opportunity (bearing in mind the same limitations as the ones mentioned earlier, that is, that we can never truly assess opportunities but only results). The crucial question here is not so much "Who gets what?" but rather "How much more does X get compared with the others?" Education is primarily seen as a product, the value of which is relative to what other pupils receive.

It is clear that social inequalities may evolve or differ between countries, either because the overall distribution of educational means changes or because the process of "allocation" (e.g., inequalities in academic progress or tracking) becomes less unequal. So, from a political point of view, policy makers may attempt to improve access to certain educational levels, which may lead to a reduction of social inequalities at these particular levels at the risk of passing on the problem to subsequent levels (which, ultimately, may prove to be very costly). This again shows that reducing social inequalities is not straightforward. International comparisons tend to show that the differences in the size of social inequalities in education are more strongly influenced by the overall distribution of educational means than by differences in the relative impact of parents' background characteristics on pupils' educational careers (Müller & Karle, 1993). The same holds true when observing the size of the gap between boys and girls in secondary education in developing countries: The gap has declined over time but this is due entirely to the expansion of the educational system (Mingat, 2007).

Anyway, in spite of the dominant trend to use odds ratios, one should not forget the advice of Swift (2004):

Social justice is not simply about securing equal chances of access to unequally rewarded positions. Fair access is an important part of the story but it is not all of it. It matters also that the inequalities in rewards attached to those positions are themselves justified. (p. 3)

Concretely, researchers and policy makers will generally consider an increase in the level of education achieved by the majority of a generation as an indicator of progress, even if the odds ratios have remained unchanged, in the same way as, in a population, the fact that the average level of resources increases is considered as progress even while inequalities remain constant.

A VARIETY OF PERSPECTIVES

Even if parameters of equity and excellence have been carefully selected, the analysis of the data that are generated is a time-consuming and challenging endeavor that needs to be put in the proper perspective. A first perspective relates to the time dimension: After all, educational systems organize sustained efforts stimulating individuals to acquire human capital over an extended period of time. A second perspective relates to the scope of the educational system: Even when assessing equity in specific educational contexts, a global and system-wide perspective cannot be neglected.

Cross-Sectional Studies versus Time Series

For practical reasons, researchers have to focus on analyzing inequalities at precise points in the educational system; however, it is crucial to identify the magnitude and structure of the data that are generated and to include cross-sectional descriptions. For example, we may identify certain inequalities between groups (boys and girls, for instance) in upper secondary education. This type of conclusion should be regarded as a starting point for further analysis, because what is really at stake is to figure out the patterns by which those inequalities were created. To illustrate this point, let us take an example in which access is regulated by a tracking process. When facing inequalities in the access to a certain educational level or strand, it is important to disentangle (a) which inequalities are generated specifically at this particular moment through the process of tracking itself (e.g., as a result of families' demands or teachers' bias in decisions) and (b) which variables related to previous educational levels contributed to the inequalities that are observed. By putting the initial results in a broader time perspective, the empirical analysis attempts to reconstruct the patterns that gave rise to the inequalities that can be observed at a given point in the system; as such, the full picture of pupils' school careers is taken into account.

As such, a mechanism observed at a given point in time (e.g., tracking at some stage) may appear to be "fair" and unbiased (so, in our example, showing no significant differences between groups in the tracking process per se, beyond those connected with their level of present achievement). However, because achievement may itself be a socially unequal construct, the seemingly fair process of tracking may mask previous inequalities in the system. So, even if some inequalities may be considered as fair at a given period of time, this does not entail any overall judgment of fairness when the whole educational process or system is considered.

This way of conducting analyses is worth considering even if no inequalities are observed at a given point in time. For example, if no inequalities in learning results are visible between high-SES and low-SES children at a given stage, this may be the outcome of unequal selection in previous steps in the educational cycle, for instance, as a result of a process of formal selection (generated by the system) or a process of self-selection (generated by the individuals themselves). So the seeming homogeneity in the sample in a particular study may mask a more problematic heterogeneity that fell outside the scope in that study. Although an empirical analysis at a given point of the system is necessary, the results need to be considered in a larger time perspective. This calls for the collection of more data and for the use of more sophisticated modelling techniques that will allow researchers to assess how inequalities evolved over time. For example, when observing inequalities in boys' and girls' access to upper secondary education, it may be useful to sort out which proportion is derived from disparities in (a) academic achievement in primary education, (b) academic achievement at the level of lower secondary education, and (c) tracking between lower and upper secondary education. Carrying out these kinds of holistic analyses may be of the utmost importance if the research results function as the basis for political action. Obviously, different policy measures need to be taken according to whether tracking or early academic achievement has the greatest impact on the observed inequalities.

The time perspective is also useful when researchers take into account both variables with an impact (a) that is limited to a specific period of time (e.g., a teacher effect), (b) that accumulates across extended periods of time (e.g., social background variables, the social mix of the school population, etc.). A cross-sectional perspective may lead researchers to the conclusion that the first type of variables are crucial, whereas an extended-time perspective may lead to radically different conclusions: For instance, the teacher effect may be mitigated because students in secondary education will be taught by different teachers showing different degrees of efficiency; social background variables, on the other hand, tend to have a generally constant impact, so that social effects may accumulate over the whole schooling career.

Narrow versus Broad Perspectives

Studies of equity in education, whether stretching over more or less extended periods of time, often focus on specific samples. The accepted division of labor between researchers (and even the rules of sound research themselves, which incite researchers to focus on specific topics and research questions) leads to a narrowing down of the focus of much empirical work in the educational field.

For instance, studies focusing on higher education in developing countries often lead to the basic observation that social inequalities are very strong, and that the introduction of scholarships for the most-disadvantaged students might enhance fairness and equity. This may hold for that particular educational level. However, if we would assume a broader perspective, and take into account the fact that the available educational resources are severely restricted, researchers may reach different conclusions: Using resources for scholarships would unavoidably result in fewer resources being available for earlier levels of education, for instance, primary education, thus increasing the number of poor children who are not enrolled.

In a similar vein, the assessment of equity may differ according to the groups that are involved in the studies. When policy makers are confronted with inequalities between groups and strive to reduce them, it seems straightforward to target the most-disadvantaged groups ("positive discrimination"). Assuming that the selected measures are successfully implemented, it may be tempting to conclude that the inequalities existing at the start have now been reduced. This would be the case if the profits that the measures yield have no negative impact on the academic achievement of other students. For instance, at first sight, aiming to improve the poorest pupils' reading comprehension skills does no harm to other students' reading skills. But in most cases (given the fact that a certain degree of scarcity is always present in educational contexts), measures directed at certain groups interact with the educational careers of other groups. If, for instance, measures are taken that allow all students more time to acquire target reading skills, bright students who learn at a faster rate may be slowed down and hindered in their progress. In general, any one-sided or homogeneous policy or pedagogical design will probably be unfair when it addresses a heterogeneous population, as one size seldom fits all.

Another consideration concerns the supply of available positions in selective schools, in higher education, or on the job market. While focusing on the benefits gained by the "lucky" or privileged students, researchers should also study the (unintentional) consequences of the measures at stake for other individuals. For instance, in a country in which 30% of the pupils drop out from compulsory education, a successful measure raising students' chances on the labor market and addressing, even randomly, 10% of these pupils may leave the remaining 20% at an even greater disadvantage than before, especially if the labor market does not offer more jobs.

The previously mentioned examples illustrate that a judgment about the equity of educational systems is necessarily of a global nature. In the end, empirical analyses must cover the overall organization of the system. This perspective is quite uncommon, because analyses predominantly focus on specific inequalities between groups within the system. Especially when educational systems of different countries are compared, or when the effectiveness of the same system is evaluated at different periods of time, this global perspective becomes crucial. For equity, the share of the population that participates at different levels of the system ("the survival pattern"), as well as the distribution of educational resources across the different levels, should be taken into consideration. For example, for two countries mobilizing the same volume of educational resources and showing similar patterns in terms of the amount of resources spent per pupil, structural inequalities may strongly differ according to the share of the population participating ("covered") at each level of education. If, in country A, about 50% of the children are enrolled in primary schools and only 20% of the student population enter higher education (whatever the social composition of the student body may be), its educational system is structurally less equitable than the system in country B, in which enrollment in primary education reaches 80% and participation in higher education amounts to 15%. The concentration of educational resources is much stronger in country A than in country B.

Conclusions

Equity is obviously an important concept in educational policy making and educational research, but the study of equity in education raises a vast number of methodological and practical challenges. Even if the time, expertise, and funds are available to carry out high-quality research, numerous choices must be made. Researchers will often have to restrict their study to a limited set of questions involving a limited sample of subjects, which means that a great number of instrumental decisions will accompany the analyses. Value judgments, even of a moral kind, will be inevitable. For individual researchers, the main rule of thumb is to make their choices explicit and transparent. Good research practice involves testing the extent to which the results are dependent on the specific methodological choices that were made (Leamer, 1983). For the benefit of the scientific community, the impact of specific variables should be evaluated in a careful manner, and research results should be integrated in a body of knowledge that by definition is dynamic, serving as a sound basis for further research and policy making.

While adopting a global research perspective, value judgments necessarily interfere, whereas they could have been more easily discarded as long as more specific research questions were being investigated. For instance, it is a delicate choice to decide up to which level the educational system should be guided by equity considerations. The question is: For how many years of schooling do we want to achieve universal coverage? How long will equity considerations prevail? As much as this decision should be inspired by moral judgments, efficiency matters too. A primary concern for each government is to decide the scope of basic education that will be secured for every single child in the country. Because resources are always limited, this decision will need to take into account efficiency considerations. Allotting a tiny fragment of the educational resources to everybody out of equity considerations is absurd if the amount is too small to be effective. Equity alone cannot be the sole argument governments depend on: Much depends on what can be achieved at a high level of performance.

At a later stage, governments will need to decide at what age it will be socially acceptable that schooling is no longer compulsory, and that only a proportion of the age group remains at school. Despite accepting the general principle that the right to receive education is universal, problems arise when governments try to make this principle operational and implement it in real life. This is particularly true in countries where many people have to compete for scarce resources: The rights of some individuals necessarily compete with the rights of others.

Excellence itself is at the core of this tension, giving rise to conflicts regarding the rights of individuals. Because the student body is heterogeneous from an academic point of view, each pupil should be stimulated to make the most of his or her capacities. Ultimately, the excellence of the whole system is assessed by evaluating its capacity to cope with this diversity. These conflicts also have a structural dimension, especially when the educational system is composed of different cycles. For instance, if governments aim to boost participation to higher education in a country where resources are quite scarce and the job market is limited in size, some regulation of the student flow will be necessary. This can take a variety of forms. For instance, governments can choose to raise private costs (in view of the fact that beyond a certain stage, education at least partly becomes a private good) or to organize some sort of academic competition. These two mechanisms clearly have different consequences in terms of promoting equity. In the case of higher education, raising the costs will hurt the poor and have negative consequences on equity. A more global perspective may lead to complex challenges, particularly when the public resources that are saved in higher education are used for the benefit of the children who are not participating in primary education yet.

Formulating a balanced synthesis on these issues remains a necessarily transitory and incomplete exercise, which researchers might be unable to translate in any straightforward way into down-to-earth policy making. It is transitory and incomplete because the current research relies heavily on studies that are limited in scope and sometimes do not meet certain quality standards and that yield (as a result) possibly contradictory results. Policy makers cannot wait to take action until the definitive and perfect knowledge base is created. This is all the more so because, however sophisticated analyses may become, research results will always be based on the evaluation of a momentary state-of-the-art. For example, we may find out whether a class of 20 students is more equitable in terms of academic achievement than a class of 25 students, but then we still may not know whether reducing the size of the class to only 10 students will have an equally positive impact. Furthermore, it will not suffice to observe that a certain action has a certain impact; we need to establish whether this action is better than any other action that we could have implemented with the same resources. This will require a variety of experiments and intervention studies, and a fair share of pedagogical imagination, and the continuous awareness that any educational process or intervention is embedded in a specific historical and social context.

NOTES

1. PISA data (OECD Programme for International Student Assessment) assess 15-year-old students' competencies in reading, mathematics, and sciences in a vast sample of countries.
2. At this point, we will not raise the controversial issue of the distinction between merit that is "deserved" (through the will of persons) and merit "not deserved," corresponding to innate ability.
3. The Gini coefficient is a concentration index. It varies from 0 (in an equitable case in which x% of the population receives x% of the resources devoted to education), to 1 (a situation in which one single pupil would receive the total resources), which reveals the maximal degree of concentration.
4. Odds ratios aim at estimating the relative chances of different groups to achieve some outcome. For example, if P is the probability of children from the upper socioeconomic status (SES) group to enter university, and Q that of children from the lower SES group, the odds ratio is computed as $[P*(1-Q)]/[Q*(1-P)]$. This indicator is not dependent on the initial value of the numbers that are compared. An odds ratio of 1 implies that the event is equally likely in both groups. An odds ratio greater than 1 implies that the event is more likely in the first group.

REFERENCES

Barry, B. (2005). *Why social justice matters*. Cambridge: Polity Press.

Benadusi, L. (2007). Education Equality Indicators in the nations of the European Union. In R. Teese, S. Lamb, & M. Duru-Bellat (Eds.), *International studies in educational inequality: Theory and policy* (pp. 155–190). Dordrecht: Springer.

Crahay, M. (2000). *L'école peut-elle être juste et efficace?* Bruxelles: de Boeck.

Danish Technological Institute. (2005). *Explaining student performance. Evidence from the international PISA, TIMSS and PIRLS surveys*. Paris: Organisation for Economic Co-operation and Development.

Duru-Bellat, M. (2009). *Le mérite contre la justice*. Paris: Presses de Sciences Po.

Duru-Bellat, M., & Suchaut, B. (2005). Organization and context, efficiency and equity of educational system: What PISA tells us. *European Educational Research Journal, 4*, 181–194.

Gamoran, A., & Long, D. (2007). Equality of educational opportunity: A 40-year retrospective. In R. Teese, S. Lamb, & M. Duru-Bellat (Eds.), *International studies in educational inequality: Theory and policy* (pp. 23–47). Dordrecht: Springer.

Hanushek, E. (1997). Assessing the effects of school resources on student perfor-
  mance: An update. *Educational Evaluation and Policy Analysis, 19*, 141–164.
Hellevik, O. (1997). Class inequality and egalitarian reforms. *Acta Sociologica,
  40*, 377–397.
Leamer, E. E. (1983). Let's take the con of econometrics. *American Economic
  Review, 73*, 31–43.
Mare, R. D. (1981). Change and stability in educational stratification. *American
  Sociological Review, 46*, 72–87.
Marshall, G., & Swift A. (1999). On the meaning and measurement of inequality.
  Acta Sociologica, 42, 241–250.
Mickelson, R. A. (2007). First- and second-generation school segregation and the
  maintenance of educational inequality. In R. Teese, S. Lamb, & M. Duru-Bel-
  lat (Eds.), *International studies in educational inequality: Theory and policy*
  (pp. 21–37). Dordrecht: Springer.
Mingat, A. (2006). Options pour une allocation coût-efficace des ressources. In A.
  M. Vespoor (Ed.), *Le défi de l'apprentissage: Améliorer la qualité de l'éducation
  de base en Afrique subsaharienne* (pp. 115–147). Paris: L'Harmattan.
Mingat, A. (2007). Social disparities in education in sub-Saharan African coun-
  tries: Gender, geographical location and family income. In R. Teese, S. Lamb, &
  M. Duru-Bellat (Eds.), *International studies in educational inequality: Theory
  and policy* (pp. 223–256). Dordrecht: Springer.
Mons, N. (2007). *Les nouvelles politiques éducatives.* Paris: PUF.
Müller, W., & Karle, W. (1993). Social selection in educational systems in Europe.
  European Sociological Review, 9, 1–22.
Shavit, Y., & Blossfeld, H.-P. (Eds.). (1993). *Persistent inequality: Changing educa-
  tional attainment in thirteen countries.* Boulder, CO: Westview Press.
Swift, A. (2004). Would perfect mobility be perfect? *European Sociological review,
  20*, 1–11.
Thrupp, M. (1995). The school mix effect: The history of an enduring problem in
  educational research, policy and practice. *British Journal of Sociology of Education, 16*, 183–203.
Wössmann, L. (2003). European education production functions: What makes a
  difference for students' achievement in Europe? *Economic Papers, 190.* Brussels: European Commission.

3 School Competition, Institutional Differentiation, and the Quality and Equity of Education Systems
Evidence from PISA 2006

Karin Zimmer, Miyako Ikeda, and Elke Lüdemann

INTRODUCTION

Competition fosters performance. This is the credo of proponents of market-oriented education policies who point out that enhancing the possibilities to choose between different schools will create competition among schools, which, in turn, will lead to overall improvement in student achievement. However, competition may also enhance inequity: This is the concern of opponents of school choice, who fear that segregation will increase, leaving behind disadvantaged students while students from better-informed and better-off families alone profit, and popular schools have the possibility to cream-skim their clientele.

Enhancing educational quality while equity suffers: This argument is also made when debating early tracking, that is, the institutional differentiation of students into schools with different curricula according to their perceived ability at a certain age. Whereas some claim that creating more homogeneous learning environments by tracking students will lead to better overall performance more efficiently, others assert that if this can be done at all, quality will come at the expense of the equality of opportunities. These critics fear that the earlier students are tracked, the less it is possible for them to fully develop their abilities and show their educational potential independently of the educational and socioeconomic background of the family they grow up in.

This chapter investigates how competition between schools and institutional differentiation relate to the quality and equity of education systems, looking across 54 countries and economies that have participated in the Programme for International Student Assessment (PISA) in 2006. The analysis presented here utilizes, and extends, results reported in the initial international report for PISA 2006 (Organisation for Economic Co-operation and Development [OECD], 2007a, 2007b), by looking at both factors separately, as well as in combination.

Whereas the extent of school competition may vary across local authorities, there typically is little variation in policies of institutional differentiation in an education system. In general, school policies differ more between countries (or provinces, regions, states in a federated system) than within. To shed light on the impact of institutional differentiation, ideally, quasi-experimental designs are utilized, for example, focusing on instances of policy reform implemented in a country. Instances of such policy reforms are rare, however. International assessments are administered more commonly and lend themselves to an investigation of the role school policies and practices play with regard to the quality and equity of educational systems by introducing variation on the level of the education system. This comes at a cost: As international assessments typically are cross-sectional in design, causal inferences can be drawn only to the extent that the variables of interest are uncorrelated with other relevant but unobserved variables not included in the analysis. Furthermore, a cross-country analysis cannot do full justice to the intricacies of any one education system. What can be achieved in the present analyses, however, is to give an indication of the association of institutional differentiation and school competition with measures of performance and equity while controlling for a number of potentially confounding variables such as the students' socioeconomic background, the school's socioeconomic intake, or the country's overall wealth.

Countries tend to differ largely in terms of curricular content. Therefore, to achieve international comparability, the performance measures employed should not so much look at whether the students have learned what they were supposed to (which varies from country to country), but whether they have achieved key competencies that they will need in their future everyday and work lives and that will support their lifelong learning. It is assumed that demand for these competencies will not be idiosyncratic or nation-bound, but will be shared among industrialized societies (Baker & LeTendre, 2005).

This chapter first looks at the existing empirical evidence and describes the database upon which the analysis is built. This is followed by the presentation of the analyses and outcomes.

SCHOOL COMPETITION: EXISTING EVIDENCE

When parents have a choice of more than one school they can decide to send their child to, then schools compete with each other for students. It must be noted that competition and choice, while being related, cannot be equated. It is assumed that increasing choice will stimulate school competition, which, in turn, mediates student performance (Bayer & McMillan, 2005). The nature of the competition among schools varies, depending, among other things, on the degree of school autonomy in the education system, and on funding policies with regard to privately managed schools. Economic models suggest that competition and parental choice between private and public schools—as well as competition within the public school sector itself—create incentives that increase the performance in all schools, as parents are free to choose the schools that supply the best quality of schooling. This is especially true if the financing of private schools is such that not only the more affluent families can afford private school attendance for their offspring. The following paragraphs will review national as well as international evidence and will first look at competition between public schools, before turning to the question of whether the existence of private schools—which may be government-funded or independent—influences outcomes in the education system in general.

School Competition and Student Achievement

In many countries, parents are restricted in their choice of public schools by the residential choice the family has made, as children typically have to attend the school that is closest to their home. In the United States, this residential choice among local school districts, called the *Tiebout choice*, was investigated by Hoxby (2000), who found a positive effect on student achievement among schools in the public school system. Again looking at the United States, Belfield and Levin (2002) reviewed cross-sectional evidence on the effects of competition among public schools, as well as among public and private schools, concluding that, controlling for other influences, increased competition and higher educational quality are positively, although modestly, correlated.

These findings are corroborated when looking at countries who have introduced policy instruments such as school vouchers to increase parental choice and competition among schools. School vouchers allow independent schools to receive similar government funding as public schools. Following the introduction of school vouchers in Sweden in 1992, for example, Sandström and Bergström (2005) found improved performance in public schools. Evaluating different experimental school voucher programs targeted at low-income students in the United States, Howell, Wolf, Campbell, and Peterson (2002) reported performance increases among African American students who switched from a public to a private school. Neal (1997) reported similar evidence for students from urban minority groups attending private Catholic schools. Evidence supporting the positive effects of school vouchers was also provided for Colombia (Angrist, Bettinger, Bloom, King, & Kremer, 2002). In her review of empirical evidence for the United States, Hoxby (2003) concluded that school choice and school competition (e.g. as supported by the introduction of school vouchers and the founding of highly autonomous public charter schools) had a positive impact on student achievement (see, however, Cullen, Jacob, & Levitt, 2005, for contrary evidence within the school district of Chicago).

Turning to evidence from international assessments, Wößmann, Lüdemann, Schütz, and West (2009) utilized indirect proxies for the competition of other schools in the area, namely, the proportion of students attending their school because it is local, and the proportion of students attending their school because it is better than other schools in the area, in 37 countries participating in PISA 2003. Wößmann et al. (2009) found no association between these two measures of school choice and mathematics performance.

Studies on the effects of competition by private schools show that countries combining relatively high shares of private operation with relatively high shares of government funding perform best. This finding suggests that the positive effects of competition induced by the existence of private schools are the larger the more students can afford to attend private school (Wößmann, 2001, 2003, 2009; Wößmann et al., 2009).[1]

School Competition and Equity

Compared to studies on the relationship of school competition and student achievement, the role of school competition with regard to equity is less extensively investigated, and findings are not conclusive. On the national level, some studies in the United States demonstrated sorting effects according to socioeconomic background (Ladd, 2002), increased segregation by race or class (Bifulco, Ladd, & Ross, 2008), or other adverse effects on disadvantaged students (Cullen et al., 2005). Moreover, Bradley and Taylor (2002) reported an increase in social segregation between schools following a British reform increasing parental school choice in secondary education. Similarly, Söderström and Uusitalo (2010) found school choice in Swedish upper secondary schools to increase segregation by socioeconomic background, as well as migration background. In contrast to these findings, equalizing effects have been reported for the United States, in that disadvantaged students benefit particularly strongly from school competition (for an overview, see Hoxby, 2003).

Evidence from international assessments is limited to outcomes related to the existence of private schools. Using data from PISA 2000, Ammermüller (2005), not distinguishing between public or private funding of privately managed schools, found higher inequality was associated with higher shares of private schools. Taking public versus private funding into account, Schütz, Ursprung, and Wößmann (2008) showed that higher shares of private management were related to higher equity in TIMSS (Trends in International Mathematics and Science Study) and TIMSS-Repeat, whereas higher shares of private funding in a country went hand in hand with higher inequity, as measured in the relationship between student performance and student socioeconomic background. Wößmann et al. (2009) replicated this finding with data from PISA 2003 and conclude that "the equity-enhancing effect of private operation stems from their greater access to government funds in countries with large private sectors" (p. 30).

Summing up the evidence as reviewed in this section, the majority of studies support a positive relationship between school competition, on the one hand, and performance in education systems, on the other. As for the equity of education systems, empirical outcomes are not unequivocal. The measures used in these investigations (e.g., the share of public versus private funding and management of schools, the share of students attending their school because it is local or because it is better than other public schools in the area) are rather indirect and address only part of the issue of school competition, namely, in as far as it relates to school choice. The analysis presented in this chapter will shed further light on the role of school competition by using direct measures: For each school, the school principal's response is available as to whether their school is competing with one or more school(s) in the area for students—be they public or private. At the country level, the school principals' individual responses are combined to provide the proportion of schools which thus face competition.

INSTITUTIONAL DIFFERENTIATION: EXISTING EVIDENCE

Studies on the effect of early tracking on the quality and equity of education systems draw on national policy reforms or on one of several cross-sectional international data collections. The majority of empirical investigations so far have failed to find any (statistical) impact of early tracking on average student performance but provide evidence that early tracking increases inequity in education systems.

Countries that abolished or deferred tracking to a later point in compulsory schooling include Sweden in the 1940s; the United Kingdom, Italy, and Norway in the 1960s; and Spain and Portugal in the 1990s. Evaluating the policy reform in Sweden, for example, Meghir and Palme (2005) found that students who showed high ability and came from a disadvantaged socioeconomic background (operationalized by the occupational status of the father) particularly benefited from the change toward a more comprehensive school system—a result pointing at the positive impacts of late tracking on equity.

Drawing on data from PIRLS 2000 (Progress in International Reading Literacy Survey) and PISA 2000 in 12 countries, Ammermüller (2005) studied the effect of changes in the institutional structure of education systems between primary and secondary school on the relationship between the student's socioeconomic background and student performance, and found early tracking to be related to inequity. Average performance was not associated with the timing of tracking in the analysis of data from TIMSS 1995 and TIMSS 1999 of 54 countries performed by Schütz, Ursprung and Wößmann (2008), and the authors found evidence that later tracking reduced the impact of the family socioeconomic background on performance. Hanushek and Wößmann (2006) reported that early tracking did not have a consistent effect over the countries and domains investigated but tended to reduce average performance overall, while it generally increased inequity. Their findings were based on data from PIRLS 2000, PISA 2000 and 2003, and TIMSS 1995, 1999, and 2003. Similarly, using data from PISA 2003, Wößmann et al. (2009) found no effect of tracking on average mathematics performance but more inequity in countries with an early-tracking system. These findings were also corroborated in the initial international report for PISA 2006 (OECD, 2007a, 2007b).

Extending these findings beyond the school years and the performance of students at school, Brunello and Checchi (2007) focused on later outcomes based on data from the European Community Household Panel (ECHP 1995 and 2000), the International Social Survey Programme (ISSP 1991 and 1999), the International Adult Literacy Survey (IALS 1994, 1996, and 1998) and PISA 2003. The authors found that tracking increased the effect of the home socioeconomic background on the final educational attainment and wages of young adults. This was not the case, however, when looking at reading skills as measured by IALS. Although not investigated in this chapter, studies on a related issue—namely, ability grouping within schools—suggest that within-school tracking reduces achievement among disadvantaged students (see Figlio & Page, 2002, for an overview of research in the United States).

In sum, there is no clear-cut evidence that placing students in different tracks at an early stage of their educational career is related to higher performance. Some studies, however, have shown that early tracking increases the impact of socioeconomic background on performance.

RESEARCH QUESTIONS

To the authors' knowledge, no empirical study has as yet investigated whether school competition plays a different role in institutionally tracked as opposed to comprehensive education systems, nor analyzed the combined effects of school competition and institutional tracking on the performance and equity of education systems. It is hypothesized that in comprehensive systems, schools from one area compete for more students and/or for higher-performing students. Tracked systems are more regulated in that school competition will only take place within a track, not between. Similarly, students do have but a partial choice in that they may attend the track for which they are deemed qualified or any lower track. In this sense, the existence of tracking limits school competition and choice. It may also be speculated that greater competition among schools may be observed in higher than in lower tracks. The following analysis will address these issues, using data from the recently published 2006 cycle of PISA (OECD, 2007a, 2007b).

With regard to the quality of performance, in line with previous findings, it is hypothesized that the average level of student performance in a country does not relate to early-tracking policies but that it increases with the number of competing schools in the local area. The analysis will also shed light on the question of whether the impact of enhanced parental choice through competition among schools is similar in education systems that practice early versus late tracking. Furthermore, addressing the equity issue, it is expected that both early tracking and school competition are associated with higher inequity. Again, the analysis will also provide results on possible interactions between these two variables.

Looking at ability grouping within schools in the United States, Epple, Newlon, and Romano (2002) found that public schools retain a greater proportion of higher-ability students by tracking but lose more wealthy, low-ability students to the private sector. Although ability grouping within school is not part of the present investigation, this outcome is seen as supportive of the hypothesis that school competition and institutional differentiation may work together in their (statistical) effects on student achievement and equity.

DATA AND METHODS

Data Source and Variables

The international database from the Programme for International Student Assessment (PISA) 2006 is utilized in this report. PISA is a 3-yearly survey that assesses the performance in reading, mathematics, and science of 15-year-old students, who are near the completion of their compulsory education. The present analysis builds on responses from 382,585 students from 13,885 schools in 54 countries/economies, with between 3,781 and 30,885 students assessed per country.

The main focus of the PISA 2006 assessment was science literacy, which involves an understanding of scientific concepts, as well as the ability to apply a scientific perspective and to think scientifically about evidence. Each participating student spent 2 hours carrying out pencil-and-paper tasks, which were typically organized in units based on a written passage or graphic, of the kind that students might encounter in real life. The assessment contained both tasks requiring students to construct their own answers as well as multiple-choice questions. Students also answered a questionnaire that focused on their personal background, their learning habits, attitudes toward science, engagement, and motivation. Furthermore, school principals completed a questionnaire about their school that included demographic characteristics and their evaluation of the learning environment at school.

Data from two countries that participated in PISA 2006 did not enter the analysis presented in this chapter. In France, no data were collected on school-level variables from school principals. In Qatar, the student's index of economic, social, and cultural status (ESCS) was found to be unreliable. All but one indicator used for the analysis come from the PISA 2006 student and school questionnaires. The age at which students experience the first selection in the education system was taken from *Education at a Glance 2006* (OECD, 2006) for the OECD countries and from a system-level questionnaire for non-OECD participants, submitted by the National Project Manager for PISA 2006 of these countries or economies.[2]

The measures of student performance, the student's ESCS and its relationship with student performance, as well as the variables indicating competition among schools and early selection in the education system, will be characterized in turn. For the analysis, educational quality will be operationalized as the mean level of student performance in a country, whereas educational equity will be defined as the relationship between student performance, on the one hand, and the socioeconomic background of the student and school, on the other. The weaker this relationship is, the more equally distributed is educational opportunity. This follows a proposal by Roemer (1998; cited in Betts & Roemer, 2007), who suggests that the educational achievement of children should be independent of family socioeconomic background because it is beyond the student's control. Descriptive statistics are presented in Table 3.1 for all countries for which valid information is available.

Table 3.1 Descriptive Statistics for the Explanatory and Outcome Variables Used in the Models

	Student performance on the science scale		Standard deviation		PISA index of economic, social, and cultural status (ESCS) of students		Slope of the socioeconomic gradient[a]		Number of schools competing for students in the same area						First age of selection in the education system
							Score point difference associated with one unit on the ESCS		Two or more other schools		One other school		No other schools		
	Mean	S.E.	S.D.	S.E.	Mean index	S.E.		S.E.	%	S.E.	%	S.E.	%	S.E.	
OECD															
Australia	527	(2.3)	100	(1.0)	0.21	(0.01)	43	(1.5)	88.4	(1.5)	5.2	(1.1)	6.4	(1.1)	16.0
Austria	511	(3.9)	98	(2.4)	0.20	(0.02)	46	(3.1)	45.2	(3.7)	19.2	(3.1)	35.6	(3.4)	10.0
Belgium	510	(2.5)	100	(2.0)	0.17	(0.02)	48	(1.9)	71.9	(2.9)	18.6	(2.8)	9.4	(2.0)	12.0
Canada	534	(2.0)	94	(1.1)	0.37	(0.02)	33	(1.4)	58.8	(2.5)	18.5	(2.4)	22.7	(2.2)	16.0
Czech Republic	513	(3.5)	98	(2.0)	0.03	(0.02)	51	(2.6)	73.9	(3.2)	12.1	(2.1)	14.1	(2.5)	11.0
Denmark	496	(3.1)	93	(1.4)	0.31	(0.03)	39	(2.0)	59.2	(3.9)	18.2	(3.1)	22.6	(3.3)	16.0
Finland	563	(2.0)	86	(1.0)	0.26	(0.02)	31	(1.6)	40.5	(4.2)	15.5	(2.9)	44.0	(3.7)	16.0
Germany	516	(3.8)	100	(2.0)	0.29	(0.03)	46	(2.1)	68.8	(3.3)	14.2	(2.2)	17.0	(2.6)	10.0
Greece	473	(3.2)	92	(2.0)	-0.15	(0.03)	37	(2.2)	44.8	(3.9)	14.9	(3.1)	40.3	(3.4)	15.0
Hungary	504	(2.7)	88	(1.6)	-0.09	(0.03)	44	(1.8)	59.7	(3.9)	15.9	(3.1)	24.4	(3.6)	11.0
Iceland	491	(1.6)	97	(1.2)	0.77	(0.01)	29	(1.8)	22.8	(0.2)	5.0	(0.1)	72.2	(0.2)	16.0
Ireland	508	(3.2)	94	(1.5)	-0.02	(0.03)	39	(2.2)	73.8	(3.5)	9.8	(2.4)	16.4	(2.7)	15.0

Italy	475	(2.0)	96	(1.3)	-0.07	(0.02)	31	(1.6)	68.8	(2.6)	12.0	(1.7)	19.2	(2.5)	14.0
Japan	531	(3.4)	100	(2.0)	-0.01	(0.02)	39	(2.7)	82.0	(2.8)	7.6	(1.8)	10.4	(2.2)	15.0
Korea	522	(3.4)	90	(2.4)	-0.01	(0.02)	32	(3.1)	75.7	(3.6)	8.7	(2.2)	15.6	(3.0)	14.0
Luxembourg	486	(1.1)	97	(0.9)	0.09	(0.01)	41	(1.2)	51.0	(0.1)	15.7	(0.0)	33.3	(0.1)	13.0
Mexico	410	(2.7)	81	(1.5)	-0.99	(0.04)	25	(1.3)	67.6	(2.7)	16.7	(2.8)	15.7	(2.0)	12.0
Netherlands	525	(2.7)	96	(1.6)	0.25	(0.03)	44	(2.2)	74.2	(3.0)	15.3	(2.5)	10.5	(2.2)	12.0
New Zealand	530	(2.7)	107	(1.4)	0.10	(0.02)	52	(1.8)	82.1	(2.7)	7.1	(2.0)	10.8	(2.0)	16.0
Norway	487	(3.1)	96	(2.0)	0.42	(0.02)	36	(2.5)	21.8	(3.3)	12.4	(2.6)	65.9	(3.6)	16.0
Poland	498	(2.3)	90	(1.1)	-0.30	(0.02)	39	(1.8)	44.4	(3.1)	20.5	(3.3)	35.1	(3.5)	16.0
Portugal	474	(3.0)	89	(1.7)	-0.62	(0.04)	28	(1.4)	48.2	(4.3)	24.7	(3.7)	27.1	(3.9)	15.0
Slovak Republic	488	(2.6)	93	(1.8)	-0.15	(0.02)	45	(2.6)	85.0	(2.7)	6.4	(1.9)	8.6	(2.1)	11.0
Spain	488	(2.6)	91	(1.0)	-0.31	(0.03)	31	(1.3)	62.1	(2.6)	17.7	(2.2)	20.2	(2.2)	16.0
Sweden	503	(2.4)	94	(1.4)	0.24	(0.02)	38	(2.1)	49.6	(3.6)	13.5	(2.5)	36.8	(3.7)	16.0
Switzerland	512	(3.2)	99	(1.7)	0.09	(0.02)	44	(1.8)	27.5	(2.8)	14.1	(2.0)	58.4	(2.7)	12.0
Turkey	424	(3.8)	83	(3.2)	-1.28	(0.04)	31	(3.2)	52.7	(4.5)	15.6	(3.5)	31.7	(3.9)	11.0
United Kingdom	515	(2.3)	107	(1.5)	0.19	(0.01)	48	(1.9)	83.7	(2.3)	8.7	(1.9)	7.6	(1.5)	16.0
United States	489	(4.2)	106	(1.7)	0.14	(0.04)	49	(2.5)	63.6	(3.7)	10.5	(2.6)	25.9	(3.1)	16.0
OECD total	491	(1.2)	104	(0.6)	-0.10	(0.01)	45	(0.6)	66.3	(1.2)	12.6	(0.9)	21.1	(1.0)	14.0
OECD average	500	(0.5)	95	(0.3)	0.00	(0.00)	40	(0.4)	60.3	(0.6)	13.6	(0.5)	26.1	(0.5)	
Partners															
Argentina	391	(6.1)	101	(2.6)	-0.64	(0.07)	38	(2.4)	71.3	(4.0)	9.4	(2.4)	19.3	(3.5)	12.0
Brazil	390	(2.8)	89	(1.9)	-1.12	(0.03)	30	(1.9)	28.4	(2.3)	38.8	(2.6)	32.8	(2.4)	17.0
Bulgaria	434	(6.1)	107	(3.2)	-0.21	(0.05)	52	(3.6)	67.4	(3.9)	17.4	(2.7)	15.2	(3.2)	11.0
Chile	438	(4.3)	92	(1.8)	-0.70	(0.06)	38	(1.8)	63.9	(3.6)	17.3	(3.4)	18.8	(3.3)	13.0

(continued)

Table 3.1   (continued)

| | Student performance on the science scale | | | | PISA index of economic, social, and cultural status (ESCS) of students | | Slope of the socioeconomic gradient[a] | | Number of schools competing for students in the same area | | | | | | First age of selection in the education system |
| | Mean score | | Standard deviation | | | | Score point difference associated with one unit on the ESCS | | Two or more other schools | | One other school | | No other schools | | |
	Mean	S.E.	S.D.	S.E.	Mean index	S.E.		S.E.	%	S.E.	%	S.E.	%	S.E.	
Colombia	388	(3.4)	85	(1.8)	-1.00	(0.05)	23	(1.6)	57.6	(5.9)	18.2	(3.9)	24.2	(5.0)	15.0
Croatia	493	(2.4)	86	(1.4)	-0.11	(0.02)	34	(1.9)	65.4	(4.1)	11.6	(2.2)	23.0	(3.5)	14.0
Estonia	531	(2.5)	84	(1.1)	0.14	(0.02)	31	(2.0)	56.4	(2.8)	22.2	(2.6)	21.4	(2.6)	15.0
Hong Kong-China	542	(2.5)	92	(1.9)	-0.67	(0.03)	26	(2.3)	89.6	(2.5)	9.2	(2.4)	1.2	(0.9)	15.0
Indonesia	393	(5.7)	70	(3.3)	-1.52	(0.05)	21	(2.6)	90.0	(2.6)	4.8	(2.1)	5.2	(1.4)	15.0
Israel	454	(3.7)	111	(2.0)	0.22	(0.02)	43	(2.7)	69.1	(3.8)	13.6	(3.4)	17.4	(3.2)	15.0
Jordan	422	(2.8)	90	(1.9)	-0.57	(0.03)	27	(1.8)	36.4	(3.9)	19.4	(3.0)	44.1	(3.9)	16.0
Kyrgyzstan	322	(2.9)	84	(2.0)	-0.66	(0.02)	27	(2.6)	47.6	(3.2)	17.3	(3.0)	35.1	(2.9)	15.0
Latvia	490	(3.0)	84	(1.3)	-0.02	(0.02)	29	(2.3)	80.7	(3.1)	15.2	(2.9)	4.1	(1.6)	16.0
Liechtenstein	522	(4.1)	97	(3.1)	0.19	(0.05)	49	(5.5)	c		c		c		11.0
Lithuania	488	(2.8)	90	(1.6)	0.04	(0.03)	38	(2.0)	42.1	(3.6)	30.4	(3.2)	27.5	(2.9)	15.0
Macao-China	511	(1.1)	78	(0.8)	-0.91	(0.01)	13	(1.5)	80.8	(0.1)	8.6	(0.1)	10.6	(0.1)	12.0
Montenegro	412	(1.1)	80	(0.9)	-0.02	(0.01)	24	(1.4)	73.6	(0.2)	24.9	(0.1)	1.5	(0.1)	14.0

Romania	418	(4.2)	81	(2.4)	-0.37	(0.04)	35	(3.4)	31.1	(4.5)	23.7	(4.0)	45.2	(5.4)	14.0
Russian Federation	479	(3.7)	90	(1.4)	-0.10	(0.03)	32	(2.6)	51.1	(4.8)	16.9	(2.6)	32.0	(4.3)	14.5
Serbia	436	(3.0)	85	(1.6)	-0.14	(0.03)	33	(1.8)	49.6	(4.4)	23.4	(3.8)	27.1	(3.6)	14.0
Slovenia	519	(1.1)	98	(1.0)	0.13	(0.01)	46	(1.6)	40.2	(0.5)	12.2	(0.3)	47.6	(0.5)	14.0
Chinese Taipei	532	(3.6)	94	(1.6)	-0.31	(0.02)	42	(2.1)	80.9	(3.4)	12.7	(2.8)	6.4	(2.1)	15.0
Thailand	421	(2.1)	77	(1.5)	-1.43	(0.03)	28	(1.6)	65.8	(4.4)	22.5	(3.9)	11.7	(2.9)	16.0
Tunisia	386	(3.0)	82	(2.0)	-1.20	(0.07)	19	(2.2)	29.3	(4.5)	21.8	(3.7)	48.9	(5.1)	16.0
Uruguay	428	(2.7)	94	(1.8)	-0.51	(0.03)	34	(1.4)	34.5	(2.4)	13.5	(2.0)	52.0	(2.9)	12.0

[a] Single-level bivariate regression of science performance on the ESCS, the slope is the regression coefficient for the ESCS. Note. The symbols c, m, and w denote missing data. The symbol c indicates that there are too few observations to provide reliable estimates, m signifies that data are not available for technical reasons, and w stands for data that have been withdrawn at the request of the country concerned.

Source: PISA 2006 database, except last column: "First age of selection" is taken from Education at a Glance (OECD, 2006) for OECD countries. For non-OECD participants, information is from a system-level questionnaire to the National Project Managers of PISA 2006. Data refer to the education system of the country, as a whole.

Student Performance

The following analysis focuses on student performance in science, which was measured on a scale that had a mean value of 500 and a standard deviation of 100 across OECD countries. The average level of science competencies varied largely across countries, from 563 score points in Finland to 322 in Kyrgyzstan (the first column in Table 3.1). The performance gap between the countries with the fifth highest and the fifth lowest mean performance was 143 score points.

From the 28 OECD countries in which a sizable number of 15-year-old students in the PISA sample were enrolled in at least two different grades, the score point difference that is associated with one school year was estimated at an average of 38 points on the science scale. This score point difference is called the *grade-level equivalent* (OECD, 2007a).

Socioeconomic Background and Its Relationship to Performance

The socioeconomic background of a student was measured by the PISA index of economic, social, and cultural status (ESCS). The ESCS is a composite index derived from the highest international socioeconomic index of occupational status of the parents (HISEI), the highest index of the education level of the parents (HISCED), and the index of household possessions, as a proxy for family wealth (OECD, 2009). The open-ended responses regarding the parents' occupational status were coded to four-digit ISCO codes (ILO, 1990) and then mapped to the international socioeconomic index of occupational status (Ganzeboom, de Graaf, & Treiman, 1992). The educational level of parents was classified using ISCED (OECD, 1999), with the index on the highest educational level of parents corresponding to the higher ISCED level of either parent. The index of home possessions is a summary index of all household items, which was scaled according to the methods established in Item Response Theory (de Ayala, 2009; Embretson & Reise, 2000; Masters & Wright, 1997; Wilson, 2005). Student scores on the ESCS index are factor scores derived from a Principal Component Analysis of the three component indices which are again standardized to have a mean of 0 and a standard deviation of 1 across the OECD countries[3] (for further details, see the PISA 2006 Technical Report, OECD, 2009). Across all participating countries, the mean ESCS index ranged from –1.52 in Indonesia to 0.77 in Iceland (third column in Table 3.1).

The relationship between socioeconomic background and student performance in science is characterized by the score point difference in performance that is associated with one unit change in the ESCS index. On average across OECD countries, student performance rises by 40 score points with a one-unit increase in ESCS, but this score point difference ranges from less than 15 in Macao-China to more than 50 in the Czech Republic, Bulgaria, and New Zealand (fourth column in Table 3.1).[4]

Apart from the student ESCS, the following analyses will take into account the socioeconomic intake of each school. The school ESCS is defined as the average student ESCS of the 15-year-old students in this school.

Number of Competing Schools in the Local Area

In the school questionnaire, school principals were asked to indicate whether there are other schools in the local area with which they compete for students. Thus, the measure depends on the school principal's report, and its validity rests on the assumption the school principals are able and willing to provide veridical information on the issue.

As is illustrated in Table 3.1, across OECD countries, 74% of the students were attending schools where parents had a choice of at least one other school in the area; for 60%, two or more schools were competing for students. In some countries, school choice is pronounced: In Australia, Hong Kong-China, Indonesia, and the Slovak Republic, more than 85% of students are enrolled in schools that compete with two or more other schools in the local area. On the other hand, in Norway, Switzerland, and Uruguay, the parents of fewer than half of the students have any choice at all.

The share of schools competing with other schools within the country or economy will enter the analysis to investigate any compositional effects that competition among schools may have at system-level, over and above the effect of individual schools competing for students within a given country or economy.

Institutional Differentiation

The rightmost column in Table 3.1 presents the age at which countries divide students into separate types of education for the first time. This is when students and their parents are faced with choices, as students will follow different curricula and reach different qualifications upon program completion, which are usually associated with different expectations regarding the transitions to further education or to work. In some countries like Austria and Germany, these decisions are taken already at the age of 10, whereas in other countries institutional differentiation takes place only after students have completed secondary education, at age 16.

Multilevel Analyses

Next, the effects of competition between schools and early selection on student performance (the *quality* model) and its relationship to student socioeconomic background (the *equity* model) are investigated employing multilevel regression analyses.[5] This approach is able to take into account the specific data structure of PISA, that is, a two-stage stratified sample design, with the first stage consisting of schools with 15-year-old students and the second stage consisting of students within the sampled schools.

As a result of the sampling strategy used, the residuals are generally not independent; that is, the assumptions of conventional Ordinary Least Squares regression models are not met. In PISA, the science achievement scores of students within a school are likely to be more similar than would be the case in a simple random sample, because students in the same school share common school and peer characteristics, for example. Moreover, the estimation technique needs to take into account the fact that the effective sample size and the degrees of freedom vary with the variables being measured at the student, school, and system levels. As mentioned earlier, there are 382,585 observations at the student level, whereas there are data from 13,881 schools at the school level and only 54 observations at the level of countries/economies.

The three-level regression analysis in this report includes student variables at Level 1 (marked with the prefix *student_* in the variable name), school variables at Level 2 (prefix *school_*), and system variables of countries and economies at Level 3 (prefix *system_*). The model coefficients and statistics are estimated using a full maximum likelihood procedure.

Outcome Variables

The dependent variable for the quality model is the science performance at student level. Each student's performance is characterized by five plausible values that are inferred from the observed item responses, following scale construction according to the mixed-coefficients multinomial logit model (Adams & Wu, 2007), with the item parameters anchored at their international scale-values. The reliability of the science scale is 0.92 at the international level; national reliabilities vary from 0.84 to 0.94 in the PISA 2006 participating countries and economies. A detailed description of the models and procedures used in the international scaling of the raw data can be found in the PISA 2006 technical report (OECD, 2009).

In the equity model, the magnitude of the impact of the PISA index of economic, social, and cultural status at the student level (*student_ESCS*) and at the school level (*school_ESCS*) on the students' science performance is estimated by the explanatory variables of interest. The quality model is an "intercepts-as-outcome model" or "random intercepts model," whereas the equity model is equivalent to a "random slopes model" in the multilevel analysis literature (Raudenbush & Bryk, 2002; Snijders & Bosker, 1999). In other words, the quality model estimates the relationship between the variability in intercepts and the explanatory variables at one level higher (e.g., the variability of the Level 1 intercept is estimated by the explanatory variables at Level 2; and the variability of the Level 2 intercept is estimated by the explanatory variables at Level 3). The equity model estimates the relationship between the variability in the slope of the *student_ESCS* (i.e., the regression coefficient) as well as the slope of *school_ESCS* (i.e., the regression coefficient for the ESCS at school level) and the explanatory variables.

Explanatory Variables

The three explanatory variables of interest in the quality model are located at the school and system levels. The existence of competing schools in the local area at school level *(school_competition)* is coded as a dummy variable. A value of 1 indicates that there is at least one other school competing for students. A value of 0 signifies that no other schools compete for students in this area. Second, the variable *system_competition* gives the share of schools competing with other schools within the country or economy. As mentioned before, this variable is introduced to be able to account for any compositional effects that competition among schools could have at the system level, over and above the effect of individual schools competing for students.

Finally, the institutional differentiation in a country or economy is assessed by looking at the age at which students are tracked in the education system for the first time. The system-level variable *system_yearsseparate* used in the current analysis is computed by subtracting the age of first selection from the age at which students were tested in PISA (i.e., age 15). For example, for education systems where students are placed in different tracks at age 11, the variable *system_yearsseparate* is equal to 4, subtracting 11 from 15. For school systems that track their students into different types of secondary school at or after age 15, this variable is set to zero.

It is important to note that the socioeconomic and demographic factors could have an effect on performance through individual, school, and system factors other than the ones that are of prime interest here. For instance, students attending schools with more competition in the area might differ systematically from those attending schools without competition. This would be the case, for example, if more competition exists in affluent areas, and families with an advantaged socioeconomic background could choose among schools more often than families who could not afford to live in those neighborhoods. Similarly, the school intake (i.e., the aggregate socioeconomic context that individual students find in their learning environment at school) has been shown to have a causal impact on students' academic performance (e.g., Ammermüller & Pischke, 2009) and could thus potentially distort the outcomes of the present analysis. In order to be able to account for such instances of selection bias, both gross models and net models of the relationship between school competition and institutional differentiation, on the one hand, and the quality and equity of performance, on the other hand, will be examined.

The gross quality model does not take into account various socioeconomic and demographic background factors, and provides an estimate of the overall effects of school competition and tracking, thus including the effects jointly attributable to these as well as to other (background) factors. Conversely, the net quality model provides the net effect of competitive school and tracking by controlling for the differences in the composition of schools and the country context. Such an adjustment allows a comparison of schools and education systems under the assumption that they would be operating in similar socioeconomic and demographic contexts.

Gross and net effects are relevant to different stakeholders. Parents, for example, will be most interested in the overall performance results of the education system as it operates in the country, and this would include any effects that are mediated by the socioeconomic intake of schools or other differences that may exist at school or system level. Policy makers, on the other hand, will be primarily interested in any effects net of preexisting background variables that are not likely to be readily amenable by school policies and practices. Background variables that were controlled for in the net quality model were selected based on previous empirical findings (OECD, 2007a), and included the student's index of economic, social, and cultural status (*student_ESCS*), the student's gender, and migration status, as well as the language spoken at home at the student level. At the school level, school size and location in a rural or city area and the school's average socioeconomic intake (*school_ESCS*, operationalized as the school's average student ESCS) were accounted for. At the system level, the relative wealth of countries and economies was controlled for by means of the country average (*system_ESCS*). The background variables that are taken into account in the net quality model are listed in Appendix 3.1, together with descriptive statistics. For the equity model, the explanatory variables include institutional differentiation, the existence of competing schools in the area (at the school and system levels), and the student and school average *ESCS*. The other (background) variables listed for the net quality model serve again as controls.

Model Specification

The model coefficients and statistics are estimated in the three-level Hierarchical Linear and Nonlinear Modelling (HLM) analysis using a full maximum likelihood procedure. Normalized student final weights are used, so that the sum of the weights is equal to the number of students in the data set, and each country contributes equally to the analysis. All variables in the model are grand-mean centered, and all interaction terms are computed using grand-mean centered variables.

The data set is complete with respect to data on student performance and the age of first selection (*system_yearsseparate*), and the missing rate for the number of competing schools in the local area is 2.66% and the missing rates for the control variables used in the net models are given in Appendix 3.1. The missing values were imputed for all variables in order to include the maximum number of cases in analysis. Because the missing rates were generally not high, a dummy variable adjustment (Cohen & Cohen, 1983) was used, creating a "missing dummy" variable for all variables with missing values at the student and school levels and setting the dummy to 1 if the data were missing on that variable or 0 else. In the model equations presented later, the variables with the first letter "*M*" in their variable names are missing dummies. After creating missing dummies, missing values were replaced by 0 for dichotomous variables and by the weighted school (country or international) average of the variable for continuous variables.

In the following section, the results from three models—including early tracking, school competition, and their interaction as explanatory variables—are presented in detail. These are the gross and net quality models, and the equity model. An effect is considered statistically significant if the *p*-value is below 0.1 at country level and below 0.005 at school level. Different criterion values were chosen for the two levels to counterbalance statistical significance and statistical power, that is, to account for the fact that at the country level there are only 54 cases, while there are nearly 14,000 observations at school level.

EFFECT OF INSTITUTIONAL DIFFERENTIATION AND SCHOOL COMPETITION ON AVERAGE PERFORMANCE

Gross Quality Model

The gross quality model is analytically specified by the three following equations, one each for the student, school, and system levels:

Model at the student level (Level 1):

$$Y = P0 + E$$

Model at the school level (Level 2):

$$P0 = B00 + B01*(school\_competition) + B02*(Mschool\_competition) + R0$$

Model at the system level (Level 3):

$$B00 = G000 + G001(system\_yearsseparate) + G002(system\_competition) + G003(system\_competition*system\_yearsseparate) + U00$$

$$B01 = G010 + G011(system\_yearsseparate) + U01$$

In these, as well as the following model equations, the first letters *P*, *B*, and *G* denote intercepts and regression coefficients on the level of the student, school, and education system, respectively. The letters *E*, *R*, and *U* signify the respective error components, and *M* stands for the missing dummy.

Table 3.2   Results of the Gross Quality Model

Fixed Effect	Coefficient	S.E.	t-ratio	Approx. d.f.	p-value
Intercept, G000	471.75	(14.03)	33.619	50	<0.001
School_competition, G010	18.20	(2.25)	8.075	52	<0.001
School_competition * system_yearsseparate, G011	7.40	(1.67)	4.419	52	<0.001
System_yearsseparate, G001	1.02	(10.04)	0.102	50	0.920
System_competition, G002	0.05	(1.01)	0.05	50	0.961
System_yearsseparate* system_competition, G003	–0.38	(0.73)	–0.519	50	0.605
Missing dummy					
Mschool_competition, B02	6.10	(5.19)	1.177	13878	0.240

Note. All regressors are grand-mean centered.

Table 3.2 presents the results for the gross quality model, in which socio-economic and demographic background variables were not accounted for. Consistent with previous empirical findings, early tracking is not related to student performance in science (system_yearsseparate; G001 = 1.02; p = 0.920). Also consistent with related investigations, students in schools that compete for students with one or more other schools in the same area perform significantly better than students in schools not competing for students with other schools (school_competition; G010 = 18.20; p < 0.001). The difference amounts to 18 score points, which is equivalent to little less than half a grade-level equivalent (estimated at 38 score points). Moreover, early tracking and school competition interact: The performance difference between competing schools and noncompeting schools is wider in education systems that practice early tracking (school_competition*system_yearsseparate; G011 = 7.40; p < 0.001). One may thus hypothesize that the earlier students are separated into different school types, the more important is the possibility of parental choice between schools that compete for students in the same local area.

Figure 3.1 illustrates this outcome, using the model coefficients estimated for the gross quality model for early tracking (at age 11, system_yearsseparate = 4) and late tracking (at age 15, system_yearsseparate = 0). The data points on the left indicate the average performance level for schools that do not face competition in the local area, whereas on the right, the average performance level of schools that compete with other schools for students are given. In both early- and late-tracking systems, illustrated by the dotted and solid lines, respectively, competition among schools goes hand in hand with higher average performance, but the gap is much wider in early-tracking systems. Early tracking and school competition is associated with higher average performance than late tracking and school competition.

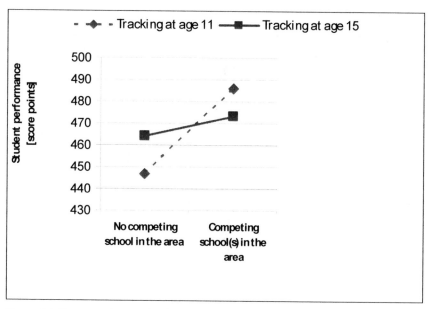

Figure 3.1 Gross quality model: Illustration of outcomes.

Looking at the system level, the results show that there is no statistically significant compositional effect; that is, education systems with a bigger share of school competition do not necessarily perform better, over and above the effect of school competition at the school level (*system_competition*; G002 = 0.05; p = 0.961). Neither can an interaction between early tracking and the share of school competition in a country be found (*system_competition* system_yearsseparate*; G003 =−0.38; p = 0.605).

Net Quality Model

The formal specification of the net quality model takes into account various socioeconomic and demographic background factors, characterized in Appendix 3.1. The net quality model thus provides an estimate of the (statistical) effects of the variables of interest while controlling for the differences in the composition of schools and the country context in general.

Model at the student level (Level 1):

$$Y = P0 + P1*(student\_ESCS) + P2*(Mstudent\_ESCS) + P3*(student\_ESCS^2) + P4*(student\_female) + P5*(student\_native) + P6*(Mstudent\_native) + P7*(student\_samelanguage) + P8*(Mstudent\_samelanguage) + E$$

Model at the school level (Level 2):

P0 = B00 + B01*(*school_ESCS*) + B02*(*Mschool_ESCS*) + B03*(*school_rural*) + B04*(*school_city*) + B05*(*Mschool_rural*) + B06*(*school_size*) + B07*(*school_size^2*) + B08*(*Mschool_size*) + B09*(*school_competition*) + B010*(*Mschool_competition*) + R0

Model at the system level (Level 3):

B00 = G000 + G001(*system_yearsseparate*) + G002(*system_competition*) + G003(*system_ESCS*) + G004(*system_yearsseparate * system_competition*) + U00

B09 = G090 + G091(*system_yearsseparate*) + U09

Table 3.3   Results of the Net Quality Model

Fixed Effect	Coefficient	S.E.	t-ratio	Approx. d.f.	p-value
Intercept, **G000**	470.42	(11.96)	39.339	49	<0.001
School_competition, **G090**	1.16	(1.49)	0.778	52	0.440
*School_competition*system_ yearsseparate*, **G091**	3.16	(0.97)	3.253	52	0.002
System_yearsseparate, **G001**	0.56	(5.54)	0.102	49	0.920
System_competition, **G002**	0.46	(0.68)	0.684	49	0.497
*System_yearsseparate *system_competition*, **G004**	−0.33	(0.32)	−1.025	49	0.311

Background variables

Student_ESCS, **P1**	16.89	(1.14)	14.795	382561	<0.001
Student_ESCS^2, **P3**	1.89	(0.41)	4.651	14897	<0.001
Student_female, **P4**	−6.21	(1.05)	-5.918	3852	<0.001
Student_native, **P5**	10.99	(3.51)	3.135	55754	0.002
Student_samelanguage, **P7**	25.84	(2.86)	9.038	3833	<0.001
School_ESCS, **B01**	54.19	(3.63)	14.944	13870	<0.001
School_rural, **B03**	6.53	(1.68)	3.888	2834	<0.001
School_city, **B04**	−6.32	(1.44)	−4.375	13870	<0.001
School_size, **B06**	1.96	(0.33)	6.012	13870	<0.001
School_size^2, **B07**	−0.03	(0.01)	−4.11	13870	<0.001
System_ESCS, **G003**	5.95	(33.17)	0.18	49	0.859

Missing dummies

Mstudent_ESCS, **P2**	−16.52	(5.43)	−3.044	13932	0.003
Mstudent_native, **P6**	−23.53	(4.51)	−5.215	4842	<0.001
Mstudent_samelanguage, **P8**	−1.15	(3.85)	−0.298	21186	0.766
Mschool_ESCS, **G010**	10.96	(36.24)	0.302	1071	0.762
Mschool_rural, **B05**	5.44	(5.41)	1.006	1380	0.315
Mschool_size, **B08**	−4.11	(3.31)	-1.24	345	0.216
Mschool_competition, **B010**	−6.85	(3.78)	−1.814	7554	0.069

The pattern of outcomes changes when looking at the results of the net quality model, which accounts for the socioeconomic and demographic background of students, schools, and countries. As shown in Table 3.3, the performance advantage that associates with school competition at the school level in the gross model disappears in the net model (*school_competition*; G090 = 1.16; p = 0.440). With the socioeconomic background variables for students and schools based on the *ESCS* index showing the strongest effect on performance, one may conclude that students in schools that face more competition come from more advantaged backgrounds, and the schools themselves are located in more advantaged neighborhoods. The interaction between institutional differentiation and school competition, however, remains significant in the net model (*school_competition*system_yearsseparate*; G091 = 3.16; p = 0.002) even though the effect decreases by more than half, from 7.40 to 3.16 score points. Similar to the gross model, none of the variables considered at system level is statistically significant.

Figure 3.2 illustrates the outcomes of the net quality model, for education systems in which tracking occurs at age 11 compared to age 15. It shows that even while accounting for socioeconomic and demographic background factors, the combination of a high level of competition among schools in the local area and early tracking is associated with higher student performance, even though the statistical effects become smaller. It is, however, also important to note that this analysis does not permit causal attribution. Whether this result indicates that early tracking coupled with school competition leads to better average student performance, or whether it signifies that in early-tracking education systems more competition can be found among schools in the academically oriented tracks cannot be decided from the database available from PISA.

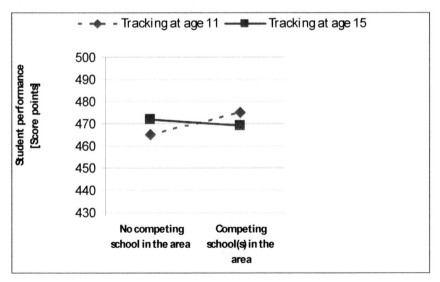

Figure 3.2   Net quality model: Illustration of outcomes.

In sum, early tracking in general is not associated with higher performance, and the performance advantage of school competition disappears after accounting for socioeconomic and demographic background factors. There is a performance advantage for schools competing with other school(s) in early-tracking systems, however, and this advantage remains even after adjusting for the socioeconomic and demographic background factors of students, schools, and countries. The data provided in PISA are cross-sectional in nature; therefore, it cannot be decided whether this result indicates that the combination of school competition and early tracking leads to higher performance or that more school competition exists in academically oriented tracks (where students show higher performance on average).

EFFECT OF INSTITUTIONAL DIFFERENTIATION AND SCHOOL COMPETITION ON THE RELATIONSHIP OF SOCIOECONOMIC BACKGROUND AND PERFORMANCE

Turning to the effects of school competition and early tracking on educational equity, it was found that early tracking is related to inequality of learning opportunities (OECD, 2007a). Furthermore, opponents of school competition argue that school competition will increase inequity. In addition to these questions, the following section examines whether school competition augments inequity in early-tracking systems.

As mentioned earlier, educational equity is defined as the relationship between socioeconomic background and performance both at the student and at the system level. The following analysis takes into account the same background variables as in the net quality model. Contrary to the net quality model, however, the socioeconomic background of students as measured by the *ESCS* index and the school's socioeconomic intake (i.e., the average *ESCS* of the students at the school) are no longer considered as background variables but rather as outcome variables (slopes-as-outcome models)[6]. The statistical analysis is formalized as follows:

Model at the student level (Level 1):

$Y = P0 + P1*(student\_ESCS) + P2*(Mstudent\_ESCS) + P3*(student\_ESCS^2) + P4*(student\_female) + P5*(student\_native) + P6*(Mstudent\_native) + P7*(student\_samelanguage) + P8*(Mstudent\_samelanguage) + E$

Model at the school level (Level 2):

$P0 = B00 + B01*(school\_ESCS) + B02*(Mschool\_ESCS) + B03*(school\_rural) + B04*(school\_city) + B05*(Mschool\_rural) + B06*(school\_size) + B07*(school\_size^2) + B08*(Mschool\_size) + B09*(school\_competition) + B010*(Mschool\_competition) + B011*(school\_ESCS*school\_competition) + R0$

P1 = B10 + B11*(*school_competition*) + R1

Model at the system level (Level 3):

B00 = G000 + G001(*system_yearsseparate*) + G002(*system_competition*) + G003(*system_ESCS*) + G004(*system_yearsseparate*system_ competition*) + U00

B01 = G010 + G011(*system_yearsseparate*) + G012(*system_competition*) + G013(*system_yearsseparate*system_competition*) + U01

B09 = G090 + G091(*system_yearsseparate*) + U09

B011 = G0110 + G0111(*system_yearsseparate*) + U011

B10 = G100 + G101(*system_yearsseparate*) + G102(*system_competition*) + G103(*system_yearsseparate*system_competition*) + U10

B11 = G110 + G111(*system_yearsseparate*) + U11

The results are presented in Table 3.4. They are consistent with the findings in the initial international report of PISA 2006 (OECD, 2007a) in that early institutional tracking is related to a higher impact of the socioeconomic composition of schools on performance (*school_ESCS*system_ yearsseparate*; $G011 = 10.80$; $p < 0.001$). Within schools, this effect goes hand in hand with a smaller impact of the individual student's socioeconomic background on performance in education systems with early institutional tracking (*student_ESCS*system_yearsseparate*; $G101 = -1.79$; $p = 0.006$). The gain in equity within schools is much smaller than the loss in equity between schools, however. Thus, on balance, early selection into different institutional tracks reinforces socioeconomic inequalities in learning opportunities.

Turning to school competition, the analysis shows that enhanced parental choice through school competition is associated with more inequitable learning opportunities at the school level but not at the system level (*school_ESCS*school_competition*; $G0110 = 8.85$; $p < 0.001$, and *school_ESCS*system_competition*; $G012 = 0.34$; $p = 0.156$, respectively).

Furthermore, over and above the effect on the school level, the share of schools that face competition at the system level interacts with institutional differentiation in its impact on equity (*school_ESCS*system_ yearsseparate*system_competition*; $G013 = -0.35$; $p = 0.035$), in that in a country or economy that practices early tracking, a higher share of school competition is more equitable than a lower share, whereas in late-tracking systems, it is the other way around.

Table 3.4   Results of the Equity Model

Fixed Effect	Coefficient	S.E.	t-ratio	Approx. d.f.	p-value
Estimates of within-school effect of the PISA index of economic, social, and cultural status on performance (slope of student_ESCS)					
Student_ESCS, G100	16.98	(1.22)	13.896	50	<0.001
Student_ESCS*school_competition, G110	0.35	(0.74)	0.473	52	0.638
Student_ESCS*system_competition, G102	−0.03	(0.07)	−0.522	50	0.603
Student_ESCS*system_yearsseparate, G101	−1.79	(0.62)	−2.899	50	0.006
Student_ESCS*school_competition* system_yearsseparate, G111	−0.09	(0.52)	−0.168	52	0.867
Student_ESCS*system_competition* system_yearsseparate, G103	0.02	(0.04)	0.52	50	0.605
Estimates of compositional effect of the school average PISA index of economic, social and cultural status on performance (slope of school_ESCS)					
School_ESCS, G010	61.72	(3.67)	16.812	50	<0.001
School_ESCS*school_competition, G0110	8.85	(2.11)	4.187	362	<0.001
School_ESCS*system_competition, G012	0.34	(0.24)	1.441	50	0.156
School_ESCS*system_yearsseparate, G011	10.80	(2.33)	4.626	50	<0.001
School_ESCS*school_competition* system_yearsseparate, G0111	0.84	(1.36)	0.618	13869	0.537
School_ESCS*system_competition* system_yearsseparate, G013	−0.35	(0.16)	−2.16	50	0.035
Estimates of the performance level in science (Intercept)					
Intercept, G000	464.22	(5.68)	81.682	49	<0.001
School_competition, B09	0.02	(1.54)	0.014	52	0.989
System_competition, G002	0.45	(0.32)	1.419	49	0.162
System_yearsseparate, G001	−2.31	(2.50)	−0.923	49	0.361
School_competition*system_ yearsseparate, G091	0.46	(1.06)	0.435	52	0.665
System_competition*system_ yearsseparate, G004	−0.20	(0.15)	−1.313	49	0.195

(continued)

Table 3.4   (continued)

Fixed Effect	Coefficient	S.E.	t-ratio	Approx. d.f.	p-value
Background variables					
Student_ESCS², **G300**	−0.04	(0.29)	−0.149	1318	0.882
Student_female, **G400**	−6.38	(1.07)	−5.965	3787	<0.001
Student_native, **G500**	10.83	(3.31)	3.271	48749	0.001
Student_samelanguage, **G700**	23.80	(2.79)	8.52	5713	<0.001
School_rural, **B03**	3.88	(1.54)	2.523	2280	0.012
School_city, **B04**	−6.02	(1.43)	−4.201	13869	<0.001
School_size, **B06**	1.69	(0.29)	5.779	13869	<0.001
School_size², **B07**	−0.02	(0.01)	−3.573	13869	0.001
System_ESCS, **G003**	12.82	(10.84)	1.183	49	0.243
Missing dummies					
Mstudent_ESCS, **G200**	−18.20	(5.50)	−3.307	16938	0.001
Mstudent_native, **G600**	−23.32	(4.40)	−5.298	4374	<0.001
Mstudent_samelanguage, **G800**	−2.22	(3.82)	−0.582	45600	0.560
Mschool_competition, **B010**	−5.32	(3.66)	−1.454	7501	0.146
Mschool_ESCS, **B02**	7.80	(35.43)	0.22	1110	0.826
Mschool_rural, **B05**	4.28	(5.20)	0.824	1358	0.410
Mschool_size, **B08**	−3.10	(3.10)	−0.999	332	0.319

Figure 3.3 illustrates the outcomes of the equity model on the system level, for educational systems that practice tracking at ages 11 and 15, respectively, and for which the share of schools competing for other schools in the area is relatively high (1 standard deviation above the average over all countries and economies) or relatively low (1 standard deviation below).

First of all, the dotted line is placed above the solid line, which illustrates the overall effect of the age at which students are institutionally tracked in the education system for the first time: The (statistical) impact of the school's socioeconomic intake (as measured by the variable *school_ESCS*) on performance is higher in early-tracking systems than in late-tracking systems. Second, the dotted line declines with an increase in the proportion of school competition at the system level, while the solid line increases, showing that among early-tracking systems, a higher share of school competition in the country or economy relates to less impact of the school's socioeconomic intake on performance, that is, to more equitable

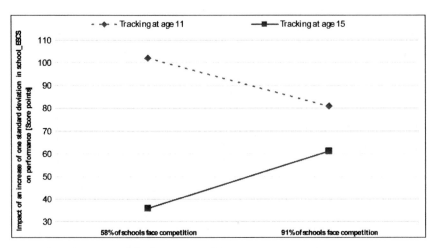

Figure 3.3   Equity model: Illustration of outcomes.

conditions. In contrast to this, a higher degree of equity is related to a lower share of school competition in late-tracking systems.

ROBUSTNESS OF OUTCOMES

Inclusion of Further Predictor Variables

This chapter investigated the effects of school competition and institutional differentiation on the quality and equity of performance. Because only a small selection of the characteristics of schools and school systems have been addressed, it is possible that the results are biased. This would be the case if, for example, an institutional factor that has an impact on the quality or equity of education systems, and that is correlated with the competition between schools or institutional differentiation, was not included in our multilevel modelling equations. To minimize the risk of bias caused by omitted variables, the robustness of the results was tested by including other school and system characteristics that were found to be significant predictors of the quality or equity of educational outcomes in the international initial report for PISA 2006 (OECD, 2007a, 2007b).

For the net quality model, these additional predictors include, at the school level, the variables *Ability grouping for all school subjects (within school)*, *High and low academic selectivity of school admittance*, *Public posting of school achievement data*, the *Index of school autonomy in budgeting* (derived from the school principal's responses on whether the school has a considerable responsibility in formulating the school budget and deciding on budget allocations within the school), *Learning time (for regular lessons, out-of-school lessons, and self-study or homework)*, as well as *School activities to promote the students' learning of science*, and, at the system level, the average of the *Index of school autonomy in budgeting* in the country or economy (OECD, 2007a). When these predictors are included, the interaction effect of institutional differentiation and school competition on performance is reduced slightly from 2.71 to 2.24 score points but retains statistical significance ($p = 0.016$). The change in results is not considerable, when taking into account the number of additional predictors (eight variables and their eight missing dummies) that have entered the analysis.

For the equity model, the initial international report of PISA 2006 (OECD, 2007a, 2007b) found two predictors: *Institutional differentiation* at the system level and *Learning time for regular lessons in school* at the school level. Inclusion of this latter predictor in the equity model affects one result, namely, the statistical impact of school competition at the school level (*school_ESCS*school_competition*), which is greatly reduced from 8.85 to 3.78 score points and fails to reach statistical significance ($p = 0.068$). This outcome gives an indication that the relationship of the schools facing competition from other schools and the schools' socioeconomic intake is mediated by learning time or by other factors for which learning time may serve as a proxy, such as different school curricula, for example.

Public and Private Schools

The PISA data provide information on whether a school competes with other schools for students in the local area. The data do not provide information on whether those (other) schools are privately or publicly managed or funded, which previous investigations have identified as an important dimension with regard to differences in the quality and equity of educational systems. Therefore, a further robustness analysis addressed the hypothesis that any effects of school competition in the present analysis may be related exclusively to privately managed and privately funded schools. As shown in Appendix 3.2, school principals of government-independent private schools[7] and government-dependent (i.e. government-funded) private schools,[8] as well as government or public schools,[9] reported to have one or more other schools in local areas that compete for their students so that parents have options to choose a school for their children. School competition in government or public schools varies across countries: from 27% in Iceland, where the majority of schools are government or public schools, to 100% in Hong Kong-China. The median value for the share of public schools facing competition in the local area is 72%.

It was tested whether the interaction effect of institutional differentiation and school competition on student performance varies for government-independent private schools, government-dependent private schools, and government or public schools. No significant differences in the interaction effect of institutional differentiation and school competition are found for the three school types, neither at school level nor at the system level. This result suggests that the joint effect of institutional tracking and school competition on performance does not change when differentiating between government-independent private schools, government-dependent private schools, and government or public schools. Neither does it change when taking into account the prevalence of the different school types in the countries and economies.

In the same way, the robustness of the outcomes of the equity model was tested. Although the point estimates for the effect of institutional tracking and the interaction of tracking and the share of schools facing competition on the system level change but slightly (from 10.80 to 10.53 for the effect of institutional tracking and from -0.35 to -0.36 for the interaction of tracking and the share of schools facing competition in the country or economy), these estimates turn statistically insignificant. Bearing in mind the very minor change in point estimates, however, one may conclude that the present analysis is reasonably robust with respect to the public versus private management and funding of schools. The private management of schools is a prevalent proxy for parental school choice, and it is interesting to note that the pattern of outcomes reported in this chapter does not change when including this proxy in the analysis.

CONCLUSIONS

This chapter looked at the effect of school competition and institutional differentiation into different school types, as well as the combined effect of these two factors on educational quality and equity. Based on previous empirical evidence, two hypotheses were tested using the PISA 2006 international database: (1) that institutional differentiation in the form of early tracking does not have any positive impact on the average student performance within a country, but competition between schools does; and (2) that both institutional differentiation and competition between schools increase the inequality of learning opportunities in education systems. Additionally, it was explored whether a combination of institutional differentiation and competition between schools is associated with an additional performance advantage, or with an additional detrimental impact on equity within education systems. When looking at the outcomes of the multilevel regression analyses, it has to be borne in mind that the PISA 2006 data set is cross-sectional in nature, thus precluding any causal interpretation of the statistical effects found. The

analyses give an indication, however, of how institutional differentiation of students, on the one hand, and the competition of schools with
other schools in the area, on the other, relate to student performance in
the 54 countries and economies for which the data are available.

Concurring with previous findings, in the present analyses, institutional differentiation does not affect student performance on average.
Furthermore, students from areas where schools compete for students
perform significantly better. This effect, however, is largely due to differences in the socioeconomic background of students and schools. After
accounting for socioeconomic and demographic background variables,
the general advantage of school competition is no longer visible. This
result points to the possible existence of sorting effects, in that (a) students
with an advantaged socioeconomic home background attend schools that
compete with other schools in the local area, and (b) competition among
schools is especially prevalent in schools with an advantaged socioeconomic intake.

On the other hand, even after accounting for background variables,
it is found that the more positive the effect is of school competition on
student performance, the earlier the age is at which students are institutionally differentiated for the first time. The net effect is approximately
3 score points for each year before the age of 15; that is, in education
systems in which institutional differentiation occurs at age 11, it is 12
score points, or almost one third of a grade-level equivalent. Further
studies will need to investigate whether this effect rests on more school
competition leading to higher performance in early-tracking systems, or
whether more competition can be found among schools in the higher
tracks of early-tracking education systems. What can be safely concluded
from the present analysis is that giving parents the possibility to choose
between different schools competing in the local area does not automatically lead to a performance advantage. In sum, our first hypothesis is
partly supported.

Turning to issues of equity, in corroboration with previous findings,
institutional differentiation is found to increase the impact of the schools'
socioeconomic intake on performance by approximately 11 score points for
every year that is tracked before the age of 15, while the impact of students'
socioeconomic background on performance within schools decreases by 2
score points. It should be noted that this effect of early tracking on inequity
is much stronger than the combined benefit of school competition and early
tracking on performance.

Similarly, school competition has an influence on the relationship
between performance and socioeconomic background. The higher impact
of the schools' socioeconomic intake on performance that comes with
schools competing for students is mediated, however, by the time students
spent in regular lessons at school. When including learning time in the
analysis, the contribution of school competition is greatly reduced from

8.85 to 3.78 score points. It is for future studies to investigate whether differences in school curricula, or other school policies and practices that are proxied by learning time, produce this effect.

Interestingly, in the present analysis, the share of schools competing with other schools in a country or economy does not play a role per se, but there is a strong interaction effect with institutional differentiation (for an illustration, see Figure 3.3). Although inequity is generally higher with earlier institutional differentiation of students, a higher share of schools competing with other schools for students weakens this effect: An increase by 16% (one standard deviation) in early-tracking countries or economies corresponds to a decrease of the impact of the school's socioeconomic intake on performance by 10 score points. Thus, competition among schools for students can be seen as beneficial to equity in early-tracking systems. In late-tracking educational systems, however, higher shares of schools that compete for students in the area are related to greater inequality of learning opportunities. Our second hypothesis is thus partly confirmed.

The results presented in this chapter point to a trade-off between the quality and equity of school systems: On the one hand, the combination of school competition and early institutional differentiation into different school types is associated with higher overall student performance. On the other hand, early institutional differentiation is detrimental to the equality of learning opportunities. It is found that this effect is milder when there is a high share of school competition in the country or economy, which may point to the different nature of school competition in educational systems that track their students into different institutions at an early versus late stage. It may be hypothesized that in late-tracking systems, competition among schools is influenced directly by the socioeconomic resources of the parents choosing a school for their children. In the early-tracking systems in which parents cannot choose among different schools in the area, the case would be similar, albeit at a higher impact level of the school's socioeconomic intake on performance overall. (From the present analysis, as well as from previous research, it is well-known that socioeconomic background and attendance of students in higher, academically oriented tracks is particularly closely related in early-tracking systems; therefore, a large part of the variation would already be taken up by the choice of the track the child attends.) If there is competition among schools in early-tracking systems, one may further assume that there would be more of it in the higher, academically oriented tracks and for better-performing students, thereby counteracting part of the high impact of the school's socioeconomic intake on performance in these countries or economies. For the time being, this interpretation is pure speculation. Future studies are needed to further address the issue by investigating, for example, the joint effect of school competition and school admission policies, while taking policies of institutional differentiation into account.

Appendix 3.1 Descriptive Statistics of the Background Variables Feeding into the Net Analysis Models

Variable Description	Variable Name	Mean	S.D.	Min.	Max.	% missing
STUDENT LEVEL						
Student's index of economic, social, and cultural status (ESCS)	*Student_ESCS; Mstudent_ ESCS*	–0.21	1.08	–5.67	3.35	0.95
Student's index of economic, social, and cultural status squared	*Student_ESCS²*	1.22	1.81	0.00	32.14	0.95
Student is female	*Student_female*	0.50	0.50	0.00	1.00	<0.01
Student is native student (not first- or second-generation migrant student)	*Student_native; Mstudent_ native*	0.88	0.33	0.00	1.00	2.40
Student speaks the test language or other national language most of the time or always at home	*Student_same-language; Mstudent_ samelanguage*	0.93	0.26	0.00	1.00	3.45
SCHOOL LEVEL						
School located in a small town or village (fewer than 15,000 people)	*school_rural; Mschool_rural*	0.32	0.47	0.00	1.00	1.52
School located in a city (with over 100,000 people)	*school_city*	0.36	0.48	0.00	1.00	1.52
School size	*school_size; Mschool_size*	8.43	7.45	0.03	100.00	2.63
School size squared	*school_size2*	126.58	385.35	0.00	10000.00	2.63
School average index of economic, social, and cultural status	*school_ESCS; Mschool_ESCS*	–0.21	0.74	–3.67	1.75	<0.01
SYSTEM LEVEL						
Mean ESCS of the country or economy	*system_ESCS*	–0.21	0.51	–1.52	0.77	–

Note: For the computation of the percentages of missing values, equal country weights were used. The first letter "*M*" in variable names signifies a missing dummy. As only four (un-weighted) cases are missing in the variable "*female*," the missing value was imputed to 0 and no missing dummy was created for this variable.

Appendix 3.2   School Competition by Type of School

	Government-independent private schools		Government-dependent private schools		Government or public schools	
	%	S.E.	%	S.E.	%	S.E.
OECD						
Australia	w	w	w	w	w	w
Austria	c	c	68	(12.7)	64	(3.7)
Belgium	77	(20.9)	91	(2.5)	94	(2.5)
Canada	97	(1.9)	98	(1.8)	76	(2.4)
Czech Republic	c	c	100	(0.0)	85	(2.7)
Denmark	c	c	83	(6.3)	76	(3.9)
Finland	m		92	(7.4)	55	(3.8)
Germany	c	c	100	(0.0)	82	(2.7)
Greece	100	(0.0)	m	m	57	(3.5)
Hungary	c	c	90	(6.8)	73	(4.1)
Iceland	c	c	c	c	27	(0.2)
Ireland	100	(0.0)	91	(2.8)	72	(5.2)
Italy	64	(15.3)	98	(0.8)	81	(2.6)
Japan	98	(1.8)	c	c	86	(3.1)
Korea	75	(9.5)	90	(4.2)	84	(4.3)
Luxembourg	m	m	87	(0.1)	63	(0.1)
Mexico	99	(0.6)	m	m	82	(2.3)
Netherlands	m	m	90	(2.9)	88	(4.4)
New Zealand	100	(0.0)	m	m	89	(2.2)
Norway	m	m	100	(0.0)	33	(3.6)
Poland	100	(0.0)	100	(0.0)	64	(3.5)
Portugal	100	(0.0)	73	(19.5)	72	(4.0)
Slovak Republic	c	c	95	(5.1)	91	(2.3)
Spain	74	(7.1)	98	(1.3)	73	(3.1)
Sweden	m	m	100	(0.2)	60	(4.0)
Switzerland	93	(5.2)	78	(19.0)	39	(2.8)
Turkey	c	c	m	m	67	(4.0)
United Kingdom	100	(0.0)	c	c	92	(1.6)
United States	100	(0.0)	c	c	72	(3.3)

(continued)

Appendix 3.2   (continued)

	Government-independent private schools		Government-dependent private schools		Government or public schools	
	%	S.E	%	S.E.	%	S.E.
Partners						
Argentina	100	(0.0)	91	(5.8)	74	(4.2)
Brazil	93	(4.5)	m	m	64	(2.7)
Bulgaria	w	w	w	w	w	w
Chile	92	(7.8)	86	(4.5)	72	(6.2)
Colombia	95	(4.6)	91	(13.2)	72	(6.1)
Croatia	c	c	c	c	77	(3.5)
Estonia	c	c	100	(0.0)	78	(2.7)
Hong Kong-China	c	c	99	(1.0)	100	(0.0)
Indonesia	99	(1.2)	100	(0.0)	92	(2.3)
Israel	58	(15.3)	89	(7.7)	84	(3.7)
Jordan	91	(6.2)	c	c	50	(4.5)
Kyrgyzstan	c	c	m	m	64	(2.9)
Latvia	m	m	m	m	96	(1.6)
Liechtenstein	c	c	m	m	56	(0.7)
Lithuania	m	m	c	c	72	(2.9)
Macao-China	76	(0.1)	97	(0.0)	c	c
Montenegro	c	c	m	m	98	(0.1)
Romania	m	m	m	m	55	(5.4)
Russian Federation	m	m	m	m	68	(4.3)
Serbia	m	m	c	c	73	(3.7)
Slovenia	c	c	c	c	53	(0.6)
Chinese Taipei	98	(1.5)	m	m	91	(2.8)
Thailand	100	(0.0)	88	(11.2)	87	(3.3)
Tunisia	m	m	c	c	50	(5.2)
Uruguay	90	(1.8)	m	m	41	(3.5)

Note: The symbols *c*, *m* and *w* denote missing data. The symbol *c* indicates that there are too few observations to provide reliable estimates; *m* signifies that data are not available for technical reasons; and *w* stands for data that have been withdrawn at the request of the country concerned.

NOTES TO CHAPTER 3

1. The important distinction between privately managed, government-funded schools and privately managed independent schools is also highlighted when comparing the relative effectiveness of public versus private schools. Although students in private schools are typically found to perform significantly better than those in public schools (see, e.g., Fuchs & Wößmann, 2007; Toma, 1996; Vandenberghe & Robin, 2004), the performance difference is mainly due to the difference in the socioeconomic composition of their students (e.g., OECD, 2007a, 2007b); remaining net performance differences between private and public schools have been related to better school climate in private schools, for instance (Dronkers & Robert, 2008).
2. In correspondence to the question put before OECD countries, the exact wording of the question to the National Project Managers of non-OECD countries and economies reads: "At which age do students experience the first selection in the education system, that is, at which age are decisions between different school types generally made for the first time?"
3. As documented in the PISA 2006 Technical Report (OECD, 2009), a comparison of within-country Principal Component Analyses has shown that the patterns of factor loadings are generally similar across countries and economies. The national scale reliabilities for z-standardized variables (Cronbach's Alpha) range between 0.52 and 0.80.
4. These results are based on single-level bivariate regression, whereas the analysis later in this chapter is based on multilevel multivariate regression.
5. The commercial software Hierarchical Linear and Nonlinear Modelling (HLM) 6.08 was used in the computations.
6. Performing the computations without the background factors led to very similar results; thus, the outcomes are not reported separately.
7. Schools that receive less than 50% of their core funding (i.e., funding that supports the basic educational services of the institution) from government agencies.
8. Schools that receive 50% or more of their core funding (i.e., funding that supports the basic educational services of the institution) from government agencies.
9. Schools that are directly controlled or managed by (a) a public education authority or agency, or (b) a government agency directly, or (c) a governing body, most of whose members are either appointed by a public authority or elected by public franchise.

REFERENCES

Adams, R. J., & Wu, M. L. (2007). The mixed-coefficients multinomial logit model: A generalized form of the Rasch model. In M. von Davier & C. H. Carstensen (Eds.), *Multivariate and mixture distribution Rasch models: Extensions and applications* (pp. 57–75). New York: Springer.

Ammermüller, A. (2005). *Educational opportunities and the role of institutions* (ZEW Discussion Paper 05–44). Mannheim: Centre for European Economic Research.

Ammermüller, A., & Pischke, J.-S. (2009). Peer effects in European primary schools: Evidence from the Progress in International Reading Literacy Study. *Journal of Labor Economics, 27*, 315–348.

Angrist, J., Bettinger, E., Bloom, E., King, E., & Kremer, M. (2002). Vouchers for private schooling in Colombia: Evidence from a randomized natural experiment. *American Economic Review, 92*, 1535–1558.

Baker, D., & LeTendre, G. (2005). *National differences, global similarities: World culture and the future of schooling.* Stanford, CA: Stanford University Press.

Bayer, P., & McMillan, R. (2005). *Choice and competition in local education markets* (NBER Working Paper Series 11802). Cambridge, MA: National Bureau of Economic Research.

Belfield, C. R., & Levin, H. M. (2002). The effects of competition between schools on educational outcomes: A review for the United States. *Review of Educational Research, 72,* 279–341.

Betts, J. R., & Roemer, J. E. (2007). Equalizing opportunity for racial and socio-economic groups in the United States through educational-finance reform. In L. Wößmann & P. E. Peterson (Eds.), *Schools and the equal opportunity problem* (pp. 209–237). Cambridge, MA: MIT Press.

Bifulco, R., Ladd, H. F., & Ross, S. (2008). *Public school choice and integration: Evidence from Durham, North Carolina* (Center for Policy Research Working Paper No. 109). Syracuse, NY: Syracuse University, Center for Policy Research.

Bradley, S., & Taylor, J. (2002). The effect of the quasi-market on the efficiency-equity trade-off in the secondary school sector. *Bulletin of Economic Research, 54,* 295–314.

Brunello, G., & Checchi, D. (2007). Does school tracking affect equality of opportunity? New international evidence. *Economic Policy, 22,* 781–861.

Cohen, J., & Cohen, P. (1983). *Applied multiple regression/correlation analysis for the behavioral sciences* (2nd ed.). Hillsdale, NJ: Erlbaum.

Cullen, J. B., Jacob, B. A., & Levitt, S. D. (2005). The impact of school choice on student outcomes: An analysis of the Chicago public schools. *Journal of Public Economics, 89,* 729–760.

de Ayala, R. J. (2009). *The theory and practice of item response theory.* New York: Guilford Press.

Dronkers, J., & Robert, P. (2008). Differences in scholastic achievement of public, private government-dependent, and private independent schools: A cross-national analysis. *Educational Policy, 22,* 541–577.

Embretson, S. E., & Reise, S. P. (2000). *Item response theory for psychologists.* Mahwah, NJ: Erlbaum.

Epple, D., Newlon, E., & Romano, R. E. (2002). Ability tracking, school competition, and the distribution of educational benefits. *Journal of Public Economics, 83,* 1–48.

Figlio, D. N., & Page, M. E. (2002). School choice and the distributional effects of ability tracking: Does separation increase inequality? *Journal of Urban Economics, 51,* 497–514.

Fuchs, T., & Wößmann, L. (2007). What accounts for international differences in student performance? A re-examination using PISA data. *Empirical Economics, 32,* 433–464.

Ganzeboom, H. B. G., de Graaf, P. M., & Treiman, D. J. (1992), A standard international socioeconomic index of occupational status. *Social Science Research, 21,* 1–56.

Hanushek, E. A., & Wößmann, L. (2006). Does early tracking affect educational inequality and performance? Differences-in-differences evidence across countries. *Economic Journal, 116,* C63–C76.

Howell, W. G., Wolf, P. J., Campbell, D. E., & Peterson, P. E. (2002). School vouchers and academic performance: Results from three randomized field trials. *Journal of Policy Analysis and Management, 21,* 191–217.

Hoxby, C. M. (2000). Does competition among public schools benefit students and taxpayers?. *American Economic Review, 90,* 1209–1238.

Hoxby, C. M. (2003). School choice and school competition: Evidence from the United States. *Swedish Economic Policy Review, 10,* 9–65.

International Labour Organisation (ILO). (1990). *International standard classification of occupations: ISCO-88*. Geneva: International Labour Office.

Ladd, H. F. (2002). School vouchers: A critical view. *Journal of Economic Perspectives, 16*, 3–24.

Masters, G. N., & Wright, B. D. (1997). The partial credit model. In W. J. van der Linden & R. K. Hambleton (Eds.), *Handbook of Modern Item Response Theory* (pp.101–121). New York: Springer.

Meghir, C., & Palme, M. (2005). Educational reform, ability, and family background. *American Economic Review, 95*, 414–424.

Neal, D. (1997). The effects of Catholic secondary schooling on secondary achievement. *Journal of Labor Economics, 15*, 98–123.

Organisation for Economic Co-Operation and Development (OECD). (1999). *Classifying educational programmes: Manual for ISCED-97 implementation in OECD countries*. Paris: Author.

Organisation for Economic Co-operation and Development (OECD). (2006). *Education at a glance: OECD indicators 2006*. Paris: Author.

Organisation for Economic Co-operation and Development (OECD). (2007a). *PISA 2006 science competencies for tomorrow's world: Vol. 1. Analysis*. Paris: Author.

Organisation for Economic Co-operation and Development (OECD). (2007b). *PISA 2006 science competencies for tomorrow's world: Vol. 2. Data*. Paris: Author.

Organisation for Economic Co-operation and Development (OECD). (2009). *PISA 2006 technical report*. Paris: Author.

Raudenbush, S. W., & Bryk, A. S. (2002). *Hierarchical linear models: Applications and data analysis methods*. London: Sage.

Sandström, F. M., & Bergström, F. (2005). School vouchers in practice: Competition will not hurt you. *Journal of Public Economics, 89*, 351–380.

Schütz, G., Ursprung, H., & Wößmann, L. (2008). Education policy and equality of opportunity. *Kyklos, 61*, 279–308.

Snijders, T., & Bosker, R. (1999). *Multilevel analysis: An introduction to basic and advanced multilevel modelling*. London: Sage.

Söderström, M., & Uusitalo, R. (2010). School choice and segregation: Evidence from an admission reform. *Scandinavian Journal of Economics, 112*, 55–76.

Toma, E. F. (1996). Public funding and private schooling across countries. *Journal of Law and Economics, 39*, 121–148.

Vandenberghe, V., & Robin, S. (2004). Evaluating the effectiveness of private education across countries: A comparison of methods. *Labour Economics, 11*, 487–506.

Wilson, M. (2005). *Constructing measures: An item response modelling approach*. Mahwah, NJ: Erlbaum.

Wößmann, L. (2001). Why students in some countries do better: International evidence on the importance of education policy. *Education Matters, 1*, 67–74.

Wößmann, L. (2003). Schooling resources, educational institutions and student performance: The international evidence. *Oxford Bulletin of Economics and Statistics, 65*, 117–170.

Wößmann, L. (2009). Public-private partnerships and student achievement: A cross-country analysis. In R. Chakrabati & P. E. Peterson (Eds.), *School Choice International: Exploring public-private partnerships* (pp. 13–45). Cambridge, MA: MIT Press.

Wößmann, L., Lüdemann, E., Schütz, G., & West, M. R. (2009). *School accountability, autonomy, and choice around the world*. Cheltenham: Edward Elgar.

4 So Where's the Teacher in School Effects Research?

The Impact of Teachers' Beliefs, Culture, and Behavior on Equity and Excellence in Education

Mieke Van Houtte

INTRODUCTION

From the 1960s on, educational sociologists have examined how schools contribute to the achievement of students and to stated inequalities between students. Many of these studies deal with the striving for effective and high-quality schooling on the one hand and equal opportunities on the other hand, coinciding with the belief in a meritocratic society. The assumption is that true meritocracy depends upon equal access to educational and occupational mobility. Ascribed features such as socioeconomic status should not be of any importance, but reality shows that children of socially subordinated groups—the poor, the ethnic minorities—attain less in the educational domain and on the labor market. An important question, then, is whether schools really provide equal opportunities. Because research shows that children with different socioeconomic or ethnic backgrounds attend different schools, it is necessary to examine whether differential achievement may result from differential school features (Hallinan, 2002).

The green light for school effects research was given in the beginning of the 1960s when the U.S. Congress ordered an investigation into the educational opportunities of students of different ethnic backgrounds, religions, or nationalities. That research program (Coleman et al., 1966) aimed at examining unequal educational opportunities by comparing objective school features, such as resources and general measures of quality, and linking these to students' outcomes on different cognitive tests. This study has been reproduced numerous times, with the use of increasingly sophisticated methods and techniques. These studies generally confirm that school features do not, or hardly, affect school achievement (e.g., Jencks et al., 1972), but in view of the strong commonsense feeling that exists about this issue, these findings stimulated more research into school effects. In the footsteps of Coleman et al. (1966) and Jencks et al. (1972), many research studies started from the assumption that "schools can make a difference" (e.g., Mortimore, Sammons, Stoll, Lewis, & Ecob, 1988). From the 1970s on, scholars were no longer merely interested in whether schools affect achievement or not, but aimed to identify the school features that are connected with good academic performance (Reynolds, Teddlie, Creemers, Scheerens, & Townsend, 2000). Furthermore, researchers no longer simply related inputs with outputs. Initially, school effects research applied an input-output perspective, considering the school itself as a black box, but more and more, school processes came to the fore as possible differentiators between schools and as influences on students' achievement (Good & Weinstein, 1986). The black box of the school was opened (Reynolds et al., 2000).

School effectiveness research endured a lot of criticism, which was both theoretically and methodologically inspired. One critique pertains to the choice of input and process variables. It is claimed that the selection of variables more often leans on availability rather than on theoretical grounds (Coe & Fitz-Gibbon, 1998). Nowadays, school effectiveness research usually takes the shape of replication research—indeed, using ever more sophisticated techniques—and traditionally starts with an enumeration of school features that were systematically linked in former research with effectiveness, such as school size, expenditures per student, or academic climate. As a consequence, research presents the same correlates again and again, without any progress. Some school features are systematically forgotten or neglected; in fact, these are features that need to be taken into account when dealing with equity, namely, the socioeconomic and ethnic composition of the student population (Thrupp, 2001). The critique most relevant to the present chapter is the one-sided concentration of school effectiveness research on cognitive outcomes of students (Coe & Fitz-Gibbon, 1998). Systematic, integrated research into the effects of structural and compositional school features on teachers' outcomes—such as job satisfaction, expectations, self-efficacy, well-being—in the tradition of school effects research is nonexistent, as far as we know. This is not to say that teacher outcomes have never been related to school features, but this kind of research is rather shattered. The schools' student composition has been rarely related to teachers' attitudes, beliefs, and other teacher characteristics, although it is not too far-fetched to hypothesize about the impact of teachers' attitudes and beliefs on students' achievement. This chapter aims to shed more light on this issue. The focus of the chapter is on how the existing knowledge regarding student–teacher relations can be incorporated in school effects research, enhancing our understanding of the mechanisms impacting upon excellence and equity in education.

STUDENT–TEACHER INTERACTIONS AND ACHIEVEMENT

Whereas teachers are seldom taken into account in traditional school effects research, the links between individual student and teacher characteristics have been the subject of studies into student–teacher relations and student–teacher interactions, showing that student features (such as gender, ethnicity, age, socioeconomic status) and teacher features (gender, ethnicity, age) correlate with (1) differences in teachers' verbal and non-verbal behavior (Simpson & Erickson, 1983), (2) teachers' perceptions of students' (problematic) behavior (Borg, 1998; Kokkinos, Panayiotou, & Davazoglou, 2005), and (3) teachers' perceptions of their relations with students (Saft & Pianta, 2001). This kind of research might surely inspire school effects research.

The Impact of Gender in the Classroom

In this respect, probably the feature examined the most is student gender. From the 1970s, research has been demonstrating gender differences in teacher–student interaction patterns. Teachers tend to interact more with boys and, as such, girls tend to receive less teacher attention (Einarsson & Granström, 2002; Jones, 1989; Sadker, Sadker, & Klein, 1991; Simpson & Erickson, 1983). These gender differences may result from the differential behavior that boys and girls exhibit. Boys are found to be more active in class and to interact more with the teachers, which leads to more teacher contact and feedback for boys than for girls (Francis, 2000; Good & Findley, 1985; Gurian, 2001; Irvine, 1986; Mosconi, 1998; Sadker et al., 1991; Warrington, Younger, & Williams, 2000). At the same time, it is stated that boys get more disciplined and controlled than girls (Davies, 1979; Good, Cooper, & Blakey, 1980; Good & Findley, 1985; Irvine, 1985, 1986), due to their less study-oriented culture (cf. Van Houtte, 2004b) and the fact that inconvenient or undesirable behaviors typical for girls—of a more internalizing and emotional nature—generally are perceived less problematic and less disturbing than those typical for boys—more externalizing and antisocial (Francis, 2000; Irvine, 1986; Kokkinos et al., 2005). In sum, compared with girls, boys more often enter into positive as well as negative interactions with their teachers.

Furthermore, Davies (1979, 1984), Schneider and Coutts (1979), and Warrington and Younger (2000) found that, in general, teachers prefer boys, because they consider boys to be less catty and sly, more open to reason, more honest, and a more interesting audience. If teachers judge boys and girls that way, one can expect them to trust boys more than girls. On the other hand, teachers have higher normative and academic expectations of girls than boys. Teachers appreciate girls more because of their better-adjusted school-related attitudes. Teachers prefer students who are responsible, punctual, and cooperative; those are traits that are more characteristic of girls than of boys (Clifton, Perry, Parsonson, & Hryniuk, 1986; Dusek & Joseph, 1985; Hughes, Cavell, & Willson, 2001; Ingleby & Cooper, 1974; Warrington & Younger, 2000). As Schneider and Coutts (1979, p. 108) suggest, teachers seem to display a synchronous adherence to two contrasting systems of values: one, the educational milieu, emphasizing feminine

behaviors, and the other, the wider social context, emphasizing the importance of masculine traits. But what does this mean for student–teacher
relations? According to Hughes et al. (2001), peers view girls as receiving
higher levels of teacher support than do boys, who are perceived as more
likely to be involved in conflictual interactions with teachers. Myhill and
Jones (2006) record that among male and female students, there is a strong
and significant perception that teachers treat boys more negatively than
girls: Girls are treated gently, whereas boys are treated firmly—confirming
social stereotypes. Teachers themselves rate their relationships with girls as
closer and less discordant than their relationships with boys (Birch & Ladd,
1998; Murray & Murray, 2004). My own research (Van Houtte, 2007) has
demonstrated that the more girls there are at school, the more students are
trusted, indicating a profound distrust of boys. This finding is not surprising in view of the previously mentioned literature but is nonetheless striking
if one keeps in mind the recent concerns about the underachievement of
boys (cf. Van Houtte, 2004b; see also Francis & Skelton, Chapter 5, this
volume) and the knowledge that teacher trust affects students' achievement
(Goddard, Tschannen-Moran, & Hoy, 2001).

Most research concerning classroom interaction has focused on student
gender, neglecting the gender of the teachers (Einarsson & Granström,
2002). Nevertheless, researchers point to the necessity of considering teachers' gender, preferably in combination with students' gender (Saft & Pianta,
2001; Simpson & Erickson, 1983). It has been shown that, irrespective of
the gender composition of the student population, female teachers tend to
stress quiet, order, obedience, and cooperation more than male teachers do.
Male teachers seem more tolerant of restlessness and aggressiveness and
attach more importance to freedom and autonomy (Schneider & Coutts,
1979). Conversely, Borg (1998) states that male teachers appear to be primarily concerned with disruptive forms of behaviors (e.g., disorderliness,
restlessness), whereas female teachers seem to be more preoccupied with
moral forms of behaviors (e.g., cruelty, bullying, obscene notes, lying). Given
this evidence, it might be expected that teacher gender affects the teacher–
student relationship. In general, female teachers seem to have less trust in
their students than male teachers do (Van Houtte, 2007). This squares with
the finding that female teachers are less tolerant and more directed to discipline and obedience in class (Schneider & Coutts, 1979). Einarsson and
Granström (2002) report that, in general, teacher gender does not seem to
affect the interaction with students. However, we have to take into account
that the grade and gender of the students has yielded some statistically
significant interactions indicating that (1) male teachers engage in more
interaction with their students at the intermediate level (ages 10–12) than
their female colleagues, but this pattern changes at the upper level when
female teachers engage in more interaction with their students than male
teachers; and (2) boys, in general, are given more attention than girls, but
at the upper level (ages 13–16), male teachers pay relatively more attention

to female students. The research of Myhill and Jones (2006) shows that students consider female teachers to be more fair than male teachers in the way they treat the different gender groups. This is supported by the finding that the gender composition of the student population at school influences female teachers' trust less than male teachers' trust. The more girls there are at school, the more trust male teachers report (Van Houtte, 2007).

Ethnicity, Age and Socioeconomic Status in the Classroom

In a similar vein, it has been demonstrated that student and teacher ethnicity are related to student–teacher relationships in complex ways. Student ethnicity can influence the teachers' perceptions and judgments of the students and, as such, the way teachers interact with students (Gillborn, 1990; Mac an Ghaill, 1988; Murray & Murray, 2004; Saft & Pianta, 2001; Stevens, 2005). Teachers' own ethnicity has also been shown to be related to their perceptions of students, independent of the child's ethnicity (see Saft & Pianta, 2001; Simpson & Erickson, 1983). Finally, it has been found that when students and teachers share ethnic backgrounds, the teachers are more likely to perceive their relationship with students as positive (Saft & Pianta, 2001), although other research has demonstrated that teachers gave more praise and less criticism to students of the opposite race (see Simpson & Erickson, 1983).

Another feature that is considered with respect to student–teacher relationships is the age of both student and teacher. Evidently, as affective and behavioral problems and competencies are conceptualized in different ways at different ages, teachers will have different expectations of younger versus older students, and their relations and interactions with students might expectedly vary according to the age of the students (Saft & Pianta, 2001). This hypothesis has been empirically substantiated by Einarsson and Granström (2002). Unfortunately, most research has involved samples of a limited age range (e.g., Hughes et al., 2001; Simpson & Erickson, 1983), and the impact of student age on teacher–student relationships has not been fully explored, although it has been suggested that teachers report greater conflicts with younger children (Saft & Pianta, 2001). The teacher's length of service and teaching experience, usually corresponding with age, appear to exert a strong influence on student–teacher relationships. Experienced teachers become more tolerant of most undesirable behaviors (Borg, 1998). Inexperienced teachers probably feel more helpless or anxious when confronted with disruptive classroom behavior compared with experienced teachers, who might be more inclined to see such behaviors as falling within the normal limits (Kokkinos et al., 2005). Consequently, it seems reasonable to expect experienced teachers to get along better with their students (cf. Brousseau, Book, & Byers, 1988; Ennis & McCauley,

2002). By contrast, Angelides (2004) observed that younger primary school teachers seemed to have closer bonds with students than the older teachers did. Older teachers appeared to be stricter than the younger ones, punishing the children more readily.

Finally, socioeconomic status (SES) can be an important determinant of teacher behavior in the classroom (Simpson & Erickson, 1983). It has been well documented that students' SES determines, in great measure, the teachers' expectations (Adams & Cohen, 1976; Baron, Tom, & Cooper, 1985; Cox, 1983; Harvey & Slatin, 1975; Rist, 1970; Solomon, Battistich, & Hom, 1996; Van Matre, Valentine, & Cooper, 2000). Teachers believe that students with higher SES achieve better, are more talented, and work harder than students with a lower SES background (Jussim, Eccles, & Madon, 1996). Bourdieu (1966) and Bourdieu and Passeron (1970) stated that teachers insufficiently take into account the existing differences between lower- and higher-SES students, as such perpetuating lower-SES students' cultural deprivation. In the same vein, Bowles and Gintis (1976) contended that, because working-class kids are expected to become workers themselves, teachers prepare them for this future by stressing discipline and obedience. Recent research demonstrates that schools with a lower-SES context pay more attention to control and discipline (Metz, 1993; Solomon et al., 1996; Thrupp, 1999; Walker, 1993). Moreover, the cultural differences arising from differences in SES seem hard to overcome in establishing relations of trust, as was shown by Goddard et al. (2001). These scholars find that teacher trust is systematically associated with student economic status: The larger the proportion is of poor students in the school, the lower the teachers' trust will be. The question here is of course whether, and to what extent, analogous to gender and ethnicity, the (in)congruence of students' and teachers' SES will influence student–teacher relationships.

STUDENT–TEACHER INTERACTIONS AND ACHIEVEMENT: EXPECTANCY EFFECTS

There can be no doubt that students' characteristics influence teachers' expectations and attitudes in the classroom. But does this also have consequences for the students' achievement? Or put differently, do these different interaction patterns bring about different levels of achievement?

It is clear that certain student characteristics raise certain expectations in teachers, who will behave in accordance with these expectations (McLaughlin, 1993; Metz, 1993); these teacher behaviors have been claimed (for many decades) to have a strong impact on students' achievement. Rosenthal and Jacobson (1968) were the first to demonstrate an association between teachers' expectations and students' achievement. They showed that teachers' perceptions of students' capabilities influence the students' achievement, irrespective of whether these beliefs are true or false. In this respect, it appears to be quite important how teachers communicate their expectancies to the students.

Brophy and Good (1970) developed a general model comprising five steps to describe the consequences of teachers' expectancies: (1) The teacher has specific expectancies regarding different students. (2) As a consequence, the teacher addresses students differently. (3) Because students are addressed differently, they respond to the teacher in a different way. (4) In responding to the teacher, each student will act according to what he or she thinks the teacher expects. (5) As a consequence, the student's behavior and achievement will be in line with teachers' expectancies. Brophy and Good (1970) empirically substantiated that teachers behave differently toward students of whom they expect more: Those students receive more praise and support. Other researchers as well (e.g., Clifton et al., 1986; Kester & Letchworth, 1972; Page & Rosenthal, 1990; Richardson, 2002) demonstrated that teachers tend to communicate more positively and more supporting with students of whom they have higher intellectual expectations. Moreover, they tend to spend more time on them. From the moment teachers have formed certain images—"mental maps"—and expectations of their students, they tend to adjust their way of teaching in various ways. Brophy and Good (1974) listed 11 mechanisms by which teachers might hinder students' educational progress, such as not allowing students to speak, demanding less from them, and so forth. Rosenthal (1973) distinguished four mediating factors between teachers' expectancies and students' achievement. In the first place, teachers' expectations create a certain climate because they are more likely to maintain warm socioemotional relationships with promising students. Second, teachers give more feedback to students they find promising. Third, promising students receive more input: They are offered more subject material and also more difficult and challenging material. And fourth, promising students get more chances to ask questions or to answer questions, which can be seen as a differential output.

As such, differential expectancies are communicated in a verbal and nonverbal manner. It is believed that the nonverbal mediators—which pertain to the climate factor—are more effective in conveying expectancies, although they produce higher variance. Teachers do not have the same capacity to communicate nonverbally, and students vary in sensitivity to nonverbal messages (Rosenthal, 1985; Zuckerman, Defrank, Hall, & Rosenthal, 1978). It must be added that the creation of a cold climate does not always happen in a subtle way. Often students are informed rather explicitly that teachers are not expecting much from them.

In sum, when teachers have rather low academic expectations of students, they will not be inclined to devote much time and energy to these students (Brookover, Beady, Flood, Schweitzer, & Wisenbaker, 1979). Obviously, when differential expectancies lead to a differential treatment of students, this will have direct consequences for the cognitive development of the child. When students receive less feedback, for example, they will be unable to distinguish between good and bad performances and so will be thwarted to improve (Jussim, 1986). So, the teachers behave in correspondence with their expectations, and the students respond to this behavior in a way that corresponds to the teachers' expectations (Brophy & Good, 1970).

STUDENT–TEACHER RELATIONS IN
SCHOOL EFFECTS RESEARCH

As indicated before, questions regarding educational excellence and equity are often dealt with in school effects research. School effects research is one of the three pillars in the broader field of School Effectiveness Research (SER) and refers to the large-scale research that relates school features to specific outcomes of students, usually students' achievement. This research tradition is quantitative in nature, leaning on large-scale surveys to explain students' educational attainment. The previously mentioned research into teacher–students relations is largely qualitative in nature, very often leaning on ethnographic case studies, which makes this research difficult to integrate in the classic school effects research. In order to develop more insight in how to achieve excellence and equity alike, it is important that school effects research takes into account the student composition of the school and relates this feature to the teachers' beliefs and judgments about these students. School effects researchers working in the SER tradition usually do not pay much attention to compositional features of the school (Thrupp, 2001). Technically, it appears very difficult to integrate information on teacher–student relationships into the school effects models, especially at the level of secondary education. Exemplary in this matter is the research into the consequences of educational stratification (tracking, streaming, or other forms of ability grouping), which occupies an important position within the sociology of education.

The Merging of Two Traditions: The Case of Tracking Research

Broadly speaking, there are two lines of research addressing tracking. One is largely quantitative and examines the effect of educational stratification on school achievement (e.g., Hallinan & Kubitschek, 1999). Students in lower tracks tend to achieve less than students in higher tracks, independently of their personal abilities. Explanations for this finding are often suggested but almost never tested. As a result, these quantitative survey analyses offer little insight into how tracking effects on achievement occur.

The other line of research is largely characterized by ethnographic case studies and focuses on the consequences of tracking on students' and teachers' attitudes and behavior, such as the way teachers and principals view their students and deal with subject material (e.g., Page, 1991). It is quite obvious that teachers in different tracks need to teach different content, but even the way they deal with it is different. In lower tracks, teaching often comes down to entertaining. Subjects are approached in a far less theoretical and academic manner, while facts and basic skills are emphasized. In higher tracks, by contrast, much emphasis is put on concepts, processes, and more complicated skills. Students in higher tracks are offered more difficult tasks and, consequently, have more opportunities to learn. In lower tracks, the subject matter is presented in a less interesting and less challenging way (Hargreaves, 1967; Metz, 1978; Murphy & Hallinger, 1989; Oakes, 1985; Persell, 1977; Rosenbaum, 1976). In addition, less is required in academic terms from lower-track students than from higher-track students. In higher tracks, students are expected to work and study at home, and extra attention is devoted to problem solving and critical thinking. In lower tracks, exercises in memorization are emphasized (Evertson, 1982; Goodlad, 1984; Hargreaves, 1967; Oakes, 1985; Page, 1991; Persell, 1977; Schwartz, 1981). In higher tracks, students' academic achievement is stressed, whereas in lower tracks, students' behavior receives most of the attention (Murphy & Hallinger, 1989; Schwartz, 1981). As such, in lower tracks, more time is spent on disciplining, at the expense of pursuing genuinely academic goals (Ball, 1981; Gaziel, 1997; Goodlad, 1984; Metz, 1978).

Generally speaking, the whole attitude of teachers in higher tracks is more apt to promote learning than in lower tracks and streams (Oakes, 1985). Students in lower tracks get fewer explanations and directions with regard to expectations and goals (Evertson, 1982; Goodlad, 1984; Oakes, 1985; Schwartz, 1981). Teachers in higher tracks or streams are more enthusiastic, and as a consequence, their lessons are better prepared (Goodlad, 1984; Oakes, 1985; Rosenbaum, 1976). An obvious reason for this is the response teachers get from their students in the respective tracks. Another reason is that the appreciation teachers receive from the outside world depends on the students' ability level. In a way, teachers acquire the status of their students: Teachers themselves become tracked (DeLany, 1998; Finley, 1984). An obvious reason for the lackluster approach demonstrated in lower tracks is that teachers have to deal with troublesome students who have developed lower levels of key competencies. As such, one can easily imagine that teaching in lower tracks also has consequences for teacher satisfaction (Van Houtte, 2006b). Job satisfaction is generally defined as the feelings that an individual holds toward his or her job (Taylor & Tashakkori, 1995). Job satisfaction is often connected to extrinsic and intrinsic rewards at work. Because teachers usually do not have many extrinsic rewards to count on (e.g., high salaries, promotional opportunities, job security, etc.), they need to achieve satisfaction from intrinsic sources, such as their work and their contact with students (Conley & Levinson, 1993; Holdaway, 1978; Kalekin-Fishman, 1986; Kasten, 1984; Lortie, 1975; Taylor & Tashakkori, 1995). This implies that working with difficult students may have negative repercussions on teacher satisfaction (Kalekin-Fishman, 1986; Kasten, 1984; Taylor & Tashakkori, 1995). It is not surprising that job satisfaction increases when teachers deal with academically capable students who behave well (Sweeney, 1981, 1982; Taylor & Tashakkori, 1995). Teachers' job satisfaction is determined to a great extent by their expectations with respect to their students' achievement (Gaziel & Maslovaty, 1998). In lower tracks, teachers do not seem to be confident that their expectations with respect to student achievement will be met. In organizational studies (Bradach & Eccles, 1989; Rousseau, Sitkin, Burt, & Camerer, 1998) as well as in educational studies (Bryk & Schneider, 2002; Goddard et al., 2001; Smith, Hoy, & Sweetland, 2001; Tschannen-Moran & Hoy, 2000), the "confidence that expectations will be met" constitutes the essence of how trust is defined. One of the causes of distrust is the belief that others are too incompetent to do what is required (Bryk & Schneider, 2002; Govier, 1992). As such, the feelings of distrust in lower tracks resulting from the less study-oriented culture of lower-track students, may be responsible for lower teacher satisfaction in the lower tracks (Van Houtte, 2006b).

In this line of research, a link with school achievement has often been suggested, although it has never been empirically documented. Considering both research traditions—that is, the quantitative research into tracking effects on student achievement, on the one hand, and the qualitative research into tracking effects on students' and teachers' attitudes and behaviors, on the other hand—an obvious approach would be to try and merge them, as has been suggested by Gamoran (1989), whose guiding perspective suggests that achievement is closely tied to students' opportunities for learning (Barr & Dreeben, 1983; Bidwell & Kasarda, 1980; Sørensen & Hallinan, 1977, 1986). The question is how the merging can be realized. As for primary education, where usually one teacher is responsible for a class of students, it seems quite feasible to study particular teacher–student relations. Individual teachers could be asked to give a judgment on each individual student, and this judgment could be related to the student's achievement. Given the intensity of this procedure, the willing cooperation of teachers would be required, though. As for secondary education, this way of working may become difficult, because commonly several teachers are instructing several classes, and students have different teachers for each subject. One option might consist of asking each teacher to give his or her judgment on each individual student and then centralizing (per student) the judgments of different teachers. However, each researcher involved in large-scale survey research will notice immediately that this is not a very convenient procedure, and therefore it will probably not be feasible. A more practicable alternative would be to consider teachers' classroom practices as a manifestation of culture and, as such, as a school feature that can be related to structural and compositional school features.

TEACHER CULTURE AND ACHIEVEMENT

Teachers' instructional practice and their visible behavior can be seen as the surface manifestation of the prevailing teacher culture (cf. Schein,

1984, 1985). In general, culture is defined as "a set of cognitions shared by members of a social unit" (Rousseau, 1990, p. 154). Over the years, colleagues (in the same school, for instance) develop common ideas and views to respond to the circumstances and problems that are particular to their work (Hargreaves, 1992). Teachers and principals share certain beliefs concerning the nature of the students, education, and school (Metz, 1978). Teacher culture consists of the work-related beliefs and knowledge teachers share—beliefs about appropriate ways of acting on the job and rewarding aspects of teaching, and about knowledge that enables teachers to do their work (Feiman-Nemser & Floden, 1986). Lower tracks, then, are often characterized by a less academically oriented teacher culture. Similar to the origin of polarization into an anti-school and a preschool culture with respect to students in respectively lower and higher tracks (Ball, 1981; Hargreaves, 1967; Lacey, 1970; Schafer & Olexa, 1971), the origin of teacher culture can be regarded as an application of Cohen's (1955) theory on the origin of (sub)cultures (Van Houtte, 2006a).

Teachers end up in specific tracks characterized by a specific group of students. This situation constitutes a problem with which teachers have to deal. Because changing the situation is not an option, they have to adjust their frame of reference (cf. Cohen, 1955). Teachers have certain general conceptions about teaching, but they need to adjust them to the contextual factors they are confronted with (Fang, 1996). To do this, they appeal to common stereotypes. The allocation of students into different tracks, for example, is an established fact for teachers and principals. Their evaluation of students starts from the stereotype that lower-track students are good for little, academically speaking (Ball, 1981; Rosenbaum, 1976). Teachers and principals believe that certain groups of students will make little headway at school. Even before they have met their students, they have built a strong image of their academic abilities (Ball, 1981; Finn, 1972; Jussim, 1986; Midgley, Feldlaufer, & Eccles, 1988; Page, 1991), and they will be inclined to adjust their educational goals to these expectations (McLaughlin, 1993; Metz, 1993). The prior conditions for the origin of a culture are clearly fulfilled: a group of people with communal problems in a communal situation. The same reasoning can be applied to different kinds of student compositions, be it with regard to ethnic composition, gender composition, or SES composition (Van Houtte, 2003).

It has been argued that educational stratification determines academic staff culture, but in order to assume that teacher culture intermediates between certain structural and compositional school features and the students' achievement, it must still be clarified how teacher culture is connected to achievement. There are at least two ways in which teacher culture may influence students' achievement. First, students may be socialized into the culture of the staff (cf. Stockard & Mayberry, 1992), as has been described by Metz (1978) with respect to order. More specifically, teachers influence students' motivation to achieve academically. They communicate socially valued goals to their students and provide contexts conducive to learning and the pursuit of these goals

(Wentzel, 1999). Parents, peers, and teachers have been studied as relatively distinct sources of influence on student outcomes, but students must often struggle to balance competing socialization influences (Wentzel, 1999). Students' perspectives are likely to be a blend of the perspectives that are fostered in the students' community (or subunits within a community), those fostered by the student body itself, and those fostered by the school staff (Metz, 1990). The group a student identifies with the most defines the culture in which the student will be socialized (Fine & Kleinman, 1979). As such, teachers may function as a normative reference group for the student. A reference group is a group, a collectivity, or even an individual person which an actor takes into account when choosing a certain manner of behavior (Kemper, 1968; Merton, 1957/1968). A normative reference group is a reference group that determines the standards individuals set for themselves (Kelley, 1952). An actor does not necessarily need to belong to the reference group. The normative aspects of a group to which one does not belong may also influence behavior (Kelley, 1952; Merton, 1957/1968; Shibutani, 1955). As such, teachers, as a normative group, may set standards for the proper level of performance internalized by the students (Kemper, 1968; Wentzel, 1999).

This is not the only way that staff culture may influence the students' achievement. More important are the surface manifestations of culture, namely, the actual behavior of the teachers in the classroom. As indicated, the staff culture encompasses teachers' shared beliefs about the students, including shared expectations, and it is well known that teachers' expectations of students determine the way that teachers behave in the classroom (e.g., Brophy & Good, 1970; Clifton et al., 1986; Kester & Letchworth, 1972; Metz, 1993; Page & Rosenthal, 1990; Rist, 1970; Rosenthal, 1973). Thus, the images of students that are typical for the teacher culture influence students' achievement because they translate into behavior that is visible to the students (Good, 1980). The traditional literature concerning expectancy effects concentrates on individual students (cf. the pioneering work by Rosenthal & Jacobson, 1968), but Finn (1972), for example, has demonstrated that sometimes teachers may have specific expectations for particular groups of students. According to Brophy (1983), teachers' differential treatment of groups of students is as widespread as the differential treatment of individual students within a classroom, and it is an equally strong mediator of expectancy effects on achievement. Expectations with respect to a whole group are communicated quite directly (Cooper, 1985). For example, students in lower tracks are often explicitly compared with students in higher tracks, and point-blank insults are not exceptional (Rosenbaum, 1976). To Brophy (1983), the fact that students in different tracks are instructed differently constitutes evidence of the existence of expectancy effects in groups. Furthermore, when students are separated in different classrooms or different schools, the chance of an expectancy effect increases, because low expectations become deep-seated norms that are never questioned (Brophy, 1983). It must be noted, though, that this does not necessarily mean that teachers are prejudiced. Very often, if not always, teachers' expectations are fairly accurate. So, it is likely that teachers react consistently to the students' behavior they are confronted with. In that case, the students are affecting the teachers, rather than the other way around. Very often, teachers assess the students' attitudes, motivations, intelligence, and behavior in class correctly and adjust their teaching to it (Brophy, 1983; Jussim, 1989; Jussim & Eccles, 1995; Jussim et al., 1996).

TEACHER CULTURE IN SCHOOL EFFECTS RESEARCH

By considering teachers' instructional practice as a surface manifestation of teacher culture, it can be linked to various structural and compositional school features, on the one hand, and to the individual student's achievement, on the other hand. In considering the way that teachers in a school deal with their students as collective, as something that is shared, that is, as culture, it becomes a school feature that can be related to other school features and to individual students' outcomes. As such, it becomes an obvious mediating variable to explain the effect of school features on the behavior of members of the organization. In this respect, Hargreaves (1995) stated that school culture needs to become a variable within school effectiveness studies but wondered whether it is possible to develop models of school culture that are potentially open to quantification to permit their inclusion in studies of school effectiveness and school improvement. In my opinion, this is possible by simply treating aspects (e.g., trust or study orientation) of the culture of a group at school (e.g., teachers or students) as plain school features, for instance by aggregating the individual beliefs after it has been established that these are truly shared at the school level (for a workable procedure, see, e.g., Van Houtte, 2004a).

In this way, Van Houtte (2004a) has demonstrated by means of a multilevel analysis that the poor academic culture of teachers in technical and vocational tracks is partly responsible for the fact that students in technical and vocational tracks have a higher chance to fail than students in academic tracks. Teachers working in technical and vocational tracks share the belief that these students are good for little, academically speaking, and they adjust their academic goals to this belief. As a consequence, the students achieve less and have a higher chance to fail. Similarly, it has been shown that that the academic teacher culture mediates the relation between the socioeconomic context of the school and individual students' chance to fail, taking into account their personal socioeconomic status and other personal characteristics (Van Houtte, 2003).

CONCLUSION

From the 1960s on, equity and excellence in education has been a major issue of concern in different parts of the world. School effectiveness research is a research tradition dealing with enhancing effectiveness, and as such, excellence, at the school level. In this line of research, equity has never really been of central concern; among others, this is demonstrated by the fact that most studies within this tradition fail to take into account the compositional features of the schools. Moreover, strikingly little attention is paid to teacher–student relations and their effects on student achievement.

In this chapter, I discussed how student characteristics and, as such, compositional school features can be associated with teachers' attitudes and instructional practices and how these can be incorporated in school effectiveness research. Teachers' images of students inform the way they interact with their students and instruct them, which in turn influences students' achievement. Obviously, specific teacher expectations of different groups—for example, boys, ethnic minority students, students with a poor socioeconomic background, lower-track students—may give rise to feelings of distrust, enhancing difficulties in teacher–student relationships; these should be taken into account when attempts are made to understand and remedy the student' difficulties to perform up to academic standards (cf. Saft & Pianta, 2001). Usually teachers are not conscious of their interaction patterns with students or their images of students (cf. Jones, 1989). Nevertheless, the viability of proposed solutions for the underachievement of particular groups of students is dependent upon teachers' beliefs about the educational chances of these groups (Avery & Walker, 1993). As such, teachers must be made aware of their personal beliefs and the role of their own attributes in this respect. This is crucially important for prospective and novice teachers, given the finding that distrust decreases with increasing teaching experience. Teacher education should make prospective teachers aware of the beliefs they bring from society into the classroom and should offer them the opportunity to develop the knowledge and skills needed to work with diverse student populations (cf. Avery & Walker, 1993; Nieto, 2000). As the existence of teacher culture shows, far too often teacher colleagues adjust their general conceptions about teaching—acquired in teacher preservice training—to the contextual factors they are confronted with by developing common ideas and views (Fang, 1996; Hargreaves, 1992). Teachers share certain beliefs concerning the nature of their students, education, and school, often falling back on common stereotypes. It can be argued that this process is facilitated by the segregation of students—be it in terms of gender, ethnicity, socioeconomic background, or ability—creating homogeneous groups, which make it easier to approach students as a unity with certain features. On the other hand, heterogeneous groups may enhance the stigmatization of individual deviant students.

In any case, teacher education may help to overcome certain stereotypes and prepare prospective teachers for teaching students with characteristics and needs different from their own. According to Darling-Hammond (2000), the most important task of teacher education is to develop in teachers the ability to see beyond one's own perspective and, as such, to understand the experiences, perceptions, and knowledge bases that influence students' approaches to learning. Briefly, future teachers, and those already in the profession, need to learn how to promote the learning of *all* students (Nieto, 2000), in order to achieve excellence and equity simultaneously.

REFERENCES

Adams, G., & Cohen, A. (1976). An examination of cumulative folder information used by teachers in making differential judgments of children's abilities. *Alberta Journal of Educational Research, 22*(3), 216–225.

Angelides, P. (2004). Generation division in Cyprus education? Different attitudes to education from younger and older teachers. *Educational Review, 56*(1), 65–76.

Avery, P. G., & Walker, C. (1993). Prospective teachers' perceptions of ethnic and gender differences in academic achievement. *Journal of Teacher Education, 44*(1), 27–37.

Ball, S. (1981). *Beachside comprehensive: A case-study of secondary schooling.* Cambridge: Cambridge University Press.

Baron, R., Tom, D., & Cooper, H. (1985). Social class, race, and teacher expectations. In J. Dusek (Ed.), *Teacher expectancies* (pp. 251–269). Hillsdale, NJ: Erlbaum.

Barr, R., & Dreeben, R. (1983). *How schools work.* Chicago: University of Chicago Press.

Bidwell, C., & Kasarda, J. (1980). Conceptualizing and measuring the effects of schools and schooling. *American Journal of Education, 88,* 401–430.

Birch, S. H., & Ladd, G. W. (1998). Children's interpersonal behaviors and the teacher-child relationship. *Developmental Psychology, 34*(5), 934–946.

Borg, M. G. (1998). Secondary school teachers' perception of students' undesirable behaviours. *British Journal of Educational Psychology, 68,* 67–79.

Bourdieu, P. (1966). L'école conservatrice. Les inégalités devant l'école et devant la culture. *Revue française de sociologie, 7,* 325–326.

Bourdieu, P., & Passeron, J. C. (1970). *La réproduction. Eléments pour une théorie du système d' enseignement.* Paris: Les Éditions de Minuit.

Bowles, S., & Gintis, H. (1976). *Schooling in capitalist America. Educational reform and the contradictions of economic life.* London: Routledge & Kegan Paul.

Bradach, J., & Eccles, R. (1989). Price, authority, and trust: From ideal types to plural forms. *Annual Review of Sociology, 15,* 97–118.

Brookover, W., Beady, C., Flood, P., Schweitzer, J., & Wisenbaker, J. (1979). *School social systems and student achievement. Schools can make a difference.* New York: Praeger.

Brophy, J. (1983). Research on the self-fulfilling prophecy and teacher expectations. *Journal of Educational Psychology, 75,* 631–661.

Brophy, J., & Good, T. (1970). Teachers' communication of differential expectations for children's classroom performance: Some behavioral data. *Journal of Educational Psychology, 61,* 365–374.

Brophy, J., & Good, T. (1974). *Teacher-student relationships. Causes and consequences.* New York: Holt, Rinehart & Winston.

Brousseau, B. A., Book, C., & Byers, J. L. (1988). Teacher beliefs and the cultures of teaching. *Journal of Teacher Education, 39*(6), 33–39.

Bryk, A., & Schneider, B. (2002). *Trust in schools. A core resource for improvement.* New York: Russell Sage Foundation.

Clifton, R., Perry, R., Parsonson, K., & Hryniuk, S. (1986). Effects of ethnicity and sex on teachers' expectations of junior high school students. *Sociology of Education, 59,* 58–67.

Coe, R., & Fitz-Gibbon, C. T. (1998). School effectiveness research: Criticisms and recommendations. *Oxford Review of Education, 24*(4), 421–438.

Cohen, A. (1955). *Delinquent boys: The culture of the gang.* New York: Free Press.

Coleman, J., Campbell, E., Hobson, C., Mcpartland, J., Mood, A., Weinfeld, F., & York, R. (1966). *Equality of educational opportunity.* Washington, DC: U.S. Department of Health, Education, and Welfare, Office of Education, U.S. Government Printing Office.

Conley, S., & Levinson, R. (1993). Teacher work redesign and job satisfaction. *Educational Administration Quarterly, 29,* 453–478.

Cooper, H. (1985). Models of teacher expectation communication. In J. Dusek (Ed.), *Teacher expectancies* (pp. 135–158). Hillsdale, NJ: Erlbaum.

Cox, T. (1983). The educational attitudes and views about school of a sample of disadvantaged fifteen-year-olds. *Educational Studies, 9,* 69–79.

Darling-Hammond, L. (2000). How teacher education matters. *Journal of Teacher Education, 51*(3), 166–173.

Davies, L. (1979). Deadlier than the male? Girl's conformity and deviance in school. In L. Barton & R. Meighan (Eds.), *Schools, pupils and deviance* (pp. 59–73). Driffield: Nafferton Books.

Davies, L. (1984). *Pupil power. Deviance and gender in school.* London: Falmer Press.

DeLany, B. (1998). The micro-politics of school, teacher, and student failure: Managing turbulence. In B. Franklin (Ed.), *When children don't learn: Student failure and the culture of teaching* (pp. 134–159). New York: Teachers College Press, Columbia University.

Dusek, J., & Joseph, G. (1985). The bases of teacher expectancies. In J. Dusek (Ed.), *Teacher expectancies* (pp. 229–249). Hillsdale, NJ: Erlbaum.

Einarsson, C., & Granström, K. (2002). Gender-biased interaction in the classroom: The influence of gender and age in the relationship between teacher and pupil. *Scandinavian Journal of Educational Research, 46*(2), 117–127.

Ennis, C., & McCauley, M. (2002). Creating urban classroom communities worthy of trust. *Journal of Curriculum Studies, 34*(2), 149–172.

Evertson, C. (1982). Differences in instructional activities in higher- and lower-achieving junior high English and math classes. *Elementary School Journal, 82,* 329–350.

Fang, Z. (1996). A review of research on teacher beliefs and practices. *Educational Research, 38,* 47–65.

Feiman-Nemser, S., & Floden, R. (1986). The cultures of teaching. In M. Wittrock (Ed.), *Handbook of research on teaching* (3rd ed.). New York: Macmillan.

Fine, G., & Kleinman, S. (1979). Rethinking subculture: An interactionist analysis. *American Journal of Sociology, 85,* 1–20.

Finley, M. (1984). Teachers and tracking in a comprehensive high school. *Sociology of Education, 57,* 233–243.

Finn, J. (1972). Expectations and the educational environment. *Review of Educational Research, 43*(3), 387–410.

Francis, B. (2000). *Boys, girls and achievement. Addressing the classroom issues.* London: RoutledgeFalmer.

Gamoran, A. (1989). Measuring curriculum differentiation. *American Journal of Education, 97,* 129–143.

Gaziel, H. (1997). Impact of school culture on effectiveness of secondary schools with disadvantaged students. *Journal of Educational Research, 90,* 310–318.

Gaziel, H., & Maslovaty, N. (1998). Predictors of job satisfaction among teachers in religious schools. *Education and Society, 16*, 47–56.

Gillborn, D. (1990). *"Race," ethnicity and education. Teaching and learning in multi-ethnic schools.* London: RoutledgeFalmer.

Goddard, R., Tschannen-Moran, M., & Hoy, W. (2001). A multilevel examination of the distribution and effects of teacher trust in students and parents in urban elementary schools. *Elementary School Journal, 102*(1), 3–17.

Good, T. (1980). Classroom expectations: Teacher-pupil interactions. In J. McMillan (Ed.), *The social psychology of school learning* (pp. 79–122). New York: Academic Press.

Good, T., Cooper, H., & Blakey, S. (1980). Classroom interaction as a function of teacher expectations, student sex, and the time of year. *Journal of Educational Psychology, 72*(3), 378–385.

Good, T., & Findley, M. (1985). Sex role expectations and achievement. In J. Dusek (Ed.), *Teacher expectancies* (pp. 271–300). Hillsdale, NJ: Erlbaum.

Good, T., & Weinstein, R. (1986). Schools make a difference: Evidence, criticisms and new directions. *American Psychologist, 41*, 1090–1097.

Goodlad, J. (1984). *A place called school: Prospects for the future.* New York: McGraw-Hill.

Govier, T. (1992). Distrust as a practical problem. *Journal of Social Philosophy, 23*, 52–63.

Gurian, M. (2001). *Boys and girls learn differently! A guide for teachers and parents.* San Francisco: Jossey-Bass.

Hallinan, M. T. (2002). Equality in education. In D. L. Levinson, P. W. Cookson, & A. R. Sadovnik (Eds.), *Education and sociology. An encyclopedia* (pp. 241–246). New York: RoutledgeFalmer.

Hallinan, M. T., & Kubitschek, W. (1999). Curriculum differentiation and high school achievement. *Social Psychology of Education, 3*, 41–62.

Hargreaves, D. (1967). *Social relations in a secondary school.* London: Routledge & Kegan Paul.

Hargreaves, A. (1992). Cultures of teaching: A focus for change. In A. Hargreaves & M. Fullan (Eds.), *Understanding teacher development* (pp. 000–000). New York: Teachers College Press, Columbia University.

Hargreaves, D. (1995). School culture, school effectiveness and school improvement. *School Effectiveness and School Improvement, 6*(1), 23–46.

Harvey, D., & Slatin, G. (1975). The relationship between child's SES and teacher expectations: A test of middle-class bias hypothesis. *Social Forces, 54*, 140–159.

Holdaway, E. (1978). Facet and overall satisfaction of teachers. *Educational Administration Quarterly, 14*, 30–47.

Hughes, J. N., Cavell, T. A., & Willson, V. (2001). Further support for the developmental significance of the quality of the teacher–student relationship. *Journal of School Psychology, 39*(4), 289–301.

Ingleby, J., & Cooper, E. (1974). How teachers perceive first-year school children: Sex and ethnic differences. *Sociology, 8*(3), 463–473.

Irvine, J. (1985). Teacher communication patterns as related to the race and sex of the student. *Journal of Educational Research, 78*(6), 338–345.

Irvine, J. (1986). Teacher student interactions: Effects of student race, sex, and grade level. *Journal of Educational Psychology, 78*(1), 14–21.

Jencks, C., Smith, M., Acland, H., Bane, M., Cohen, D., Gintis, H., et al. (1972). *Inequality: A reassessment of the effect of family and schooling in America.* New York: Basic Books.

Jones, M. G. (1989). Gender issues in teacher education. *Journal of Teacher Education, 40*(1), 33–38.

Jussim, L. (1986). Self-fulfilling prophecies: A theoretical and integrative review. *Psychological Review, 93*, 429–445.

Jussim, L. (1989). Teacher expectations: Self-fulfilling prophecies, perceptual biases, and accuracy. *Journal of Personality and Social Psychology, 57*, 469–480.

Jussim, L., & Eccles, J. (1995). Are teacher expectations biased by students' gender, social class, or ethnicity? In Y. Lee, L. Jussim, & C. McCauley (Eds.), *Stereotype accuracy: Toward appreciating group differences* (pp. 245–271). Washington, DC: American Psychological Association.

Jussim, L., Eccles, J., & Madon, S. (1996). Social perception, social stereotypes, and teacher expectations: Accuracy and the quest for the powerful self-fulfilling prophecy. *Advances in Experimental Social Psychology, 28*, 281–388.

Kalekin-Fishman, D. (1986). Burnout or alienation? A context specific study of occupational fatigue among secondary school teachers. *Journal of Research and Development in Education, 19*, 24–34.

Kasten, K. (1984). The efficacy of institutionally dispensed rewards in elementary school teaching. *Journal of Research and Development in Education, 17*, 1–13.

Kelley, H. (1952). Two functions of reference groups. In G. Swanson, T. Newcomb, & E. Hartley (Eds.), *Readings in social psychology* (pp. 410–415). New York: Holt.

Kemper, T. (1968). Reference groups, socialization and achievement. *American Sociological Review, 33*, 31–45.

Kester, S., & Letchworth, G. (1972). Communication of teacher expectations and their effects on achievement and attitudes of secondary school students. *Journal of Educational Research, 66*, 51–55.

Kokkinos, C. M., Panayiotou, G., & Davazoglou, A. M. (2005). Correlates of teacher appraisals of student behaviors. *Psychology in the Schools, 42*(1), 79–89.

Lacey, C. (1970). *Hightown grammar: The school as a social system.* Manchester: Manchester University Press.

Lortie, D. (1975). *Schoolteacher: A sociological study.* Chicago: University of Chicago Press.

Mac an Ghaill, M. (1988). *Young, gifted and black. Student–teacher relations in the schooling of black youth.* Buckingham: Open University Press.

McLaughlin, M. W. (1993). What matters most in teachers' workplace context? In J. W. Little & M. W. McLaughlin (Eds.), *Teachers' work. Individuals, colleagues, and contexts* (pp. 79–103). New York: Teachers College Press, Columbia University.

Merton, R. (1968). *Social theory and social structure.* Glencoe, IL: Free Press. (Original work published 1957)

Metz, M. (1978). *Classrooms and corridors: The crisis of authority in desegregated secondary schools.* Berkeley: University of California Press.

Metz, M. (1990). How social class differences shape teachers' work. In M. McLaughlin, J. Talbert, & N. Bascia (Eds.), *The contexts of teaching in secondary schools: Teachers' realities* (pp. 40–107). New York: Teachers College Press, Columbia University.

Metz, M. (1993). Teachers' ultimate dependence on their students. In J. Little & M. McLaughlin (Eds.), *Teachers' work: Individuals, colleagues, and contexts* (pp. 104–136). New York: Teachers College Press, Columbia University.

Midgley, C., Feldlaufer, H., & Eccles, J. (1988). The transition to junior high school: Beliefs of pre- and post-transition teachers. *Journal of Youth and Adolescence, 17*, 543–562.

Mortimore, P., Sammons, P., Stoll, L., Lewis, D., & Ecob, R. (1988). *School matters.* Berkeley: University of California Press.

Mosconi, N. (1998). Réussite scolaire des filles et des garçons et socialisation différentielle des sexes à l'école. *Recherches féministes, 11*(1), 7–17.

Murphy, J., & Hallinger, P. (1989). Equity as access to learning: Curricular and instructional treatment differences. *Journal of Curriculum Studies, 21,* 129–149.

Murray, C., & Murray, K. M. (2004). Child level correlates of teacher–student relationships: An examination of demographic characteristics, academic orientations, and behavioral orientations. *Psychology in the Schools, 41*(7), 751–762.

Myhill, D., & Jones, S. (2006). "She doesn't shout at no girls": Pupils' perceptions of gender equity in the classroom. *Cambridge Journal of Education, 36*(1), 99–113.

Nieto, S. (2000). Placing equity front and center—Some thoughts on transforming teacher education for a new century. *Journal of Teacher Education, 51*(3), 180–187.

Oakes, J. (1985). *Keeping track: How schools structure inequality.* New Haven, CT: Yale University Press.

Page, R. (1991). *Lower track classrooms: A curricular and cultural perspective.* New York: Teachers College Press, Columbia University.

Page, S., & Rosenthal, R. (1990). Sex and expectations of teachers and sex and race of students as determinants of teaching behavior and student performance. *Journal of School Psychology, 28,* 119–131.

Persell, C. (1977). *Education and inequality: The roots and results of stratification in America's schools.* New York: Free Press.

Reynolds, D., Teddlie, C., Creemers, B., Scheerens, J., & Townsend, T. (2000). An introduction to school effectiveness research. In C. Teddlie & D. Reynolds (Eds.), *The international handbook of school effectiveness research* (pp. 3–25). London: Falmer Press.

Richardson, R. (2002). Expectations great and small: The mental maps of teachers and systems. *Race Equality Teaching, 20*(2), 15–20.

Rist, R. (1970). Student social class and teacher expectations: The self-fulfilling prophecy in ghetto education. *Harvard Educational Review, 40,* 411–451.

Rosenbaum, J. (1976). *Making inequality: The hidden curriculum of high school tracking.* New York: Wiley.

Rosenthal, R. (1973). The Pygmalion effect lives. *Psychology Today, 7,* 56–63.

Rosenthal, R. (1985). From unconscious experiments bias to teacher expectancy effects. In J. Dusek (Ed.), *Teacher expectancies* (pp. 37–65). Hillsdale, NJ: Erlbaum.

Rosenthal, R., & Jacobson, L. (1968). *Pygmalion in the classroom: Teacher expectation and pupils' intellectual development.* New York: Holt, Rinehart & Winston.

Rousseau, D. M. (1990). Assessing organizational culture: The case for multiple methods. In B. Schneider (Ed.), *Organizational climate and culture* (pp. 153–192). San Francisco: Jossey-Bass.

Rousseau, D. M., Sitkin, S. B., Burt, R. S., & Camerer, C. (1998). Not so different after all: A cross-discipline view of trust. *Academy of Management Review, 23*(3), 393–404.

Sadker, M., Sadker, D., & Klein, S. (1991). The issue of gender in elementary and secondary education. *Review of Research in Education, 17,* 269–334.

Saft, E. W., & Pianta, R. C. (2001). Teachers' perceptions of their relationships with students: Effects of child age, gender, and ethnicity of teachers and children. *School Psychology Quarterly, 16*(2), 125–141.

Schafer, W., & Olexa, C. (1971). *Tracking and opportunity: The locking-out process and beyond.* Scranton, PA: Chandler.

Schein, E. H. (1984). Coming to a new awareness of organizational culture. *Sloan Management Review, 25*(2), 3–16.

Schein, E. H. (1985). *Organizational culture and leadership*. San Francisco: Jossey-Bass.

Schneider, F., & Coutts, L. (1979). Teacher orientations towards masculine and feminine: Role of sex of teacher and sex composition of school. *Canadian Journal of Behavioural Science, 11*(2), 99–111.

Schwartz, F. (1981). Supporting or subverting learning: Peer group patterns in four tracked schools. *Anthropology and Education Quarterly, 12*, 99–121.

Shibutani, T. (1955). Reference groups as perspectives. *American Journal of Sociology, 60*, 562–569.

Simpson, A. W., & Erickson, M. T. (1983). Teachers verbal and nonverbal-communication patterns as a function of teacher race, student gender, and student race. *American Educational Research Journal, 20*(2), 183–198.

Smith, P., Hoy, W., & Sweetland, S. (2001). Organizational health of high schools and dimensions of faculty trust. *Journal of School Leadership, 11*(2), 135–151.

Solomon, D., Battistich, V., & Hom, A. (1996). Teacher beliefs and practices in schools serving communities that differ in socioeconomic level. *Journal of Experimental Education, 64*(4), 327–347.

Sørensen, A., & Hallinan, M. (1977). A reconceptualization of school effects. *Sociology of Education, 50*, 273–289.

Sørensen, A., & Hallinan, M. (1986). Effects of ability grouping on growth in academic achievement. *American Educational Research Journal, 23*, 519–542.

Stevens, P. A. J. (2005). *An ethnography of teacher racism and discrimination in Flemish and English classrooms with Turkish secondary school pupils*. Unpublished doctoral thesis, Warwick University, Coventry.

Stockard, J., & Mayberry, M. (1992). *Effective educational environments*. Newbury Park, CA: Corwin.

Sweeney, J. (1981). Professional discretion and teacher satisfaction. *High School Journal, 65*, 1–6.

Sweeney, J. (1982). Teacher dissatisfaction on the rise: Higher level needs unfulfilled. *Education, 102*, 203–208.

Taylor, D., & Tashakkori, A. (1995). Decision participation and school climate as predictors of job satisfaction and teachers' sense of efficacy. *Journal of Experimental Education, 63*, 217–230.

Thrupp, M. (1999). *Schools making a difference: Let's be realistic!* Buckingham: Open University Press.

Thrupp, M. (2001). Sociological and political concerns about school effectiveness research: time for a new research agenda. *School Effectiveness and School Improvement, 12*(1), 7–40.

Tschannen-Moran, M., & Hoy, W. K. (2000). A multidisciplinary analysis of the nature, meaning, and measurement of trust. *Review of Educational Research, 70*(4), 547–593.

Van Houtte, M. (2003). Reproductietheorieën getoetst. De link tussen SES-compositie van de school en onderwijscultuur van leerkrachten en directie. *Mens en Maatschappij, 78*(2), 119–143.

Van Houtte, M. (2004a). Tracking effects on school achievement: A quantitative explanation in terms of the academic culture of school staff. *American Journal of Education, 110*(4), 354–388.

Van Houtte, M. (2004b). Why boys achieve less at school than girls: The difference between boys' and girls' academic culture. *Educational Studies, 30*(2), 159–173.

Van Houtte, M. (2006a). School type and academic culture: Quantitative evidence for the differentiation-polarisation theory. *Journal of Curriculum Studies, 38*(3), 273–292.

Van Houtte, M. (2006b). Tracking and teacher satisfaction: The role of study culture and trust. *Journal of Educational Research, 99*(4), 247–254.

Van Houtte, M. (2007). Exploring teacher trust in technical/vocational secondary schools: Male teachers' preference for girls. *Teaching and Teacher Education, 23(6),* 826–839.

Van Matre, J., Valentine, J., & Cooper, H. (2000). Effect of students' after-school activities on teachers' academic expectancies. *Contemporary Educational Psychology, 25*(2), 167–183.

Walker, J. (1993). Cultural perspectives on work and schoolwork in an Australian inner-city boys' high school. In L. Angus (Ed.), *Education, inequality and social identity* (pp. 128–159). Washington, DC: Falmer Press.

Warrington, M., & Younger, M. (2000). The other side of the gender gap. *Gender and Education, 12*(4), 493–508.

Warrington, M., Younger, M., & Williams, J. (2000). Student attitudes, image and the gender gap. *British Educational Research Journal, 26*(3), 393–407.

Wentzel, K. (1999). Social-motivational processes and interpersonal relationships: Implications for understanding motivation at school. *Journal of Educational Psychology, 91,* 76–97.

Zuckerman, M., Defrank, R., Hall, J., & Rosenthal, R. (1978). Accuracy of nonverbal communication as determinant of interpersonal expectancy effects. *Environmental Psychology and Nonverbal Behavior, 2*(4), 206–214.

5   A Feminist Analysis of Gender and Educational Achievement

Becky Francis and Christine Skelton

INTRODUCTION

Gender and achievement is a controversial issue. Whereas second-wave feminists attended to the underachievement of girls, in recent years an international concern has developed in relation to the apparent underachievement of boys, to the extent that many commentators have identified the fervor in media and policy surrounding this issue as a moral panic. The debate around "boys' underachievement" is well established in the United Kingdom and in Australia, and is rapidly developing in many other OECD nations (Francis & Skelton, 2005; Hayes & Lingard, 2003; Jha & Kelleher, 2006). Educational policy concerns with this issue have precipitated an unprecedented amount of energy, resources, targets, and recommendations to schools to "narrow the gender gap," with feminists often voicing concern that such policies (a) are misguided and (b) marginalize the continuing needs of girls. In this chapter, then, we seek to analyze the figures on gender and achievement, and to unpick some of the assumptions and explanations underpinning commentary on "boys' underachievement," in order to provide a more balanced account of the field.

In Britain, a concern at boys' apparent underperformance in mainstream education was precipitated by the introduction of school "league tables" in 1992, which recorded pupil performance at General Certificate of Secondary Education (GCSE) exams (exams that mark the end of compulsory schooling at 16 in the United Kingdom) and which included a breakdown of results according to gender. League tables are widely accessed by parents and the media. The statistics suggested that, overall, girls were catching up with boys at math and science (and by the mid-1990s they had caught up) and were outperforming boys in many other subject areas. These findings caused a furor in the national media, with journalists speculating wildly about the supposed size of the "gender gap" and about the various explanations for this apparently sudden turn of events (Delamont, 1999; Epstein, Elwood, Hey,

& Maw, 1998). In fact, as Arnot, David, and Weiner (1999) discuss, girls had been outperforming boys at a majority of subjects prior to the introduction of the National Curriculum in 1988, but because they tended to pursue less prestigious subject areas, this point went unattended. The introduction of the mandatory curriculum forced girls to pursue science subjects to GCSE level for the first time, leading to a rapid improvement in their performance in science subjects that was not matched by a simultaneous improvement at language subjects among boys.

The size of any "gender gap" has been debated, and there have been academic discussions about the validity of different interpretations of the statistics (Connolly, 2006, 2008; Gorard, Rees, & Salisbury, 1999). Further, the validity of attention to gender as a discrete variable has also been critiqued, with researchers drawing attention to the (stronger) impact of other social variables on educational achievement (see, e.g., Archer & Francis, 2007; Arnot et al., 1999; Epstein et al., 1998; Francis & Skelton, 2005; Gillborn & Mirza, 2000). Yet, as the OECD PISA (Programme for International Student Assessment) studies reveal, there are significant gender gaps in particular curriculum areas. In England and Australia, and increasingly in other countries too, policy makers and practitioners have driven targets, resources, and classroom strategies geared toward "raising boys' achievement," which are having very direct impacts in schools (although not in the ways intended; see Skelton et al., 2009).

Hence in this chapter we provide an analysis of the patterns in gender (and other social factors) in relation to achievement, using figures for England to provide an account of the English case, contextualized by the PISA figures for the OECD more broadly. Having looked at the numerical picture, we then turn to examine the different explanations for apparent gender gaps in achievement that underpin different approaches to the issue in policy and practice. We show how many of the commonsense explanations on which strategies have been built are premised on unevidenced, and often stereotypical and even misogynist, assumptions.

COMPULSORY EDUCATION ACHIEVEMENT PATTERNS IN ENGLAND

We will consider the data from the compulsory education sectors to identify some of the patterns that are occurring for gender and achievement.[1] Data for the following discussion are drawn from DfE (Department for Education, until recently titled the Department for Children, Schools and Families, or DCSF); HESA (Higher Education Statistics

Agency); and the OECD (Organisation for Economic Co-operation and Development).

Messages from the DCSF website have tended to perpetuate the view that boys are underperforming in comparison with girls across the curriculum (see analysis in Skelton, Francis, & Valkanova, 2007). However, in fact, of the three subject areas presented as key in the English compulsory curriculum—maths, science, and literacy/English—there is no significant gender gap for maths and science. Throughout the assessed compulsory education stages, boys and girls in England perform fairly evenly at maths and science, and there actually remains a trend toward boys as a group outperforming girls at higher-level maths. Table 5.1 depicts the results in 2007 for the Keys Stage 2 (KS2) exams taken at the end of primary schooling (ages 10–11).

As we can see from Table 5.1, boys and girls are performing roughly evenly at Level 4 for Key Stage 2 at both maths and science, and at the more challenging Level 5, boys are somewhat outperforming girls at maths. But the most substantial gap is at English (particularly at Level 5), where girls as a group outperform boys.

The consistency of this trend is confirmed by the GCSE exam results taken at the end of compulsory schooling in England, at 16. Table 5.2 shows the percentage of pupils gaining the important A*–C grades at these key subjects:

Table 5.1   Key Stage 2 Results for England, 2007

	Percentage of Pupils Achieving Level 4 or above in KS2 National Curriculum Test			*Percentage of pupils Achieving Level 5 or above in KS2 National Curriculum Test*		
	English	*Maths*	*Science*	*English*	*Maths*	*Science*
Boys	76	78	87	28	35	46
Girls	85	76	88	39	30	46

Source: DCSF. Department for Education, Gender and Achievement: Introduction and Key issues, www.standards.dfes.gov.uk/genderandachievement/understanding/analysis/

Table 5.2   Percentage of Pupils Achieving A*–C at GCSE for Key Subjects, 2006/2007

	English	*Maths*	*Science*
Boys	53	53	50
Girls	68	56	52

Table 5.2 broadly confirms this trend. Analysis shows that when these figures are broken down further, again males tend to enter more specialized science subjects than females, and to achieve higher grades for maths (National Science Board, 2006). But here again we see the very substantial gender gap for English. These patterns play out across the OECD more broadly. The OECD produces data that show the performance of pupils in various countries. PISA is an internationally standardized assessment in reading, mathematics, and scientific literacy which is administered to 15-year-olds in schools in participating countries. The survey takes place every 3 years. The 2003 PISA study of educational achievement at maths, science, and national language in OECD and "partner" nations found a trend toward gender equality in performance at maths and science, but where there were significant gender gaps for science these tended to favor boys (OECD, 2004). The 2006 PISA study found a similar trend to gender equality in performance at maths and science, but this time found more gaps for maths, again favoring boys (OECD, 2007). Average science performance for 15-year-olds showed no gender difference in the majority of countries (22 of the 30 OECD countries), and where there were differences in either direction, these were small. But there remain gendered trends in perceptions of science and science ability that may explain later trends in subject take-up: Males performed substantially better than females when answering "physical systems questions," and in the United Kingdom, boys had significantly more positive attitudes to science than girls. The largest gender difference was in self-concept regarding science: Males tended to think significantly more highly of their own science abilities than did females (echoing a raft of feminist work showing how boys tend to articulate greater confidence in their academic abilities than do girls). And males tend to outperform females at maths: In 35 of 57 countries, males performed significantly better at the PISA assessments, including in the United Kingdom, whereas females performed better in only one country, Qatar.

However, both portions of the study identified a significant and consistent gender gap for national language. This substantial gap is reflected in all European nations (indeed the gap for England, although substantial, is relatively small in comparison to many other nations). We have argued elsewhere that it is the size of this gender gap at language that skews results so that policy makers and commentators can make claims to girls outperforming boys "across the board" (Francis & Skelton, 2005). And indeed, we have also suggested that the disproportionate underachievement among boys at literacy is likely to impact on their achievement in other curriculum areas: One will struggle at exams in many curriculum areas if one's literacy is weak. Cassen (2008) also raises this hypothesis, noting how many of the underachieving boys in his study struggled with literacy (see Cassen & Kingdon, 2007).

Yet in recognizing this gender gap for literacy/national language, it is important to note that, in contrast to the presumptions made by many

Table 5.3   English Language Pass Rates—GCE/GCSE Grades A*–C

_	Girls	Boys
1976	65	56
2006	69	55

commentators on the subject, this issue is not new. Table 5.3 compares pass rates for English at grades C-A in England, in the prior GCE O-level exams, and in the contemporary GCSE, which replaced them.

Table 5.3 vividly illustrates how this gender gap was already substantial in the 1970s, although it has grown slightly in the interim, reflecting the improved attainment of girls as a group.

What feminist researchers in the United Kingdom and elsewhere have been quick to point out is that other factors are stronger predictors of educational achievement than is gender. Ethnicity and social class, taken on their own, have a stronger impact on attainment (although it is also the case that within every social group, there is a gender gap at literacy which favors girls). The pioneering work done by feminists in this area (see, e.g., Arnot et al., 1999; Epstein et al., 1998) has now been elaborated by many different researchers from a variety of disciplines.[2] The impact of social class on achievement is particularly acute in the United Kingdom, as illustrated by the OECD PISA studies. Table 5.4 illustrates this point in the case of England, using the indicator of Free School Meals (FSM) as a proxy for relative poverty.[3]

Table 5.4 shows a gender gap for both pupils receiving Free School Meals (FSM) and those not taking Free School Meals (non-FSM) (a gap of 9 percentage points for FSM pupils; 10 for non-FSM pupils). But the gap it

Table 5.4   Achievements at Key Stage 4 GCSE Qualifications in 2006, by FSM and Gender

GCSE	Five or more A*–C					
	Eligible Pupils			% Achieving		
	Boys	Girls	Total	Boys	Girls	Total
FSM	39,498	38,589	78,087	28.7	37.4	33.0
Non-FSM	261,971	252,545	514,516	56.2	66.0	61.0
Unclassified	814	717	1,531	42.3	47.7	44.8
All pupils	302,283	291,851	594,134	52.6	62.2	57.3

Source: www.standards.dfes.gov.uk/genderandachievement/understanding/analysis/

reveals for FSM is far wider. The figures show that nearly double the proportion of girls and boys not taking FSM (indicatively middle-class pupils) achieve 5 or more GCSE A*–C grades than their counterparts taking FSM (indicatively working-class pupils). This includes a gap of 19 percentage points between boys not taking FSM (56%) and girls taking FSM (37%). This gap illustrates how (indicatively) middle-class boys tend to outperform (indicatively) working-class girls. So Table 5.4 illustrates two points: first, how in England the social class gap dwarfs the gender gap for achievement, and following from this, how nonsensical it is to discuss gender as an isolated factor in relation to achievement.

Gender and "race" inflect with social class in sometimes unpredictable ways: Social class and gender have a less significant impact on the achievement of some ethnic groups than others. The complexity at stake once ethnicity and social class (as indicated by FSM) are taken into account with gender in patterns of achievement is demonstrated by Table 5.5.

Even if we direct our attention exclusively to the most substantial pupil groups (given that the numbers for some ethnic groups are very small), Tables 5.5a and 5.5b show the diversity of achievement patterning by ethnicity, social class, and gender. The trend to smaller social class gaps for achievement in minority ethnic groups (see Archer & Francis, 2007) is illustrated by these figures. This is in comparison to the huge social class gap for the White British majority, of 35 percentage points between White British girls gaining 5 A*–C (non-FSM 66%, FSM 31%), and of 32 percentage points for White British boys (non-FSM 56%; FSM 24%). Pupils of Indian heritage, and the smaller group of pupils of Chinese heritage, continue to outperform other groups: Although girls in these ethnic groups are outperforming boys, boys from these groups outperform nearly all other groups of girls (including the majority group of White British girls). Mirza (2008) has warned against this kind of analysis of "achieving" and "underachieving" ethnic groups, arguing that such approaches set up groups as discrete and as in competition, pathologizing particular groups (such as Black boys) and creating "model minorities" (such as pupils of Chinese and Indian heritage).

Actually, there is little evidence to suggest that relatively high-achieving minority ethnic groups in Britain are "celebrated"; rather, their attainment tends to be problematized by teachers as "achieved in the wrong way." In other words, in spite of their high attainment, doubts are cast on their methods of achievement, with suggestions that this achievement is produced by inauthentic and even problematic means of hyper-diligence and/or parental pressure (Archer & Francis, 2005, 2007; Brah, 1994). Indeed we would suggest that use of the term "model minorities," even in a critical sense, risks ignoring the ongoing pathologizing and racism, which such "achieving" minority ethnic pupils continue to experience (see, e.g., Archer & Francis, 2006). However, Mirza's critique does alert

Table 5.5 Achievements at Key Stage 2 (for English) in 2006 by Ethnicity, Free School Meals, and Gender

Key Stage 2 English	Non-FSM						FSM					
	Eligible Pupils			% Achieving			Eligible Pupils			% Achieving		
	Boys	Girls	Total	Boys	Girls	Total	Boys	Girls	Total	Boys	Girls	Total
White	**208,080**	**198,748**	**406,828**	**79**	**88**	**83**	**34,258**	**32,742**	**67,000**	**52**	**66**	**59**
White British	201,597	192,597	394,194	79	88	83	32,280	30,936	63,216	52	66	59
Irish	798	790	1,588	85	92	88	236	202	438	54	66	59
Traveller of Irish Heritage	53	53	106	30	32	31	128	108	236	20	30	25
Gypsy/Roma	212	188	400	38	44	41	184	178	362	19	38	28
Any other White background	5,420	5,120	10,540	75	82	78	1,430	1,318	2,748	55	65	60
Mixed	**6,817**	**6,670**	**13,487**	**81**	**90**	**85**	**2,313**	**2,250**	**4,563**	**61**	**77**	**69**
White and Black Caribbean	2,221	2,229	4,450	77	87	82	1,030	992	2,022	58	76	67
White and Black African	637	621	1,258	80	90	85	213	274	487	67	72	70
White and Asian	1,497	1,442	2,939	86	92	89	326	315	641	62	77	69
Any other mixed background	2,462	2,378	4,840	83	90	86	744	669	1,413	64	79	71
Asian	**15,798**	**14,779**	**30,577**	**75**	**84**	**79**	**5,571**	**5,405**	**10,976**	**62**	**74**	**68**
Indian	5,892	5,528	11,420	83	90	86	680	718	1,398	69	80	75
Pakistani	5,989	5,456	11,445	68	79	73	2,844	2,653	5,497	57	70	63

Bangladeshi	2,021	1,973	3,994	73	81	77	1,577	1,593	3,170	68	78	73
Any other Asian background	1,896	1,822	3,718	76	83	79	470	441	911	64	71	68
Black	7,788	7,646	15,434	72	85	78	4,529	4,480	9,009	56	70	63
Black Caribbean	3,211	3,096	6,307	69	84	76	1,214	1,203	2,417	55	75	65
Black African	3,694	3,806	7,500	74	85	79	2,869	2,849	5,718	56	67	62
Any other Black background	883	744	1,627	72	85	78	446	428	874	57	73	65
Chinese	890	917	1,807	83	90	86	119	89	208	76	90	82
Any other ethnic group	1,853	1,655	3,508	69	78	73	1,070	1,010	2,080	57	66	62
All pupils	245,446	234,421	479,867	78	88	83	48,701	46,755	95,456	54	68	61

Source: standards.dfes.gov.uk/genderandachievement/understanding/analysis/

us to the dangers of such analyses in potentially reifying difference and stereotyping certain groups as either "achieving" or "underachieving." A tension emerges, then, between a need to analyze achievement patterns in order to identify (and potentially address) inequalities and the danger of exacerbating inequalities by doing so. We would maintain that analysis of the figures provides a means to explode the myths surrounding, say, "boys' underachievement" (or indeed "Black underachievement," as Mirza herself undertook so successfully in the early 1990s; see Mirza, 1992[4]). And clearly, in the British case, such analysis plays a vital role in highlighting the impact of wealth/poverty on educational achievement. However, it is important that such analyses are attuned to the relationship and intersection of multiple social indices. Moreover, it can never be reiterated too often that patterns identified are *only* patterns. Many individual pupils continue to buck the trends; hence, it is vital that patterns do not lead to stereotyping.

Perhaps illustrating the importance of such statistical analysis, however, Table 5.5 highlights how, among groups of girls taking FSM, the largest group—White British girls—have virtually the lowest achievement figure at 31% (excluding the 102 girls of traveler/gypsy/Roma background). Hence, this substantial group of girls are attaining below the achievement of virtually all groups of boys not taking FSM, illustrating again the significance of social class for the White majority of pupils in the English education system. Clearly this shows how the discourse of "boys' underachievement" to which we have been subject in the media and in educational policy over the past 15 years ignores and masks the needs of many girls. And the tables also illuminate the marginalization of working-class White British boys and those of Caribbean heritage.

Having illustrated the complexity in achievement patterns, and the importance of considering multiple factors of identity, we turn now to the various assumptions and explanations upon which notions of "boys' underachievement", and strategies to address this, have been premised.

EXPLANATIONS UNDERPINNING THE PANIC OVER "BOYS' UNDERACHIEVEMENT"

There are three main explanations that underpin debates about "boys' underachievement" (sometimes focusing on literacy, sometimes as conceived more broadly):

- Feminization of schooling
- Essential differences between boys and girls
- The social construction of masculinity and femininity

We shall look at each of these in turn.

A "feminization of schooling"?

We have argued that the very term "feminization" is both inaccurate and misogynist, and that its application in educational contexts appears to compound both aspects (e.g., Francis & Skelton, 2005). However, this concept certainly propagates many strategies to "raise boys' achievement," so it is important that we examine it here.

Most frequently, the phrase "feminization of schooling" is used simply to refer to the fact that in the United Kingdom (and increasingly in many other EU nations) there are more female teachers than male, especially in the primary sector. Women primary teachers outnumber men by roughly five to one, but it continues to be the case that men are disproportionately represented at the headteacher level (Francis & Skelton, 2005). Indeed, male teachers in both primary and secondary schools are statistically far more likely to become headteachers than are their female colleagues (Hutchings, 2002).

Further, since the introduction of state schooling in 1870 in the United Kingdom, numbers of women teachers have always exceeded the numbers of men teachers (Thornton & Bricheno, 2006). Commentators concerned at the number of women teachers in the primary workforce rarely seem aware of this point, regarding it rather as a new phenomenon. The relative lack of men teachers is often presented as one that is detrimental to the educational experiences and opportunities of boys (Biddulph, 1997; Sewell, 1997) and a factor in the perceived "underachievement" of boys, with the implication that boys do better when taught by men teachers. What is never explained is why the greater numbers of women teachers was not considered a problem for boys in previous decades when they were seen to be outperforming girls.

In the meantime, a raft of empirical research has been developed that investigates the presumption of a correlation between a pupil–teacher gender match and pupils' achievement but finds little evidence to support that hypothesis. Indeed, some work has even found correlations between gender match and underachievement (see Carrington et al., 2007, or Carrington, Tymms, & Merrill, 2008, for discussion). Our own research supports this. The evidence from our large-scale qualitative study on the topic of "gender match" (see, e.g., Carrington et al., 2007; Francis et al., 2008; Skelton et al., 2009) found primary pupil and teacher respondents consistently tending to reject gender as a salient factor in primary pupil–teacher relations, or as an issue in engaging boys in schooling (Francis et al., 2008). Hence, it provides overwhelming support for Lahelma's (2000) and Ashley and Lee's (2003) finding that children tend not to perceive the gender of their teacher as salient, and Lahelma's finding that children's concern is with the quality/ability of the teacher, rather than whether the teacher is male or female. The consistency in responses to various questions probing the notion of gender match, in our study, provides particularly strong evidence to corroborate the lack of correlation between teacher–student gender match demonstrated across a range of quantitative work (see Carrington et al., 2007, 2008, for review). Further, in the minority of cases where children believed teacher gender is salient, no single explanation emerged as primary. Certainly no clear themes emerged in relation to enhanced pupil–teacher relations or to support the notion of gender match. Indeed, our findings that children tend to reject teacher gender as a salient factor in pupil–teacher relations is especially intriguing given how children can and do draw on gender discourses to construct difference in so many other aspects of interaction.

Another use of the phrase the "feminization of schools" is in relation to the idea that the predominance of females has led to the management and organization of the classroom, the delivery of the curriculum, and assessment practices becoming more "feminine" in nature. But what does it actually mean for schools to take on "feminized practices"? Research shows that the reality is that, far from becoming more progressively "feminized," primary schools are increasingly "masculinized" in terms of management regimes (Mahony & Hextall, 2000). The Education Reform Act 1988 introduced a quasi-market in English schooling, wherein the teachers' role has become increasingly focused on ensuring pupils achieve proscribed stages in public tests, set down in a state-regulated curriculum. Haywood and Mac an Ghaill (2001) have argued that one consequence of a restructured authority system, together with intensified surveillance, disciplinary codes, curriculum and testing stratification technologies, subject allocation and knowledge selection, has been to remasculinize schooling.

A Feminized Curriculum?

The curriculum itself has come under criticism within the notion of "feminization." Particularly, it has been argued that the literacy and English curriculum disadvantages boys. It is certainly the case that many researchers maintain that within dominant constructions of gender, writing and the content of the English curriculum at school is positioned as feminine and hence as inappropriate focus for boys/men (see, e.g., Marsh, 2003; Millard, 1997). It is interesting to see how the policy debates in this area tend to problematize teachers, teaching practice, or the curriculum for boys' underperformance, rather than boys themselves. For example, teachers are criticized for being too boring and not sufficiently stimulating, or for their onus on presentational issues in writing. A focus on subjects that boys may find embarrassing and out of keeping with their constructions of masculinity (such as poetry and many novels) is problematized within these arguments. These approaches acknowledge that it is boys' constructions of masculinity that impede their writing, but rather than challenge these constructions, they seek to better accommodate them (i.e., by altering the curriculum to reflect what are seen as "boys' interests").

Such arguments have been challenged by many feminist researchers working on gender and literacy, who argue that boys' and girls' preferences and constructions of gender should be challenged and diversified, rather than stereotyped and narrowed by teachers. Brownyn Davies and her colleagues have adopted a more radical critique, arguing that researchers tend to ignore the way in which literacy is implicated in facilitating and producing traditional constructions of gender. She maintains that within such approaches, literacy tends to be presented as "a desirable but innocent generic skill," whereas in fact, "being gendered shapes individual interest and engagement in literate practices. Literate practices in turn shape the ways in which one becomes gendered" (Davies & Saltmarsh, 2006, p. 238). In their study, Davies and Saltmarsh show how boys and girls tend to produce themselves in particular gendered ways through writing (both in their writing practices and in the subject matter about which they write): boys as active and girls as passive/obedient. For example, they describe how girls tend to regulate and discipline themselves through writing, both in their neat productions but also in the embodied ways in which they physically practice writing, whereas boys tend to exercise more territorial ownership in such practices. In light of their analysis of children's writing practices, Davies and Saltmarsh (2006) argue that many boys resist the kind of diligence, passivity, and obedience required to produce beautiful handwriting and work that "fits" the demands of the school. Such work, and the diligent application required to produce it, would require feminine working practices that they tend to avoid (see also Kanaris, 1999; Millard, 1997). Davies and Saltmarsh (2006) note, however, that boys "may on the other hand invest considerable effort in maintaining dominant positions in the social order of classrooms and playgrounds, which in turn map on to the masculine primacy at work in the broader social and economic order" (p. 238).

Feminized Assessment?

The final argument emerging within a notion of "feminization of schooling" is that assessment procedures are biased in favor of girls. In England, an increased amount of assessed coursework has been suggested to explain boys doing less well at GCSE and A levels, with the argument being that boys do less well at coursework because of their preferred learning styles. Girls are seen to do better with sequential assessment methods that reward consistent application (Smithers & Robinson, 1995)—what Bleach (1998) controversially terms the "diligent and plodding approach that is a characteristic of girls" (p. 14). Girls do less well at "sudden death" exams (timed exams previously unseen by the candidate), which rely on last-minute revision and require self-confidence. This latter form of assessment has been argued to favor boys (Bleach, 1998) and was the basis for O-level exams (the exams that preceded GCSEs in Britain). In fact, however, girls' results were already improving *before* the GCSE assessment model was introduced

(Bleach, 1998). And further, Arnot et al. (1999) discuss how a reduction in the coursework component in public examinations in the 1990s did little to alter the pattern of gender achievement. Hence, this evidence contests the idea that gender achievement gaps can be explained by changes in assessment models at school.

On the other hand, as gender imbues all aspects of social interaction, it clearly does impact on aspects of assessment more generally. So, for example, various research has analyzed practices by which gendered teacher perceptions dictate the level of exam to which pupils are entered (e.g., Elwood & Murphy, 2002; Harlen, 2004). These tendencies for social and cultural expectations to impact on assessment are of course influenced by other aspects of social identity, such as social class and ethnicity, as well as gender. A body of work has shown how many teachers read the behaviors of pupils differently depending on their "race" and social class (e.g., Archer & Francis, 2005; Crozier & Reay, 2005; Majors, 2001; Reay, 2001; Sewell, 1997; Wright, 1987). All of this complex information needs to be taken into account in any judgment about the impact of gender on assessment outcomes, but the evidence demonstrates that a simplistic attribution of girls' outperformance of boys in some subject areas to "feminized assessment tools" is unfounded.

Essential Gender Differences

Some authors subscribing to theories of inherent "brain difference" as explaining gender differences maintain that boys are biologically disadvantaged at writing and communication. These authors tend to believe that babies are born with an inbuilt biological and/or genetic predilection which, for example, pushes them toward some curriculum subjects while avoiding others. Such positions include "brain sex" theories, which see male and female brains as "wired" differently, resulting in different abilities that impact on learning.

One pragmatic problem with such perspectives on differences in achievement as "natural" is that they close down the possibility of change. But it is also noticeable that among proponents of such views, it tends to be *boys* that are presented as more in need of support than girls. But is the gender gap attributable to "nature"? Diane Halpern's (1992) overview of the research concludes that both "nature and nurture" have a part to play. We have debated this elsewhere, each of us taking a slightly different perspective (Francis & Skelton, 2005). Neuroscientists themselves admit that the science is in its infancy, and many are keen to point out that more difference *within* the groups labeled the girls, and the boys, than *between* them (see Slavin, 1994). Also important for educators to note is that the brain is not "fixed" prior to birth, but is a tensile organ that responds to external stimuli. Neuroscientist Lesley Rogers (2000) has explained that even hormones may be affected by environmental factors. So even if a relationship were to be found between patterns of brain difference and gendered patterns in educational achievement, these gender differences in the brain might still be the result of social experiences rather than innate (and unalterable) factors. That practice in a skill, or attempts to learn a particular skill, develops certain parts of the brain has been demonstrated by Blakemore and Frith (2005). Thus, teaching practices aimed at playing to boys' and girls' perceived strengths and weaknesses in any one curriculum area or to a preferred learning style would be intensifying the differences between the genders.

Indeed, there is far more evidence pointing to the significance of social factors in shaping children's abilities, rather than biological factors. And given that it is this aspect which educationalists can control, one might have thought the onus would be centered here. Yet in recent years in response to the panic around "boys' underachievement," there has been increasing attention to the concept of "gendered learning styles" and of drawing on these as a strategy to "raise boys' achievement" (Skelton et al., 2009).

Gendered Learning Styles

Interest in learning styles has grown rapidly in recent years (Coffield, Moseley, Hall, & Ecclestone, 2004), and perceived differences in the learning styles of boys and girls are one of the most frequently expressed explanations for the gender gap in achievement (Duffy, 2003; Maby, 2004). This argument is also based on the presumption that if boys are naturally different to girls because of their biological make-up, then it follows that they will have different approaches to learning (Gurian, 2002; Noble & Bradford, 2000). It is these preferred learning styles which are said to explain why boys are attracted to science subjects with their emphasis on the memorization of rules, facts, and short, abstract responses and girls toward humanities subjects, which are related more to real-life situations and demand elaborate and detailed responses (Arnot et al., 1999; Gipps & Murphy, 1994). Of course it has been shown that, as groups, there are tendencies for boys and girls to prefer different approaches to learning. But it is imperative to remember that these are trends, rather than true of all girls or all boys. Moreover, these tendencies can be explained by social accounts, and indeed, girls' better performance at maths and science in recent years might be one example of how social phenomena change (whereas, if down to inherent differences, such developments could not occur).

But if it is the case that there are gendered preferences for learning, should single-sex classes be encouraged, and/or should teachers develop strategies that cater to these different learning styles? We examine these queries in turn. With regard to single-sex classes as a method of addressing achievement, the findings are inconclusive to say the least. It has been shown that teachers tend to adopt curriculum-as-usual approaches and utilize the same teaching practices whether in mixed-sex or single-sex classes

(Jackson, 2002; Warrington & Younger, 2001). And where teachers *are* found to address the gender of their pupils, such approaches tend to draw on gender stereotypes likely to increase, rather than dissemble, current gendered trends (Ivinson & Murphy, 2007; Jackson, 2003). Findings are sometimes contradictory, but evidence suggests that even within coeducational schools (where single-sex classes have sometimes been introduced recently to boost boys' achievement), it tends to be girls achievement rather than boys' that improves (Warrington & Younger, 2002, 2003). Boys have been found especially unlikely to enjoy or support single-sex classes (Jackson, 2002).

As to the issue of "gendered learning styles," there remains much skepticism about the identification of distinct learning styles at all (see Coffield et al., 2004), let alone those associated with gender. The extent of gendered tendencies in learning preference remains highly contested (Elwood, 2005; Younger, Warrington, & McLellan, 2005), with many pupils bucking the trends. Drawing on the evidence in the literature, we would suggest that teachers should be aware of pupils' preferred ways of learning, but these should not be labeled as "boys' learning styles" and "girls' learning styles," as this will only reinforce traditional gender stereotypes.

Social Construction of Gender

The single explanation for the gender gap to emerge strongly and consistently from the various large-scale studies (from a range of perspectives) that have been carried out on gender and achievement is that pupils' constructions of gender produce different behaviors, which in turn impact on achievement. Children actively construct their own gender identities as relational (masculinity being what femininity is not, and vice versa) and adopt different behaviors to express their gender allegiance (Davies, 1989). Gendered behavior is habitual and often unconscious. Multiple factors impact on pupils' constructions of gender, including their age, school type and location, social class, and ethnicity (e.g., Ali, 2003; Archer & Francis, 2006; Connolly, 1998, 2004; Reay, 2001, 2006).

Feminist researchers have demonstrated how the production of gender difference and gender inequality pervades the whole of the schooling system, including, for example, the curriculum, management and disciplinary practices, staffing, teaching and assessment, teacher expectations, staff–pupil interaction, and pupil interaction. In terms of the social construction of gender by pupils, the peer group is seen as of central importance. As any teacher knows, given the choice pupils usually sit in same-gender groups, and friendship groups tend to be composed of pupils of the same gender (Thorne, 1993). Davies (1989) and Lees (1993) show in detail how primary and secondary pupils respectively "police" the gendered behavior of their peers and punish failure to conform to traditional gender norms. Many researchers have found that a particular construction of masculinity is invested with high status among peer groups in the secondary school (and even in the later years of primary schooling). This construction is what has commonly been referred to as the "laddish" construction of masculinity. The notion of being "one of the lads" evokes a group of young males engaged in hedonistic practices (including "having a laugh," disruptive behavior, alcohol consumption, objectifying women, and an interest in pastimes and subjects constructed as masculine). Such hedonistic practices and constructions of being "too cool for school" have also been observed to be adopted by some young women (Jackson, 2006).

The key point in relation to gender and educational achievement is that the "laddish" construction is seen as "anti" academic application (it is not "cool" to work hard or to achieve at school), hence having a negative impact on achievement. Some researchers see this as due to the conflict between "laddish" values and school culture: "Laddish" behaviors have a negative affect on the achievement of the boys concerned and of their classmates due to the "lads'" disruptive and distracting behaviors, and prioritization of other interests over schoolwork (Francis, 2000; Salisbury & Jackson, 1996; Skelton, 2001). Other writers see "lads" as *specifically* "anti-swot" and "anti-work" (Mac an Ghaill, 1994; Martino, 1999; Willis, 1977): school work, diligence, and application are constructed as feminine, and hence some boys seek to disassociate themselves from it as part of their efforts to bolster their constructions of masculinity. Martino (1999) maintains that where previously it had been particularly working-class boys who saw academic application as feminine and consequently sought to disassociate themselves from learning, these attitudes are increasingly being adopted by some middle-class boys.

Again, such constructions have been shown to be "raced" as well as socially classed and gendered (Haynes, Tickly, & Caballero, 2006; Wright, Weekes, & McGlaughlin, 2000). In relation to Black boys in the British education system, Warren (2005) points out that it is a mistake to read the anti-authority positions adopted by some Black boys in school as a sign that school or education is being rejected; rather it is the perceived "inequality of respect" that is being contested, as these boys tend to be stereotyped as problematic by teachers (Connolly, 1998). Indeed, some research suggests that some boys (Black and/or working-class) produce "laddish" behaviors as a result of their negative schooling experiences and subsequent disenchantment (Bleach, 1998; Jackson, 2002, 2003). In this view, boys take up "laddish" expressions of masculinity as an alternative method of building their self-worth, which has been damaged by their experiences of schooling. However, this assumes, like certain education policy documents, that such boys tend toward having "low self-esteem," an idea that remains controversial given a contradiction between research showing that boys express *higher* self-confidence and belief in their ability than girls.

A slightly different perspective is that which sees some boys taking up disruptive behaviors if they are not doing well in their schoolwork as a result of their competitive behaviors (rather than due to their "low self-esteem") (e.g., Epstein, 1998; Jackson, 2006; Salisbury & Jackson, 1996). In other words, such boys create different competitions to excel in (e.g., being "the most rebellious" or the best at sports, and so on), or adopt the attitude that if they can't win, then no one will (by disrupting lessons and deriding achievement). This view sees boys as needing to exercise power and "success" of one sort or another as an aspect of their masculinity.

Irrespective of the debates about the *causes* of boys' "laddish" behavior, a substantial body of work has shown how these high-status constructions of masculinity are likely to have a negative impact on attainment (of the boys concerned, and sometimes that of their classmates).[5] These various studies have shown that constructions of gendered behavior provide the key explanation for a "gender gap" in achievement. As with other explanations for gendered achievement patterns, it is extremely difficult to establish the *extent* to which boys' "laddish" constructions of masculinity adversely affect their achievement. For example, some boys seem proficient at achieving in spite of "laddish" behaviors. Few of the studies listed have examined the behaviors of individual boys in relation to any impact (or otherwise) on their educational attainment. However, the evidence does constitute a convincing explanation for the comparative underachievement of some boys, and this remains the only account that has not been challenged or discredited by counterevidence.

What is important to consider in all this is the complexity at stake in pupils' constructions of gender and the ways in which educational institutions facilitate and/or constrain these, as well as the impact of these constructions on achievement. Our own present study, funded by the Economic and Social Research Council,[6] illustrates this extremely effectively. We have been focusing on high-achieving pupils, deliberately including many pupils, both girls and boys, who are both high achieving and popular. We have found that, in contrast to the implications of research on "laddish behavior," some pupils are able to maintain popularity with peers in spite of their open production of high academic achievement. This simultaneous social and academic achievement was attained by pupils of both genders, of different ethnicities and social class groups. This provides a timely reminder that not all high-achieving pupils are derided or marginalized as "swots" and that not all boys are underperforming academically in order to preserve their social status. On the other hand, we did find that a fundamental facilitator of this "balance" for our high-achieving and popular pupils is their physical appearance (and for boys, their physical ability, at sports). As we point out in an article that elaborates our findings, notions of "attractiveness" are socially constructed, but it remains the case that some pupils have features that conform to such constructions, where others do not (see Francis, Skelton, & Read, 2010). This can also be applied to some extent to ability at sports, for boys. So our findings highlight the centrality of the body in productions of gendered subjectivity and in facilitating "balance" between popularity and academic achievement.

But appearance is not the only factor at stake. We found that the high-achieving popular pupils in our study are engaged in constant identity work to maintain their classroom subjectivities. Their behaviors are rarely excessive: Their academic achievement is performed as being attained relatively "effortlessly," and these pupils are simultaneously engaged in peer-oriented interaction as well as with the pedagogic tasks (see Francis et al., 2010). And their behaviors are not excessively disruptive: They tend to engage in good-humored "cheek" rather than overt confrontation. In these productions, then, high-achieving popular pupils are achieving the "balance" between achievement and sociability that Jackson (2006) observes as being so fragile for school pupils. But crucially, the performances involved in the production of such "effortless" achievement are themselves far from effortless: Such constructions are based on onerous identity work. This identity work is, of course, highly gendered, and we found that the high-achieving popular pupils performed gender in ways that reflected normative productions of "doing boy" and "doing girl" (Francis et al., 2010).

CONCLUSION

In looking at quantitative and qualitative evidence on gender and achievement, we hope to have shown the complexity of the field and, in doing so, illustrated the fallacy in generalized discussions of "girls" and "boys" and in assumptions about "boys' underachievement." We have examined the achievement figures to show how gendered patterns are far from straightforward and are inflected by social class and ethnicity (besides school and other variables). And we have analyzed some of the discourses and assumptions underpinning key arguments in the debates on "boys' underachievement," including notions of "feminization of schooling," "essential gender differences," and "the social construction of gender." We have shown the lack of evidence and damaging effects of some of these. Drawing out the substantive literature on the impact of social constructions of gender on patterns of subject preference and school achievement, we have also highlighted findings from our own current research to illustrate the complexity and nuance at stake and the interweaving of a raft of different factors, including physical embodiment, in pupils' performances of gender and educational achievement.

In England, policy making with respect to gender and achievement is currently experiencing something of a hiatus. Although the DCSF has been key in perpetuating myths around "boys' underachievement" and recommending strategies to address this "underachievement" which play to stereotypes rather than challenge them, there appears now to be some recognition that a change of approach is required. In 2008 and 2009, the DCSF launched a "Gender Agenda" to reappraise the issues at stake, and this has involved consultation with some academics, including ourselves. We suggest that this reappraisal may be due to various factors. First, in spite of 15 years of classroom application of their recommended "strategies to raise boys' achievement," figures for gender and achievement have nevertheless remained stable. There is also renewed education policy attention to the issue of social class. This has created an opportunity for some research input into policy documents on social identity and achievement, including instances of critique of previous policy-endorsed emphases on "boys' underachievement" and suggested methods to address this perceived underachievement (see, e.g., Moss, Francis, & Skelton, 2009a, 2009b). The message from such inputs is strongly that teachers need to be aware of gendered (and "raced" and classed) patterns in achievement and learning, but informed by an understanding of these trends as socially constructed and partial. As such, teachers should be encouraged to see their role as widening horizons and repertoires of behavior among pupils, rather than exacerbating existing stereotypes through their teaching.

As our own research has found, this reappraisal is slow to reach schools, which are still implementing "boy-friendly" strategies and teaching approaches with gusto (Skelton et al., 2009). It will be interesting to see how policy making develops from here, or whether gender inequalities will now be left aside as too entrenched and subtle an issue. But whatever the case, it seems imperative that feminists continue to research and highlight the continuing inequalities in the field and to insist on attention to the ways in which patterns in gender and achievement reflect wider social discourses that maintain the gender order.

NOTES

1. The chapter draws on data produced by the Department for Children, Schools and Families and published on its Standards website. We are aware that the way in which the statistics we refer to in this section have been arrived at and subsequently "read" have been open to criticism (see debates between Gorard et al., 1999, and Connolly, 2006, 2008), but our purpose here is to survey the information in the form that it is made available by government agencies to teachers and parents.
2. See, e.g., Archer & Francis, 2007; Cassen & Kingdon, 2007; Francis & Skelton, 2005; Gilborn & Gipps, 1996; Gillborn & Mirza, 2000; Skelton et al., 2007.
3. We acknowledged that Free School Meals is an unsatisfactory indicator of social class, and even of poverty, yet it is the only indicative record maintained by schools in England.
4. Mirza's (1992) important study showed how girls were being conflated with boys in discussion of "Black underachievement" in the 1980s, and that at the time Black girls were actually attaining relatively highly in comparison with White girls but that this pattern was hidden by the focus on the underachievement of Black boys.

5. See, for example, studies by Epstein, 1998; Francis, 2000; Francis & Skelton, 2005; Martino, 1999, 2000; Martino & Pallotta-Chiarolli, 2003; Mills, 2001; Salisbury & Jackson, 1996; Skelton, 2001; Warrington et al., 2000; Younger et al., 2005.
6. The study is titled "The Gender Subjectivities of High Achieving Pupils," ESRC project number: RES062230462.

REFERENCES

Ali, S. (2003). "To be a girl": Culture and class in schools. *Gender and Education*, *15*(3), 269–283.

Archer, L., & Francis, B. (2005). "They never go off the rails like other groups": Teachers' constructions of British-Chinese pupils' gender identities and approaches to learning. *British Journal of Sociology of Education*, *26*(1), 165–182.

Archer, L., & Francis, B. (2006). Constructions of racism by British-Chinese pupils and parents. *Race, Ethnicity and Education*, *8*(4), 387–407.

Archer, L., & Francis, B. (2007). *Understanding minority ethnic achievement*. London: Routledge.

Arnot, M., David, M., & Weiner, G. (1999). *Closing the gender gap?* Cambridge: Polity.

Ashley, M. and Lee, J. (2003). Women Teaching Boys. Stoke on Trent: Trentham.

Biddulph, S. (1997). *Raising boys*. London: Thorsons.

Blakemore, S. J., & Frith, U. (2005). *The learning brain*. Oxford: Blackwell.

Bleach, K. (Ed.). (1998). *Raising boys' achievement in schools*. Stoke-on-Trent: Trentham Books.

Brah, A. (1994). Difference, diversity and differentiation. In D. James & A. Rattansi (Eds.), *"Race," culture and difference* (pp. 126–145). London: Sage.

Carrington, B., Francis, B., Hutchings, M., Skelton, C., Read, B., & Hall, I. (2007). Does the gender of the teacher really matter? Seven- to eight-year-olds' accounts of their interactions with their teachers. *Educational Studies*, *33*(4), 397–413.

Carrington, B., Tymms, P., & Merrell, C. (2008). Role models, school improvement and the gender gap—Do men bring out the best in boys and women the best in girls? *British Educational Research Journal*, *34*(3), 315–327.

Cassen, R. (2008, April 7). *The national picture: Research findings and policy implications*. Speech presented at the Greenwich Council "Raising White Working-Class Achievement" conference, University of Greenwich, England.

Cassen, R., & Kingdon, G. (2007). *Tackling low educational achievement*. York: Joseph Rowntree Foundation.

Coffield, F, Moseley, D., Hall, E., & Ecclestone, K. (2004). *Should we be using learning styles? What research has to say to practice*. London: Learning and Skills Research Centre.

Connolly, P. (1998). *Racism, gender identities and young children*. London: Routledge.

Connolly, P. (2004). *Boys and schooling in the early years*. London: Routledge-Falmer.

Connolly, P. (2006). The effects of social class and ethnicity on gender differences in GCSE attainment: A secondary analysis of the Youth Cohort Study of England and Wales 1997–2001. British Educational Research Journal, *32*(1), 3–21.

Connolly, P. (2008). A critical review of some recent developments in quantitative research on gender and achievement in the UK. British Journal of Sociology of Education, *29*(3), 249–260.

Crozier, G., & Reay, D. (2005). Introduction. In G. Crozier & D. Reay (Eds.), *Activating participation* (pp. ix–xiv). Stoke-on-Trent: Trentham Books.

Davies, B. (1989). *Frogs and snails and feminist tales*. London: Allen & Unwin.

Davies, B., & Saltmarsh, S. (2006). Gender and literacy. In C. Skelton, B. Francis, & L. Smulyan (Eds.), *Sage handbook of gender and education* (pp. 236–248). London: Sage.

Delamont, S. (1999). Gender and the discourse of derision. *Research Papers in Education, 14*(1), 3–21.

Duffy, M. (2003). Achievement gap, TES Friday, *Times Educational Supplement*, 15/11/03, 15–18

Elwood, J. (2005). Gender and achievement: What have exams got to do with it? *Oxford Review of Education, 31*(3), 373–393.

Elwood, J., & Murphy, P. (2002).Tests, tiers and achievement: Gender and performance at 16 and 14 in England. *European Journal of Education, 37*, 395–416.

Epstein, D. (1998). Real boys don't work:'underachievement', masculinities and the harassment of 'sissies', in D. Epstein, J. Elwood, V. Hey and J. Maw (eds) Failing Boys? Buckingham: Open University Press.

Epstein, D., Elwood, J., Hey, V. & Maw, J. (Eds.). (1998). *Failing boys?* Buckingham, Open University Press.

Francis, B. (2000). *Boys, girls and achievement*. London: RoutledgeFalmer.

Francis, B., & Skelton, C. (2005). *Reassessing gender and achievement*. London: Routledge.

Francis, B., Skelton, C., Carrington, B., Hutchings, M., Read, B., & Hall, I. (2008). A perfect match? Pupils' and teachers' views of the impact of matching educators and learners by gender. *Research Papers in Education, 23*(1), 21–36.

Francis, B., Skelton, C., & Read, B. (2010). The simultaneous production of educational achievement and popularity: How do some pupils accomplish it? *British Educational Research Journal, 36*(2), 317–340.

Gillborn, D. & Gipps, C. (1996). *Recent Research on the Achievements of Ethnic Minority Pupils*. London: HMSO.

Gillborn, D., & Mirza, H. (2000). *Educational inequality: Mapping race, class and gender*. London: HMI.

Gipps, C., & Murphy, P. (1994). *A fair test? Assessment, achievement and equity*. Buckingham: Open University Press.

Gorard, S., Rees, G., & Salisbury, J. (1999). Reappraising the apparent underachievement of boys at school. *Gender and Education, 11*(4), 441–454.

Gurian, M. (2002). *Boys and girls learn differently! A guide for teachers and parents*. San Francisco: Jossey-Bass.

Halpern, D. (1992). *Sex differences in cognitive abilities*. Hillsdale, NJ: Erlbaum.

Harlen, W. (2004). *Research evidence of the impact on students of self-and peer-assessment*. Assessment and Learning Research Synthesis Group, EPPI Review. London: Eppi Centre, Institute of Education.

Hayes, D., & Lingard, B. (2003). Introduction: Rearticulating gender agendas in schooling: An Australian perspective. *International Journal of Inclusive Education, 7*(1), 1–6.

Haynes, J., Tickly, L., & Caballero, C. (2006). The barriers to achievement for White/Black Caribbean pupils in English schools. *British Journal of Sociology of Education, 27*(5), 569–583.

Haywood, C., & Mac an Ghaill, M. (2001). The significance of teaching English boys: Exploring social change, modern schooling and the making of masculinities. In W. Martino & B. Meyenn (Eds.), *What about the boys?* (pp. 24–37). Buckingham: Open University Press.

Hutchings, M. (2002). A representative profession? Gender issues. In M. Johnson & J. Hallgarten (Eds.), *From victims of change to agents of change: The future of the teaching profession* (pp. 125–149). London: IPPR.

Ivinson, G. and Murphy, P. (2007). *Rethinking Single Sex Teaching.* Maidenhead: Open University Press/McGraw-Hill Education.

Jackson, C. (2002). Can single-sex classes in co-educational schools enhance the learning experiences of girls and/or boys? An exploration of pupils' perceptions. *British Educational Research Journal, 28,* 37–48.

Jackson, C. (2003). Motives for "laddishness" at school: Fear of failure and fear of the "feminine." *British Educational Research Journal, 29*(4), 583–598.

Jackson, C. (2006). *Lads and ladettes in school.* Maidenhead: Open University Press.

Jha, J., & Kelleher, F. (2006). *Underachievement in education.* London: Commonwealth of Learning.

Kanaris, A. (1999). Gendered journeys: Children's writing and the construction of gender. *Language and Education, 13,* 254–268.

Lahelma, E. (2000) Lack of male teachers: A problem for students or teachers? *Pedagogy, Culture & Society, 8:* 173–85.

Lees, S. (1993). *Sugar and spice: Sexuality and adolescent girls.* London: Penguin.

Maby, T. (2004) How to turn boys on to studying. *Independent Education & Careers, Independent,* 21 Oct., 4–5.

Mac an Ghaill, M. (1994). *The making of men: Masculinities, sexualities and schooling.* Buckingham: Open University Press.

Mahony, P., & Hextall, I. (2000). *Reconstructing teaching.* London: Routledge-Falmer.

Majors, R. (2001). Introduction. In R. Majors (Ed.), *Educating our Black children* (1–9). London: RoutledgeFalmer.

Marsh, J. (2003). Superhero stories. In C. Skelton & B. Francis (Eds.), *Boys and girls in the primary classroom* (pp. 59–79). Maidenhead: Open University Press.

Martino, W. (1999). "Cool boys," "party animals," "squids" and "poofters": Interrogating the dynamics and politics of adolescent masculinities in school. *British Journal of Sociology of Education, 20*(2), 239–263.

Martino, W. (2000). Policing masculinities: Investigating the role of homophobia and heteronormativity in the lives of adolescent schoolboys. *Journal of Men's Studies, 8:* 213–236.

Martino, W. & Pallotta-Chiarolli, M. (2003). *So What's a Boy?* Buckingham: Open University Press.

Millard, E. (1997). *Differently literate: Boys, girls and the schooling of literacy.* London: Falmer Press.

Mills, M. (2001). *Challenging Violence in Schools.* Buckingham: Open University Press.

Mirza, H. (1992). *Young, female and Black.* London: Routledge.

Mirza, H. (2008, November 25). *Inaugural lecture: Race, gender and educational desire.* Institute of Education, London.

Moss, G., Francis, B., & Skelton, C. (2009a). *Gender and education—Mythbusters: Addressing gender and achievement: Myths and realities.* London: Department for Children, Schools and Families (DCSF).

Moss, G., Francis, B., & Skelton, C. (2009b). *Gender issue in school—What works to improve achievement for boys and girls.* London: Department for Children, Schools and Families (DCSF).

National Science Board. (2006). *Science and engineering indicators 2006: Student coursetaking in mathematics and science* Arlington, VA: National Science Foundation, Division of Science Resource Statistics. http://www.nsf.gov/statistics/seind06/c1/c1s2.htm

Noble, C., & Bradford, W. (2000). *Getting it right for boys . . . and girls.* London: Routledge.

Organisation for Economic Co-operation and Development. (2004). *Learning for tomorrow's world: First results from PISA 2003.* Paris: Author.

Organisation for Economic Co-operation and Development. (2007). *Science competencies for tomorrow's world PISA 2006*. Paris: Author.

Reay, D. (2001). "Spice girls," "nice girls," "girlies" and "tomboys": Gender discourses, girls' cultures and femininities in the primary classroom. *Gender and Education, 13*(2), 153–166.

Reay, D. (2006). Gender and class in education. In C. Skelton, B. Francis, & L. Smulyan (Eds.), *Sage handbook of gender and education* (339–349). London: Sage.

Rogers, L. (2000). *Sexing the brain*. New York: Columbia University Press.

Salisbury, J., & Jackson, D. (1996). *Challenging macho values*. London: Falmer Press.

Sewell, T. (1997). *Black masculinities and schooling: How Black boys survive modern schooling*. Stoke-on-Trent: Trentham Books.

Skelton, C. (2001). *Schooling the boys*. Buckingham: Open University Press.

Skelton, C., Carrington, B., Francis, B., Hutchings, M., Read, B., & Hall, I. (2009). Gender "matters" in the primary classroom: Pupils' and teachers' perspectives. *British Educational Research Journal, 35*(2), 187–204.

Skelton, C., Francis, B., & Valkanova, Y. (2007). *Breaking down the stereotypes: Gender and achievement in schools*. Manchester: Equal Opportunities Commission.

Slavin, R. (1994). *Educational psychology: Theory and practice* (4th ed.). Boston: Allyn & Bacon.

Smithers, A., & Robinson, P. (1995). *Co-educational and single-sex schooling*. Manchester: University of Manchester, CEER.

Thorne, B. (1993). *Gender play: Girls and boys in school*. Buckingham: Open University Press.

Thornton, M., & Brichenco, P. (2006). *Missing men in education*. Stoke-on-Trent: Trentham Books.

Warrington, M., Younger, M. and Williams, J. (2000) Student attitudes, image and the gender gap. *British Educational Research Journal, 26,* 393–407.

Warrington, M., & Younger, M. (2001). Single-sex classes and equal opportunities for girls and boys: Perspectives through time from a mixed comprehensive school in England. *Oxford Review of Education, 27,* 339–356.

Warrington, M., & Younger, M. (2002, November 17). 'Raising Boys' Achievement'. Opening speech at the 'Raising Boys' Achievement Conference', Homerton College Cambridge, 11/7/02.

Warrington, M., & Younger, M. (2003). "We decided to give it a twirl": Single-sex teaching in English comprehensive schools. *Gender and Education, 15,* 339–350.

Willis, P. (1977). *Learning to labour*. Aldershot: Saxon House.

Wright, C. (1987).The relations between teachers and Afro-Caribbean pupils. In G. Weiner & M. Arnot (Eds.), *Gender under scrutiny* (pp. 173–186). London: Hutchinson.

Wright, C., Weekes, D., & McGlaughlin, A. (2000). *"Race," class and gender in exclusion from school*. London: Falmer Press.

Younger, M., Warrington, M., & McLellan, R. (2005). *Raising boys' achievements in secondary schools: Issues, dilemmas and opportunities*. Maidenhead: Open University Press.

6 Teachers' Adaptations to Ethnic Minority Students in Belgium and England

Peter Stevens

INTRODUCTION

The question "Is the educational system meritocratic?" has dominated much sociological work in education since the 1970s. Influenced by Marxist social theory (Althusser, 1971; Bowles & Gintis, 1976), sociologists and educational researchers have paid considerable attention to the role of schools and educational systems in "reproducing social inequalities" in education. In their discourse, many researchers have used very different and sometimes contradictory notions of "inequality" and "social reproduction" (Hammersley, 2009). Whereas research in Europe has focused more on social class inequalities (Bourdieu, 1966/1974; Bourdieu & Passeron, 1977), U.S. researchers have traditionally paid closer attention to racial inequalities in education (Giroux, 1983).

However, despite the emphasis on social class over race (see, e.g., the culture versus class debate in the Netherlands: Phalet, 1998; Stevens, Clycq, Timmerman, & Van Houtte, 2010), the past decades have seen a sharp increase of research on racial/ethnic inequalities in education in Europe, particularly in the United Kingdom, in which researchers have paid considerable attention to ethnic stereotyping and discrimination in schools. Most of these studies apply a social-constructivist approach and focus mainly on students' experiences of ethnic stereotyping and discrimination, teachers' stereotypes of ethnic minority students, processes and effects of selection by teachers, the distribution of classroom resources, and the nature of the knowledge and values taught and sanctioned in schools (for reviews, see Foster, Gomm, & Hammersley, 1996; Gillborn & Gipps, 1996; Stevens, 2007).

Although research on teacher racism and discrimination constitutes a well-developed area of research, there have been few efforts to integrate existing findings into one overarching theoretical framework. Furthermore, there is a lack of research that investigates the impact of national differences between educational systems on teachers' adaptations to ethnic minority students. This study elaborates on the previously mentioned body of educational research by employing an ecological or embedded context approach in studying teachers' adaptations to ethnic minority students. Ethnographic data collected in one Flemish (Belgian) and one English secondary "sink" school are used to explore how the differences between the Flemish and English educational systems influence (a) teachers' ethnic stereotypes of Turkish minority students,[1] (b) teachers' allocation of scarce educational resources (such as personal feedback and praise) to minority pupils, and (c) teachers' ways of passing responsibility for educational success or failure to ethnic minority students. Hence, rather than addressing the question whether schools are meritocratic or not, this chapter seeks to enrich the existing research base by investigating how educational systems stimulate teachers to treat particular students in particular ways. In so doing, this chapter aims to develop a better understanding of the processes underlying the development of educational inequality and ultimately help to generate knowledge that can assist educational policy makers in promoting equity and excellence in education.

The following sections first review the literature on the factors and processes that influence students' and teachers' experiences or expressions of ethnic stereotypes and discriminating behavior. The key conclusion that will be drawn from this review is that racism in school is best understood from an ecological perspective and that there is very little research on the impact of national educational contexts on the development of racist stereotyping and discriminating behavior. Next, the methods section will briefly discuss the case-study research that was conducted. The analysis section then explores how a specific national educational system informs teachers' ethnic stereotypes and discriminating behavior toward Turkish school students. Finally, in the conclusions section, I will discuss the main findings and implications of this study for social policy and future research.

CONCEPTUALIZING INSTITUTIONAL EFFECTS

A large body of international research explores the importance of *face-to-face interactions* between young people, their teachers, and their parents to account for differences in expressions or perceptions of racism and discrimination (Stevens, 2007, 2009). Connolly showed that peer-group interactions in primary schools reinforce each other in developing specific stereotypes of Asian and African Caribbean pupils (Connolly, 1995, 2000a). A quantitative study involving 222 teachers in a Midwestern school district in the United States suggested that White teachers protect each other by remaining silent and not challenging incidents of racist behavior by White colleagues (Kailin, 1999). Furthermore, several quantitative studies conducted in the United States suggest that increased interracial interactions between young people, on the one hand, and parents' stereotypes of racial/ethnic minority people, on the other hand, inform how young people perceive such groups (Smith &

Ross, 2006; Wood & Sonleitner, 1996). These studies illustrate the importance of face-to-face interactions between students, parents/care-takers, and teachers in understanding the prevalence of (teacher) racism and discrimination and the development of students' perceptions of such incidents.

At the same time, researchers have focused on school and classroom characteristics in studying racism and discrimination in schools (Foster, 1990; Trentin, Monaci, De Lume, & Zanon, 2006; Verkuyten & Thijs, 2002). For example, a large-scale quantitative study in the Netherlands suggested that ethnic minority students experience less racism in more ethnically mixed classrooms (Verkuyten & Thijs, 2002). Furthermore, expressions of racism decrease in classrooms where teachers punish such incidents, and students are more likely to perceive incidents of racism in classrooms in which teachers teach multicultural education (maybe because multicultural teaching increases students' awareness and sensitivity to racism and, hence, their perception of it). This research suggests that multicultural programs help students to develop positive views of different ethnic groups. However, other studies show less straightforward and positive results (Hill & Augoustinos, 2001; Trentin et al., 2006), and a recent review on the effectiveness of diversity-related programs in U.S. colleges suggests that the success of such programs depend on a wide range of factors, including the level of institutional support, the comprehensiveness of such programs, the level of racial diversity, and (particularly) whether intergroup contact is a major component of the intervention (Denson, 2009). Although the findings of studies in this area are not always conclusive, they illustrate the importance of considering school and classroom characteristics in studying expressions and perceptions of (teacher) racism and discrimination in schools.

Finally, a few studies emphasize characteristics of the *larger social and institutional environment* in which schools are embedded and which interact with school-related variables in developing ethnic stereotypes and discrimination in schools (Faas, 2008; Gillborn & Youdell, 2000). Recent research in England suggests that students develop more negative attitudes to ethnic outgroups when their neighborhoods are characterized by competitive relationships between different ethnic groups over space and control in their area (Faas, 2008). Furthermore, other studies illustrate the importance of students' social and economic background (Spruyt, 2008), the influence of the educational market (Gillborn & Youdell, 2000), and international political relationships (such as the political divisions in Northern Ireland and Cyprus; see Connolly, 2000b; Spyrou, 2002) in understanding ingroup–outgroup attitudes between students. These studies emphasize the importance of taking into account the broader social and institutional contexts (such as neighborhood context, educational policies, and (inter)national political relationships) in which students and schools are embedded in view

of building a better understanding of the development of ethnic stereotypes and discrimination.

In highlighting the importance of particular institutional characteristics that are situated on different levels of analysis, these bodies of literature point to the usefulness of employing an "integrated" (Connolly,
2000b) or "ecological" approach (Feinstein, Duckworth, & Sabates,
2004) in studying the expression and perception of ethnic stereotyping
and discrimination in schools. This approach has its origins in developmental psychology (Bronfenbrenner, 1979) and classifies environmental
context measures according to the level in which they are situated. In line
with such an approach, the different institutional variables considered
in the literature can be classified as political/socioeconomic institutional
contexts (such as national or local government school policies, ethnic/
racial mix, and segregation neighborhood); characteristics of institutions
(such as school mix and adoption of multicultural and anti-racist policies);
and proximal school processes (such as face-to-face interactions between
students, their parents/caretakers, and staff). These various institutional
characteristics interact with and inform *teachers' mental frames of reference*, including their (stereotypical) attitudes and motivations for discriminating or treating ethnic minority students less favorably than majority
students. Based on the research literature, the conceptual scheme shown
in Figure 6.1 was developed to study racial/ethnic stereotyping and discrimination in school.

This chapter builds on existing research in this area by exploring,
through case-study research, the impact of nationally specific educational
contexts on teachers' ethnic stereotypes of and discriminatory practices
toward Turkish minority students. Whereas racial/ethnic stereotypes usually refer to negative emotions or feelings toward a target racial/ethnic
group, discrimination is manifest in behavior and refers to unequal treatment among racial groups (Pettigrew & Tropp, 2005; Quillian, 2006).
More specifically, this chapter explores the impact of the Flemish (Belgian) and English educational system on teachers' negative and generalized
views and their differential allocation of scarce educational resources and
blame for educational "failure" to Turkish minority students.

METHODS

This chapter employs data collected as part of case-study research conducted between 2001 and 2003 on ethnicity and educational inequality in
English and Flemish multicultural secondary school classrooms. It involves
the analysis of semi-structured interviews with teachers and naturalistic
observations in one English (*Park Lane*) and one Flemish (*Riverside*) secondary multicultural school.[2]

Although comparing settings in case-study research is difficult because
researchers often cannot control for relevant characteristics (Le Compte

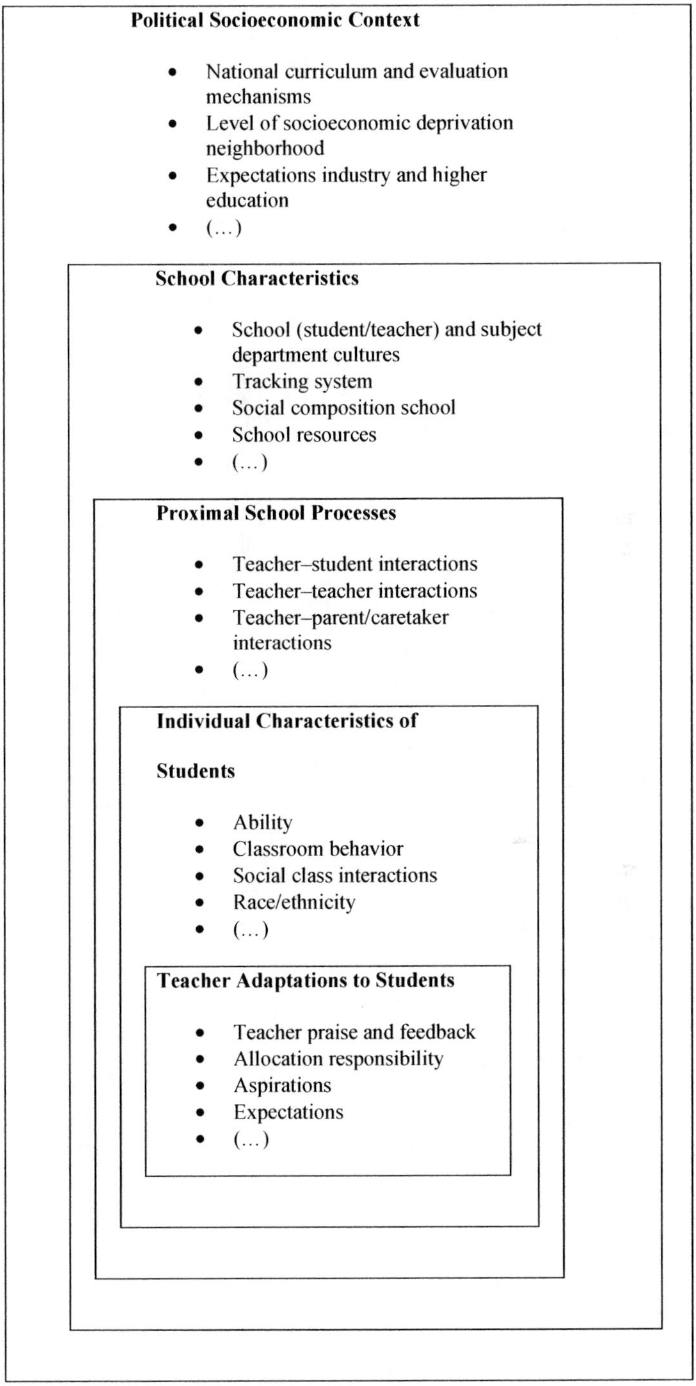

Political Socioeconomic Context

- National curriculum and evaluation mechanisms
- Level of socioeconomic deprivation neighborhood
- Expectations industry and higher education
- (…)

School Characteristics

- School (student/teacher) and subject department cultures
- Tracking system
- Social composition school
- School resources
- (…)

Proximal School Processes

- Teacher–student interactions
- Teacher–teacher interactions
- Teacher–parent/caretaker interactions
- (…)

Individual Characteristics of

Students

- Ability
- Classroom behavior
- Social class interactions
- Race/ethnicity
- (…)

Teacher Adaptations to Students

- Teacher praise and feedback
- Allocation responsibility
- Aspirations
- Expectations
- (…)

Figure 6.1   Conceptual model of embedded institutional contexts.
Source: Adapted from Feinstein et al., 2004; Stevens, 2007.

& Goetz, 1982), special care was taken to ensure that the Flemish and English schools selected for this study were similar in important ways to better explore the potential impact of a national context on teacher adaptations to ethnic minority students. *Riverside* and *Park Lane* are similar in that they attract a substantial number of working-class and ethnic minority students, including a large group of second-generation Turkish minority students whose parents migrated from mainland Turkey. Furthermore, both schools are situated in a highly urbanized environment and share a relatively poor reputation in their neighborhood. The latter is related to the problems experienced by *Riverside* and *Park Lane* in terms of behavioral and academic standards, the high proportion of students with special educational needs, a decline in the number of students enrolled, and a high turnover of both student and staff populations. Finally, because of these problems, both schools were in danger of being closed down by higher educational authorities and experienced a change in management at the start of the fieldwork.

Despite the similarities between these schools, it appeared impossible to select two identical schools. *Riverside* and *Park Lane* appeared different in numerous ways. *Park Lane* had 1,142 students; only an estimated 15% of the student population was of "White English" descent. In contrast, *Riverside* had only 355 students, and native Flemish students made up 72% of the student population. Furthermore, whereas *Park Lane* was a coeducational school (40% girls), *Riverside* counted very few female students because it offered programs (such as mechanics, electricity, and computer science) that appealed more to boys than girls. Finally, whereas the teaching staff in *Riverside* had only one part-time teacher of Turkish background, the *Park Lane* teaching staff were ethnically very diverse and had more teachers of ethnic minority background than of White English background, including many teachers of Turkish, Kurdish, African Caribbean, and Somali backgrounds. In sum, although the selected schools are similar in important ways, they are also different in ways other than the national context in which they situated. The latter constituted the main focus of this study.

The researcher conducted naturalistic observations in classroom settings in the two schools over the course of one school year, observing lessons of students and their teachers mainly as a "participant observer" (Gold, 1969). Four tutor groups in *Riverside* and three in *Park Lane* were followed for a period of 3 to 4 weeks each before being invited for interviews, which allowed the researcher to build rapport with interview participants. Observations took place in classrooms, playgrounds, staffrooms, and outside school (e.g., lunch-time, sport, and social events) and focused increasingly more on issues related to ethnic stereotyping and discrimination.

Qualitative, semi-structured face-to-face interviews were conducted with 11 teachers in *Riverside* and 8 teachers in *Park Lane*. The qualitative interviews in both countries usually lasted for 40 to 50 minutes and were guided by the same set of questions. Interviews started with questions on the teachers' definition of an ideal student and an ideal teacher and then continued to address the teachers' general adaptations to students, their experiences with teaching ethnic minority students, their employed evaluation standards and mechanisms, and their experiences with the school more generally. Although the participating teachers were all asked the same questions in both countries, often additional questions were asked to pursue interesting issues raised by respondents. Only those teachers who taught students who were observed during lesson time and gave the impression that they trusted the researcher were invited for an interview.[3] The sample of interviewed teachers reflected the sex and ethnic distribution of staff in both schools. In *Riverside* all informants were of White Flemish descent, and most of them were male. In contrast, the sample of teachers interviewed at *Park Lane* included more ethnic minority teachers than White teachers and more female than male teachers (see Table 6.1 in Appendix). Although the small sample of teachers selected for interviews does not allow generalization of the findings to the two educational settings, the analysis involved triangulation of the interview data with observations and informal conversations with staff to make inferences about the schools on a whole.

The data analysis used a grounded theory approach, in which a substantive theory, related to a particular setting, is developed through mainly inductive analyses of qualitative data (Glaser & Strauss, 1967). The qualitative data analysis used a word processing program and N6 qualitative analysis software. Because the ethnographic research underlying the data analysis did not focus initially on *explaining* differences in teachers' ethnic stereotypes and allocation of scarce educational resources, the initial findings emerged from the analysis in line with Glaser's (1992) "open coding" approach to grounded theory. However, in line with Strauss and Corbin's (1990) "coding paradigm," the data were analyzed increasingly more in a systematic way, by continuously focusing on the potential importance of particular (national) and school contexts, and causal conditions more generally in explaining differences between teachers' adaptations to particular students.

KEY DIFFERENCES IN EDUCATIONAL POLICY IN FLANDERS AND ENGLAND

Before exploring differences between teachers' ethnic stereotypes and discriminatory behavior toward Turkish minority students in our Flemish and English case-study schools, I will first discuss some key differences between the Flemish and English secondary school systems in terms of how teachers evaluate their students and the importance attached to multicultural and anti-racist policies.

Nationally Specific School and Student Evaluation Systems

The Flemish educational system is particular in that schools cannot be compared in public in terms of quality or output indicators. Furthermore, teachers have considerable power to determine the educational career of their students. In Flemish secondary education, students have to take an examination twice a year (in December and June) for every subject that is taught. Teachers are responsible for designing, administering, and marking the examinations of the students they teach. At the end of the school year in Flanders, teachers come together to discuss the progress of every student and decide whether a student is allowed to pass the year or not; this event is called "deliberation." Although the schools are free to decide the criteria for evaluation and procedures that are used during the deliberations, the results of the students' examinations are generally considered important in deciding whether the students will be allowed to pass the school year. A deliberation meeting is secret by law, and only the headteacher and/or deputy headteacher, the teachers who teach the student, the teachers who are responsible for providing pastoral support, and members of the external social and psychological school-counseling team are allowed to attend this event. (It should be noted, however, that parents in Flanders have the right to legally challenge the outcome of the deliberation process.)

At the end of compulsory secondary education in England, students can sit General Certificate of Secondary Education (GCSE) exams for each subject taught (usually at the ages of 15–16). Most of these exams are standardized and centrally administered and are taken in a variety of subjects, which are usually decided by the students themselves in Year 9 (ages 13–14). Although grades can vary from A* to G, the "A*–C economy" sets the benchmark for educational success for all secondary school institutions and students at five GCSEs of grade level A*–C. Receiving five or more A*–C grades, including GCSEs in English and maths, is often a requirement for taking Advanced levels (A levels) in the school's sixth form, at a sixth form college, or at a further education college after leaving secondary school. However, regardless of a student's performance in their A level, most universities typically require students to obtain five GCSEs of level C or better, including English and mathematics. Every year, popular media in England publish league tables of secondary schools, based on the percentage of students in secondary schools obtaining at least five GCSE grade levels A*–C. Hence, students' entrance to colleges and universities and the perceived performance and status of schools depends on students' success in meeting the standard of five GCSEs grade levels A*–C (Gillborn & Youdell, 2000). Compared to their colleagues in Belgium, teachers in England have relatively little power in the process of evaluating their students. Exams are standardized and administered nationally to all students, and teachers are not involved in designing, administering, and marking the examinations of the students they teach. Furthermore, students in England pass the school year automatically and, unlike their peers in Belgium, they are not subject to a deliberation process in which their teachers decide whether they should be allowed to pass the year.

National Context and Diversity Policies

The particular cultural characteristics and needs of members of ethnic minority groups, especially in education, became increasingly more recognized on a political level in England during the late 1970s and early 1980s (Foster et al., 1996). Whereas in the 1970s the English government adhered to an integration policy and tried to subsume problems experienced by ethnic minorities under those of the poor and disadvantaged, the committee chaired by Rampton in 1979 and Swann in 1981 emphasized the importance of racism in explaining racial/ethnic underachievement (Nehaul, 1996). The public outrage and media attention that followed the publication of the *Stephen Laurence Inquiry* into the racist murder of a Black British teenager (Gillborn, 2008) stimulated the government to implement the Race Relations (Amendment) Act in 2000 to ensure that "all public authorities provide services in a way that is fair, accessible and nondiscriminatory on the grounds of 'race,' ethnicity or colour" (NASUWT, 2002). This act puts responsibility on schools to provide services that is nondiscriminatory in its operation and impact, which includes a series of measures, such as the development and implementation of a race equality policy, training of staff, and monitoring development and success of their policies (NASUWT, 2002).

In sharp contrast, Flanders only started to implement a comprehensive policy to improve educational outcomes of ethnic minorities in 1991. This policy largely reduced the educational problems experienced by ethnic minorities to their lower socioeconomic position (De Wit & Van Petegem, 2000).[4] Although schools were encouraged to recognize specific minority needs by allocating extra resources to "Intercultural Education" and "Teaching in Home Language and Culture," in practice very few schools implemented such measures and instead adopted an assimilation perspective by focusing almost exclusively on "Dutch Second Language Development." Furthermore, teachers who took responsibility for these particular courses in school often lacked experience, were given a lower status by the teaching staff, and even experienced overt resistance from other members of staff (De Wit & Van Petegem, 2000). Finally, in part because of the historical tension between the Dutch-speaking (Flanders) and French-speaking (Wallonia) communities in Belgium, Belgian legislation does not allow teachers in each of the two language regions to communicate with parents in any other language than the official language of the region (Dutch in Flanders and French in Wallonia). All this suggests that whereas British educational policy emphasizes the importance and value of multiculturalism and anti-racism and discrimination, the Flemish government adopts a policy of assimilation with regard to ethnic and cultural diversity in education (see also Blommaert & Verschueren, 1998).

One area in which these national differences in multicultural policies appeared very strong concerns the language policies adopted in these two educational settings. In *Riverside,* school students were only allowed to communicate in Dutch, and expressions of ethnic minority languages were generally regarded by teaching staff as inappropriate at best and offensive at worst. School staff in *Riverside* were not allowed to communicate formally with parents in any other language than Dutch. A recent study conducted in three inner-city multicultural primary schools in Flanders (Blommaert, Creve, & Willeart, 2006) suggests that such views on ethnic minority languages are not restricted to *Riverside* school. The Flemish teachers interviewed in these three schools considered students as "literate" only when they spoke standard Dutch or possessed the specific literacy skills associated with Dutch orthography. Students who failed to develop proficiency in these skills were defined as language-poor and illiterate, even if they were proficient multilingual individuals (Blommaert et al., 2006).

In sharp contrast, students in *Park Lane* could follow Turkish language education as part of their curriculum and obtain recognized educational qualifications (GCSE and A level) in their mother tongue. Students were allowed to communicate in their own language during playtime, and some teachers asked Turkish students with stronger English language skills to translate course material to Turkish students with poor English language skills. Major signs in school were written in English, Turkish, Kurdish, and Somali. Finally, the school employed official documents written in different minority languages to improve communication between school and parents. Teachers were expected to take initiative in communicating with parents and, in doing so, made use of colleagues who were proficient in different languages.

In sum, whereas Flemish educational policy does not allow schools to be compared in public and offers teachers considerable power in evaluating their students, English policy is characterized by public and standardized assessment procedures in which teachers have relatively little power in determining the educational career of their students. In addition, whereas English educational policy shows a strong awareness of linguistic and cultural diversity and puts much more emphasis on anti-racism and discrimination, Flemish educational policy emphasizes the importance of social class inequalities over ethnicity and does not have strong anti-racist or discriminatory policies. The following sections explore how these differences in national educational policies with regard to multiculturalism, anti-racism, and school and student evaluation systems influence teachers' stereotypes of Turkish minority students and their allocation of scarce educational resources and blame for failure to ethnic minority students.

TEACHERS' ADAPTATIONS TO ETHNIC MINORITY STUDENTS

The previous sections highlighted a number of key differences between the English and Flemish educational system in terms of their evaluation systems and the importance and implementation of multicultural and anti-racist policies in schools. The following sections explore the significance of these national educational systems in explaining teachers' adaptations to Turkish minority students in terms of (a) their allocation of scarce educational resources and the extent to which they blame the Turkish students for educational failure and (b) their stereotyping of Turkish minority students.

Teachers' Allocation of Scarce Educational Resources and Blame for Failure

Teachers in *Riverside*, particularly those teaching in the vocational strands in which most of the ethnic minority students were enrolled, perceived their students as less capable and motivated to do well in school. In reaction to this, they adapted their evaluation methods in order to increase the students' chances of demonstrating their knowledge and skills successfully.

> MR. ALONSO: "I have the impression that some of them are really not interested in the course material, but then there are also students who . . . cannot process too much information at a time. It's as if their computer crashes. It's finished. You might say: 'Yeah, they will have remembered something' but no: it's 'deleted totalement.' But what can you do about it? That's the problem. The only thing I have learned this year is to change the way I ask questions: Never ask two questions, you ask one thing at a time, otherwise they will definitely get it wrong."
>
> **(Male Flemish teacher, *Riverside*, car mechanics)**

Similarly, some teachers asked multiple-choice questions to help students who had poor Dutch writing skills. Many teachers offered students a "second chance" to submit certain assignments after having failed to meet the initial deadline. Some ethnic minority students in vocational education said that certain teachers even offered them the answers to some questions during their re-examination period. However, although observations suggest that such measures were employed on a large scale in *Riverside* by teachers in the vocational strand, teachers' adaptations in the evaluation criteria they used appeared even more dramatic. Teachers in vocational education not only lowered their standards in terms of the curriculum they taught, or the kind of skills and knowledge students had to develop, but also seemed to attach less importance to reaching educational goals, while valuing pro-school orientated attitudes and behavior much more.

RESEARCHER: "What kind of criteria are taken into account during the deliberations? How important is it that a student is considered motivated?"

MR. DUDEK: "300%! That student is almost certain to obtain a A-certificate and allowed to pass the year, even if his marks are poor!"

(Male Flemish teacher, *Riverside*, practice and theory car mechanics)

The strong tendency among vocational education teachers to value school-related attitudes and behavior more highly than students' acquired knowledge or skills shows that these teachers had not abandoned educational standards and related evaluation criteria altogether. Although these teachers felt obliged to lower the curriculum and evaluation standards to fit their evaluation of students' ability and interests, their students still had to demonstrate a willingness to do well in school. Students who managed to demonstrate a minimal ability and pro-school-related values and behavior were not only perceived as successful but were also allocated more educational resources than those who failed to meet these expectations.

RESEARCHER: "And Shakur (ethnic minority student)?"

MR. GERRARD: "Look, you know I don't have any favorites, but there is one . . . even if he had his setbacks during the second term. But he isolates himself completely from the others . . . he wants to achieve, he wants to achieve. He doesn't join the others, he calls them 'drivellers.' And for students like him I have a lot more respect than for the others. I will also tolerate more from those students than from others. Tolerate in the sense of repeating something, not in that they would receive better marks, that's something I don't do: you earn marks. But when they ask for explanations, you are more likely to give it to them, because they are interested, they want to know, they don't just ask you to butter you up, or to make you explain it again so that they don't have to study the material. No, Shakur is not like that."

(Male Flemish teacher, *Riverside*, practice and theory car mechanics)

RESEARCHER: "Like Aldo (ethnic minority student)?"

MR. BABEL: "Yes, now that's an example, that boy, it takes time, but I remember when he came in and he didn't know almost anything, but now he's doing much better, especially his verbal skills . . . but writing, no, he can't."

RESEARCHER: "So on the basis of what will you evaluate such a student?"

MR. BABEL: "On progress, progress, even if his marks are not very good. So progress . . . and effort! Aldo shows enormous effort, enormous! He always pays attention, is never distracted! He wants to move up! No, progress and effort, absolutely. And they can still fail their exams, they can pass to the next year for me."

(Male Flemish teacher, *Riverside*, Dutch language)

Hence, these vocational education teachers defined success in terms of students' progress in achievement and lowered their expectations and standards of assessment to a point where ethnic minority students merely had to show a strong motivation to do well in school. As a result, these students were held responsible for their own success and motivated students were more likely to receive scarce educational resources.

Teachers interviewed at *Park Lane* appeared to have mixed feelings about the meaning and importance of GCSE outcomes. On the one hand, they seemed to accept the social significance of GCSEs as important selection and evaluation tools employed in English society, but on the other hand, they questioned the validity of these tools as adequate measures of student or school "success."

MS. RIISE: "They ACHIEVE well, even though their attainment is well below national standards. They achieve well from where they are. They do better—lots of them—than their SATS from Key Stage 3 would suggest they were going to do. But some of these students don't even get an F or a G grade. If they come here with no English at all, and if they end up with an F or G at GCSE, that IS an achievement. (. . .). [Well, I think] it is not fair. And I think it's now beginning to be recognized that a school like this might be MUCH more successful than a school which has not an intake of children who cannot read and write, or speak English and so on. And they end up with—what shall we say—with 70% five A's to C's. Well, you should ask them: Why is it not 90%? But on paper, it looks as if we aren't successful, but we gradually move on."

(Female English teacher, *Park Lane*, religious education)

Teachers interviewed at *Park Lane* school appeared to acknowledge that the benchmark of five GCSE levels A*–C constituted an important evaluation standard for students and schools. However, at the same time, they did not seem to find it feasible for them and their students to reach this goal, and they defined students' success more in terms of progress or added value rather than outcome. Several teachers explain a change in, or lowering of, their expectations by referring to the nature of their student population, in particular the large proportion of students who recently arrived in the United Kingdom and as a consequence lack proficiency in English. Hence, just like in *Riverside* school, especially in vocational streams, teachers appeared to redefine success and lower their student expectations in the light of the perceived interests and especially the ability of their students.

However, whereas teachers in vocational education at *Riverside* school lowered their standards to such a level that underachieving was considered mainly a result of "unwillingness" on the students' part, the teachers interviewed in *Park Lane* school could not lower the standards to a level that they thought attainable by most students, as the standards are fixed nationally at five GCSE levels A*–C. As a result, they felt that many students were simply "unable" to reach such standardized goals. At the same time, the English educational system is characterized by a culture of ability testing, in which decisions regarding students' educational careers are strongly informed by their performance on standardized ability tests (Gillborn & Youdell, 2000). This suggests that teachers' perception of students' failure is influenced by the nationally specific evaluation system: Whereas teachers from vocational streams in *Riverside* mainly pointed to (and criticized their ethnic minority) students' lack of motivation or willingness in explaining underachievement, teachers in *Park Lane* mainly stressed the unrealistic nature of the expectations imposed on certain students by the educational system. The former blame the students, whereas the latter blame the educational system and the specific social conditions in which these students are growing up.

> RESEARCHER: "Ehm, do you feel that, it's a school with a lot of different kids from a lot of different backgrounds, and do you feel that you have to be a different teacher, a different kind of teacher for different groups, different students?"
>
> MS. MELLOR: "I feel in a sense that, you have to be quite nurturing, and quite, sort of motherly to a lot of the kids, I mean, they've just been yanked out of the country, brought into a foreign country, they don't know the language—a lot of the time—feel very alienated, they feel very, sort of, alone and isolated, you know, it's not a system that they're used to, so in a sense, although I am quite firm, I try and be as nurturing as possible and as understanding with their behavior, because there is so much baggage that they bring with them, so that's sort of pressure I think, that if perhaps I was in a different school, then I might be a bit different, I would expect more of them I think, but here, any little thing that they do, I, you know, reward them, I, I point out their success because I feel that's so important, you know."

(Female Turkish teacher, *Park Lane*, mathematics)

Although this teacher claims to be more "nurturing" and "understanding with their behavior" to students she regards as victims of their social situation, like her colleagues, she cannot lower the standards of evaluation in order to increase these students' chances of succeeding. As a result, these students can only hope to achieve inferior educational qualifications.

> MS. ANNA: "Well, obviously, the biggest success for a child is to actually leave the school with some qualifications, whether that is GCSC, certificate of achievement, you know, as long as they come out with something, and they can use that later on in their lives, and I would say that they've been successful."
>
> RESEARCHER: "Right, and do you think they can use, all those qualifications, for something?"
>
> MS. ANNA: "Yes, of course, I mean a certificate of achievement, that's about it for kids, ehm, who have just recently come into the country. But they're like saying Year 10, they're not allowed to do a GCSC when they're just learning the language, so obviously that way they don't feel useless, you know. But it's just a way of actually getting them to achieve something really, and that's the reason why we do it. Obviously, they wouldn't be able to cope with GCSC, it'd be too difficult for them."
>
> (Female African Caribbean teacher, *Park Lane*, mathematics)

Like Mr. Babel in *Riverside* (see extract with Aldo), this teacher in *Park Lane* teaches secondary school students who have only recently arrived in England and have very little knowledge of the English language. However, unlike Mr. Babel, this teacher cannot lower her standards of expectations to help such students obtain valued educational qualifications. Instead, such students are expected to achieve lower levels of educational qualifications ("certificates of achievement"), which, according to many teachers in *Park Lane,* seem to have relatively little value in the labor market (compared to GNVQs and especially GCSEs) and sometimes merely function as a consolation prize for those who are not allowed to participate or who fail the qualifying race for access to high-status education and employment.

Furthermore, teachers in *Riverside* not only lowered the standards of assessment to the perceived ability and interest of their students, they allocated scarce educational resources to those students perceived as willing or motivated to be successful. However, the "A*–C economy" appeared to stimulate *Park Lane* school to adopt specific policies to increase their GCSE output. In line with Gillborn and Youdell's research (2000), it seems that the school implemented a form of "educational triage," or initiatives that allocate scarce educational resources to a limited number of students who were expected to benefit most from support in terms of reaching the benchmark of five GCSE levels A*–C.

For example, a project called "GAP" aimed to boost the GCSE output of *Park Lane* school by allocating extra support to students who were considered intermediate, or students who were expected to obtain a level C-D on their GCSE exams. The students selected for this program received additional help during the 2 years prior to their GCSE exams. First, they were given "in-class support" in Years 10 and 11, which meant that a support teacher offered them individual help in their main subjects such as English, maths, sciences, ICT, history, and geography during regular lesson time. Second, GAP students were also assigned a mentor teacher in Year 11 who helped these students improve their GCSE results by developing their organizational and learning skills. The support staff viewed the positive increase in GCSE output over time as proof that the program "paid off." By excluding those students who were not expected to have the ability to obtain five GCSEs levels A*–C (even with additional support), the support team was effectively implementing a system of educational triage that disadvantaged students regarded as unable to achieve. Although the support staff recognized this unfairness, they felt pressured to implement such measures in the light of the school's poor GCSE output.

> MR. FOY: "It is unfair to the lower-achieving students, but the school has to show that it can get rid of its special status, where it's considered as a school that needs special measures, it has to show that it can get the GCSE results. (. . .). Unfortunately, it is impossible for us to give support to every individual student."
>
> (Male Somali teacher, *Park Lane*, support teacher)

In sum, in both educational settings, Turkish students were among the lowest-achieving groups. In response to this problem, teachers in the Flemish school lowered their standards of assessment to a point where success was considered to be a function of students' willingness to be successful and scarce educational resources were allocated to those students perceived as willing or motivated to be successful. In contrast, teachers in the English case-study school could not lower their standards of assessment and perceived Turkish students largely as victims of a social situation in which they had to reach impossible standards imposed from above. Whereas teachers in *Park Lane* expressed more positive views and knowledge of Turkish minority students, the "GCSE A*–C economy" in the English educational context stimulated teachers to consider and implement specific measures that allocate scarce educational resources only to those students who are most likely to reach the national benchmark of achievement with the help of such additional educational resources. All this suggests that national educational evaluation systems can have an important impact on the ways teachers treat and perceive their students. The following section will explore teachers' stereotypes of Turkish students in *Riverside* and *Park Lane* and the importance of nationally specific educational policies in shaping these stereotypes.

TEACHERS' STEREOTYPES OF TURKISH STUDENTS

In *Riverside*, structured interviews and informal conversations with teachers and administrative staff revealed strong, negative attitudes toward Turkish and Moroccan (both mainly Muslim) students. Turkish students in particular were often criticized for having low educational aspirations, for not communicating in Dutch, and for being lazy and arrogant or disrespectful toward teachers.

> "On my way to the workshop of metal-working, I pass by a teacher who is sitting outside. He seems to be a senior teacher in electricity. When I ask him if there are differences between native and Turkish and Moroccan students, he explains that 'immigrant students' have a different, more negative attitude towards studying, they also cause more behavioural, discipline problems, apart from the language problems. Nevertheless, there are differences between the different immigrant groups, Moroccan people are *even more* lazy and hypocritical than Turkish people" (emphasis added).
>
> (Fieldnotes, *Riverside*, playground)

Not only did teachers attach such negative attributes to general categories like "Turkish" or "Moroccan" students, they also framed such views within a discourse of "us against them" in which the ethnic outgroup was expected but deliberately failed to adapt to the dominant ingroup culture.

> **RESEARCHER:** "And why don't they want to learn Dutch?"
> **MR. AGGER:** "They just want to be Belgian to take advantage of the benefits of living in Belgium. That's why they want to be Belgian, but apart from that? That's it, the rest doesn't matter, they don't need that. They just need Belgium for the money, for luxury, and they think 'we are not going to adapt to you, you just adapt to us,' and it starts to turn that way, slowly, we will have to adapt."
>
> (Teacher interview: White, male, Flemish senior teacher, *Riverside*)

Teachers in *Riverside* not only criticized Turkish students for not *wanting* to speak Dutch and for being arrogant to (Flemish) teachers, they also criticized these students for somehow taking advantage of Flemish people and society. During my fieldwork I talked to at least 50% of all staff in *Riverside,* and the vast majority explicitly subscribed to such a view, with the other staff members usually refraining from expressing their opinion. Although most members of staff expressed such views to me in confidence or in a safe "backstage" area where no ethnic minority students or less familiar colleagues were present, some teachers also expressed such views in the classroom in front of Turkish students.

> *Context:* Mr. Gerrard is irritated because some Turkish pupils communicate in Turkish and ask the teacher to go slower and to translate words in Dutch.

MR. GERRARD: "If you think that Europe will become like Turkey
. . . it won't happen!"

HAGI: "Yes, but I want to copy . . ."

PEPSI: "Yes, why do you always have to talk about Turkey!?!"

MR. GERRARD: "Hagi is a Turk, isn't he?!"

HAGI: "(serious) No, I am Belgian!"

MR. GERRARD: "You don't behave like a Belgian!"

HAGI: (Keeps on talking about his map and that he cannot follow the
teacher.)

CIMI: (Says something in Turkish to Hagi.)

MR. GERRARD: (Angry because Cimi talks in Turkish.) "Cimi, I've got
a job for you . . . they need monkeys in the zoo of Antwerp!"

(Fieldnotes, *Riverside*—5VC during theory lessons auto-
mechanics in workshop)

Teachers interviewed and observed at *Park Lane* also criticized Turkish students for having low educational aspirations and lacking proficiency in the
language of instruction. However, it should be noted that these teachers did
not perceive all Turkish students as such, but mainly attached such negative
perceptions to Turkish students from a less educated and (associated with
this) more rural background.

RESEARCHER: "And why do you think they don't [achieve their
potential]?"

MS. TORRES: "Cause they haven't [practiced for their GCSE exams so
far]. And also, perhaps, because their parents don't understand
education, they don't encourage them. Some of our students
here, while talking about the Turkish students and Kurdish students, there are differences between them, you can pick them
out. You can pick out those who come from an educated background, come from the city, have high expectations, and then
there are others, who just come from the stage of looking after
the goats on the mountains and they fall straight into this, they
don't adapt very well. And then there are students here who are
not literate in their OWN language, never mind in English."

(Teacher interview: White, female English teacher, *Park Lane*)

I rarely experienced teachers in *Park Lane* blaming "Turkish" or "Kurdish"
students for something negative. Instead, they focused their criticism on
individual students and their particular circumstances or (like the teacher
in the previous excerpt) on particular subgroups within these communities
(e.g., "the more traditional families"). Furthermore, whereas this was common practice in *Riverside*, I did not experience any teacher in *Park Lane*
(where I communicated with at least one third of staff on a regular basis)
criticizing Turkish students for not wanting to adapt to the English society,
let alone express such views in front of their Turkish students.

Furthermore, teachers in *Riverside* showed less consideration and knowledge of Turkish students' particular interests and social situation, and they also appeared to have more stereotypical views of the Turkish parents' involvement with the schooling of their children. Although teachers in both schools claimed that Turkish parents did not often take initiative in liaising with their school to discuss issues related to the education of their child, teachers interviewed in *Park Lane* showed a deeper understanding of the motivations and implications behind this.

> RESEARCHER: "Do you think there is a difference in the contact you have between Flemish and foreign parents?"
>
> MR. MACHERANO: "Em the foreigners, they are ignorant you know."
>
> RESEARCHER: "And do you sometimes talk to them, do they come to school?"
>
> MR. MACHERANO: "Not a lot! Very rare, they either have an interpreter or a brother or sister, and that doesn't go very smooth you know. No, that doesn't work. And they don't come very spontaneously. I am talking about my own experiences. I don't know if there are others . . . that's possible. Are they scared? Are they insecure? Definitely insecure, but scared, I don't know . . . it's weird."
>
> (Teacher interview: White, male, Flemish senior teacher, *Riverside*)

————-

> MR. LEIVA: "In Africa, Turkey, West Indies, and India, teachers are held in a very, very high regard. Your profession is like to be a doctor or a lawyer, a very, very good job. And they trust us, they trust us 100%. As long as we are—you know—not beating their children or not abusing them in some way, they'll do whatever you say. And they say: 'You're the teacher, you do it.' Sometimes when you phone them up, you say: 'I've got a problem with your son or daughter," the reaction you get is 'So what?'. Sometimes you think they are not very supportive, but the fact is, it's them being VERY supportive, cause they say: 'Why are you phoning me, you deal with it, and whatever you do, I'll support you.' And that's the attitude that they bring here, 'You're the teacher, you do what you have to do,' because immigrant parents know how important education is. It's the ONLY chance for a lot of them."
>
> (Teacher interview: White, male, English senior teacher, *Park Lane*)

In line with previous research on parental participation in school and its relationship to social class and ethnicity (Lareau, 1987/1999; Lareau & Horvat McNamara, 1999), this study indicates that Turkish-speaking parents did not always possess the cultural and social capital necessary to interact more effectively with schools compared to White middle-class parents. Furthermore, Turkish-speaking parents also adhered to a different, more passive model of parent–teacher relationships (see also Timmerman, 1999), in which the teachers are given considerable authority, autonomy, and responsibility to manage their children's educational progress (for similar findings on Mexican American parents, see Lopez, 2001; Trinkler, 2002). However, the staff members interviewed in *Park Lane* did not perceive this as ignorance or a lack of interest on the part of Turkish-speaking parents.

In sum, teachers in both *Riverside* and *Park Lane* criticized Turkish students for having low educational aspirations and for lacking sufficient skills in the language of instruction. In addition, teachers in both schools criticized Turkish-speaking parents for not taking enough initiative in communicating with school staff members. However, compared to the teachers observed and interviewed in *Park Lane*, teachers at *Riverside* showed less awareness and consideration of Turkish students' social background and blamed Turkish students (and their parents) for not showing enough willingness to do well in school or adapting to Flemish society more generally and for having a disrespectful attitude to teachers.

These differences in teachers' knowledge and stereotypes of ethnic minority students can be explained in part by the different national education context in which these teachers operate. The analysis in the previous section suggests that the particular student evaluation system in Flanders allowed teachers to lower their standards of assessment to a point where educational failure was explained by students' lack of willingness to achieve. This can explain in part why teachers in *Riverside* had such negative views of Turkish students (who as a group were among the lowest-achieving students in both schools). In addition, given the emphasis on anti-racism and discrimination in British educational policy, it could be expected that teachers in *Park Lane* felt more pressured not to be seen as racist. Furthermore, English educational policy allowed and stimulated the *Park Lane* school to value ethnic minority cultural capital, for example, by introducing GCSE courses in Turkish and teaching in and communicating with parents in Turkish. In sharp contrast, *Riverside* lacked the stimulus of such political legislation to stimulate teachers in emphasizing the importance of ethnic minority cultures and interests. As a result, teachers in *Riverside* were found to have less knowledge of and more negative views of Turkish minority students and perceived these students as unwilling to integrate in Flemish society.

CONCLUSIONS AND DISCUSSION

Whereas a considerable body of research has explored how racism operates in educational settings to the disadvantage of racial/ethnic minority students, there has been little research that investigates the importance of differences between national educational systems in shaping teachers' stereotypes and discriminatory behavior to ethnic minorities. Furthermore, there has been very little research that has specifically focused on Turkish students, who constitute a relatively large and underachieving (predominantly) Muslim minority group in Europe.

This chapter elaborated on the existing research base in this area by illustrating the usefulness of an ecological approach in studying racism in schools and by investigating the importance of a national education context in the way teachers' racist stereotypes and discriminatory behavior to Turkish minority students are shaped. Ethnographic data from a multicultural, inner-city "sink" school in Belgium and in England were used to explore how teachers perceive their Turkish minority students and allocate scarce educational resources (such as personal feedback and praise) and "blame" for educational failure.

The findings suggest that the Flemish teachers had more negative views and less knowledge of Turkish minority students and blamed these students for underachieving in education. In contrast, teachers in the English case-study school appeared to have more knowledge and positive views of Turkish minority students and held the educational system responsible for their underachievement. However, whereas teachers interviewed and observed in Flanders allocated scarce educational resources to those students considered as motivated to do well in school, the English school appeared to devise strategies of educational triage (Booher-Jennings, 2005; Gillborn & Youdell, 2000) through which scarce educational resources were targeted to those students perceived as likely to achieve the benchmark of success imposed by the educational system. In sum, whereas the Flemish teachers adapted their standards and responsibility for success to their Turkish students, English teachers were more likely to adapt their standards and responsibility of success to the educational system.

The findings of this study suggest that future research and educational policy should continue to take racial stereotyping and discrimination serious. However, the particular ways in which teachers disadvantage students, as expressed in their development of stereotypes and allocation of scarce educational resources and blame of failure, seem to depend, at least partly, on the nature of the educational system. In Flanders, schools could benefit from adopting more anti-racist and multicultural policies to improve teachers' knowledge and attitudes of ethnic minority students and parents. In England, centralized educational market principles seem to disadvantage particular groups of students by limiting the power of teachers to allocate scarce educational resources to particular groups of students considered likely to achieve.

An answer to the question "Which system is best?" ultimately depends on the definition of notions like "equality" or "equity." For example, does equality mean that we treat everybody the same way or that we direct resources in such a way that everybody achieves equally? When do social groups "achieve equally"? When they have on average the same exam results and/or progress in equal proportions to the same programs in higher education? Such questions relate not only to particular definitions of equality but also to the (alleged) extent to which schools are or should be held responsible for particular observed inequalities (Hammersley, 2009). This study does suggest that empowering teachers in lower-status educational programs and tracks makes it more likely that those teachers will adapt to the level of students they teach but, at the same time, assign higher responsibility to students in realizing educational outcomes valued by the educational system. If such a system would be combined with a greater awareness of the challenges multiculturalism entails and the difficulties experienced by certain minority ethnic groups in society (e.g., by making this an essential feature in inspecting schools and allocating resources to schools and teacher training to address this challenge), students of racial/ethnic minority groups in school could be given not only more responsibility but also greater opportunities to become successful in education. However, such changes will not necessarily result in greater equity or equality, as this depends on how such concepts are defined and which institutions are considered responsible for realizing this (e.g., schools and/or families and/or religious groups and/or society in general and/or the international community).

Because the social processes that were identified in this study relate to the experiences of a small group of teachers in one Flemish and one English school, the findings of this study cannot be generalized beyond the cases studied in this research. Furthermore, the two schools compared in this study are similar in important ways but also differ significantly (e.g., ethnic and gender composition and size of staff and student population), which makes it difficult to disentangle and assess the influence of each of these characteristics. Finally, although case-study research is particularly strong in exploring, identifying, and illustrating complex processes and interactions that seem important to our understanding of teachers' adaptations (and as a result help researchers to develop hypotheses on the development of such phenomena), its power is restricted in terms of estimating the effects of such processes on teachers' adaptations to students on a larger, more representative scale. As a result, large-scale quantitative studies have an important role to play in this field, by testing the effects of various embedded institutional contexts through multilevel analysis. The findings of this study underline the future potential of nationally comparative studies, using quantitative, representative, and qualitative case-study research, employing similar measurement instruments and starting from the same underlying theoretical assumptions and hypotheses, to investigate how particular educational systems inform decision-making processes in specific schools and how this can in turn affect the opportunities for social mobility of various social groups in society.

Appendix 6.1   Background Characteristics of Staff Population in Schools and
Sample Interviewed

School	Riverside		Park Lane	
Characteristics	Sample	School	Sample	School
Number of teachers	10	42	8	74
Proportion women staff	2/10	12/42	5/8	55/74
Proportion ethnic minority staff	0/10	1/42	5/8	49/74
Proportion senior staff (> 10 years teaching experience)	9/10	35/42	6/8	36/74

ACKNOWLEDGMENTS

I would like to thank Bob Carter, Jonathan Tritter, Martyn Hammersley, Andrew Parker, and three anonymous referees for their very useful comments and suggestions on earlier drafts of this chapter. Finally, I am indebted to the Economic and Social Research Council (UK), Belgian Royal Benevolent Society, and Scientific Research Foundation Flanders for providing the funding on which this research is based.

NOTES

1. Whereas Turkish immigrants constitute the largest group of non-EU immigrants in Flanders and have settled in all the major cities (Timmerman, 1999), they are only a small ethnic minority group in England, where they have settled mainly within particular neighborhoods in London. Furthermore, the group of Turkish immigrants in England is much more diverse, including Kurdish people and people from mainland Turkey and Cyprus (Kucukcan, 1999).
2. The names of the participating schools and individuals are pseudonyms.
3. Although the researcher interviewed many more teachers than the 19 teachers included in this analysis, time and resource constraints did not allow for transcription and analysis of additional interviews. The 19 interviews included in this study were selected for transcription and analysis because the researcher perceived those to provide richer data compared to the other interviews.
4. The Flemish "educational priority policy" (*onderwijsvoorrangsbeleid*) was built up around five target domains: prevention of underachievement and remedial support, parental involvement, intercultural education, education in own language and culture, and (Dutch) second language teaching.

REFERENCES

Althusser, L. (1971). Ideology and ideological state apparatus. In B. Cosin (Ed.), *Education, structure and society* (pp. 242–280). Middlesex: Penguin.

Blommaert, J., Creve, L., & Willeart, E. (2006). On being declared illiterate: Language-ideological disqualification in Dutch classes for immigrants in Belgium. *Language & Communication, 26*(1), 34–54.

Blommaert, J., & Verschueren, J. (1998). *Debating diversity: Analysing the discourse of tolerance.* London: Routledge.

Booher-Jennings, J. (2005). "Educational triage" and the Texas accountability system. *American Educational Research Journal, 42*(2), 231–268.

Bourdieu, P. (1974). The school as a conservative force: Scholastic and cultural inequalities. In J. Eggleston (Ed.), *Contemporary research in the sociology of education* (pp. 32–46). London: Harper & Row. (Original work published 1966)

Bourdieu, P., & Passeron, J.-C. (1977). *Reproduction in education, society and culture.* London: Sage.

Bowles, S., & Gintis, H. (1976). *Schooling in capitalist America.* London: Routledge and Kegan Paul.

Bronfenbrenner, U. (1979). *The ecology of human development.* Cambridge, MA: Harvard University Press.

Connolly, P. (1995). Racism, masculine peer-group relations and the schooling of African/Caribbean infant boys. *British Journal of Sociology of Education, 16*(1), 75–92.

Connolly, P. (2000a). Racism and young girls' peer-group relations: The experience of South Asian girls. *Sociology, 34*(4), 499–519.

Connolly, P. (2000b). What now for the contact hypothesis? Towards a new research agenda. *Race, Ethnicity and Education, 3*(2), 169–191.

Denson, N. (2009). Do curricular and cocurricular diversity activities influence racial bias? A meta-analysis. *Review of Educational Research, 79*(2), 805–838.

De Wit, K., & Van Petegem, P. (2000). *Gelijke kansen in het Vlaamse onderwijs. Het beleid inzake kansengelijkheid.* Leuven/Apeldoorn: Garant.

Faas, D. (2008). Constructing identities: The ethno-national and nationalistic identities of White and Turkish students in two English secondary schools. *British Journal of Sociology of Education, 29*(1), 37–48.

Feinstein, L., Duckworth, K., & Sabates, R. (2004). A model of inter-generational transmission of educational success. *WBL Research Report Series.* London: Centre for Research on the Wider Benefits of Learning.

Foster, P. (1990). *Policy and practice in multicultural and anti-racist education.* London: Routledge.

Foster, P., Gomm, R., & Hammersley, M. (1996). *Constructing educational inequality: Aan assessment of research on school processes.* London: Falmer Press.

Gillborn, D. (2008). *Racism and education. Coincidence or conspiracy?* London: Routledge.

Gillborn, D., & Gipps, C. (1996). *Recent research on the achievements of ethnic minority pupils.* London: Institute of Education and Office for Standards in Education.

Gillborn, D., & Youdell, D. (2000). *Rationing education: Policy, practice, reform and equity.* Buckingham: Open University Press.

Giroux, H. A. (1983). Theories of reproduction and resistance in the new sociology of education: A critical analysis. *Harvard Educational Review, 53*(3), 257–394.

Glaser, B. G. (1992). *Emergence vs. forcing: Basics of grounded theory analysis.* Mill Valley, CA: Sociology Press.

Glaser, B. G., & Strauss, A. L. (1967). *The discovery of grounded theory: Strategies for qualitative research*: New York: Aldine.

Gold, R. L. (1969). Roles in sociological field observations. In G. J. McCall & J. L. Simmons (Eds.), *Issues in participant observation: A text and reader* (pp. 217–223). Reading, MA: Addison-Wesley.

Hammersley, M. (2009, September). *Can social science tell us whether Britain is a meritocracy? A Weberian critique.* Paper presented at the British Educational Research Association (BERA) conference, University of Manchester, UK.

Hill, M. E., & Augoustinos, M. (2001). Stereotype change and prejudice reduction: Short- and long-term evaluation of a cross-cultural awareness programme, *Journal of Community and Applied Social Psychology, 11*(4), 243–262.

Kailin, J. (1999). How White teachers perceive the problem of racism in their schools: A case study in "liberal" Lakeview. *Teachers' College Records, 100*(4), 724–750.

Kucukcan, T. (1999). *Politics of ethnicity, identity and religion. Turkish Muslims in Britain.* Aldershot: Ashgate.

Lareau, A. (1999). Social-class differences in family-school relationships: The importance of cultural capital. In A. H. Halsey, L. Hugh, B. Philip, & A. S. Wells (Eds.), *Education: Culture, economy, and society* (pp. 703–717). Oxford: Oxford University Press. (Original work published 1978)

Lareau, A., & Horvat McNamara, E. (1999). Moments of social inclusion and exclusion. Race, class, and cultural capital in family-school relationships. *Sociology of Education, 72*(1), 37–53.

Le Compte, M. D., & Goetz, J. P. (1982). Problems of reliability and validity in ethnographic research. *Review of Educational Research, 52*(1), 31–60.

Lopez, G. R. (2001). The value of hard work: Lessons on parent involvement from an (im)migrant household. *Harvard Educational Review, 71*(3), 416–437.

NASUWT. (2002). *Race Relations (Amendment) Act 2000 and the Code of Practice. Implications for schools and colleges.* Birmingham: Author.

Nehaul, K. (1996). *The schooling of children of Caribbean heritage.* Stroke-on-Trent: Trentham Books.

Pettigrew, T. F., & Tropp, L. R. (2005). Allport's intergroup contact hypothesis: Its history and influence. In J. F. Dovidio, P. Glick, & L. Rudman (Eds.), *On the nature of prejudice. Fifty years after Allport.* Oxford: Blackwell.

Phalet, K. (1998). Minderheden en schoolsucces. In C. H. M. Geuijen (Ed.), *Werken aan ontwikkelingsvraagstukken. Multiculturalisme* (pp. 97–114). Utrecht: Uitgeverij Lemma B.V.

Quillian, L. (2006). New approaches to understanding racial prejudice and discrimination. *Annual Review of Sociology, 32*(-), 299–328.

Smith, S. T., & Ross, L. T. (2006). Environmental and family associations with racism. *Journal of Applied Social Psychology, 36*(11), 2750–2765.

Spruyt, B. (2008). Ongelijkheid en segregatie in het onderwijslandschap: Effecten op etnocentrisme. *Tijdschrift Voor Sociologie, 29*(1), 60–87.

Spyrou, S. (2002). Images of "the other": "The Turk" in Greek Cypriot children's imaginations. *Race, Ethnicity and Education, 5*(3), 255–272.

Stevens, P. A. J. (2007). Researching race/ethnicity and educational inequality in English secondary schools: A critical review of the research literature between 1980 and 2005. *Review of Educational Research, 77*(2), 147–185.

Stevens, P. A. J. (2009). Pupils' perspectives on racism and differential treatment by teachers: On stragglers, the ill and being deviant. *British Educational Research Journal, 35*(3), 413–430.

Stevens, P. A. J., Clycq, N., Timmerman, C., & Van Houtte, M. (2010). Researching race/ethnicity and educational inequality in the Netherlands: A critical review of the research literature between 1980 and 2008. *British Educational Research Journal, 36*(4).

Strauss, A. L., & Corbin, J. (1990). *Basics of qualitative research. grounded theory procedures and techniques.* Newbury Park, CA: Sage.

Timmerman, C. (1999). *Onderwijs maakt het verschil.* Leuven/Amersfoort: Acco.

Trentin, R., Monaci, M. G., De Lume, F., & Zanon, O. (2006). Scholastic integration of gypsies in Italy—Teachers' attitudes and experience. *School Psychology International,* 27(1), 79–103.

Trinkler, B. (2002). *A review of literature on Hispanic/Latino parent involvement in K–12 education.* New York: ERIC Clearinghouse on Urban Education.

Verkuyten, M., & Thijs, J. (2002). Racist victimisation among children in the Netherlands: The effect of ethnic group and school. *Ethnic and Racial Studies,* 25(2), 310–331.

Wood, P. B., & Sonleitner, N. (1996). The effect of childhood interracial contact on adult antiblack prejudice. *International Journal of Educational Development,* 20(1), 1–17.

7 Early Childhood Education and Care

Equity and Excellence in the Foundational Stage

Michel Vandenbroeck

INTRODUCTION

There is a growing attention for early childhood education and care in general and for the role of preschool education in fighting poverty, inequality, and social exclusion in particular. Both policy makers and researchers agree on the importance of educational investment in the stages of early development. In the affluent world and beyond, early childhood provisions are expanding because an early start is generally believed to reduce the educational divide that runs along socioeconomic as well as ethnic and linguistic lines. Major studies such as the Programme for International Student Assessment (PISA) and the Effective Provisions of Pre-School Education (EPPE) study in the United Kingdom have strengthened the claims about the potentially beneficial impact of early childhood education (e.g., Sylva, Melhuish, Sammons, Siraj-Blatchford, & Taggart, 2004). Yet, as a recent report from a European Commission network of experts (Penn, 2009) made clear, this apparent consensus may hide a diversity of perspectives on actual policy making, leading to diverse approaches to promoting equity and excellence in the foundational stage.

In this chapter, I will present a social pedagogical framework to analyze these issues, which includes an analysis of how pedagogical actions and provisions are linked to the social context and to broader structures of society (Coussée, Bradt, Roose, & Bouverne-De Bie, 2008). This implies that an educational "problem" is never taken for granted, but calls for an analysis of how the problem was socially constructed. Such an analysis reveals that the problem of inequality (cf. "la nouvelle question sociale") tends to be addressed predominantly from an *economical* perspective. From this perspective, the educational divide in postindustrial societies (or knowledge economies) is worrying to governments because it conjures up doom scenarios of massive unemployment and excessive government spending in the welfare state of future. This approach reframes early childhood education as an investment in future society. In the first part of this chapter, I will briefly summarize what the "problem" may look like from this economic point of view.

Yet, however relevant this perspective may be, a merely quantitative approach may not suffice. Penn (2009) showed that a purely economic perspective often leads to investments in promoting the accessibility of early childhood provisions, without paying sufficient attention to *what kind of* early childhood education is necessary. Even though it may be an established fact that early childhood education matters, not all early childhood education matters in the same way (see, e.g., UNICEF Innocenti Research Centre, 2008, for an overview of research on this issue). Therefore, in the second part of this chapter, I will address the problem of inequity in education from a *pedagogical* angle. More particularly, I will discuss one particular aspect of the quality of early childhood education that may be very salient with respect to equity and excellence: respect for (cultural, social) diversity. This is a crucial dimension of any educational perspective, because children can only learn and fully develop in settings that are highly contextualized and in which their family values, beliefs, and living conditions are taken into account. This implies a choice for a child-centered curriculum that fosters multiple belongings as well as the agency of children and their families to shape their own identities.

Because a social pedagogical perspective also takes into consideration the broader structures of society, the third part of this chapter will address a *social* perspective and examine different aspects of structural inequality. This part of the chapter will be based on quantitative and qualitative research carried out in Brussels and will also be linked to the international literature.

The final part of this chapter will describe ways in which the challenge of fostering equity through the organization of early childhood education can be met, looking at early childhood provisions as transitional spaces between the home and society (or between the private and the public sphere). Some general guidelines will be given, based on the work of a European network of experts in this field (Diversity in Early Childhood Education and Training [DECET]). However, we will need to be continuously aware of the endless complexities that are inherent to working in contexts of diversity, as will be illustrated by the narratives of newly arriving immigrant mothers at the end of this chapter.

The term most commonly used in this chapter is "early childhood education and care" (ECEC); I prefer this term for a number of reasons. First, it is the term that is used in EU documents nowadays, as well as in the European Early Childhood Education Research Association. Second, the term emphasizes that one cannot distinguish care from education: Profound educational issues are raised in the context of what has traditionally been considered as "care" (such as taking care of the basic needs of physical and psychological safety of very young children); in a similar vein, education needs to adopt a caring attitude (rather than merely focusing on teaching pre-academic skills). However, the use of the term "ECEC" may also lead to misunderstandings. Whereas some countries (e.g., Denmark) have structurally integrated the care for very young children and the education of toddlers before the compulsory school age, many other countries still have a "split system" (Bennett, 2003). This is also the case in Belgium, and in the northern part of Belgium (Flanders), in which the research that will be reported in this chapter was carried out. In Flanders, the split system has led to an undervaluation of the provisions for the youngest children (0 to 3 years). In comparison with the provisions for kindergarten education for children between 3 and 6 years old, the provisions for the youngest children are generally characterized by a lower-qualified workforce, poorer working conditions, fewer public investments, fewer provisions, and, consequently, more problems of accessibility (Vandenbroeck, 2006b). Because my own working experience of the past 25 years has been predominantly situated in *child care* for infants and toddlers, I will focus on these provisions in this chapter. I will deliberately use the term "ECEC," however, not only because it is the commonly used official term but also because I want to emphasize that this undervalued sector is both concerned with care *and* education.

THE VALUE OF EARLY CHILDHOOD EDUCATION

In education in general, and in early childhood education in particular, educational issues are increasingly entangled with economic issues. Discussions on educational issues such as equity and excellence need to take into account the wider societal context, including changes in welfare states and their social, economic, and political contexts (e.g., Vandenbroeck, 2006a, 2006b). ECEC has received growing attention in recent years, and many countries are currently investing in the expansion of their early years provisions, including the United Kingdom, the Netherlands, and Germany (OECD, 2001, 2006). These efforts can be viewed as economic investments in the future of the welfare state. Indeed, the aging of the population challenges welfare states insofar as they will need to invest in care for the (growing) oldest populations as well as for the youngest. One of the major European strategies to respond to the challenges of the aging population is to invest in the employability of its younger population and particularly in the employment of women. The Lisbon strategy puts forward clear objectives on employment rates to be reached by European nation-states. In order to reach these objectives, the gender gap in the labor market needs to be reduced; therefore, continuous investments in early childhood education are increasingly perceived from an economic perspective as urgent and necessary (Cameron & Moss, 2007; Peeters, 2008).

Recent findings about the educational divide have further legitimized the investments in ECEC. In different countries (including Belgium, Germany, and Greece), the PISA studies have profoundly shocked the educational communities as well as policy makers, especially where the results showed a societal gap in educational achievements. In some countries that have a longer tradition in researching the educational gap (such as the United Kingdom), there is a long-standing concern about the underachievement of children from ethnic minorities, nurturing fears about the emergence of a "two-tier system," although this has been overshadowed lately by concerns about the underachievement of boys (Connolly 2006a, 2006b; Gorard & Smith, 2004; see also Francis & Skelton, Chapter 5, this volume). In the case of the PISA results, but also in many other studies, including the EPPE study (Sylva et al., 2004), the educational divide seems to run along socioeconomic and ethnic-cultural lines. In countries like Belgium, children from ethnic minorities and children from poor families (and these are often,—but not always—overlapping categories) perform less well at school. This poses a major threat to social cohesion (Nicaise, 2008). According to Leseman (2002), in all OECD countries, some 10% to 20% of the children belong to "category C": children with presumably normal potential but who show developmental delays or are at risk of educational failure due to socioeconomic, cultural, and/or sociolinguistic factors. Yet, research also shows that early childhood care and education can make a difference (for an overview of the impressive literature on this issue, see Duncan & Brooks-Gunn, 2000; Leseman, 2002; OECD, 2006; UNICEF Innocenti Research Centre, 2008). In short, early childhood education matters for the employability of the present workforce (i.e., getting more women at work), as well as for the employability of future cohorts in late modern, postindustrial societies, where employability is closely linked with academic achievement. Boldly speaking, late modern, postindustrial societies cannot afford anymore not to invest in ECEC or to leave ECEC to the private market of individual arrangements between parents and provisions, because the societal (including economic) costs of doing so may soon become outrageous.

Hence, in many countries, strong investments in the expansion of ECEC go hand in hand with investments in the quality of care, in curriculum development, and/or in the professionalization of the workforce. In Germany, a lot of energy and money are invested in the development of curricula, some of them (e.g., in Berlin) focusing explicitly on diversity issues (Preissing, 2004). In France, a new curriculum is constructed for the Éducateur Jeunes Enfants, a project that has been expanded to a 3-year study (Décret No. 2005–1375). In the United Kingdom, investments in leadership courses as well as in raising the levels of qualification of the caring workforce have been made (Brown, 2009). Unfortunately, this is not (yet) the case in Belgium (Peeters, 2008). However, the recent decision to invest in a newly created bachelor programme in early childhood education and care may reverse this trend.

Scholars have argued that early childhood education matters for later academic achievement. However, the previously mentioned studies also clearly show that not all early childhood education matters in the same way. Since the publication of the work of scholars like Bronfenbrenner and Vygotsky, but also thanks to recent work of Barbara Rogoff and colleagues

(2005), researchers know that cultural contexts play a major role and that the learning contexts of ECEC may not be optimally adapted to the needs of children from ethnic minorities and/or children with lower socioeconomic status (SES). The ongoing EPPE study in England shows that academic achievement runs along ethnic-cultural lines as well as SES lines. However, according to Iram Siraj-Blatchford (2006), one of the researchers involved in this study, the ethnic variation seems to be limited, when controlled for SES. Additionally, the EPPE study clearly shows that ECEC experiences may make a substantial difference, but only in those cases where the ECEC environment is of high quality. The study provides some indications of what is meant by "high quality." The rating scale with the strongest power in predicting early learning experiences and later school achievement is respect for diversity (Siraj-Blatchford, 2006). Apart from this, the level of staff qualifications also seems to matter. This is consistent with a recent U.S. study, showing that staff qualifications significantly predict quality of care, also with regard to home-based care (family day care providers), whereas the caretakers' years of experience do not (Doherty, Forer, Lero, Goelman, & LaGrange, 2006). In conclusion, ECEC may contribute to a closing of the educational gap in our societies. Yet, it can only do so provided (a) substantial investments in high staff qualifications are made, and (b) a child-centered curriculum that takes into account respect for diversity is developed. In the following section, I will go into more detail as to what respect for diversity actually means.

MULTIPLE BELONGINGS

Issues of (cultural) identity are at the core of concerns about the quality of ECEC, because they pertain to essential and existential questions such as "Who am I?" and "Is it okay to be who I am?" A positive self-image is closely linked to well-being. Scholars such as Laevers (1997) have argued that well-being and involvement are essential process variables that may mediate educational outcomes. However, these essential and existential questions regarding identity may be problematic for children from ethnic minorities when ECEC providers fail to take into account family cultures in their curriculum (for a concise overview, see Vandenbroeck, 2001a, or www.decet.org). In short, children need to "belong" and to have their identity recognized in the educational setting (Brooker & Woodhead, 2008).

Traditionally, it was generally accepted that children gradually construct their identity through enculturation, or in other words, through socialization, both terms referring to a unidirectional and gradual adaptation of the growing child to the prevailing norms and values of their primary educators, that is, the family and, later on, their caretakers and teachers in other (educational) environments. Since the turn of the century, the traditional views on identity construction and socialization have been challenged by two important evolutions: the profound changes in societies that are linked with globalization, individualization, and detraditionalization, on the one hand, and the emergence of the new sociology of childhood, on the other hand. In today's society, individuals (including children) do not belong to one clearly defined cultural group anymore. Individuals in the posttraditional society have multiple belongings and thus construct their autobiographies themselves (Beck, 1994, 1997; Beck & Beck, 1995). This evolution is sometimes referred to as the "dynamics of identity," "multiple identities," "hyphenated identities," or "hybrid identities" (Vandenbroeck, 2001, 2007; Vandenbroeck & Bouverne-De Bie, 2006) or, from a poststructural perspective, "nomadic identities" (Roets & Goedgeluck, 2007). Today individuals can belong to many different and changing reference groups, including ethnic and language communities; professional groups; advocacy groups; gender, political, or religious groups; gay or lesbian groups; and many others. This may very well be one of the most important effects of globalization on the individual's level: Belonging to a certain reference group does not automatically entail a belonging to other "cultural" groups. Important decisions in life, such as choosing a specific job, marrying or not, staying married or not, living with a person of the same or the opposite sex, having children or not, or voting for this or that party at the elections, tend to be far less dominated by the fact that people belong to a specific subgroup in society. Instead, they tend to be perceived as highly individual decisions, which are influenced by a personal and dynamic mix of multiple belongings. History and tradition have a far weaker impact on people's decisions than ever before, at least in our perception. Consequently, these evolutions profoundly affect family relationships, because households now consist of individuals, making their individual choices and having to negotiate continually with other household members and to compromise, for instance, between their commitment to the family, their duties as parents or children or spouses, their professional ambitions, and their personal emotional development (Beck & Beck, 1995).

Some contemporary authors, such as Ulrich Beck seem to welcome this evolution for the degree of individual freedom it brings and are pleased that the old Eriksonian concept of identity is replaced by the concept of "writing one's own autobiography." From the perspective of diversity and equity, this seems to be an oversimplified analysis, because the educational challenge is to foster multiple belongings and processes of hybrid or nomadic identity construction in an unequal society. There are indeed many documented examples of young children that are sincerely hurt in the development of their multiple belongings in cases where early years provisions do not take into account the culture of their families (Brougère, Guénif-Souilamas, & Rayna, 2007; Preissing & Wagner, 2003; Vandenbroeck, 2001). One nice example of this was reported by Rajae, a mother of Moroccan descent. When she went to pick up her 4-year-old daughter Dounia from kindergarten, the girl jumped into her arms, put her hand on Rajae's mouth and whispered in her ear: "Please, Mum, never speak Arabic to me again when the other kids can hear you" (reported in Brooker & Woodhead, 2008). Another example is the case of Maricella, a 2½-year-old girl from Latin American descent, who spoke Spanish and was not yet acquainted with Dutch, the dominant language in the center. When distributing jig-saw puzzles, a peer (of the same age) gave her a baby puzzle. When the educator asked the girl why she gave this baby puzzle to a toddler, the girl replied that Maricella was not very smart (reported in Vandenbroeck, 2001).

Such examples describe apparently insignificant micro-events, in which children receive an implicit message that it is not okay to be who they are, their home language is devaluated, their gender inappropriate, their skin color not suitable for playing Peter Pan, or their physical abilities not adapted to playing with the other kids in the toddler group they wish to belong to. The accumulation of these micro-events, however, may be claimed to significantly affect the children's well-being (as well as their parents'), and in doing so, they may make the early childhood environment an inappropriate learning environment for them, as well as for the majority children (for examples of studies showing the impact on the identity development of ethnic minority children, see Mac Naughton, 2006).

Yet, ECEC may offer unique possibilities to foster the development of multiple and nomadic identities. For many children, it represents their first transition to society. It presents them with a mirror on how society looks at them and thus how they may be looking at themselves, because it is only in a context of sameness *and* difference that identity can be constructed. Indeed, what it is to "be" a boy and how one may perform one's "boyness" can only be explored in an environment where both boys and girls are present and where this difference can be enacted (at least symbolically) in multiple ways. Similarly, having Berber as a home language can only acquire social meanings in a multilingual context, just as being "White" has no meaning without the presence of "Blacks."

However, many children today still are overwhelmingly confronted with conceptions of the "average" child, being the "good" child, and have difficulties connecting with this ideal self. This may particularly be the case when their origins are ignored (i.e., when the new environment, the language spoken there, and the food and rituals do not reflect any of the familiarities of the home environment). This may also be the case when the children's identities are reduced to their origin (i.e., associated with typical and often stereotypical images of their ancestors' culture of origin, with their "disability," or with their gender). The issue therefore is not that ECEC should be a "home away from home," as similar to the home as possible, yet it needs to take the home culture into account.

Consequently, pedagogies of diversity cannot be derived from presumed knowledge of what constitutes "Muslim culture" or "African values" or "autism," because essentialist views would imprison children in a construction of their past or a diagnosis that does not take into account their own choices and dreams for the present, let alone for the future. Therefore, pedagogies of diversity will need to be constructed in a continuous negotiation with the parents, in order to build bridges between the institutional cultures and parental cultures and beliefs. Only then can ECEC enable children to avoid the dichotomous approach that would force them to choose between either the dominant or the home culture and, on the contrary, foster the construction of multiple and nomadic belongings. The European DECET network has developed interesting expertise on how such pedagogies can be shaped in day-to-day practice as well as in the professionalization of staff. Interestingly, their approach is not focused on ethnic minority children but on *all* children. This seems to be more and more crucial.

Another line of thought that can be inspiring when discussing the quality of early childhood education is the sociology of childhood (Hendrick, 1997; James, Jenks, & Prout, 1998; Mayall, 2002), which forces us to reconsider how we view children. It challenges us to leave behind the image of passive children "in need" and to look at the agency of children and their capability for shaping their own identities, in relationship to both peers and adults. Children are no longer perceived as passive recipients of culture, knowledge, and identity but as human beings who are actively involved in reshaping their cultural heritage, as well as their educational environment. Research that embraces this image of a "rich" child clearly documents young children's capabilities for building relations, researching and solving problems (e.g., Rinaldi, 2005; Singer & De Haan, 2007). Child-centered programs that build on these capacities may be more effective in reaching their educational objectives than more traditional programs that focus on the transmission of early academic skills and adopt a more adult-oriented approach, the latter being the case, according to Bennett (2005), for both child care and kindergarten education.

THE OTHER

Obviously, ECEC as an educational environment cannot suffice with fostering multiple identities in order to enable children to grow up as happy individuals with a sound image of themselves. Educational goals regarding respect for diversity and social inclusion reach beyond individualism and autonomy, well-being and involvement, but also comprise issues of connectedness, solidarity, or interdependence. The question is not only "Am I okay? but also "Are you okay?" A concern for early socialization cannot ignore the emergence of prejudice and exclusion within the centers. From a very early age on, children begin to notice differences that have to do with gender, family compositions, ability, skin color, language, dress codes, food habits, abilities, and so forth (Vandenbroeck,

2001). Research shows that from 3 years on (and sometimes earlier), these observations challenge children's image of the self as well as of the other. They raise implicit or explicit questions about diversity and may develop into prejudices against those who are "different" or do not belong to their ingroup (Connolly, Kelly, & Smith, 2009; Mac Naughton, 2006). The attitude and the response of the educator may contribute to children's vision of the world, a process that German pedagogues have labeled "Bildung." One can observe that when adults fail to deal with these emerging questions, children may take over racist representations that are present in society (Connolly, 2000). They may begin to associate observed differences with value-laden, dominant discourses on who is a "good" child and who is not (Vandenbroeck, 2001). The old Adornian hypothesis—that early contact with diversity would prevent stereotypical thinking, prejudices, and exclusion from emerging—has proven to be false.

One of the most difficult challenges for early childhood teachers is that education does not take place outside the real world, and there is no reason to assume that prevailing inequities or prejudices would be left in the corridor together with the children's coats. When a Turkish-speaking child is regularly taken apart by the teachers' assistant to promote his knowledge of the dominant language and, conversely, his fluency in Turkish is not used as an asset, the socially constructed hierarchy of languages tends to be reproduced in the classroom. There are many examples and observations of unspoken, implicit messages that convey societal inequalities in the cultural or social capital of the children and their families, that is, micro-events that may influence the peer relations among children (e.g., Bekerman & Tatar, 2009). As Meertens (1997) points out in his meta-analysis of empirical studies in this field, adults should take a clear stand against racism and discrimination and explicitly promote norms and values that foster equality.

In addition, pedagogies of diversity should be developed, making different forms of diversity (racial, ethnic, gender, ability, age) visible in the school infrastructure through the use of decorations and respectful representations of the families and the local communities, as well as embedding these within school activities (reading, music, arts, and drama, etc.). Pedagogies of diversity should reach beyond the mere explicit visibility of diversity; this is not a prime objective in its own right. Rather, the visibility of diversity may serve as a trigger for children's questions, remarks, and observations and for the interactions and discussions that grow out of them. In fact, these interactions give shape to pedagogies of diversity, rather than the images on the wall or the black doll in the play corner. Again, making such pedagogies operational cannot succeed without involving the families and the local communities. Ample opportunity for in-depth discussions on parental involvement should be created. Examples of good practice in Belgium (Vandenbroeck, Roets, & Snoeck, 2009), France (Blanc

& Bonabesse, 2008), Italy (Sharmahd, 2007), and many other countries have shown that during the first weeks when the child comes to the day care provision (and even the weeks prior to enrollment), it is crucial to establish a degree of reciprocity in what is fundamentally an asymmetric relationship between parents and professionals. Continuous efforts in day-to-day contacts can help turn the day care center into a mutual learning community in which shared repertoires of practices are constructed (Moreau & Brougère, 2007). When focusing on parent involvement in contexts of diversity, it is especially important to avoid the pitfalls of essentialism, which were described earlier in this chapter. There is indeed a world of difference between asking a parent to bring along a piece of music "of his or her culture" and asking the same parent if there is some music they often listen to at home and they would wish to share with the group.

In conclusion, this means that we need child-centered curricula that are, at the same time, family centered. Staff members should actively involve parents and need to be trained and supported in negotiating their daily practice with parents from diverse backgrounds. In the final paragraphs of this chapter, an example will be given of how challenging this may be. Teams that are diverse themselves (including staff members from diverse backgrounds as well as representing gender diversity) are an important asset to achieve these goals. This calls for positive actions in the area of human resources management.

STRUCTURAL INEQUITIES IN ACCESSIBILITY

Quite often, literature on "tolerance education" or "anti-bias education" stops here, ignoring structural inequities and power relations, and failing to pay heed to issues of affordability and accessibility that affect ethnic minority and poor families. Accessibility of ECEC services is a growing topic of interest. It is well documented that children from lower-income families receive lower-quality care than those from middle-income and higher-income families in the United States (Phillips & Adams, 2001; Pungello & Kurtz-Costes, 1999) as well as in Europe (Vandenbroeck, De Visscher, Van Nuffel, & Ferla, 2008; Wall & José, 2004). Some researchers (e.g., Peyton, Jacobs, O'Brien, & Roy, 2001; Vanpée, Sannen, & Hedebouw, 2000) focus on characteristics of the families to explain why their children receive low-quality care more often, suggesting that poor parents attach less importance to ECEC in general or to high-quality criteria.

Recently, several authors have criticized the construct of rational choice because it does not sufficiently take into account the impact of environmental constraints, such as availability and affordability (Henly & Lyons, 2000; Himmelweit & Sigala, 2004; Shlay, Tran, Weinraub, & Harmon, 2005; Weinraub, Shlay, Harmon, & Tran, 2005). Perceived differences in preferences very often reflect restricted child care options or problems of affordability for some groups. These scholars argue that inequalities in the use of high-quality care cannot be solely explained by differences in parental attitudes, which in turn are linked with demographic variables. On the contrary, environmental constraints, including costs, supply, and quality, should also be taken into account, as well as mothers' working conditions (for an overview of this discussion, see Vandenbroeck et al., 2008).

A first aspect of the analysis of structural exclusion has to do with affordability and thus with funding policies. In countries that are labeled "liberal welfare regimes," such as the United States, the United Kingdom, Canada, or Australia (Avdeyeva, 2006; Esping-Andersen, 2001), states hardly interfere with market operations and funding; when available, it is more often directed to the users. In contrast, in "democratic welfare regimes" (such as the Scandinavian countries), funding is directed more often to the providers. Funding parents through voucher systems is less effective in combating inequality than funding provisions. First, vouchers do not necessarily influence the quality of the services the parents have access to, whereas funding providers may have that effect (Weinraub et al., 2005). Second, vouchers or individual measures for underprivileged parents do not guarantee equal access for families living in very precarious conditions, as the bureaucracy of the system may exclude the most marginalized families and local interpretations may have a strong impact on the implementation of central policies, as was documented in the case of Flanders (Roelandt, 2006) and the Netherlands (Schreuder, 2005). Third, voucher systems position early childhood education on the free market, a choice that tends to be legitimized with the contestable concept of free choice. This may influence the educational approach of the center and the curricula of provisions that are seemingly adapted to individual parents' preferences (Lee, 2006). Finally, a market-oriented approach tends to favor highly populated and richer areas, at the cost of rural and poorer areas, as was shown in the case of the Netherlands (Noailly, Visser, & Grout, 2007; see also Moss, 2008).

Yet, political systems that fund provisions do not necessary fulfill all criteria that are necessary to guarantee equal access to high-quality ECEC. In fact, in some cases, it may even reinforce existing inequalities. Studies in the three major cities in Flanders (Brussels, Antwerp, and Ghent) have shown that high-quality infant care is unequally distributed and that poor families have fewer high-quality provisions in their neighborhood than parents who are better off (Rotthier, 2007; Vandenbroeck et al., 2008). This is shown in Figure 7.1, which maps the 19 municipalities of the Belgian capital, Brussels, according to the parents' average income and the coverage of funded provisions for child care.

The study we carried out in Brussels also showed that center directors tend to give priority to parents at work and to those who subscribe first. A survey among a sample of 100 parents (who were representative for the

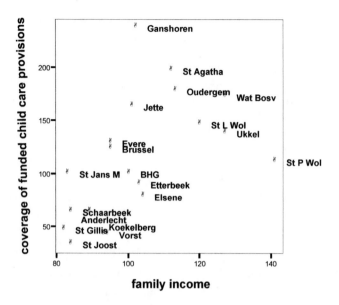

Figure 7.1   Coverage of funded child care providers related to family income in the municipalities of Brussels.

diversity of the Brussels population) about their search for a child care center revealed that this access criterion had a significant impact on the exclusion of specific groups of parents. The parents in our sample began to look for child care 5 to 6 months prior to the birth of the child (i.e., 9 to 12 months prior to the end of parental leave). Our findings indicate the following:

1. Ethnic minority parents (mean = 5.6 months after birth) started their search significantly later than Belgian parents (mean = 5.9 months before birth) $(F(1,68) = 13.187; p = 0.001)$.
2. Single-parent families (mean = 0.50 months after birth) started their search significantly later than two-parent families (mean = 4.65 months before birth) $(F(1,69) = 5.726; p = 0.019)$.
3. Low-educated families (mean = 0.94 months after birth) also started their search later than high-educated parents (mean = 5.51 months before birth) $(F(1,67) = 10.992; p = 0.002)$.

A two-way ANOVA, including education and ethnicity, showed that the main effects of education persist, when controlling for the interaction with ethnicity $(F(1,64) = 4.927; p = 0.030)$ and there were no interaction effects. High-educated parents started their search significantly earlier than low-educated parents, regardless of their ethnicity. A GLM procedure showed that low-educated parents also made less use of Internet sites providing information about available care providers than high-educated parents, regardless of their ethnicity ($F(1,66) = 8.396$; $p = 0.005$). Half of the parents subscribed to two or more waiting lists to enhance their chances of access. Ethnicity was not significantly linked with this behavior, although the language spoken at home was, indicating that foreign language families subscribed less often to multiple waiting lists than families using the dominant languages ($t(71) = 2.029$; $p < 0.001$) (for a full account of the study, see Vandenbroeck et al., 2008).

The effect of the unequal distribution of funded care, in combination with the access policies of the management, results into a structural discrimination of lower-educated parents, ethnic minority parents, and single-parent families, who tend to start their search later and who wish access for other reasons than reconciling work with family life (e.g., to follow training, to apply for a job, or to socialize their young children in an educational environment of the dominant language).

A study by Wall and José (2004) shows that this is particularly salient for immigrants in low-paid jobs in different European countries, such as Finland, France, Italy, and Portugal. These analyses of the weak regulatory function of different welfare states, with regard to the protection of families who have low-paid jobs and simultaneously have to take care of young children, may have important consequences for policy making. In defining and supervising quality, policy makers might wish to consider not only structural criteria, such as group size, adult–child ratio, and staff qualifications, but also process variables, such as adult–child interaction and the languages that are used. In addition, they should also acknowledge accessibility for mixed groups as a crucial criterion for high-quality care. Merely assuming that parent education could solve the problem at hand (i.e., low-income children are offered low-quality care) pays no due homage to the complexity of parental choice and the bidirectional character of the decision-making process. As Himmelweit and Sigala (2004) found, enabling policies that lift existing constraints and make more options available are more likely to have long-term effects than coercive policies that impose new behavior, as the use of child care also influences maternal beliefs. In order to achieve these goals, structural policies that fund provisions seem to be the most effective.

ECEC AS A TRANSITIONAL SPACE

In this chapter, I have tried to show how respect for diversity and social inclusion is related with policy making on macro, meso, and micro levels. It may be obvious by now that provisions that respect diversity and social inclusion cherish a child-centered approach and that this includes both a family-centered and a community-centered approach. A good summary of the guiding principles of such a curriculum is given by the DECET network (www.decet.org):

- Every child, parent, and staff member should feel that he/she belongs. This implies an active policy to take into account home cultures when constructing the project.
- Every child, parent, and staff member is empowered to develop the diverse aspects of his/her identities. This implies that the curriculum fosters multiple identity building and multilingualism by building bridges between the home and the institutional environment as well as between the institutional environment and the local community.
- Everyone can learn from each other across cultural and other boundaries.
- Everyone can participate as active citizens. This implies that staff members develop an explicit anti-bias approach and take appropriate actions to involve all parents.
- Staff, parents, and children work together to challenge institutional forms of prejudice and discrimination. This includes a critical study of access policies and structural inequities.

Two pitfalls should be avoided when implementing policies on diversity and social inclusion in education in general and in early childhood education in particular: the "deculturalization of education" and the "culturalization of inequalities." The former refers to the risks associated with the formulation of quality criteria or educational outcomes (i.e., achievement measures) that deny cultural diversities. Anyone who describes excellence in ECEC without analyzing whom it serves and whom it does not serve may contribute to the perpetuation of existing inequalities in the educational system. It may be beneficial to impose minimal quality standards on all services, in order to monitor the appropriate use of public funds and to avoid the previously mentioned problem that poor families tend to make use of child care of poorer quality. Setting minimal quality standards is also in line with the International Convention on the Rights of the Child. Yet, these general quality criteria should also include criteria on accessibility and affordability for diverse populations as well as take into account the possibilities for local meaning making in a dialogical process with children, families, and local communities.

The second pitfall ("culturalizing inequities") refers to the danger that structural inequalities that are linked with socioeconomic variables may be reframed as cultural issues and consequently be rephrased as individual parents' responsibilities. In the past, the underrepresentation of ethnic minority families in ECEC or the underachievement of ethnic minority children in the educational system were attributed to cultural values, masking structural inequities in the accessibility of services or in the curricula. We continuously need to strike a delicate balance between the denial of cultural differences, on the one hand, and a narrow view on these differences, on the other.

A FINAL WORD ON COMPLEXITY

Addressing the issues described in this chapter in day-to-day interactions is a matter of endless complexity and subtlety, because they deal with macropolitics as well as with realizing democracy and citizenship on the microlevel. Democratic participation is an important criterion of true citizenship: It is a means by which children and adults can participate with others in shaping decisions that affect themselves, the groups they join, and the wider society (Moss, 2007). This implies that neither children nor parents should be merely seen as the clients of ECEC or that quality can be assessed by consumer satisfaction ratings. On the contrary, our view calls for a continuous co-construction and reconstruction of daily practice in an endless negotiation procedure with all who are involved (children, families, local communities, and policy makers). According to Moss (2007), this includes the respect for diversity; the recognition of multiple perspectives and diverse paradigms; welcoming curiosity, uncertainty, and subjectivity; and critical thinking.

In our opinion, one of the main challenges in this domain is to redefine what expertise in ECEC actually stands for, in order to avoid the subtle inequities and exclusion mechanisms between the "expert knowledge" of the staff and the "layman's knowledge" of the parents. Adopting multiple perspectives may help to overcome these inequities, without necessarily having to dismiss expert knowledge. In a study on evolving parental ideas on a "good life" for their children, we interviewed newly arrived immigrant mothers with young children attending day care centers (Vandenbroeck et al., 2009) and analyzed these interviews from a constructivist (Super & Harkness, 1996) and a postconstructivist (Foucault, 1990) perspective. One of the mothers in this study, whom we will call Neamat, is from Lebanese origin and arrived in Belgium in 2003. She says that she lives rather isolated and that they do not have many friends. She regularly speaks on the telephone with a niece in London and her aunt and a friend in Lebanon, with whom she discusses educational matters regarding her daughter. Her niece is worried about the sexual education of Neamat's daughter in Belgium and advises her to send her daughter to her grandparents in Lebanon when she is 10, in order to prevent her from dating boys. Neamat does not agree and thinks she should, as a mother, talk with her daughter rather than ban her from the Western world. After 6 months, the mother and her daughter went to stay with her family in Lebanon for 1 month. About this period, she says:

> *Yeah my aunts, they had a lot of impact (laughs). And it was really a good one, because it's really nice when you are surrounded by people*

who already raised children and who know how to deal. It's not how to deal, but they already know what to expect and what should be done or not. Even though we say they have very ancient methods and I don't know whatever and maybe the modern methods they are better, but it's really . . . it gives you a lot of insight and a lot of things you think about. Ancient people, they always feel that children should eat a lot, and I don't feel that they should eat a lot.

This narrative, together with some others, shows the agency of this mother, constructing changing and multiple and nomadic identities, in relation to different belongings, that do not need to generate conflicts but may involve to a highly personal mix of parental ethnotheories.

After the stay in Lebanon, the mother had a discussion with the day care staff members. Her daughter slept with her in the parental bed. Neamat did not think this was a problem, but the day care staff members claimed that this was not good for the child's sense of autonomy. About this discussion, the mother said:

I love my daughter very much, not only in my heart, as they say, but everywhere inside and that feeling is very big and warm. It is beyond my comprehension. I never loved someone like that.

In the last interview, she looks back at the first months in the nursery, when her daughter was almost 1 year old. She had repeatedly asked the staff to put her daughter on a potty after her nap. After many discussions, the staff partially accepted to do what the mother was asking for.

In the day care centre they are against it, because she's very young and . . . they don't train the baby's until they are 2. Sometimes in the day care centre when she wakes up, they put her on the potty, but it's always too late. Because the moment the child has to wake up, you have to take him, take his diaper and put it on the potty, you see. But in the day care centre for example a child . . . many children would wake up at the same time, so you have to deal with one child at the time. And until now she don't know that she has to control her muscles, maybe she, I think that she can do it now. So she has to learn how to do it. So most of the time it's too late, but they try to . . . I think even though they don't agree with me, but they do it. And I think it's amazing you know, because for them, err . . ., when you put a child of 2 years on a potty, there's not a lot of responsibility. Because you don't have to watch him. You don't have to sit, and he has to finish and he will call you when he's done. But with X [names her daughter], she's very young so someone has to keep an eye on her. And it is not really logic when you have 21 children. You see, so I think it's amazing even if they don't do it every day. The fact that they do it from time to time. I think it's amazing, yeah.

A developmental perspective may have focused on this "developmentally appropriate practice," which may have led to ongoing explanations to the mother about why it is wrong to potty-train a 1-year-old girl. However valuable this knowledge may be, a social constructivist perspective aims to discover what the meaning of potty training is for this mother. Is it about the potty, or rather about individual attention, or something else? Is it connected to beliefs this mother shares with her Lebanese peers, or is it ridiculous to search for cultural associations in this matter? A poststructural perspective may consider the subtle power relations that are enacted in this interview. From that point of view, we see a strong mother who asks to be heard by the "experts" of the day care center. Once she has experienced that different expertise does not necessary imply a hierarchy of knowledge, she has no problem saying that her daughter may be too young for the potty. This implies that even though we may never entirely grasp the meaning of this scene, we may ask ourselves how we can welcome this mother's perspective without fully understanding it, as well as look at the effects of our own attitudes and behavior on the relationship between this mother and her daughter.

Taking into account these subtleties of the daily encounters in ECEC calls for new kinds of professionalism that do not focus only on technical knowledge, with regard to children's development and developmentally appropriate practices, but also on support staff members in uncovering the meaning parents and the local community make of ECEC practice. Policies that frame ECEC professionals both within the domains of educational and social work (e.g., the French Éducateur Jeunes Enfants in France) provide interesting examples of this newly emerging professionalism.

REFERENCES

Avdeyeva, O. (2006). In support of mothers' employment: Limits to policy convergence in the EU? *International Journal of Social Welfare, 15*(1), 37–49.

Beck, U. (1994). The reinvention of politics: Towards a theory of reflexive modernization. In U. Beck, A. Giddens, & S. Lasch (Eds.), *Reflexive modernization. Politics, tradition and aesthetics in the modern social order* (pp. 1–55). Cambridge: Polity Press.

Beck, U. (1997). Democratisation of the family. *Childhood, 4*(2), 151–168.

Beck, U., & Beck, E. (1995). *The normal chaos of love.* Cambridge: Polity Press.

Bekerman, Z., & Tatar, M. (2009). Parental choice of schools and parents' perceptions of multicultural and co-existence education: The case of the Israeli Palestinian-Jewish bilingual primary schools. *European Early Childhood Education Research Journal, 17*(2), 171–186.

Bennett, J. (2003). Starting strong: The persistent division between care and education. *Journal of Early Childhood Research, 1*(1), 21–48.

Bennett, J. (2005). Curriculum issues in national policy making. *European Early Childhood Education Research Journal, 13*(2), 5–24.

Blanc, M. C., & Bonabesse, M. L. (2008). *Parents et professionnels dans les structures d'accueil de jeunes enfants: Enjeux et limites des interactions.* Paris: ASH.

Brooker, E., & Woodhead, M. (Eds.). (2008). *Developing positive identities: Diversity and young children.* Milton Keynes: Open University.

Brougère, G., Guénif-Souilamas, N., & Rayna, S. (2007). De l'usage de l'altérité pour comprendre le préscolaire. In G. Brougère & M. Vandenbroeck (Eds.), *Nouveaux paradigmes pour repenser l'éducation des jeunes enfants* (pp. 263–284). Bruxelles: Peter Lang.

Brown, G. (2009). *New opportunities. Fair chances for the future.* London: HM Government.

Cameron, C., & Moss, P. (2007). *Care work in Europe. Current understandings and future directions.* London: Routledge.

Connolly, P. (2000). Racism and young girls' peer-group relations: The experience of South Asian girls. *Sociology, 34*(3), 499–519.

Connolly, P. (2006a). The effects of social class and ethnicity on gender differences in GCSE attainment: A secondary analysis of the Youth Cohort Study of England and Wales 1997–2001. *British Educational Research Journal, 32*(1), 3–21.

Connolly, P. (2006b). Summary statistics, educational achievement gaps and the ecological fallacy. *Oxford Review of Education, 32*(2), 235–252.

Connolly, P., Kelly, B., & Smith, A. (2009). Ethnic habitus and young children: A case study of Northern Ireland. *European Early Childhood Education Research Journal, 17*(2), 217–232.

Coussée, F., Bradt, L., Roose, R., & Bouverne-De Bie, M. (2008). The emerging social pedagogical paradigm in the UK child and youth care: Deus ex machina or walking the beaten path? *British Journal of Social Work, 43*(3), 789–805.

Doherty, G., Forer, B., Lero, D. S., Goelman, H., & LaGrange, A. (2006). Predictors of quality in family child care. *Early Childhood Research Quarterly, 21*, 296–312.

Duncan, G., & Brooks-Gunn, J. (2000). Family poverty, welfare reform, and child development. *Child Development, 71*(1), 188–196.

Esping-Andersen, G. (2001). Quel état-providence pour le XXIe siècle? Convergences et divergences des pays européens. *Esprit, 2*, 122–150.

Foucault, M. (1990). *Politics, philosophy, culture. Interviews and other writings 1977–1984.* London: Routledge.

Gorard, S., & Smith, E. (2004). An international comparison of equity in education systems. *Comparative Education, 40*(1), 15–28.

Hendrick, H. (1997). Constructions and reconstructions of British childhood: An interpretative survey, 1800 to present. In A. James & A. Prout (Eds.), *Constructing and reconstructing childhood* (pp. 34–62). London: Falmer Press.

Henly, J., & Lyons, S. (2000). The negotiation of child care and employment demands among low-income parents. *Journal of Social Issues, 56*(4), 683–706.

Himmelweit, S., & Sigala, M. (2004). Choice and the relation between identities and behaviour for mothers with pre-school children: Some implications for policy from a UK study. *Journal of Social Policy, 33*(3), 455–478.

James, A., Jenks, C., & Prout, A. (1998). *Theorizing childhood.* Cambridge: Polity Press.

Laevers, F. (1997). Assessing the quality of childcare provision: "Involvement" as criterion. *Researching Early Childhood, 3*, 151–165.

Lee, I. F. (2006). Illusions of social democracy: Early childhood educational voucher policies in Taiwan. In M. Bloch, D. Kennedy, T. Lightfoot, & D. Weyenberg (Eds.), *The child in the world/The world in the child. Education and the configuration of a universal, modern, and globalized childhood*. New York: Palgrave Macmillan.

Leseman, P. (2002). *Early childhood education and care for children from low-income or minority backgrounds*. Paris: OECD.

Mac Naughton, G. (2006). *Respect for diversity. An international overview*. The Hague: Bernard Van Leer Foundation.

Mayall, B. (2002). *Towards a sociology for childhood. Thinking from children's lives*. Buckingham: Open University Press.

Meertens, R. (1997). Verminderen van vooroordelen en discriminatie. Een overzicht van de sociaal-pedagogische literatuur. In H. De Witte (Ed.), *Bestrijding van racisme en rechts-extremisme*. Leuven: Acco.

Moureau, A., & Brougère, G. (2007). *Participation parentale et pédagogie de la diversité*. Paris: Université Paris Nord.

Moss, P. (2007). Bringing politics into the nursery: Early childhood education as a democratic practice. *European Early Childhood Education Research Journal, 15*(1), 5–20.

Moss, P. (2008). *Early childhood education. Markets and democratic experimentalism: Two models for early childhood education and care* (Discussion paper). Gütersloh: Bertelsmann Foundation.

Nicaise, I. (2008). Ongelijkheid en sociale uitsluiting in het onderwijs: een onuitroeibare kwaal? In I. Nicaise & E. Desmedt (Eds.), *Gelijke kansen op school: Het kan!* (pp. 21–53). Mechelen: Plantyn.

Noailly, J., Visser, S., & Grout, P. (2007). *The impact of market forces on the provision of childcare: Insights from the 2005 Childcare Act in the Netherlands*. The Hague: CPB Netherlands Bureau for Economic Policy Analysis.

Organisation for Economic Co-operation and Development. (2001). *Starting strong: Early childhood education and care. Education and skills*. Paris: OECD.

Organisation for Economic Co-operation and Development. (2006). *Starting strong II: Early childhood education and care*. Paris: OECD.

Peeters, J. (2008). *Een internationaal perspectief op professionaliteit in de kinderopvang in Vlaanderen. Proefschrift ingediend tot het behalen van de academische graad van Doctor in de Pedagogische Wetenschappen*. Gent: Vakgroep Sociale Agogiek, UGent.

Penn, H. (2009). *Early childhood education and care. Key lessons from research for policy makers*. Brussels: European Commission, NESSE.

Peyton, V., Jacobs, A., O'Brien, M., & Roy, C. (2001). Reasons for choosing child care: associations with family factors, quality, and satisfaction. *Early Childhood Research Quarterly, 16*, 191–208.

Phillips, D., & Adams, G. (2001). Child care and our youngest children. *Future of Children, 11*(1), 35–51.

Preissing, C. (2004). *Berliner Bildingsprogramm für die Bilding, Erziehung und Betreuung von Kindern in Tageseinrichtungen bis zu ihrem Schuleintritt*. Berlin: Senatsverwaltung für Bildung, Jugend und Sport.

Preissing, C., & Wagner, P. (2003). *Kleine Kinder, keine Vorurteile? Interkulturelle und vorurteilsbewusste Erziehung in Kindertageseinrichtungen*. Freiburg: Verlag Herder.

Pungello, E., & Kurtz-Costes, B. (1999). Why and how working women choose child care: A review with a focus on infancy. *Developmental Review, 19*, 31–96.

Rinaldi, C. (2005). *In dialogue with Reggio Emilia: Listening, researching and learning*. London: Routledge.

Roelandt, A. (2006). *De toegankelijkheid van initiatieven voor buitenschoolse kinderopvang. Onuitgegeven scriptie*. Gent: Vakgroep Sociale Agogiek, UGent.

Roets, G., & Goedgeluck, M. (2007). Daisies on the road: Tracing the political potential of our postmodernist, feminist approach to life story research. *Qualitative Inquiry, 13*(1), 85–112.

Rogoff, B., Moore, L., Najafi, B., Dexter, A., Correa-Chávez, M., & Solis, J. (2005). Children's development of cultural repertoires through participation in everyday routines and practices. In J. Grusec & P. Hastings (Eds.), *Handbook of socialization* (pp. 490-515). New York: Guilford Press.

Rotthier, P. (2007). *Omgevingsanalyse kinderopvang in Antwerpen*. Antwerpen: Stad Antwerpen.

Schreuder, L. (2005). Kinderopvang in Nederland: van welzijn tot markt. In M. Vandenbroeck (Ed.), *Pedagogisch management in de kinderopvang* (pp. 63–73). Amsterdam: SWP.

Sharmahd, N. (2007). *La relazione tra educatrici e genitori al nido*. Pisa: Editione del Cerro.

Shlay, A., Tran, H., Weinraub, M., & Harmon, M. (2005). Teasing apart the child care conundrum: A factorial analysis of perceptions of child care quality, fair market price and willingness to pay by low-income, African-American parents. *Early Childhood Research Quarterly, 20*, 393–416.

Singer, E., & De Haan, D. (2007). *The social lives of young children. Play, conflict and moral learning in day-care groups*. Amsterdam: SWP.

Siraj-Blatchford, I. (2006, October 26–28). *The impact of early childhood settings and families on children's development*. Paper presented at the Promoting Diversity through Education conference, Bratislava.

Sylva, K., Melhuish, E., Sammons, P., Siraj-Blatchford, I., & Taggart, B. (2004). *The Effective Provision of Pre-School. Final report*. London: DfES, EPPE.

Super, C., & Harkness, S. (1996). *Parents' cultural belief systems: Their origins, expressions and consequences*. New York: Guilford Press.

UNICEF Innocenti Research Centre. (2008). *The child care transition. A league table of early childhood education and care in economically advanced countries*. Florence: Author.

Vandenbroeck, M. (2001). *The view of the Yeti*. The Hague: Bernard Van Leer Foundation.

Vandenbroeck, M. (2006a). *Globalisation and privatisation: The impact on childcare policy and practice* (Vol. 38). The Hague: Bernard Van Leer Foundation.

Vandenbroeck, M. (2006b). The persistent gap between education and care: A "history of the present" research on Belgian child care provision and policy. *Paedagogica Historica. International Journal of the History of Education, 42*(3), 363–383.

Vandenbroeck, M. (2007). Beyond anti-bias education: changing conceptions of diversity and equity in European early childhood education. *European Early Childhood Education Research Journal, 15*(1), 21–35.

Vandenbroeck, M., & Bouverne-De Bie, M. (2006). Children's agency and educational norms. A tensed negotiation. *Childhood, 13*(1), 127–143.

Vandenbroeck, M., De Visscher, S., Van Nuffel, K., & Ferla, J. (2008). Mothers' search for infant care: The dynamic relationship between availability and desirability in a continental European welfare state. *Early Childhood Research Quarterly, 23*, 245–258.

Vandenbroeck, M., Roets, G., & Snoeck, A. (2009). Immigrant mothers crossing borders: Nomadic identities and multiple belongings in early childhood education. *European Early Childhood Education Research Journal, 17*(2), 187–202.

Vanpée, K., Sannen, L., & Hedebouw, G. (2000). *Kinderopvang in Vlaanderen. Gebruik, keuze van de opvangvorm en evaluatie door de ouders.* Leuven: Katholieke Universiteit Leuven, HIVA.

Wall, K., & José, J. S. (2004). Managing work and care: A difficult challenge for immigrant families. *Social Policy and Administration, 38*(6), 591–621.

Weinraub, M., Shlay, A., Harmon, M., & Tran, H. (2005). Subsidizing child care: How child care subsidies affect the child care used by low-income African-American families. *Early Childhood Research Quarterly, 20,* 373–392.

8 Bilingualism for Equity and Excellence in Minority Education
The United States[1]

Ofelia García and JoAnne Kleifgen

INTRODUCTION

The use of the home language in educating language minority students throughout the world is often fraught with controversy. But, as this chapter will show, educating students bilingually is the most effective way to provide these students with an equitable education that is at the same time highly challenging intellectually and academically.

The lack of understandings surrounding the bilingual practices of language minority students has led to the schooling of these students in ways that (re)produce socioeducational inequities. This chapter examines inequities in four areas of education and the resulting miseducation of language minority students: (1) curricula and programs, (2) assessment, (3) resources, and (4) parental involvement. The chapter makes clear that language minority students, whose bilingual practices are ignored in schools, experience more remedial instruction and assignment to lower curriculum tracks, higher dropout rates, poorer graduation rates, and erroneous referrals to special education classes. Different ways of using the students' home language practices in education are thus crucial to address equity and excellence in the education of *all* language minority students, but especially in the education of those who are in the process of developing the majority language and becoming bilingual.

We start by discussing the prevalence of bilingualism among students in the world and distinguishing between those who are already bilingual and those who are in the process of becoming bilingual. We call this latter group of students *emergent bilinguals*, and we include in this group all who are acquiring an additional language through school—whether a majority or minority language. We also discuss theoretical foundations that can inform the education of these students. Equity and excellence for all students in the 21st century will increasingly depend on whether they are receiving appropriate bilingual instruction, which would enable them not only to be linguistically versatile, but also to show linguistic tolerance toward others (García, 2009).

In this chapter, we focus on emergent bilinguals who are acquiring a majority language in school. And we argue that for those emergent bilinguals—whether immigrants, refugees, indigenous peoples, or autochthonous minorities—the use of their home language practices is the key to providing them with educational excellence and equity. We use the case of the United States, and the monolingual educational policies and practices in the education of these emergent bilinguals, to show how it is precisely the reluctance to use the students' home language practices that brings about their educational failure.

BILINGUAL STUDENTS AROUND THE WORLD

Few countries have ever had populations that are monolingual in their makeup, and even today there are very few countries in the world that can be considered linguistically homogenous (see Lewis, 1981). In 2000, Grimes and Grimes listed 6,809 languages in over 200 countries, making it very obvious that most states in the world are multilingual. And yet, less than 25% of the world's 200 or so countries recognize two or more official languages (Tucker, 1998). This has important consequences for education, because it turns out that, although there are more bilingual and multilingual individuals in the world than monolinguals and more languages than states, education most often takes place in the *de jure* or *de facto* official language of the state. Thus, most students in the world are educated in a language other than that of the home. The consequence of this policy for minority language communities is great. Monolingual education, as carried out by the dominant language group in the state, plays an important role in ensuring that language minority communities do not receive a fair share of educational opportunities and that their bilingual resources and their multiple voices are diminished.

Monolingual education is being ever more challenged today in the 21st century. New communication technologies and globalization resulting in the increased flow of people, goods, services, and information across borders have greatly impacted language practices. In brief, the bilingualism that had always characterized school populations has intensified with increased influx of students who do not yet know the language of the school system and who are emergent bilinguals.

Emergent bilinguals are not a separate category of students inferior to those who are monolingual speakers of a language of power. Indeed, emergent bilinguals are in sociolinguistic continua with other bilinguals. But too many schools continue to be constituted as monolingual realms where bilingualism is ignored and all students are forced to speak, read, and write the language of schooling. In this context, emergent bilinguals are seen as problematic, as having absences instead of possibilities. We argue that it is precisely the lack of understanding about bilingualism that creates the inequities in the education of these emergent bilinguals and occasions their educational failure.

THEORIZING BILINGUAL EDUCATION

Over the past four decades, researchers have developed frameworks for understanding the relationship between bilingualism and academic achievement. We describe here some of the theoretical frameworks that are useful in considering the equitable education of emergent bilinguals.

Bilingualism and Education

Lambert (1974), working in the context of Canadian immersion education for Anglophone majorities, proposed that bilingualism could be either *subtractive* or *additive*. According to Lambert (1974), language minorities usually experience subtractive bilingualism as a result of schooling in another language. Their home language is subtracted as the school language is learned. On the other hand, language majorities usually experience additive bilingualism, as the school language is added to their home language. These models of bilingualism can be rendered as in Figure 8.1.

Subsequent research by Cummins (1981a, 1981b) and Skutnabb-Kangas (1981) has explained why being immersed in a different language at school works for language majority, but not for language minority, students.

Responding to the greater bilingual complexity of the 21st century, as well as the increased understanding of the multilingualism of the "developing" world, García (2009) has proposed that bilingualism could also be seen as being *recursive* or *dynamic*. These two models of bilingualism go beyond the conception of two separate autonomous languages of additive or subtractive bilingualism, suggesting instead that the language practices of bilinguals are complex and interrelated, and are not simply linear. Language minority communities who have experienced language loss and attend bilingual schools undergo a process of recursive bilingualism. They

Subtractive Bilingualism   Additive Bilingualism

$L1 \rightarrow + L2 - L1 \rightarrow L2$ $L1 + L2 = L1 + L2$

Figure 8.1   Subtractive versus additive bilingualism.

Recursive Bilingualism   **Dynamic Bilingualism**

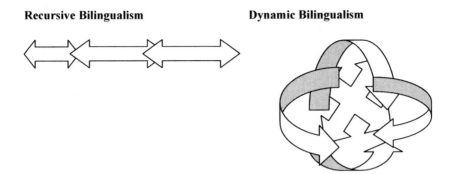

Figure 8.2   Recursive bilingualism versus dynamic bilingualism.

do not start as simple monolinguals (as in the subtractive or additive models). Instead, they recover bits and pieces of their existing ancestral language practices, as they develop a bilingualism that continuously reaches back in order to move forward. Dynamic bilingualism, on the other hand, refers to the development of different language practices to varying degrees in order to interact with increasingly multilingual communities. In some ways, dynamic bilingualism is related to the concept of *plurilingualism* proposed by the Language Policy Division of the Council of Europe. The difference is that within a dynamic bilingual perspective, languages are not seen as autonomous systems. Thus, educating for dynamic bilingualism builds on the complex and multiple language practices of students to develop new and different language practices as they interact in multilingual classrooms. These models can be rendered as in Figure 8.2.

Educators meaningfully educate when they draw upon the entire linguistic repertoire of all students, including language practices that are multiple and hybrid. Any language-in-education approach, be it monolingual or bilingual, that does not acknowledge and build upon the hybrid language practices in bilingual communities is more concerned with controlling language behavior than in educating (Cummins, 2007; García, 2009).

Linguistic Interdependence

The use of bilingualism in education in order to help language minority students do better in English is explained by the concept of *linguistic interdependence,* which means that both languages bolster each other (Cummins, 1979, 1981a, 1981b). Cummins (2000) explains linguistic interdependence by saying:

> To the extent that instruction in Lx [one language] is effective in promoting proficiency in Lx [that language], transfer of this proficiency

to Ly [the additional language] will occur provided there is adequate exposure to Ly. (p. 38)

A related theoretical construct is that of the *common underlying proficiency* (Cummins, 1979, 1981a, 1981b), which posits that knowledge and abilities acquired in one language are potentially available for the development of another. Researchers have consistently found that there is a cross-linguistic relationship between the student's first and second language, and proficiency in the native language is related to academic achievement in a second language (Riches & Genesee, 2006).

Academic Language

Skutnabb-Kangas and Toukomaa (1976) proposed that there is a difference between the way in which language is used in academic tasks as opposed to conversation and intimacy. Face-to-face communication is most often accompanied by gestural and other cues. Cummins (1981a, 1981b) has called this *contextualized language*, which is what one uses for *basic interpersonal communication* (BICS) (Cummins, 1981a, 1981b). To complete school tasks, more abstract language[2] is needed in order to participate in most classroom discourse. In speaking about the need for these abstract language skills, Cummins used the term *cognitive academic language proficiency* (CALP). Cummins (1979, 1981a, 1981b, 2000) proposes that it takes 5 to 7 years to develop these abstract skills in a second language, whereas the language of everyday communication is usually acquired in 1 to 3 years. Many programs currently provided to emergent bilinguals do not afford sufficient time to gain these language skills.

Literacy Skills and Literacy Practices:
Toward a Theoretical Synthesis

Cummins's framework has been tested, revised, and, like any ground-breaking proposal, subjected to criticism. Without rejecting the notion that the metalinguistic capacities available to learners through their first language can support the learning of spoken language and literacy skills in the second or third language, an alternative framework rejects a binary view of language and suggests that BICS and CALP are oversimplified terms. Rather, the linguistic repertoire is a complex phenomenon comprising multiple codes and modes or channels of expression (Zamel & Spack, 1998).

Brian Street, a key figure in New Literacy Studies, challenges scholars and educators to examine the uses of academic language as a series of social practices. Rather than thinking of literacy as a monolithic construct made up of a discrete set of skills, he recommends that we consider first, that literacies are multiple, and second, that they are embedded in a web of social relations that maintain asymmetries of power (Street, 1985, 1996, 2005). In other words, learning academic language is not a neutral activity, easily divided into two modes of communication—spoken and written. Instead, as recent scholarship has shown, learning academic literacy entails skills that are multimodal—spoken and written modes intricately bound up with other visual, audio, and spatial semiotic systems (Kleifgen & Kinzer, 2009; Kress, 2003; New London Group, 1996). These literacy scholars note that the acquisition of such complex technical skills is contingent upon wider societal factors beyond the school.

Taking the notion of language variation and complexity further, García, Bartlett, and Kleifgen (2007) build on the concept of plurilingualism, which accounts for the complex language practices and values of speakers in multilingual contexts, where people hold and value varying degrees of proficiency in a variety of languages, dialects, registers, and modes of communication. García et al. propose the concept of *pluriliteracy practices*, which are grounded in an understanding that equity for emergent bilinguals must take into account the benefits of having strong native language and literacy skills for attaining academic achievement in another language. Equity must also account for the power and value relations that exist around the various languages, language varieties, and literacy practices in the school setting and in society. It is thus important for schools to value emergent bilinguals' pluriliteracy practices—home, school, and community—in other contexts or countries, in other languages and scripts (Kleifgen, 2009). An equitable education for emergent bilinguals builds on all these practices and enables them to develop a powerful repertoire of multiple literacies. For a case in point, we now turn to the bilingual education situation in the United States.

A BRIEF OVERVIEW OF BILINGUAL EDUCATION IN THE UNITED STATES

The United States, a nation of immigrants, has seldom had a policy of promoting languages other than English in education or the wider society. Only for a brief period, during the late 1960s, the 1970s, and the early 1980s, following the Civil Rights era, bilingual education was conscientiously used as an alternative in the education of emergent bilinguals who were failing in the nation's schools. The rate of educational failure among these students then was alarming. Reports on the education of Mexican Americans noted that Spanish-surnamed students were, on average, 3 years below their Anglophone counterparts academically, and in the 1960s the dropout rate among Puerto Ricans in New York City schools was 60% (Castellanos, 1983). Bilingualism in education during those years was seen as a way of promoting educational equity for these students and providing them with an intellectually challenging education. Funding for academic programs that used languages other than English became available in 1968 when the U.S. Congress passed legislation known as Title VII of the Elementary and Secondary Education Act (also known as the Bilingual Education Act). Although bilingual education was not mandatory, funds were appropriated to spend on bilingual programs. There was clearly a consensus among legislators that something different had to be done to educate language minority students, and that the students' home languages were important to consider. Parents also had a hand in influencing the equitable education of their children who did not speak the language of the school. One case was taken to the Supreme Court, where, writing the majority opinion in the case of *Lau v. Nichols* brought by Chinese parents in San Francisco, Justice William O. Douglas said:

> [T]here is no equality of treatment merely by providing students with the same facilities, textbooks, teachers and curriculum; for students who do not understand English are effectively foreclosed from any meaningful education. . . .We know that those who do not understand English are certain to find their classroom experiences wholly incomprehensible and in no way meaningful. (*Lau v. Nichols*, 1974)

Although the U.S. Supreme Court did not mandate specific pedagogical approaches, it did mention bilingual education as one of a number of possible ways to provide an equitable education for these students. A year later, the government issued the "Lau Remedies," specific pedagogical directives, including the requirement that children's home language be used for instruction in primary schools with a large number of these students.

Since the 1990s, however, bilingual education in the United States has come increasingly under attack. In 2002, the Bilingual Education Act was substituted by Title III of the No Child Left Behind Act (NCLB). Significantly, although Title III also provided funding for bilingual education, the legislation was now called "Language Instruction for Limited English Proficient and Immigrant Students," silencing the word "bilingual." Under NCLB, "limited English proficient students" were those "whose difficulties in speaking, reading, writing, or understanding the English language may be sufficient to deny the individual the ability to meet the State's proficient level of achievement on State assessments" (sec. 9101 [37]). No longer was bilingualism considered important in an equitable and meaningful education, as reflected in the U.S. Supreme Court statement of 1974. Now equity was described as being able to meet English proficiency levels on assessment. The difference is telling, and it points to the growing anti-immigration sentiment and resistance to U.S. bilingualism. We turn now to describing the emergent bilingual population in U.S. schools, after which we address the educational inequities for these students in the four areas of curriculum, assessment, resources, and parental involvement.

Who are the Emergent Bilingual Students?

Between 1989–1990 and 2004–2005, the number of students classified as "limited English proficient" by the U.S. Department of Education in grades pre-K through 12 more than doubled, from 1,927,828 to 4,459,603 (National Clearinghouse of English Language Acquisition [NCELA], 2006; U.S. Department of Education, Office of the Secretary, 1991, p. 10). According to NCELA, this represents approximately 11% of the total U.S. public school student enrollment in 2005. The population of emergent bilinguals is increasing at nearly seven times the rate of total student enrollment (NCELA 2006). In 2001–2002, an estimated 45,283 of the approximately 91,000 regular K–12 public schools nationwide—approximately one half of all schools—had students who were emergent bilinguals (Zehler et al., 2003).

Emergent bilinguals are heavily concentrated in six U.S. states: California, Texas, Florida, New York, Illinois, and Arizona. But the greatest growth in the number of emergent bilinguals has been outside of these states, particularly in a new set of Southeastern states and one Midwestern state: South Carolina, Kentucky, North Carolina, Tennessee, and Indiana. It is estimated that between 75% and 80% of emergent bilinguals speak Spanish. In fact, close to half of all Spanish-speaking students going to school have been classified as emergent bilinguals (Lazarín, 2006). After Spanish, a significant number speak Vietnamese, Hmong, Korean, Arabic, Haitian Creole, and Cantonese (Kindler, 2002; Zehler et al., 2003). After Latinos, most emergent bilinguals are Asians (13%) (Hopstock & Stephenson, 2003a). Not all emergent bilinguals are immigrants. In fact, approximately half of emergent bilingual students have been born in the United States (Zehler et al., 2003). And many of these are Native Americans and Alaskan Natives.

About 75% of emergent bilinguals are poor, if we take the number of free- or reduced-price school lunch among emergent bilinguals as a proxy for poverty (Zehler et al., 2003). August, Hakuta, and Pompa (1994) have reported that the majority of emergent bilinguals live in high-poverty school districts. Emergent bilinguals frequently attend poor urban schools, which are often crowded and segregated, and where teachers lack adequate credentials (De Cohen, Deterding, & Chu Clewell, 2005).

The Education of Emergent Bilinguals in the United States

It is clear that if assessment scores in English are an indication of how these emergent bilinguals are doing, their educational situation is dire. According to the National Assessment of Educational Progress data, only a very small percentage of emergent bilinguals in the eighth grade are proficient in reading (4%) and in math (6%). They are also not graduating in proportionally the same numbers as those who are English proficient. A survey by Hopstock and Stephenson (2003b) revealed that 50% of emergent bilinguals fail their graduation tests, compared with 24% of those who are proficient in English.

Most emergent bilinguals in the United States are educated using English-only approaches. Sometimes, they are given special support in the form of so-called pull-out programs for classes in *English as a Second Language* (ESL). Usually students are pulled out daily from mainstream classrooms for 30 to 45 minutes of special ESL instruction. Other times, special English-only programs known as *Structured Immersion, Sheltered English,* or *Content-Based ESL* are developed specifically for emergent bilinguals. In these programs, subject matter is taught at the students' level of English, but the students' home language is not used.

There exist, however, several bilingual education alternatives for these students. Most students in bilingual education are in *transitional bilingual education,* meaning that students stay for only 1 to 3 years (early exit) until they become proficient in English. The home language is used to teach initial literacy and some subject instruction, and there is a strong ESL component and some subject matter instruction at the students' level of English. Very few emergent bilinguals are educated in what are called *one-way developmental bilingual education* programs. In these programs, emergent bilinguals of one language group are educated initially in the home language and eventually with a 50/50 distribution of English and the language other than English for over 5 years. Finally, there is a growing trend to develop what are called *two-way bilingual education programs* (also called *two-way dual language, two-way immersion,* and *dual immersion* programs). In these programs, emergent bilinguals are educated alongside bilingual children and monolingual children for over 5 years. These two-way bilingual education programs are of two types: 50/50 programs, in which the two languages have parity from the beginning, and 90/10 programs, in which the minority language is initially used 90% of the time until 50/50 language parity is gradually achieved. Although teachers in these programs separate the two languages strictly, in practice the complex linguistic heterogeneity of the students results in much more flexible language use than is recognized (García, 2006, in press).

EQUITY ISSUES IN THE EDUCATION OF EMERGENT BILINGUALS

The way in which most emergent bilinguals are educated in the United States today—solely through the medium of English or in bilingual education programs that mistakenly treat each of the two languages as if they were autonomous—runs contrary to what research tells us about how best to educate and assess emergent bilingual students. Drawing on research from different fields, including sociolinguistics and psycholinguistics, psychometrics and assessment, education and curriculum, sociology, and economics, we address four critical equity issues for emergent bilingual students:

1. Appropriate educational curricula and programs
2. Fair assessment
3. Adequate pedagogy and resources
4. Involvement of parents and communities

Toward Appropriate Educational Curricula and Programs

There is near consensus among researchers around the world that the use of students' home language practices and academic development are "positively related to higher long-term academic attainment" (Ferguson, 2006, p. 48). In the United States, several large-scale evaluations (Ramírez, 1992; Thomas & Collier, 1997) have demonstrated that using the home language in instruction benefits language minority students. The Ramírez study (1992) was a longitudinal study of 554 kindergarten to sixth-grade Latino students in five states (New York, New Jersey, Florida, Texas, and California) who were either in English-only structured immersion programs, transitional early-exit programs, or late-exit developmental bilingual programs. The results of the Ramírez study showed that the programs most favorable for student achievement were late-exit developmental bilingual programs, that is, programs that use bilingual students' home languages for at least 5 years. Although the data showed no differences among programs for students in the third grade, by sixth grade, students in late-exit developmental programs were performing better in mathematics, English language arts, and English reading than students in the other programs.

Collier (1995) stressed that four factors are important for the equitable and successful education of emergent bilinguals: (1) a socioculturally supportive environment, (2) the development of the students' first language to a high cognitive level, (3) uninterrupted cognitive development, which best occurs through education in the first language, and (4) teaching the second language with cognitively complex tasks. Thomas and Collier (1997) provided evidence that development of first-language skills provides a sound foundation for subsequent academic success in and through English as a second language. They stated:

> The first predictor of long-term school success is cognitively complex on-grade level academic instruction through students' first language for as long as possible (at least through grade 5 or 6) and cognitively

complex on-grade level academic instruction through the second language (English) for part of the day. (p. 15)

In 2002, Thomas and Collier released a study of the effectiveness of different kinds of educational programs for language minority student achievement. They compared the achievement on nationally standardized tests[3] of students in different kinds of programs who entered a U.S. school in kindergarten or first grade with little or no proficiency in English, following them to the highest grade level reached. They concluded that the use of the students' home languages in bilingual education produces better results in students' English reading scores than do programs that use English only.

In their recent synthesis of the research evidence in the education of emergent bilinguals, Genesee, Lindholm-Leary, Saunders, and Christian (2006) concluded that students who are in educational programs that provide extended instruction in their native language through developmental and two-way bilingual education programs outperform students who only receive short-term instruction through their native language (early-exit transitional bilingual education). They also found that students' bilingual biliteracy proficiencies were positively related to academic achievement in both languages. Finally, these researchers found that emergent bilinguals who participated in primary school programs that provided first language support acquired the same or superior levels of reading and writing skills as students in English-only programs by the end of elementary school. The National Literacy Panel on Language Minority Children and Youth, made up of individuals selected by the Bush administration, also concluded that bilingual education approaches in which the child's home language is used are more effective in teaching children to read than are English-only approaches (see August & Shanahan, 2006).[4]

Despite significant evidence supporting the use of students' home language practices in their schooling, emergent bilinguals are increasingly in classrooms where their home languages are disregarded. In fact, many more of these students are now in classrooms where nothing is being done differently to help them. Crawford (1999) estimates that in 1994–1995, 23% of all emergent bilinguals were in submersion classrooms where their home language was not used, and they were receiving the same instruction as native speakers of the school language, with no accommodation or support. Furthermore, a survey by Zehler et al. (2003) found that in the 2001–2002 academic year, 59% of emergent bilinguals were receiving all instruction in English. They also found that only 20% of these students were being educated with significant use of the home language, as in bilingual education.

The pull-out ESL approach continues to be the program of choice in the United States (Crawford, 1999). Although it has been found that ESL taught via content-area instruction (social studies, math, science, etc.) is associated with higher long-term educational attainment than ESL pull-out (which usually focuses on the development of English language and skills) (Thomas & Collier, 1997), there are more pull-out ESL programs than programs that teach English via content-area instruction.

U.S. schools also continue to emphasize bilingual education programs that cater to only one language minority group, ignoring the growing linguistic heterogeneity in classrooms. Bilingual education programs generally include emergent bilingual students of one language background (transitional or developmental bilingual education) or, in some cases, emergent bilingual students of the same language minority background alongside those of English-speaking background (two-way bilingual education). Although residential segregation as well as the large population of Spanish-speaking students have made these bilingual education programs possible (see, e.g., García & Bartlett, 2007), there is a growing need to develop educational models that take into account the chorus of multilingual voices in today's classrooms. We have personally witnessed evidence of how, even in two-way bilingual education classrooms, the home language practices of students from different language backgrounds have been ignored.

But even in bilingual classrooms that have emergent bilinguals from the same language group, educators tend to ignore bilingual language practices that go beyond monolingual language use of two languages. García (2009) refers to these bilingual education programs that treat each of the child's languages as separate and that ignore bilingual practices as *monoglossic*. By strictly separating the two languages, bilingual educators in these programs often fail to build on the students' home language practices in bilingual communities. Furthermore, these programs do not allow for cross-linguistic comparisons and other bilingual practices that are most important in the 21st century.

Unfortunately, most bilingual education programs in the United States hold a monoglossic ideology and treat each language as if each were being used in a monolingual context. Bilingual communities, however, use multiple and complex discursive practices in order to make sense of their bilingual worlds. García (2009) has referred to these discursive practices as *translanguaging*, extending Cen Williams's term, which he uses to refer to a specific pedagogic practice in bilingual Welsh classrooms (Baker, 2006). For García, translanguaging is an approach to bilingualism that is centered not on languages, but on the observable communicative practices of bilinguals. Although translanguaging may include code-switching, it also comprises other hybrid language use that is systematic and sense-making.

Until very recently, translanguaging was not seen as appropriate in bilingual classrooms. But there is now emerging evidence that keeping the two languages separate at all times and following only monolingual instructional strategies is not always appropriate (Cummins, 2007; García, 2006, 2009). Duverger (2005) has pointed out that both macro-alternation (in the sense of allocating languages to periods of the day, teacher, or subject matter) and micro-alternation (or the use of hybrid language and instructional practices by both teachers and students) are important in bilingual schools:

> Macro-alternation is programmed, institutionalized, demanding; micro-alternation adds suppleness, flexibility, and efficiency. The combination of the two is subtle. (p. 93)

Although all bilingual education programs need to have a language allocation policy, as well as a curricular arrangement for macro-alternation of languages, it is the micro-alternation, the translanguaging, which bilingual educators must learn to use.

In recent years, we have seen evidence that translanguaging, if properly understood and suitably applied in schools, can in fact enhance cognitive, language, and literacy abilities (Gajo, 2007; Heller & Martin-Jones, 2001; Lewis, 2008; Martin-Jones & Saxena, 1996; Serra, 2007; Wei, 2009). Thus far, however, most bilingual education programs in the United States, whether of the transitional, developmental, or two-way type, regard translanguaging with suspicion. Unfortunately, although the intent is to include the minority language in the classroom, many of these programs in effect exclude and stigmatize students' home language practices.

One of the key equity issues in the education of emergent bilinguals concerns the ways in which these students are assessed. Although teachers have developed instructionally embedded assessment that may measure emergent bilinguals' academic progress in more equitable ways, as we show next, large-scale fair assessments have yet to be developed for this population.

Toward Fair Assessment

The devastating effect of high-stakes testing in English for language minority students in the United States has been well documented. It has been widely demonstrated that as a result of these tests, emergent bilinguals experience more remedial instruction, greater probability of assignment to lower curriculum tracks, higher dropout rates, poorer graduation rates, and disproportionate referrals to special education classes (Artiles & Ortiz, 2002; Cummins, 1984; MacMillan & Reschly, 1998; Menken, 2008). There are important equity concerns in assessing emergent bilingual students having to do with two main issues: (1) disentangling academic language proficiency from content proficiency and (2) the validity of the tests themselves for emergent bilinguals.

Every assessment is an assessment of language skills (American Educational Research Association, American Psychological Association, & National Council on Measurement in Education, 1985), and, thus, assessment for emergent bilinguals who are still learning the language of the test is not valid unless language is disentangled from content. Shepard (1996) has argued that a fair assessment framework for emergent bilinguals should integrate the two dimensions: *academic language proficiency* and *content proficiency*. Academic performance of bilinguals should be seen as a continuum that is related to language acquisition, so that the language of the assessment is adapted according to the place along the continuum on which the student is situated.

Given the intermingling of language and content effect, there are concerns over the validity of standardized assessments for emergent bilinguals, as the test may not measure what it intends to evaluate. Furthermore, these tests have little content validity for these students because the performance of emergent bilinguals does not reveal much about their learning (Lachat, 1999). Worse still is the consequential validity of these tests for emergent bilinguals, that is, the consequences with regard to the teaching and learning process for these students (Cronbach, 1989; Messick, 1989). Because tests are constructed for monolingual populations, they always contain a built-in content bias. These monolingual tests reflect neither the language nor the language structures that the emergent bilingual students know. Furthermore, monolingual tests do not include activities, words, or concepts from both of the worlds of bilingual students (Mercer, 1989). Nor do monolingual assessments take into account the cultural norms of the bilingual students being assessed.

Formative approaches to assessment are a promising alternative to summative measures. Garcia and Pearson (1994) support the notion that emergent bilinguals be given performance-based assessment that is dynamic, in the sense that it should find out what the student can do with or without the help of the teacher. In this way, teachers are able to evaluate the kind of support that bilinguals need to complete tasks. The authors explain kinds of assessments for culturally diverse learners across a wide range of subject matters and test types. For example, teachers may assess students in English, the home language, or in both languages. They may assess their students' interpretations of material and vocabulary from diverse cultural and linguistic perspectives based on their backgrounds or build on that knowledge to assess them on their understandings of mainstream perspectives. Also, bilingual students can demonstrate their knowledge of native-language reading to assist them in their second-language reading. (See also Cummins, 2000, for alternative approaches to monitoring student progress.)

We argue that the best way to assess emergent bilingual students is for teachers to observe and listen to their students in both languages and record these observations systematically over extended periods. These ongoing descriptive reviews of students can establish a multidimensional portrait of bilingual learners. Rather than labeling emergent bilinguals as "limited," "at risk," or "deficient," these assessment approaches provide avenues for finding out what bilinguals do know. Authentic, formative assessments are much better ways of obtaining valid, reliable information that can inform teaching. But schools continue to assess language minority students exclusively in English with invalid tests. The result is the inadequate instruction and resources that we describe next.

Toward Adequate Instruction and Resources

When emergent bilinguals enter kindergarten, they already face a disadvantage. According to data from the Early Childhood Longitudinal Study (ECLS), about half of kindergartners who speak English at home perform above the 50th percentile in California, whereas no more than 17% of kindergartners who speak a language other than English at home perform at this level (Gándara, Rumberger, Maxwell-Jolly, & Callahan, 2003). This disparity has to do with the fact that emergent bilingual kindergartners cannot understand English well enough to be assessed in English only. As a result, the (mis)placement of these children into remedial education starts the moment they enter school for the first time.

Kindergartners and others who score low on tests are likely to be placed in remedial education (Gottlieb, Alter, Gottlieb, & Wishner, 1994). Because emergent bilinguals are only seen as English language learners from whom little is expected, they often go to schools that offer more remedial programs, where the emphasis is on rote instruction and remediation (De Cohen et al., 2005). The programs focus on compensating for the learners' limited English language skills (Harklau, 1994; Olsen, 1997) and offering them multiple periods of ESL instruction instead of meaningful content (García, 1999), thus creating further inequities (Anstrom, 1997; Fleishman & Hopstock, 1993). Furthermore, although it is widely accepted that a balanced approach to literacy incorporating more time to discuss, create, read, and write, as well as to learn phonics (instruction in sound–symbol correspondence) is central to literacy development (Birch, 2002; Honig, 1996), most emergent bilinguals are taught to read exclusively through heavily phonics-based approaches.

Emergent bilinguals are also regularly tracked into courses that do not provide them with challenging content (Callahan, 2003, 2005; Oakes, 1990). Sometimes they are given shortened day schedules and excused from courses that are not considered relevant to them (Olsen, 1997). Or they are given physical education or art classes rather than core subject content classes (García, 1999). In fact, often their learning of content-area academics is delayed until English has been acquired (Minicucci & Olsen, 1992). Alternatively, when newcomers are taught subject matter through English alone, instruction often takes on a slower pace, and less content is covered (Minicucci & Olsen, 1992). When the home language is used to teach academic subjects, thereby affirming these students' emergent bilingualism, challenging academic content is taught and excellent learning takes place (García & Bartlett, 2007).

English language learners are also overrepresented in some categories of special education, particularly in specific learning disabilities and language and speech impairment classes, and most especially at the secondary level (Artiles, Rueda, Salazar, & Higareda, 2002). This overrepresentation suggests the difficulty that schools have in distinguishing students with disabilities from those who are still learning English (Yates & Ortiz, 1998). Emergent bilinguals who are in bilingual programs are less likely to be in special education than those students who are in English-only programs (Artiles et al., 2002).

The other side of the coin for emergent bilinguals, when it comes to access to the most challenging educational programs, is their underrepresentation in "gifted and talented" programs. Only 1.4% of emergent bilinguals nationwide are in gifted and talented programs, in contrast to 6.4% of the English proficient population (Hopstock & Stephenson, 2003b). Although 3.2% of all high school students are enrolled in Advanced Placement (AP) mathematics and science, only 0.8% of emergent bilinguals are enrolled in AP science and 1.0% in AP math (Hopstock & Stephenson, 2003b).

Oakes and Saunders (2002) have argued that there is a clear link between appropriate materials and curriculum and student academic outcome. Emergent bilinguals need developmentally appropriate materials to learn English, but they also need appropriate content materials in their home languages. More often than not, emergent bilinguals do not have these materials. In a survey of teachers by the American Institute for Research, only 25% reported that they used a different textbook for emergent bilinguals than for their English proficient students (Parrish et al., 2002).

Research also demonstrates that teacher and principal quality are two of the most important factors in determining school effectiveness and, ultimately, student achievement (Clewell & Campbell, 2004). But few school leaders and not enough teachers are well versed in issues surrounding bilingualism. Teachers in schools with high numbers of emergent bilinguals have fewer credentials on average than teachers at schools with few or no emergent bilinguals (De Cohen et al., 2005). Although slightly more than 50% of teachers in schools with high levels of emergent bilinguals have full certification, almost 80% of teachers in other schools do. In short, in the United States, emergent bilinguals do not have the same opportunity to be in schools with highly prepared teachers and administrators and updated material resources, including new technologies, as do English-speaking students. With regard to equity in both human and material resources, there is a wide gap to close.

Toward Greater Parental Involvement

Both folk wisdom and research over the years have supported the notion of parental involvement in their children's schooling, the premise being that several caring adults (school personnel and family members), working together, can accelerate their learning. It is "the mantra of every educational reform program" (González, 2005, p. 42), including the current NCLB legislation, which requires schools to reach out to parents and involve them in their children's education. Research has shown the benefits of such collaboration: Parent involvement leads to better attendance, higher achievement, improved attitudes about learning, and higher graduation rates. In addition, children from minority and low-income families gain the most from parent involvement (Epstein, 1990; Henderson, 1987; Henderson & Berla, 1994; Henderson & Mapp, 2002; Hidalgo, Siu, & Epstein, 2004; Jordan, Orozco, & Averett, 2001). Despite these findings, the parents of emergent bilinguals, who in many cases have limited formal schooling themselves and may not communicate proficiently in English, continue to be stigmatized and considered incapable educational partners (Ramirez, 2003).

Many educators still consider family practices to be barriers to student achievement. For example, parents are often exhorted to "speak English at home," in the mistaken belief that this will improve their children's English at school. This advice, although well intentioned, devalues the home language practices and at the same time encourages inconsistent, often poor, linguistic input from nonnative-speaking parents (see Ross & Newport, 1996). In a major effort to counteract the stigmatization of families of emergent bilingual children, a group of anthropologists from the University of Arizona have developed a program of research, spanning nearly two decades, on "funds of knowledge" for schooling (e.g., Greenberg, 1989, 1990; González, Moll, & Amanti, 2005; Moll, Amanti, Neff, & González, 1992; Moll & Greenberg, 1990). The concept of "funds of knowledge" refers to different strategies and ways of knowing needed for a household to function effectively. It is based on the notion that everyday practices, including linguistic practices, are sites of knowledge construction and that these resources can be brought into the classroom. This research shows that parents of emergent bilinguals have a great deal to teach school personnel about knowledge and skills that originate in their households that can be translated into academic success in schools. Other research shows that parents want to learn how to help their children at home (Epstein, 1990), yet they have in some cases felt disregarded and left powerless in their attempts to be involved in the school (Pérez Carreón, Drake, & Calabrese Barton, 2005). Sadly, too many schools continue to ignore this research, and little effort is made to build on the strengths of the families and communities from which emergent bilinguals come.

CONCLUSION

It is clear that the inequities that surround the education of language minority students in the United States have to do with the policy makers' myopic view of education that is both monolingual and monocultural, even in a country with rapidly changing demographics and in a world that has become increasingly interdependent. The importance of bilingualism as a resource to provide an excellent education to these students is misunderstood. There is little commitment to deepen understanding of the nature of bilingualism among educators and to provide adequate instructional resources to emergent bilinguals. And the role of the linguistic and cultural practices of the home is largely ignored.

If we are going to seriously and equitably educate language minority students in the 21st century, we have to point out the inequities of the present, while forging a path for a different future. In a country that has just elected its first African American president, it is clear that the future is now. To educate for excellence means to build on strengths; to develop self-confidence and an imaginative, creative, and inquisitive intellectual spirit; and to believe in one's potential to lead and help construct a better and more just future. It is clear that this cannot be accomplished by ignoring the students' home language practices and by insisting that they give up who they are in order to receive an education. The future must include all of us, and a clear path to practices of tolerance, justice, and intellectual curiosity is through educating both language minorities and language majorities in the use of each other's multiple languages and diverse ways of knowing. Bilingual education holds the possibility of providing all students with that possibility: the opportunity of intellectual engagement and deep and rigorous academic challenge, as well as the possibility of mutual understanding and collaboration.

NOTES

1. We gratefully acknowledge the support of the Campaign for Educational Equity at Teachers College for the research that resulted in a report authored by García, Kleifgen, and Falchi (2008) and that is here summarized. The contents of the report on which this chapter is based has since been expanded into a full length book by García and Kleifgen, *Educating Emergent Bilinguals: Policies, Programs, and Practices for English Language Learners.* New York: Teachers College Press. Copyright © 2010 by Teachers College Press, Columbia University. All rights reserved.
2. Cummins called this *decontextualized language*, a term that has been controversial, as no language, however abstract, can truly be called decontextualized.
3. These included the Iowa Test of Basic Skills (ITBS), Comprehensive Test of Basic Skills (CTBS), Stanford 9, and Terra Nova.
4. Notably, the Panel's report was not released by the government. The authors were given the copyright, and the report was published by Erlbaum.

REFERENCES

American Educational Research Association, American Psychological Association, & National Council on Measurement in Education. (1985). *National Council on Measurement in Education standards for educational and psychological testing.* Washington, DC: American Psychological Association.

Anstrom, K. (1997). *Academic achievement for secondary language minority students: Standards, measures, and promising practices.* Washington DC: National Clearinghouse for Bilingual Education.

Artiles, A. J., & Ortiz, A. A. (Eds.). (2002). *English language learners with special education needs: Identification, assessment, and instruction.* Washington, DC, & McHenry, IL: Center for Applied Linguistics and Delta System.

Artiles, A. J., Rueda, R., Salazar, J., & Higareda, I. (2002). English-language learner representation in special education in California urban school districts. In D. Losen & G. Orfield (Eds.), *Racial inequity in special education* (pp. 117–136). Cambridge, MA: Harvard Education Press.

August, D., Hakuta, K., & Pompa, D. (1994). For all students: Limited English proficient students and Goals 2000. *Focus* (Vol. 10). Washington, DC: National Clearinghouse for Bilingual Education.

August, D., & Shanahan, T. (Eds.). (2006). *Developing literacy in second-language learners: Report of the National Literacy Panel on language-minority children and youth.* Mahwah, NJ: Erlbaum.

Baker, C. (2006). *Foundations of bilingual education and bilingualism* (4th ed.). Clevedon: Multilingual Matters.

Birch, B. M. (2002). *English L2 reading: Getting to the bottom.* Mahwah, NJ: Erlbaum.

Callahan, R. (2003). *Tracking and English language proficiency: Variable effects on academic achievement of high school ELs.* Unpublished doctoral dissertation, University of California, Davis.

Callahan, R. (2005). Tracking and high school English learners: Limiting opportunities to learn. *American Educational Research Journal, 42,* 305–328.

Castellanos, D. (1983). *The best of two worlds: Bilingual-bicultural education in the U.S.* Trenton, NJ: New Jersey State Department of Education.

Clewell, B., & Campbell, P. (2004). *Highly effective USI schools: An outlier study.* Washington, DC: Urban Institute & Campbell-Kibler Associates.

Collier, V. (1995). Acquiring a second language for schools. *Directions in Language and Education, 1*(4), 1–12.

Crawford, J. (1999). *Bilingual education: History, politics, theory, and practice* (4th ed.). Los Angeles: Bilingual Educational Services.

Cronbach, L. J. (1989). Construct validation after thirty years. In R. L. Linn (Ed.), *Intelligence: Measurement theory and public policy.* Urbana: University of Illinois Press.

Cummins, J. (1979). Cognitive/academic language proficiency, linguistic interdependence, the optimum age question, and some other matters. *Working Papers on Bilingualism, 19,* 121–129.

Cummins, J. (1981a). *Bilingualism & minority language children.* Toronto, Canada: Ontario Institute for Studies in Education.

Cummins, J. (1981b). The role of primary language development in promoting educational success for language minority students. In California State Department of Education (Ed.), *Schooling and language minority students: A theoretical framework* (pp. 3–50). Los Angeles: Evaluation, Dissemination and Assessment Center.

Cummins, J. (1984). *Bilingualism and special education: Issues in assessment and pedagogy.* Clevedon: Multilingual Matters.

Cummins, J. (2000). *Language, power, and pedagogy: Bilingual children in the crossfire.* Clevedon: Multilingual Matters.

Cummins, J. (2007). Rethinking monolingual instructional strategies in multilingual classrooms. *Canadian Journal of Applied Linguistics, 10*(2), 221–240.

De Cohen, C. C., Deterding, N., & Chu Clewell, B. (2005). *Who's left behind? Immigrant children in high and low LEP schools.* Washington, DC: Urban Institute, Program for Evaluation and Equity Research.

Duverger, J. (2005). *L'Enseignement en classe bilingue.* Paris: Hachette.

Epstein, J. L. (1990). School and family connections: Theory, research, and implications for integrating sociologies of education and family. In D. G. Unger & M. B. Sussman (Eds.), *Families in community settings: Interdisciplinary perspectives* (pp. 99–126). New York: Haworth Press.

Ferguson, G. (2006). *Language planning and education.* Edinburgh: Edinburgh Press.

Fleishman, H. L., & Hopstock, P. J. (1993). *Descriptive study of services to Limited English Proficient students: Vol. 1. Summary of findings and conclusions.* Arlington, VA: Development Associates.

Gajo, L. (2007). Linguistic knowledge and subject knowledge: How does bilingualism contribute to subject development? *International Journal of Bilingual Education and Bilingualism, 10*(5), 563–581.

Gándara, P., Rumberger, R., Maxwell-Jolly, J., & Callahan, R. (2003). English learners in California schools: Unequal resources, unequal outcomes. *Education Policy Analysis Archives, 11.* http://epaa.asu.edu/epaa/v11n36

Garcia, G., & Pearson, P. D. (1994). Assessment and diversity. *Review of Research in Education, 20,* 337–391.

García, O. (1999). Educating Latino high school students with little formal schooling. In C. J. Faltis & P. Wolfe (Eds.), *So much to say: Adolescents, bilingualism, & ESL in the secondary school* (pp. 61–82). New York: Teachers College Press.

García, O. (2006). Lost in transculturation: The case of bilingual education in New York City. In M. Putz, J. A. Fishman, & J. Neff-van Aertselaer (Eds.), *Along the routes to power: Exploration of empowerment through language* (pp. 157–178). Berlin: Mouton de Gruyter.

García, O. (2009). *Bilingual education in the 21st century: A global perspective.* Malden, MA: Wiley/Blackwell.

García, O., with Makar, C., Starcevic, M., & Terry, A. (In press). Translanguaging of Latino kindergarteners. In Rothman, J. and Potowski, K. *Bilingual Youth: Spanish in English speaking societies.* Amsterdam and Philadelphia: John Benjamins.

García, O., & Bartlett, L. (2007). A speech community model of bilingual education: Educating Latino newcomers in the U.S. *International Journal of Bilingual Education and Bilingualism, 10,* 1–25.

García, O., Bartlett, L., & Kleifgen, J. (2007). From biliteracy to pluriliteracies. In P. Auer & W. Li (Eds.), *Multilingualism and multilingual communication: Handbook of applied linguistics* (Vol. 5, pp. 207–228). Berlin: Mouton de Gruyter.

García, O., Kleifgen, J., & Falchi, L. (2008). *From English language learners to emergent bilinguals* (Research Review No. 1). New York: Columbia University, Teachers College, Campaign for Educational Equity. www.tc.columbia.edu/i/a/document/6468_Ofelia_ELL__Final.pdf

Genesee, F., Lindholm-Leary, K., Saunders, W. M., & Christian, D. (Eds.). (2006). *Educating English language learners.* New York: Cambridge University Press.

González, N. (2005). Beyond culture: The hybridity of funds of knowledge. In N. González, L. C. Moll, & C. Amanti (Eds.), *Funds of knowledge: Theorizing practices in households, communities and classrooms* (pp. 29–46). Mahwah, NJ: Erlbaum.

González, N., Moll, L. C., & Amanti, C. (2005). *Funds of knowledge: Theorizing practices in households, communities, and classrooms.* Mahwah, NJ: Erlbaum.

Gottlieb, J., Alter, M., Gottlieb, B. W., & Wishner, J. (1994). Special education in urban America: It's not justifiable for many. *Journal of Special Education*, 27(4), 453–465.

Greenberg, J. (1989, June). *Funds of knowledge: Historical constitution, social distribution, and transmission.* Paper presented at the annual meeting of the Society for Applied Anthropology, Santa Fe, NM.

Greenberg, J. (1990). Funds of knowledge: Historical constitution, social distribution, and transmission. In W. T. Pink, D. S. Ogle, & B. F. Jones (Eds.), *Restructuring to promote learning in America's schools: Selected readings* (Vol. 2, pp. 317–326). Elmhurst: North Central Regional Educational Laboratory.

Grimes, B. F., & Grimes, B. E. (Eds.). (2000). *Ethnologue: Vol. 1. Languages of the world* (14th ed.). Dallas, TX: Summer Institute of Linguistics.

Harklau, L. (1994). Tracking and linguistic minority students: Consequences of ability grouping for second language learners. *Linguistics and Education*, 6(3), 217–244.

Heller, M., & Martin-Jones, M. (Eds.). (2001). *Voices of authority: Education and linguistic differences.* Westport, CT: Ablex.

Henderson, A. T. (Ed.). (1987). *The evidence continues to grow: Parent involvement improves student achievement.* Columbia, MD: National Committee for Citizens in Education.

Henderson, A. T., & Berla, N. (Eds.). (1994). *A new generation of evidence: The family is critical to student achievement.* Washington, DC: Center for Law and Education.

Henderson, A. T., & Mapp, K. L. (2002). *A new wave of evidence: The impact of school, family, and community connections on student achievement.* Austin, TX: Southwest Educational Development Laboratory.

Hidalgo, N. M., Siu, S. F., & Epstein, J. L. (2004). Research on families, schools, and communities: A multicultural perspective. In J. Banks & C. Banks (Eds.), *Handbook of research on multicultural education* (2nd ed., pp. 631–655). San Francisco: Jossey-Bass.

Honig, B. (1996). *Teaching our children to read: The role of skills in a comprehensive reading program.* Thousand Oaks, CA: Corwin Press.

Hopstock, P. J., & Stephenson, T. G. (2003a). *Descriptive study of services to LEP students and LEP students with disabilities. Special Topic Rep. No. 1: Native languages of LEP students.* Washington, DC: U.S. Department of Education, Office of English Language Acquisition. http://onlineresources.wnylc.net/pb/orcdocs/LARC_Resources/LEPTopics/ED/DescriptiveStudyofServicestoLEP-StudentsandLEPStudentswithDisabilities.pdf.

Hopstock, P. J., & Stephenson, T. G. (2003b). *Descriptive study of services to LEP students and LEP students with disabilities. Special Topic Rep. No. 2: Analysis of Office of Civil Rights data related to LEP students.* Washington, DC: U.S. Department of Education, Office of English Language Acquisition.

Jordan, C., Orozco, E., & Averett, A. (2001). *Emerging issues in school, family, and community connections.* Austin, TX: Southwest Educational Development Laboratory.

Kindler, A. (2002). *Survey of the states' limited English proficient students and available educational programs and services: 2000–2001 summary report.* Washington, DC: National Clearinghouse for English Language Acquisition and Language Instruction Educational Programs.

Kleifgen, J. (2009). Discourses of linguistic exceptionalism and linguistic diversity in education. In J. Kleifgen & G. C. Bond (Eds.), *Languages of Africa and the diaspora: Educating for language awareness* (pp 1–21). Clevedon: Multilingual Matters.

Kleifgen, J., & Kinzer, C. (2009). Alternative spaces for education with and through technology. In H. Varenne & E. Gordon (Eds.), *Theoretical perspectives on comprehensive education: The way forward* (pp. 139–186). Lewiston, NY: Mellen Press.

Kress, G. (2003). *Literacy in the new media age*. New York: Routledge.

Lachat, M. (1999). *What policymakers and school administrators need to know about assessment reform for English language learners*. Providence, RI: Brown University, Northeast and Islands Regional Education Laboratory.

Lambert, W. E. (1974). Culture and language as factors in learning and education. In F. E. Aboud & R. D. Meade (Eds.), *Cultural factors in learning and education* (pp. 91–122). Bellingham: Western Washington State College.

Lau v. Nichols, 414 U.S. 563 (1974).

Lazarín, M. (2006). *Improving assessment and accountability for English language learners in the No Child Left Behind Act*. Washington, DC: National Council of La Raza.

Lewis, E. G. (1981). *Bilingualism and bilingual education*. Oxford: Pergamon Press.

Lewis, W. G. (2008). Current challenges in bilingual education in Wales. *AILA Review, 21*, 69–86.

Li, Wei (2009). Polite Chinese children revisited: Creativity and use of code-switching in the Chinese complementary school classroom. *International Journal of Bilingual Education and Bilingualism, 12*(2), 193–211.

MacMillan, D. L., & Reschly, D. J. (1998). Overrepresentation of minority students: The case for greater specificity or reconsideration of the variables examined. *Journal of Special Education, 32*(1), 15–24.

Martin-Jones, M., & Saxena, M. (1996). Turn-taking, power asymmetries, and the positioning of bilingual participants in classroom discourse. *Linguistics and Education, 8*(1), 105–123.

Menken, K. (2008). *English learners left behind*. Clevedon: Multilingual Matters.

Mercer, J. R. (1989). Alternative paradigms for assessment in a pluralistic society. In J. A. Banks & C. M. Banks (Eds.), *Multicultural education* (pp. 289–303). Boston: Allyn & Bacon

Messick, S. (1989). Validity. In R. L. Linn (Ed.), *Educational measurement* (3rd ed., pp. 13–103). Washington, DC: American Council on Education & National Council on Measurement in Education.

Minicucci, C., & Olsen, L. (1992, Spring). *Programs for secondary limited English proficient students: A California study* (Occasional Papers in Bilingual Education, No. 5). Washington, DC: National Clearinghouse for Bilingual Education.

Moll, L. C., Amanti, C., Neff, D., & González, N. (1992). Funds of knowledge for teaching: Using a qualitative approach to connect homes and classrooms. *Theory Into Practice, 31*(2), 132–141.

Moll, L. C., & Greenberg, J. (1990). Creating zones of possibilities: Combining social contexts for instruction. In L. Moll (Ed.), *Vygotsky and education: Instructional implications and applications of sociohistorical psychology* (pp. 319–348). New York: Cambridge University Press.

National Clearinghouse for English Language Acquisition (NCELA). (2006). *Fast frequently asked questions*. http://www.ncela.gwu.edu/faqs/.

New London Group. (1996). A pedagogy of multiliteracies. Designing social futures. In B. Cope & M. Kalantzis (Eds.), *Multiliteracies: Literacy learning and the design of social futures* (pp. 9–37). London: Routledge.

Oakes, J. (1990). *Multiplying inequalities: The effects of race, social class, and tracking on opportunities to learn mathematics and science*. Santa Monica, CA: RAND.

Oakes, J., & Saunders, M. (2002). *Access to textbooks, instructional materials, equipment, and technology: Inadequacy and inequality in California's public schools.* Williams Watch Series (wws-rr001–1002). Los Angeles: UCLA/IDEA.

Olsen, L. (1997). *Made in America.* New York: Free Press.

Parrish, T. B., Linquanti, R., Merickel, A., Quick, H. E., Laird, J., & Esra, P. (2002). *Effects of the implementation of Proposition 227 on the education of English learners. K–12: Year Two Report.* Palo Alto, CA: American Institutes for Research. http://www.wested.org/online_pubs/year2finalrpt.pdf.

Pérez Carreón, G., Drake, C., & Calabrese Barton, A. (2005). The importance of presence: Immigrant parents' school engagement experiences. *American Educational Research Journal, 42*(3), 465–498.

Ramirez, A. Y. F. (2003). Dismay and disappointment: Parental involvement of Latino immigrant parents. *Urban Review, 35*(2), 93–110.

Ramírez, D. (1992). Executive summary. *Bilingual Research Journal, 16,* 1–62.

Riches, C., & Genesee, F. (2006). Cross-linguistic and cross-modal aspects of literacy development. In F. Genesee, K. Lindholm-Leary, W. Saunders, & D. Christian (Eds.), *Educating English language learners: A synthesis of research evidence* (pp. 64–108). New York: Cambridge University Press.

Ross, D. S., & Newport, E. L. (1996). The development of language from non-native linguistic input. In A. Stringfellow, D. Cahana-Amitay, E. Hughs, & A. Zukowski (Eds.), *Proceedings of the 20th annual Boston University conference on language development* (Vol. 2, pp. 634–645). Somerville, MA: Cascadilla Press.

Serra, C. (2007). Assessing CLIL at primary school: A longitudinal study. *International Journal of Bilingual Education and Bilingualism, 10*(5), 582–602.

Shepard, L. A. (1996). *Research framework for investigating accommodations for language minority students.* Paper presented at the CRESST Assessment conference, University of California, Los Angeles.

Skutnabb-Kangas, T. (1981). *Bilingualism or not: The education of minorities.* Clevedon: Multilingual Matters.

Skutnabb-Kangas, T., & Toukomaa, P. (1976). Semilingualism and middle-class bias: A reply to Cora Brent-Palmer. *Working Papers on Bilingualism, 19.* Toronto: Ontario Institute for Studies in Education, Bilingual Education Project.

Street, B. V. (1985). *Literacy in theory and practice.* Cambridge: Cambridge University Press.

Street, B. V. (1996). Academic literacies. In D. Baker, J. Clay, & C. Fox (Eds.), *Alternative ways of knowing: Literacies, numeracies, sciences* (pp. 101–134). London: Falmer Press.

Street, B. V. (Ed.). (2005). *Literacies across educational contexts: Mediating, learning and teaching.* Philadelphia: Caslon Press.

Thomas, M., & Collier, V. (1997). School effectiveness for language minority students. Washington DC: National Clearinghouse for Bilingual Education, George Washington University, Center for the Study of Language and Education.

Thomas, W., & Collier, V. (2002). *A national study of school effectiveness for language minority students' long-term academic achievement.* Santa Cruz: University of California at Santa Cruz, Center for Research on Education, Diversity, and Excellence.

Tucker, G. R. (1998). A global perspective on multilingualism and multilingual education. In J. Cenoz & F. Genesee (Eds.), *Beyond bilingualism* (pp. 3–15). Clevedon: Multilingual Matters.

U.S. Department of Education, Office of the Secretary. (1991). *The condition of bilingual eduction in the nation: A report to Congress and the President,* June 30.

Yates, J. R., & Ortiz, A. (1998). Issues of culture and diversity affecting educators with disabilities: A change in demography is reshaping America. In R. J. Anderson, C. E. Keller, & J. M. Karp (Eds.), *Enhancing diversity: Educators with disabilities in the education enterprise* (pp. 21–37). Washington, DC: Gallaudet University Press.

Zamel, V., & Spack, R. (Eds.). (1998). *Negotiating academic literacies: Teaching and learning across languages and cultures.* Mahwah, NJ: Erlbaum.

Zehler, A., Fleischman, H., Hopstock, P., Stephenson, T., Pendizick, M., & Sapru, S. (2003). *Descriptive study of services to LEP students and LEP students with disabilities* (Vol. 1). Research Report. http://onlineresources.wnylc.net/pb/orcdocs/LARC_Resources/LEPTopics/ED/DescriptiveStudyofServicestoLEP-StudentsandLEPStudentswithDisabilities.pdf.

9 Finnish Basic Education
When Equity and Excellence Meet

Pirjo Linnakylä, Jouni Välijärvi, and Inga Arffman

INTRODUCTION

Judging by various international assessments, the Finnish school system seems to be successful in providing the majority of its students with a solid foundation for further and higher studies, working life, and active citizenship. The results of the Organization for Economic Co-operation and Development (OECD) Programme for International Student Assessment (PISA) studies, in particular, have shown that the Finnish education system has succeeded not only in stimulating academic excellence but also in promoting relatively high equity among 15-year-olds. For example, in reading literacy, Finnish students performed highest in PISA 2000 and 2003 and second highest in PISA 2006. In mathematics, they scored fourth in PISA 2000 and second in PISA 2003 and 2006. In science, their performance ranked third highest in PISA 2000 and highest in PISA 2003 and 2006. At the same time, when compared to other countries, the number of weak-performing students in Finland has been remarkably low in all three domains and the gap between low and high achievement relatively narrow (OECD, 2001, 2004, 2007).

For Finns, the good results in reading literacy did not come as a complete surprise, because Finnish students (9- and 14-year-olds) had already been found to be the best readers in the Reading Literacy Study conducted by the International Association for the Evaluation of Educational Achievement (IEA) in 1991 (Elley, 1994; Linnakylä, 1995). Finnish young adults (16- to 25-year-olds) had likewise outperformed their peers in other countries in the International Adult Literacy Survey (IALS) in 1998 (Linnakylä, Malin, Blomqvist, & Sulkunen, 2000; OECD, 2000).

However, in mathematical and scientific literacy, the results have been more of a surprise. In previous international assessments, Finnish students have typically performed among the highest quarter but never among the top countries (Kupari, Reinikainen, Nevanpää, & Törnroos, 2001; Martin et al., 2000; Mullis et al., 2000). This disparity is due partly to the fact that in PISA, the assessment focuses more on problems in everyday and working contexts, whereas in the Trends in International Mathematics and Science Study (TIMSS), for example, the emphasis is more on mastery of skills and knowledge learned at school. This can be inferred from the extent to which the performance of the participating countries systematically varies between the assessments. In assessments such as TIMSS, where the focus is on mathematics and science as learned at school, Asian countries typically perform extremely well, much better than European countries. However, in assessments such as PISA, not only Finland's but also several other European and also Anglo-American countries' scores approximate those of Asian countries, the difference in performance being much smaller than in TIMSS.

The success of Finnish students in PISA has been, of course, a great joy but at the same time also a somewhat puzzling experience for all those responsible for educational policy making in Finland. At a single stroke, PISA has transformed our conceptions of the quality of Finnish basic education. Traditionally, we have been used to thinking that the models for educational reforms should be adopted from abroad. For a long time, we turned to Germany for these models and later to Sweden, Great Britain, or the United States. Today, thanks to PISA and other international studies, the situation has changed, with the Finnish education system and pedagogical practices suddenly in the focus of international interest. This rapid evolution from being a country that followed the example of others to one serving as a model has prompted us to recognize and reflect seriously on the special characteristics and strengths of our basic education (Välijärvi et al., 2007).

This chapter discusses possible reasons for the high achievement of Finnish students, suggesting that it is strongly related to how the principle of equity is implemented in Finnish education. Obviously, Finland's high achievement scores should not be attributed to one decisive factor. Rather, it is the result of a whole array of interconnected factors, including variables related to students' personal interests, attitudes, and leisure activities, as well as variables pertaining to the social and cultural context of the education system, teacher education, and learning in general. The chapter rounds off with a discussion of the challenges still facing Finnish basic education.

EQUALITY OF LEARNING OUTCOMES

Providing all students with equal access to education and removing obstacles to learning, especially for students from disadvantaged backgrounds, have been leading principles in Nordic education policy for a long time (Husén, 1972, 1974). A key aim in this policy has been to attain high overall performance while at the same time evening out disparities in learning outcomes. Especially in Finland this aim seems to have been relatively well achieved (Lie & Linnakylä, 2004; Sarjala, 2008). A small country, so the reasoning goes, cannot afford to exclude anyone from high-quality education. Therefore, major efforts have been made to provide all students, population groups, and regions of the country with equal opportunities to be successful in education (Tuovinen, 2008).

These efforts have shown to be highly successful. This can be inferred, for example, from the findings of PISA studies, which show that in Finland the gap between high and low performers has been comparatively narrow (OECD, 2001, 2004, 2007). In reading literacy, for instance, Finland's standard deviation in PISA 2000 was the second smallest and in PISA 2003 and 2006 the smallest among all OECD countries. Moreover, in Finland the number of low performers, those reading at or below the PISA proficiency Level 1 (7% in PISA 2000, 6% in PISA 2003, and 5% in PISA 2006), is significantly smaller than in the OECD countries on average (18% in PISA 2000, 19% in PISA 2003, and 20% in PISA 2006) (Figure 9.1).

More or less similar results have also been shown for mathematical and scientific literacy. For mathematical literacy, Finland's standard deviation has consistently been the smallest when compared to the other OECD countries. For scientific literacy, Finland had the third smallest standard deviation in PISA 2000, the second smallest in PISA 2003, and the third smallest in PISA 2006.

As a matter of fact, many of the lowest-scoring students in Finland perform better than their fellow students in other OECD countries. On the other hand, the difference between Finnish and OECD top performers appears to be much less pronounced. This can be observed, for instance, when the reading score distributions of Finnish, Swedish, Norwegian, New Zealandian, and German students are compared with the OECD average

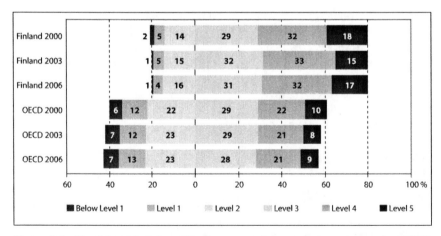

Figure 9.1   Finnish students' reading literacy performance compared to the OECD countries on average in PISA 2000, 2003, and 2006 (OECD, 2001, 2004, 2007).

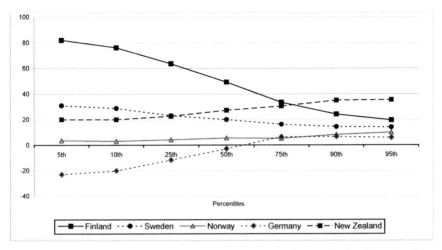

Figure 9.2   Finnish, Swedish, Norwegian, German, and New Zealandian distributions compared on the reading literacy percentile scale against the OECD average in PISA 2003 (OECD, 2004).

distribution on a percentile scale (Figure 9.2). Figure 9.2 shows that in PISA 2003, New Zealand's highest-achieving students outperformed their peers in Finland. However, the performance level of low-achieving New Zealanders was below that of their Finnish counterparts (OECD, 2004).

In PISA 2006, when scientific literacy was the focus of research, Finland fared even better in this respect. Cross-country comparisons between the lowest performers in scientific literacy showed that the differences were substantial. In addition, unlike during the previous PISA rounds, when the best performers (95th percentile) were compared, Finnish students performed highest. However, for these top performers, the difference with the other countries was much smaller than for the low performers (Figure 9.3).

The positive impact of the Finnish strategy of supporting students from disadvantaged backgrounds can be inferred from the results of PISA 2000, 2003, and 2006, which reveal that the impact of parents' PISA socioeconomic status on student performance is relatively low in Finland as compared to the other OECD countries (OECD, 2000, 2004, 2007).

In Finland, differences between schools have likewise been among the smallest in the OECD countries (Malin, 2005) and even the weakest-performing schools have achieved the OECD average scores in reading, mathematics, and science (OECD, 2001, 2004, 2007; Välijärvi et al., 2007, p. 34). Small between-school variation is a characteristic of all the Nordic countries, and of Finland in particular (Malin, 2005; Välijärvi & Malin, 2002). On the other hand, in countries where students are channeled into different kinds of schools, streams, or tracks at an early

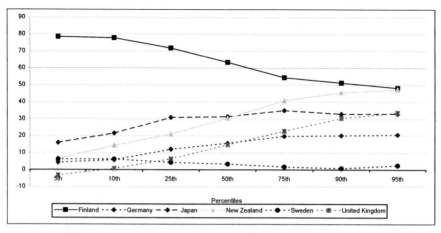

Figure 9.3   Finnish, German, Japanese, New Zealandian, Swedish, and English distributions compared on the science literacy percentile scale against the OECD average in PISA 2006 (OECD, 2007).

age, the variation tends to be more pronounced. This is quite significant because the results of PISA indicate that small between-school variation is one of the key factors associated with high performance. These results are most encouraging for Finland, where differences proved small also between different regions and between urban and rural schools (Välijärvi & Linnakylä, 2002).

Another characteristic of the Finnish education system is that there is very little or no connection between a school's social status and the average performance of its students (OECD, 2004, 2007; Välijärvi & Linnakylä, 2002). In Finland, then, it seems to make little difference where a student lives, whether in the far north, on the rural eastern boarder, or in the Helsinki capital area, or which school he or she attends. Even though school curricula may vary, the opportunities to acquire key skills are virtually the same all over the country. This may be related to the fact that in Finland, socioeconomic differences between geographic areas are relatively small. Since there is no tracking or streaming in basic education, students usually go to the nearest school. Also, Finnish universities are spread evenly across the country, which ensures that academically educated, highly skilled teachers are available in all parts of the country.

Even though between-school variation at Finnish schools is small, there are differences between students within the schools. The most prominent among these are differences between the genders, especially those found with regard to reading literacy. Among the OECD countries, Finland had the largest gender gap in reading literacy in PISA 2000. In PISA 2003, the gap was the fourth largest, and in PISA 2006, it was the second largest (OECD, 2001, 2004, 2007). Moreover, in comparison with previous international reading literacy assessments, the gender gap seems to have widened not only in Finland but also in the other Nordic and OECD countries (Linnakylä & Malin, 2003; Roe & Taube, 2003).

Another factor that appears to be associated with within-school differences between students is immigrant background, which seems to increase the risk of low achievement. More specifically, this risk tends to be more pronounced for students whose parents come from another country than for those students having one or two parents who are native citizens (Linnakylä, Malin, & Taube, 2004, 2006). Immigrant background is not a homogeneous variable in this respect. Rather, it encompasses a wide variety of native countries, mother tongues, and cultures. Students coming from Estonia or those whose families are Finnish- or Swedish-speaking "returners" from Sweden experience fewer difficulties than those coming from Russia or African countries.

STUDENTS' ATTITUDES TOWARD READING AND MATHEMATICS

In Finland, student performance is exceptionally strongly correlated with student attitudes, interests, and activities (see Figure 9.4). It would even appear that the most effective way to improve performance is to foster Finnish boys' engagement and interest in reading and Finnish girls' enjoyment and self-concept of mathematics. This implies that interest, engagement, enjoyment, and self-concept should be seen as learning outcomes as such. The challenge for the future, then, is how to construct learning environments and pedagogical practices that fully contribute to the development of students' affective domains.

In PISA 2000, Finnish students were the most engaged readers, as measured by their positive attitudes toward reading, their frequency of reading, and the diversity of their reading materials (OECD, 2002; Figure 9.4). For example, in Finland 41% of students reported that reading was one of their favorite hobbies, and 78% said that they spent at least some time each day reading for their own enjoyment. In Finland the percentage of students not reading at all for enjoyment was 22%, whereas in Sweden and Germany the corresponding percentages were 36% and 42%, respectively. Finnish students were also the most active readers of newspapers, and they reported borrowing books from the library more frequently than their peers in any other OECD country.

However, compared to Finnish girls, Finnish boys were far less engaged readers (Figure 9.5). They were also clearly overrepresented among the low achievers. Fostering boys' interest and engagement in reading thus seems to pose a particular challenge to Finnish literacy education. Responding to this challenge was one of the major objectives of the project "Reading Finland," implemented by the Finnish National Board of

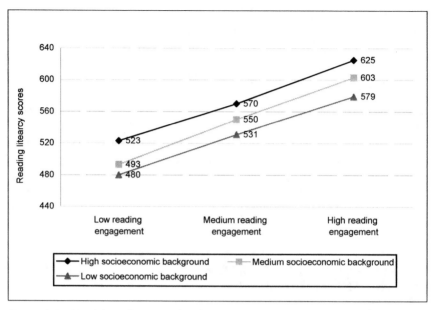

Figure 9.4   Finnish students' reading literacy performance by socioeconomic background and by reading engagement in PISA 2000 (OECD, 2001).

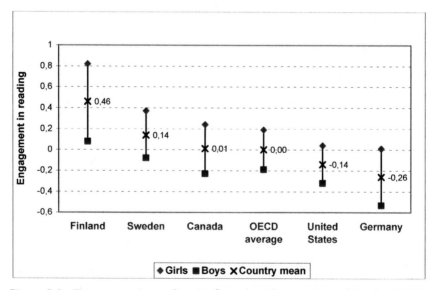

Figure 9.5   Engagement in reading in five selected countries and in the OECD on average in PISA 2000: Country means and differences between girls and boys (OECD, 2002).

Education in 2001–2004 (Sinko, 2007). Despite this and other efforts (Linnakylä & Malin, 2003; Merisuo-Storm, 2003; Murto, 2003), the gender gap in both reading engagement and performance is still inequitably large in Finland.

Interestingly, although Finnish students performed well for scientific and mathematical literacy, their attitudes toward mathematics were by and large more negative than those of their peers in the 40 countries participating in PISA 2003 on average (Törnroos & Kupari, 2005). On the index of interest in and enjoyment of mathematics, Finnish students were ranked 37th out of 40 countries. For example, in Finland only one student in four agreed with the statement "I do mathematics because I enjoy it"; the average was 38%. However, Finnish students' self-concept in mathematics was only slightly lower that their peers' in the other participating countries. For example, 40% of Finnish students agreed with the statement "I'm just not good in mathematics," the corresponding OECD average being 42%.

Also Finnish students' self-efficacy in mathematics was relatively low as compared to their peers in other countries. Self-efficacy was measured by presenting examples of different types of mathematical problems to students. They were asked how certain they would be of their success in solving these problems in real-life situations. The Finnish students only ranked 31st (see Figure 9.6). This is somewhat surprising, considering Finnish students' excellent performance in mathematical literacy.

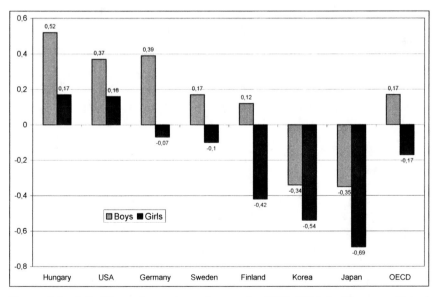

Figure 9.6 Self-efficacy in mathematics on the 2003 PISA in Hungary, United States, Germany, Sweden, Finland, Korea, and Japan (OECD, 2004).

As opposed to the other attitudinal factors, Finnish students' anxiety for learning mathematics was relatively low. In the international comparison, Finland's percentage was the fourth lowest. For example, only 7% of Finnish students agreed with the statement "I get very tense when I have to do mathematics homework." In Japan, where the value for all affective indicators was the lowest, the corresponding figure was 52%, while the OECD average was 29%.

In Finland, gender differences in attitudes toward mathematics were exceptionally large (see Figure 9.6), boys' attitudes being clearly more positive. This difference applied to all attitudinal indicators in PISA 2003 (OECD, 2004). However, unlike reading literacy, for mathematics this gender difference is not reflected in performance. This is somewhat surprising, because overall there appears to be, in Finland in particular, a fairly strong connection between student attitudes, interests, and motivation toward mathematics, on the one hand, and their mathematics performance, on the other. Somehow Finnish girls manage to compensate for their weaker attitudinal and motivational basis with regard to learning mathematics, whereas for the boys this compensation does not seem to work to a similar extent with regard to reading literacy.

In general, when looking at mathematical literacy in PISA 2003, the most powerful factor explaining the Finnish results is students' self-concept regarding mathematics. It accounts for 33% of the variance in correlation analyses (11% in the OECD countries). Similarly, 27% of the variance is explained by self-efficacy in mathematics (23% in the OECD), 20% by anxiety for mathematics (13%), and 11% by interest in and enjoyment of mathematics (2%). In contrast, socioeconomic background (7% in Finland; 12% in the OECD) and the cultural status at home (4% in Finland; 6% in the OECD) have a weaker impact.

A policy measure that has undoubtedly contributed to Finland's high performance in mathematical and scientific literacy is the national LUMA program. The program was implemented in 1996–2003 and aimed at developing knowledge and skills in mathematics and science at all levels of schooling (LUMA is an acronym for the Finnish *LUon-nontieteet* ja *MAtematiikka*, "science and mathematics"). The way to success, it was claimed, was to develop the teaching of mathematics and science in such a way that it would increase students' interest in studying these subjects.

The specific aims of the program included finding ways to support the learning of mathematics and science of the weakest and the most gifted students; increasing girls' interest and achievements in mathematics and science; diversifying teaching arrangements and methods so that more emphasis would be put on observation and experimenting and on the application of knowledge when solving problems; promoting cooperation between teachers of mathematics and science at different school levels; and promoting cooperation between mathematics and science teachers, and teachers of subjects applying mathematics and science. To reach these goals, teachers were offered in-service training both in mathematics and science and in didactics. Support was also provided by means of publications and via the Internet.

The following results of the program have been listed: updating schools' computer hardware and software and their science laboratory equipment and materials; increasing the quantity of experimental activities in teaching; setting up mathematics- and science-oriented classes and streams based on interest; developing teacher education, both when it comes to the command of mathematics and science and of pedagogical skills; promoting cooperation between teachers both within and outside schools; and adding to the number of students taking advanced courses in mathematics and to the number of girls taking advanced courses in physics. Even though it is not possible to establish a direct, causal link between the implementation of this particular program and Finnish students' performance for mathematics and science, it seems quite evident that thanks to the program, the quality of Finnish mathematics and science instruction has improved, which, in turn, is a prerequisite for better student performance for mathematics and science. The strong focus of the program on real-life experiments, problem solving, and the application of mathematical and scientific knowledge may also have contributed to Finland's success in the PISA study.

THE COMPREHENSIVE SCHOOL AS A WAY OF PROMOTING EQUITY

The high quality and comparatively high equity of Finnish basic education is firmly grounded in a publicly funded, nonselective comprehensive basic education system that involves no tracking or streaming. Until the 1960s, Finland had a traditional German-type tracked system. In this two-track system, students at the end of grade 4 at primary (elementary) school chose to continue either in an academic stream, consisting of eight further grades, leading to an matriculation examination and right to university entrance or in a civic stream of three to five grades, which was supposed to lead to entrance in the labor market or vocational schools. With the educational reform of the 1970s, the two-track system was replaced with a comprehensive basic education system.

Especially at the early stages of comprehensive school, the notion of equity was made operational by stimulating equal access to education. Accordingly, in Finland the school network covers the whole country: For 5.3 million inhabitants (the age cohort in recent years being 56,000–59,000), there are 3,100 comprehensive schools, more than 400 (academic) upper secondary schools, and a great number of vocational and adult education institutes.

Children generally start school in the year they become 7 years old. Before comprehensive school, children may participate in 1-year preschool education. This is not compulsory, but nowadays 98% of children take part in the program. Finland has nine years of compulsory schooling. Usually, for the first six years of comprehensive school (grades 1 to 6) children are taught by a class teacher, during the last 3 years (grades 7 to 9) by specialized subject teachers. Nowadays subject teachers may obtain the qualification to teach also in grades 1 through 6, but this presupposes about an additional 6 months of pedagogical training. Correspondingly, class teachers can obtain subject teacher's qualification in a specific subject by taking and additional training of approximately 6 months for that subject. All comprehensive school pupils and students are offered the same core subjects and work with similar syllabuses for these subjects. However, about 10% of the classroom hours are reserved for optional studies that are freely chosen by the pupil or student and his or her parents.

The regular education system is financed almost entirely by public funds. Nearly all educational institutions are owned by municipalities (primary- and secondary-level institutions and polytechnics) or the state (universities). Only 1.5 % of the primary and lower secondary school pupils go to private schools. The funding of the private sector is almost completely dependent on public funding (*Koulutuksen määrälliset indikaattorit*, 2008, pp. 28, 54). Comprehensive education leading to a qualification has traditionally been free of charge for students. Free education also covers instruction at the level of higher education. The responsibility for financing education is transferred via the tax system. Students at the primary and lower secondary level receive free tuition, free instructional materials, warm school meals, health and dental care, and, if necessary, transport and accommodation (Andere, 2008.)

The main educational goals and subject-specific objectives are outlined in the national curriculum. However, the national curriculum is only a general framework which has to be specified by local authorities and at each individual school; these specifications are based upon principles and cross-curricular themes that reflect the local culture, the interests of the students, and the pedagogical project of the school. School curricula, in turn, are based upon discussions between the principal, teachers, parents, and students, and these further specify the national goals, the contents of the curriculum, instructional practices, and assessment methods. However, at the level of the individual classroom, specific pedagogical objectives, subject matter content, and classroom practices are determined by the teacher, who is a trusted pedagogical professional, acquainted not only with the general policy framework and the school curriculum but also with a variety of teaching procedures, enabling him or her to fine-tune pedagogical interventions to individual students' interests and potential.

A CULTURE OF TRUST

It is not an overstatement to say that the quality of the Finnish education system is largely based on trust. When the comprehensive education system was introduced and implemented in Finland in the 1970s, the Finnish education system was highly centralized. However, in the 1980s a gradual shift toward trusting schools and teachers began and was fully carried through in the early 1990s. As a result, central control was abolished and municipalities and schools received more or less full autonomy to develop school curricula, set priorities in terms of pedagogical values and principles that the schools were supposed to respect, make designs for powerful learning environments, choose materials, and make decisions about instructional and assessment methods (Laukkanen, 1995). Nowadays schools also have a wide autonomy to take budgetary decisions, even though the frameworks for schools' financial policy are outlined by the municipality. This culture of trust involves that the system, curriculum, and pedagogy are implemented and adjusted together with schools, even though the main principles behind national policy is outlined by the Ministry of Education (Välijärvi, 2007). This culture starts from the presumption that teachers, principals, parents, and their communities know best how to provide their children and youth with the best possible education. They are the ones who know the students and who have been actively involved in school development for a long time (Aho, Pitkänen, & Sahlberg, 2006).

This means that Finland has not followed the Anglo-Saxon accountability movement in basic education, which holds schools and teachers accountable for learning outcomes. As a consequence, there are no inspection systems, centrally organized examinations, or nationwide tests in Finnish basic education, even though the quality and development of the education system has been evaluated by means of sample-based assessments.

At the same time, however, the need for other types of national and local system evaluation has increased. According to the Education Act issued in 1999, the national and municipality level evaluation of education is compulsory and concerns all areas of education. The evaluation system seeks to ensure that the objectives set in the legislation are achieved and to support the development of education as well as to improve opportunities to learn. Although the emphasis in the evaluation is on outcomes, the system does not prescribe that any allocation of funds to schools should be based upon the results they have achieved. Neither does it involve any ranking of individual schools.

The principles and targets of the national evaluation of education are determined by the Ministry of Education. The main guidelines behind the implementation of the national evaluation, together with the methodology of data collection, are negotiated in advance with the local administration and other stakeholders. The Ministry also prepares, in cooperation with the stakeholders, an evaluation program, specifying its main focus of attention well in advance.

TOWARD GREATER SCHOOL AUTONOMY

The decentralization of administration has increased the autonomy of schools. As a consequence, schools have become differentiated, offering students a substantially more elaborate range of options. All this has increased the need for the municipal educational administration and the schools themselves to design adequate evaluation programs. The main purpose of the Finnish model of evaluation is to develop and support schools, not to control them. Specific attention has been paid to the interaction between bottom-up and top-down evaluation. Taking particular schools and their local contexts into consideration is of crucial importance. On the other hand, at the national level it is equally important to monitor development with regard to between-school differences in educational outcomes, resources, the quality of teaching staff, among others, so as to be able to ensure equal educational opportunities.

Safeguarding and monitoring educational quality becomes especially important when schools are small and located in remote areas. Finnish education policy has sought to give special support to schools that are located in economically disadvantaged regions, where the environment itself can cater for less educational support. Finns have never been enthusiastic about the idea of schools competing with each other, although parents can now freely choose which school their child will attend.

It has been strongly argued, by teachers and researchers in particular, that there are wide differences in schools' competitive capacity. Therefore, it is not fair to apply the same criteria to all schools. Yet, each school can do excellent work with its students and within the boundaries of its own context. This seems to pay off: The PISA results showed that between-school differences in Finland were among the smallest in PISA countries. As a result of the strong degree of school autonomy, Finnish schools may have greatly differing profiles and curricula. Therefore, it is not reasonable to demand from each school that they use the same criteria for evaluation and focus their evaluation on the same aspects of the educational program. Nation-wide evaluation will therefore focus on general features, such as the accessibility of education or optional subject areas, the financial accountability of schools, and the differences between schools.

At the school level, the evaluation targets will often include the achievement of objectives mentioned in the school curriculum, the completion of pedagogic and curricular reforms, co-operation between the school and homes, use of resources, students' self-esteem, or students' and teachers' well-being. However, the exact focus and criteria of that area strongly depends on the choices made within the school. School-based evaluations typically rely on various questionnaires and discussions, but also school portfolios are being used. When school portfolios are placed on the Internet, this stimulates communication about the schools' performance with other interested parties, from parents to educational administration (Kankaanranta, 2002).

The main purpose of municipal and school-based evaluations is to improve the way schools function. They can lead to changes with regard to the curriculum, methodological development, intensified co-operation, and so forth. At the municipal level, evaluation may also result in the allocation of extra resources and special support being provided to some schools. On the other hand, no sanctions are imposed on schools on the basis of the evaluations. Rather, the main policy has been to offer more support to schools that are facing more problems, both financially and in terms of human resources.

Interestingly, in international comparisons, countries with greater degrees of school and teacher autonomy attain higher average levels of student performance than countries with a lower level of autonomy. A high level of school and teacher autonomy may thus be claimed to contribute in significant ways to Finland's outstanding performance in PISA. In Finland content-based prescriptions of what a teacher should teach have been replaced with a focused set of educational goals that communicate what the students should be able to do, leaving it up to the schools to design an appropriate learning environment and establish the educational content that would best help the students to reach these goals. A key principle is to link high expectations with support for schools in ways that encourage and enable teachers and principals to assume responsibility for learning outcomes for each and every student (Schleicher, 2006).

HETEROGENEOUS GROUPING AND STUDENT SUPPORT SYSTEMS

The philosophy of the comprehensive school emphasizes that each student should have equal opportunities to learn. In practice this means that all students, including students with learning problems and the most talented students, work together in heterogeneous groups. By the age 16, practically all students (99.7%) have completed comprehensive school, enabling access to further studies at the secondary level. Around 98% of students finish comprehensive school in 9 years. Nowadays, only 1.5% of students are studying at special schools for disabled children (*Framework curriculum for the comprehensive school*, 1994, 2004; *Koulutuksen määrälliset indikaattorit*, 2008).

Heterogeneous grouping, as was shown by studies conducted in the 1970s and 1980s, when the comprehensive school system was still under construction, and as has been confirmed more recently by PISA data, appears to be of the greatest benefit to the weakest students. In heterogeneous groups, low-performing students have the opportunity to see how other students approach, explore, question, and interpret information and why the perspectives and understanding of these students may differ from those of their own. In contrast, the performance of the best students seems to remain at virtually the same level irrespective of how the groups are formed (Välijärvi et al., 2007, pp. 40–41; OECD, 2007).

For educational systems that aim to maintain the heterogeneity of student groups, the size of the groups becomes a critical issue. In lower secondary schools, the average group size in core subjects (mathematics, science, mother tongue, foreign languages) is small (typically 18–20 students). At primary schools, it is slightly bigger (20–22 pupils), and in academic upper secondary schools considerably bigger (*Koulutuksen arviointisuunnitelma,* 2008; OECD, 2007).

Another way to take care of the needs of individual students in heterogeneous groups is special needs education, which is organized for students with learning and adaptation difficulties. Special needs education is usually closely integrated into mainstream teaching, which by its nature is inclusive. At the primary level, special needs education mostly focuses on reading and writing and mathematics. At the lower secondary level, a student with problems in a particular subject or subjects typically has the opportunity to study once or twice a week in a small group of two to five students or even individually with a special teacher. Alternatively, the special teacher may attend regular classes, working together with the class teacher. A student's right to special needs education is written down in the Finnish school laws. In basic education, about 20% of students receive part-time special needs education during their 9 years of schooling (Linnakylä, 2004b; *Koulutuksen määrälliset indikaattorit,* 2008).

Every student also has a right to student counseling. Schools are to provide students with guidance in study skills, choice of options (e.g., elective courses), and the planning of post-compulsory studies. The purpose of counseling is to enhance students' skills of learning to learn and to ensure that all young people leaving school are (a) aware of the higher and further education options that are open to them, (b) understand what working in the adult world entails, and (c) have a clear plan for their future. During the first six years of basic education, guidance is integrated into regular instruction, but in upper grades special counselors are available for the students. Student counselors are usually subject teachers who have attended specific training courses in guidance and counseling. Therefore, they are well acquainted with the work of the teacher and are regular members of the school personnel.

On the whole, the students' well-being is supported by "student welfare groups," made up of the principal, the counselors, the school health nurses, the psychologists, and the doctors, all working together (Välijärvi, 2007). Because education is free of charge also at higher levels, Finnish students' plans for further studies can be based on their personal potential and goals and not on their parents' wealth.

TEACHERS AS PEDAGOGICAL EXPERTS

In Finland we believe that academically educated teachers are the greatest experts and the most skillful professionals who are able to design their teaching methodologies in daily classroom practice, within the fairly loose boundaries of the national curricula. We also trust that teachers do their best in the classroom to maximally promote learning. This may sound idealistic, but in view of the results of recent international studies, the teachers have deserved this trust. It is also important to keep in mind that in terms of educational investment, Finland has clearly made a choice that is different from the choices of most other European countries. Instead of focusing on external evaluation, Finland has invested heavily in teacher education.

It seems that these investments have yielded good results and kept up the high esteem and popularity of the profession. All teachers are educated at universities, where they complete a master's degree. Although the salaries of Finnish teachers are only average from an international perspective (OECD, 2008), young people find the teacher's profession an attractive option. Thus, the students enrolling in teacher education usually make up an outstanding, highly motivated, and selected group. For instance, in classroom teacher programs, only about 15% of the candidates are admitted (Luukkainen, 2000). Teacher education attracts multitalented students who are good not only at academic subjects but also at arts, music, and physical education. However, in secondary education, where the teachers are mostly subject teachers, the situation is not as good: For example, in mathematics, science, and English, there now is a growing shortage of teachers.

The new decree of teacher education was issued in 1978 and led to the creation of degree programs for class teachers, comprehensive and upper secondary school subject teachers, as well as programs for special needs teachers and student counselors, which may be characterized as postgraduate studies. In class teacher education (300 credits), the emphasis is on the theoretical and methodological contents of educational science and the subjects taught at school and their practical applications. The main subject is educational science, which also includes teacher's pedagogical studies. During the studies, the trainees familiarize themselves with, among others, the following aspects of education: holistic human development; interaction between the teacher and the learner; and scientific theories about the educational, learning, and development process and their applications to practical educational work. The latter component enables teachers to create and design their own meaningful subjective theories and, when functioning as teachers, to promote the development of each learner's personality and the achievement of the school objectives (Niemi, 2002).

Subject teacher education includes studies in one or two teaching subjects and teacher pedagogical studies as part of a master's degree program. A "teaching subject" stands for a school subject included in the curriculum of basic education, upper secondary school, or some other educational institution. "Studies in a teaching subject" refer to studies that promote the mastery of the subject to the degree that is required for the teaching profession. Teaching subject studies consists of advanced studies in one subject and subject studies in a possible second subject. The education is divided into two tracks: The faculties of education are responsible for some part of the program, while another part of the program is carried out in a co-operation between teacher education departments and different subject departments. Students apply directly for subject teacher education (such as education for subject teachers in mathematics, physics and chemistry, or in history, religion, etc.). In addition, it is possible to graduate as a subject teacher by following teacher pedagogical studies separately after obtaining a university degree.

In Finnish culture, teachers are trusted as academic professionals. Therefore, Finnish teachers enjoy a substantial degree of pedagogical autonomy in the classroom. Compared to other OECD countries, Finnish teachers possess a relatively high degree of decision-making power in matters pertaining to the school curriculum and school management. For instance, they have an almost exclusive responsibility for the choice of teaching and assessment methods and of textbooks. They also have more authority with regard to course contents and availability within the school and school-based budget allocations, as compared to their colleagues in most other OECD countries (Jakku-Sihvonen & Niemi, 2006; OECD, 2002).

SUPPORTIVE STANDARDS

To help teachers doing their work, subject-specific standards for good learning have been set at a national level. The purpose of these standards is, above all, to help teachers in planning their work. The standards are not binding in the sense that teachers will be controlled or evaluated with regard to how well they live up to the standards. Rather, they are a supportive aid that teachers and schools may use at their own discretion. Often the standards have also been phrased in such a way that an assessment using specific measures or indicators would not even be possible. Teachers' academic education prepares them to apply the standards in a creative way and adjust them to their own teaching conditions. In addition, the strong coherence of the teacher education programs provided by different universities guarantees that teachers' conceptions about good learning and teaching will show a high degree of uniformity even without any set standards;

in the latter case, however, textbooks would probably serve as the guiding standard for many teachers.

For the time being, the standards only describe learning output. They are expected to provide teachers and students with an outlook on what is considered sufficient mastery of different subjects at the end of compulsory education. However, in the autumn of 2007, the Minister of Education set up an expert group to define standards for good teaching. The work is still under way, but it is evident that the standards will define requirements for schools as learning environments as well as describing good practices of learning at school. Again, these will not be used as criteria for evaluating the quality of teachers' work but rather should be interpreted as descriptions of educational practices that are most likely to yield good results. The standards will take the form of recommendations for municipalities and schools, describing good practices of how to design, for example, school leadership, financial policy, and evaluation programs or how to guarantee that the school curriculum, as well as student guidance and counseling, individualized teaching, involvement of students in decision making, students' well-being and cooperation with parents, are all of high quality.

In the Finnish pedagogical culture, it is not customary for teachers to strictly adhere to one instructional method only but rather to combine various pedagogical methods in order to adjust to the needs of individual students. Teachers are encouraged and supported to expand their pedagogical repertoire, to individualize their instruction and pedagogical practices, and to construct innovative approaches to timetabling. All this has fed a professional ethos that accepts and assumes that every child comes to school with different skills, attitudes, and aspirations and that their needs and potential have to be developed by applying diverse instructional strategies (Linnakylä, 2004b; Schleicher, 2006).

Finnish teachers are also considered experts when it comes to student assessment, which is usually based on students' class and homework, individual and group projects, teacher-made exams, and portfolios (OECD, 2001). Students in basic education are not assessed by national tests or examinations at the end of, or during, the school years. Rather, Finland's assessment culture can be characterized as "soft" or formative, because assessment is an ongoing part of daily school work aiming to support rather than to control students' learning. Although there are national guidelines for grading student performance, these are no strict standards. Students' efforts, interests, and activities are always taken into account. In fact, in Finland the concept "standard" has negative connotations. We do not want to standardize learning or teaching into specific cognitive tasks and skills. Rather, we want to value the capabilities, interests, and potential of individual students and regard diversity of outcomes as desirable. In knowledge-intensive societies, we need creativity, initiative, and innovation rather than ability to study for tests and examinations (Linnakylä, 2004a).

This does not mean that Finnish schools' or teachers' expectations are low. Rather, as revealed, for example, by a comparative study of the Nordic countries, Finnish teachers tend to foster high expectations for their students' literacy learning (Sommer, Lau, & Mejding, 1996). A similar finding was obtained in an international substudy of the IEA Reading Literacy Study carried out in 1991 on 11 countries, where Finnish and Swedish teachers were found to have extremely high expectations for their students' reading literacy skills. Students in the countries with the highest expectations also performed highest in the reading literacy assessment (Linnakylä, 1996).

FUTURE CHALLENGES

Even though Finnish students, generally speaking, seem to fare very well academically, there is still room for improvement. In all PISA studies conducted so far, about 20% of Finnish students have been found to have difficulties in coping with the high reading literacy demands of today's knowledge society (at or below Level 2). In mathematics the corresponding figure was 22%, and in science 18%. According to international standards these proportions are small, but from the point of view of individual students they are far too high. Often the same students are found experiencing difficulties in all three domains. Out of the group of Finnish students who were below the 5th percentile in mathematics in 2003, 65% were also below the 5th percentile in science and 56% in reading literacy. These students also tend to show low interest and engagement in their studies, tend to have low self-concepts, and low confidence in their learning compared to Finnish students on average, which, in turn, reduces their willingness to apply for further and higher studies and increases the risk that they will interrupt their studies, especially in vocational education, thereby also adding to their risk of social marginalization. Finnish schools will have to continue struggling to decrease the proportion of these students at risk.

The students at risk in any of the three domains need cognitive, affective, and social support. Such triple support can be enhanced by fostering students' curiosity, interest, and desire to learn, through catering for enjoyable real-world interaction, authentic and exciting tasks at school, personal choice of materials and methods to learn, and collaborative interaction with peers. High-quality instruction that supports interest, autonomy, and engagement in learning often also supports the development of effective cognitive strategies (Guthrie & Davis, 2003; Guthrie & Wigfield, 2000; Guthrie et al., 2006).

In reading literacy education, more attention needs to be paid to improving students' reflective and critical reading competencies, especially when it comes to evaluating the effectiveness of reasoning in a text or to comparing and contrasting texts and to making evaluative inferences. Attention also needs to be paid to students' ability to analyze the content, structure, and style of texts and to judge the quality of the texts, taking into account their purpose and intended audience (Linnakylä & Sulkunen, 2005).

Another challenge facing Finnish reading literacy education and also the teaching of several other subjects has to do with the use of electronic media, which are becoming an increasingly important part of children's and adolescents' everyday life in Finland (Leino, Linnakylä, & Malin, 2004). Working and learning in electronic environments understandably necessitates new skills and strategies. For example, searching and using information on the Internet requires skimming and scanning through large amounts of information. In addition, this information may be presented not only in linear text form but also in the shape of graphics, audiovisual signs and symbols, music, and animations; moreover, it may appear in both authored and message-based environments. Therefore, electronic learning calls for a highly critical and ethical mind (Leu, 2002) and the ability to rapidly evaluate the credibility and validity of large amounts of information. Indeed, overcoming the "digital divide" is not only a matter of achieving online access; it also involves enhancing people's ability to compare and contrast, integrate, evaluate, and communicate information (Warschauer, 1999).

Still another major challenge facing reading literacy education is the wide performance gap between boys and girls, brought about by, among other things, gender differences in values, goals, and out-of-school activities. To reduce the gap, innovations seeking to stimulate boys' interest and engagement in literary culture and helping them to find enjoyment in reading are badly needed. To this end, fuller advantage should be taken of various types of real-life texts and ICT-mediated literacy environments, for example. However, the gender gap also seems to be associated with differences in students' self-confidence and self-efficacy in reading. An intriguing question calling for further exploration, then, is why this difference is only vaguely related to students' mathematics performance, whereas for reading literacy the gender gap in performance appears to be widening.

Also in mathematics, the most demanding challenges are related to gender. Even though Finnish girls' cognitive proficiency in mathematics is only slightly lower than that of Finnish boys, their self-efficacy, self-concept, and interest in mathematics are far below those of boys. This gender gap in attitudes toward mathematics, which is one of the biggest among PISA countries, may have serious consequences for the later phases of schooling and working life. Only a few girls now take advanced courses in mathematics, physics, and chemistry when they move to upper secondary school. Later on, when students apply for higher education, there are only a few females who are eligible or motivated for studies in mathematics, technology, and hard natural sciences. All this may solidify traditional gender structures and stereotypes in working life. If we want to change these attitudes, we will have to focus our interest and research endeavors more on the lowest grades of comprehensive school. Attitudes toward mathematics seem to diverge strongly in grades 1 to 4; trying to influencing them at a later stage may prove to be extremely difficult. In a similar vein, parents' impact on student attitudes may be expected to be most powerful during the first school years.

"Gifted education pedagogy" has traditionally received scant attention in Finland, and it has often been mistaken for an alternative to the concern shown for the least-successful students. Yet, it seems possible to strengthen the development of students with widely differing levels of knowledge and skills even in heterogeneous groups, if the teacher is proficient and has sufficient resources for within-group differentiation. The latter, however, appears to be jeopardized in today's Finnish educational system by the increase in the average group size, brought about by economic retrenchment. In addition, Finnish teachers have traditionally been more concerned about weak learners than gifted students. Therefore, more emphasis has to be placed in teacher education on the challenge to also take into account the needs of gifted students.

Culturally speaking, Finland is relatively homogeneous. Linguistically, however, Finland is a bilingual state with two official languages: Finnish (spoken by 94% of the inhabitants) and Swedish (6%). Both of these language groups are equally entitled to, and have equal resources for, education in their own language from preschool up to the university. Other minorities, however, are still relatively small in Finland. The Sami language is spoken in only a few municipalities in Lapland, where there are some Sami-speaking classes in the primary grades of basic education. Altogether, the proportion of immigrants in Finland is small. For example, in the PISA 2003 data, the proportion of nonnative students amounted to about 2% of the Finnish student population (the OECD average being 4.7%). The largest immigrant groups in Finland are Russians and Estonians (National Board of Education, 2006).

Despite the relative homogeneity of the Finnish population, the pursuit of equal opportunities to learn has been put to a severe test during the past decades due to the increasing number of immigrant students coming to Finland and the growing cultural heterogeneity. This presents a special challenge to literacy education, and PISA findings show that there remains still a lot of work to be done if we want to ensure that immigrant students have a truly equal opportunity to learn, ideally both in their own mother tongue and in the language of their new country. Without adequate and diverse literacy skills, it will be difficult for them to stay in touch with their relatives and friends in their native countries, and even harder to keep up in their new home country with the highly literate culture (Linnakylä et al., 2004, 2006). In facing this challenge, Finland has a lot to learn from other countries, particularly from their experiences in educating immigrant students to communicate and build contacts and networks with various cultures, in several languages, and using a variety of media and technological tools. To pursue equal opportunities for life, we want all children to acquire key competences, learn to live together, respect each other, and take care of the weak, different, and vulnerable.

THE CONSTANTLY CHANGING SCHOOL

There has been a fairly healthy balance between reforms that were introduced from outside the schools and school-internal, bottom-up innovations and practices when renewing the Finnish education system and Finnish school culture. As a rule, the development of Finnish comprehensive basic education after the 1970s has been underpinned by an exceptionally broad cultural and political consensus about the main guiding principles of national education policy. In Finnish culture, severe political conflicts and sudden changes in educational principles have been rare, even though the educational policy has been open to change (Välijärvi et al., 2007). Of course, there are always also those who, looking back to "the good old days," demand a return to stronger centralization and control, streaming, and even to the dual school system. However, thanks to the outstanding results gained by Finnish students in recent international assessments, attesting both to high quality and equity in Finnish basic education, these demands have become much weaker. With the world in a state of constant change, a return to the past does not seem desirable. Rather, the world—and together with it, its changes—are entering the school, so schools need to develop the courage to face those changes.

In all this, we should keep in mind that high educational outcomes never come about without long-span perseverance and sustained commitment from the students, teachers, and all those involved in education. With each student age group, the work has to be resumed. To guarantee high performance in the future, schools need to be better able to cope not only with societal changes but also with the changing needs of the students. As the emphasis on lifelong learning becomes increasingly stronger, the Finnish school system, in addition to catering for the development of key competences that are required by society, also needs to find ways to enhance children's and youngster's learning motivation, self-confidence, positive attitudes toward various school subjects, social skills, and overall well-being at school.

REFERENCES

Aho E., Pitkänen, K., & Sahlberg, P. (2006). *Policy development and reform principles of basic and secondary education in Finland since 1968.* Washington, DC: World Bank.

Andere, E. (2008). The *lending power of PISA. League tables and best practice in international education* (Monograph Series in Comparative Education and Development No. 6). Hong Kong: University of Hong Kong.

Elley, W. (Ed.). (1994). *The IEA Study of Reading Literacy: Achievement and instruction in thirty-two school systems.* The Hague: IEA.

Framework curriculum for the comprehensive school. (1994). Helsinki: National Board of Education.
Framework curriculum for the comprehensive school. (2004). Helsinki: National Board of Education.
Guthrie, J. T., & Davis, M. H. (2003). Motivating struggling readers in middle school through an engagement model of classroom practice. *Reading and Writing Quarterly, 19*, 59–85.
Guthrie, J. T., & Wigfield, A. (2000). Engagement and motivation in reading. In M. L. Kamil & P. B. Mosenthal (Eds.), *Handbook of reading research* (Vol. 3, pp. 403–422). Mahwah, NJ: Erlbaum.
Guthrie, J. T., Wigfield, A., Humenick, N. M., Perencevich, K. C., Taboada, A., & Barbosa, P. (2006). Influences of stimulating tasks on reading motivation and comprehension. *Journal of Educational Research, 99*, 232–245.
Husén, T. (1972). *Social background and educational career.* Paris: OECD.
Husén, T. (1974). *Learning society.* London: Methuen.
Jakku-Sihvonen, R., & Niemi, H. (Eds.). (2006). *Research-based teacher education in Finland. Reflections by Finnish teacher educators.* Turku: Finnish Educational Research Association.
Kankaanranta, M. (2002). *Developing digital portfolios for childhood education.* Jyväskylä: University of Jyväskylä, Institute for Educational Research.
Koulutuksen arviointisuunnitelma vuosille 2009–2011 [The plan for the national evaluation of education 2009–2011] (Publication No. 38:2008). (2008). Helsinki: Ministry of Education.
Koulutuksen määrälliset indikaattorit [Quantitative indicators for school education]. (2008). Helsinki: National Board of Education.
Kupari, P., Reinikainen, P., Nevanpää, T., & Törnroos, J. (2001). *Miten matematiikkaa ja luonnontieteitä osataan suomalaisessa peruskoulussa. Kolmas kansainvälinen matematiikka- ja luonnontiedetutkimus TIMSS 1999 Suomessa* [How do Finnish comprehensive school students perform in mathematics and science? The Third International Mathematics and Science Study (TIMSS 1999) in Finland]. Jyväskylä: University of Jyväskylä, Institute for Educational Research.
Laukkanen, R. (1995). The formation of evaluation policies in education in Finland. In Y. Yrjönsuuri (Ed.), *Evaluating education in Finland* (pp. 17–40). Helsinki: National Board of Education.
Leino, K., Linnakylä, P., & Malin A. (2004). Finnish students" multiliteracy profiles. *Scandinavian Journal of Educational Research, 48*(3), 251–270.
Leu, D. J. (2002). The new literacies: Research on reading instruction with the Internet. In A. F. Farstrup & S. J. Samuels (Eds.), *What research has to say about reading instruction* (pp. 310–336). Newark, DE: International Reading Association.
Lie, S., & Linnakylä, P. (2004). Nordic PISA 2000 in a sociocultural perspective. *Scandinavian Journal of Educational Research, 3*, 227–230.
Linnakylä, P. (1995). *Lukutaidolla maailmankartalle. Kansainvälinen lukutaitotutkimus Suomessa* [Global access through reading. The IEA Study of Reading Literacy in Finland]. Jyväskylä: University of Jyväskylä, Institute for Educational Research.
Linnakylä, P. (1996, March). *High expectations—High achievement on literacy.* Paper presented at the UNESCO conference, Philadelphia.
Linnakylä, P. (2004a). Educational "'standards"' in Finland: Opportunities and threats. In T. Fitzner (Ed.), *Bildungsstandards* [Educational standards] (pp. 43–53). Bad Boll: Evangelische Akademie.
Linnakylä, P. (2004b). Finland. In H. Döbert, E. Klieme, & W. Stroka (Eds.), *Conditions of school performance in seven countries. A quest for understanding the international variation of PISA results* (pp. 150–218). Munster: Waxmann.
Linnakylä, P. (2006). How can a country manage the impact of "'excellent"' cross-national research results? In K. N. Ross & I. J. Genevois (Eds.), *Cross-national*

studies of the quality of education. Planning their design and managing their impact (pp. 241–254). Paris: UNESCO IIEP.

Linnakylä, P., & Malin, A. (2003). How to reduce the gender gap in reading literacy. In S. Lie, P. Linnakylä, & A. Roe (Eds.), *Northern lights on PISA. Unity and diversity in the Nordic countries in PISA 2000* (pp. 21–38). Oslo: University of Oslo, Department of Teacher Education and School Development.

Linnakylä, P., Malin, A., Blomqvist, I., & Sulkunen, S. (2000). *Lukutaito työssä ja arjessa. Aikuisten kansainvälinen lukutaitotutkimus Suomessa* [Reading literacy at and beyond work. The International Adult Literacy Survey in Finland]. Jyväskylä: University of Jyväskylä, Institute for Educational Research.

Linnakylä, P., Malin, A., & Taube, K. (2004). Factors behind low reading literacy achievement. *Scandinavian Journal of Educational Research, 48*(3), 231–250.

Linnakylä, P., Malin A., & Taube, K. (2006). What lies behind low reading literacy performance? A comparative analysis of the Finnish and Swedish students. In J. Mejding & A. Roe (Eds.), *Northern lights on PISA 2003—A reflection from the Nordic countries* (pp. 143–158). Copenhagen: Nordic Council of Ministers.

Linnakylä, P., & Sulkunen, S. (2005). Suomalaisnuorten lukutaito ja -harrastus [Finnish students' reading literacy performance and reading engagement]. In P. Kupari & J. Välijärvi (Eds.), *Osaaminen kestävällä pohjalla. PISA 2003 Suomessa* [Knowledge and skills on a solid basis. PISA 2003 in Finland] (pp. 37–64). Jyväskylä: University of Jyväskylä, Institute for Educational Research.

Luukkainen, O. (2000). *Teachers in 2010. Final report.* Anticipatory project to investigate teachers' initial and continuing training needs (OPEPRO Rep. No. 15). Helsinki: National Board of Education.

Malin, A. (2005). *School differences and inequities in educational outcomes. PISA 2000 results of reading literacy in Finland* (Research Rep. No. 15). Jyväskylä: University of Jyväskylä, Institute for Educational Research.

Martin, M., Mullis, I., Gonzalez, E., Gregory, K., Smith, T., Chrostowski, S., et al. (2000). *TIMSS 1999 International science report. Findings from IEA's repeat of the Third International Mathematics and Science Study at the eighth grade.* Boston: Boston College, Lynch School of Education, International Study Center.

Merisuo-Storm, T. (2003). Pojatkin voivat innostua lukemisesta ja kirjoittamisesta [Even boys can become enthusiastic readers and writers]. *Virke 4,* 36–39.

Mullis, I., Martin, M., Gonzalez, E., Gregory, K., Garden, R., O'Connor, K., et al. (2000). *TIMSS 1999 International mathematics report. Findings from IEA's repeat of the Third International Mathematics and Science Study at the eighth grade.* Boston: Boston College, Lynch School of Education, International Study Center.

Murto, M. (2003). Voi pojat [Oh boy]! *Virke 4,* 6–9.

National Board of Education. (2006). *Education in Finland.* Helsinki: Author.

Niemi, H. (2002). Active learning—A cultural change needed in teacher education and school. *Teaching and Teacher Education, 18,* 763–780.

OECD. (2000). *Literacy in the information age. Final report of the International Adult Literacy Survey.* Paris: Author.

OECD. (2001). *Knowledge and skills for life. First results from PISA 2000.* Paris: Author.

OECD. (2002). *Reading for change. Performance and engagement across countries. Results from PISA 2000.* Paris: Author.

OECD. (2004). *Learning for tomorrow's world. First results from PISA 2003.* Paris: Author.

OECD. (2007). PISA 2006. *Science competencies for tomorrow's world. Vol. 1: Analysis.* Paris: Author.

OECD (2008). *Education at a glance 2008: OECD indicators.* Paris: Author.

Roe, A., & Taube, K. (2003). Reading achievement and gender differences. In S. Lie, P. Linnakylä, & A. Roe (Eds.), *Northern lights on PISA* (pp. 21–38). Oslo: University of Oslo.

Sarjala, J. (2008). Järki hyvä herätetty [The comprehensive school and political discourse]. Helsinki: Kirjapaja.

Schleicher, A. (2006). *The economics of knowledge: Why education is key for Europe's success* (Lisbon Council Policy Brief). Brussels: Lisbon Council.

Sinko, P. (2007). Reading Finland—A priority project of the Finnish National Board of Education. In P. Linnakyä & I. Arffman (Eds.), *Finnish reading literacy. When quality and equity meet* (pp. 107–125). Jyväskylä: University of Jyväskylä, Institute for Educational Research.

Sommer, M., Lau, J., & Mejding, J. (1996). *Nordlaes—en nordisk undersögelse af laesefaerdigheder i 1.-3. klasse* [Nordlaes—A Nordic study of reading skills in grades 1 to 3]. Copenhagen: Danmarks Paedagogiske Institut.

Tuovinen, J. E. (2008). Learning the craft of teaching and learning from world's best practice. The case of Finland. In D. M. McInerney & A. D. Liem (Eds.), *Teaching and learning: International best practice* (pp. 51–77). Charlotte, NC: Information Age Publishing.

Törnroos, J., & Kupari P. (2005).Suomalaisnuorten matematiikan osaaminen [Finnish students' mathematical literacy performance]. In P. Kupari & J. Välijärvi (Eds.), *Osaaminen kestävällä pohjalla. PISA 2003 Suomessa* [Knowledge and skills on a solid basis. PISA 2003 in Finland] (pp. 7–36). Jyväskylä: University of Jyväskylä, Institute for Educational Research.

Välijärvi, J. (2007). Debate: Focus on Finland. *European Business Forum 30*, 20–21.

Välijärvi, J., Kupari, P., Linnakylä, P., Reinikainen, P., Sulkunen, S., Törnroos, J., et al. (2007). *The Finnish success in PISA—and some reasons behind it, 2.* Jyväskylä: University of Jyväskylä, Institute for Educational Research. http://ktl.jyu.fi/img/portal/8317/PISA_2003_screen.pdf.

Välijärvi, J., & Linnakylä, P. (Eds.). (2002). *Tulevaisuuden osaajat. PISA 2000 Suomessa* [Well prepared for the future. PISA 2000 in Finland]. Jyväskylä: University of Jyväskylä, Institute for Educational Research.

Välijärvi, J., & Malin, A. (2002). The two-level effect of socio-economic background. In S. Lie, P. Linnakylä, & A. Roe (Eds.), *Nordic lights on PISA* (pp. 123–131). Oslo: University of Oslo, Department of Teacher Education and School Development.

Välijärvi, J., & Sahlberg, P. (2008). Should "'failing" students repeat a grade? *Journal of Educational Change, 9*(4), 385–389.

Warschauer, M. (1999). *Electronic literacies: Language culture and power in online education.* Mahwah, NJ: Erlbaum.

10 Literacy for All

Koen Jaspaert and Kris Van den Branden

INTRODUCTION

Full participation in modern Western society requires a range of multi-faceted skills and competencies. Among them, literacy skills are generally regarded to be crucial for successful participation in education and in society at large. Lately, literacy development has received much attention from policy makers because a number of studies have shown that, despite the large amount of attention that is paid to promoting reading and writing skills in compulsory education, there are still a considerable number of citizens in modern Western societies who fail to develop a sufficient level of literacy.

In Flanders, more than 15% of the population are estimated to lack the literacy skills necessary to function adequately in different relevant domains of society (Van Damme, 1997). In 2004, the Dutch Language Union published a report on literacy skills in the Dutch language area (Flanders and the Netherlands) (Bohnenn, Ceulemans, van de Guchte, Kurvers, & Van Tendeloo, 2004). In that report, four levels of literacy were distinguished. People at the lowest level (Level 0) are not able to read and write at all. At Level 1, people have some basic notions of reading and writing but experience a lot of difficulties in applying these notions to any real-world literacy-related activity. At Level 2, people can perform simple reading and writing tasks but still are unable to perform a considerable range of functional literacy tasks that they are confronted with in modern-day society. Only at Level 3 are people able to live up to the literacy demands of society. Bohnenn et al. estimated that 16.8% of the Flemish population (of 16 years of age and older) belonged to Level 1 or lower. A quarter of the population was assigned to Level 2. At the lower levels, people older than 50 are only slightly overrepresented, indicating that Flemish literacy problems will not gradually disappear with time. Nor is the problem mainly caused by the lack of integration into Flemish society of large numbers of (illiterate or semi-literate) immigrants. Although people with an immigrant background are overrepresented in the lower levels, the problem of low literacy is by no means restricted to particular ethnic groups. In general, Bohnenn et al. estimate that about 7% of the young people leaving the Flemish compulsory educational system at the age of 18 do not perform higher than Level 1, and 27% only reach Level 2 at the most.

The fact that large numbers of people leave compulsory education with relatively low literacy levels each year adds to the necessity of developing support systems for encouraging lifelong learning in Flanders, including a wide range of adult education courses that aim to remedy reading and writing skills. In absolute numbers, Bohnenn et al. (2004) estimate that currently about 800,000 Flemish adults are not able to perform relatively simple reading and writing tasks (at Level 1 or lower). However, adult education can offer literacy courses to only 4,000 students a year. In view of the fact that about 8,000 young school-leavers join the Level 1 group each year, we can conclude that the annual influx of new candidates for adult literacy courses is about twice as large as the number of people that adult education is able to enroll. Moreover, the question can be raised whether trying to remedy young people's lack of literacy skills through adult education is the most appropriate policy in the long term. Eighteen-year-olds who enroll in adult literacy courses have just been through a 15-year period of extensive, compulsory schooling. It seems relatively naive to expect a course of 1 year in adult education to remedy a problem that 15 years of compulsory education was not able to solve or prevent. From this perspective, probably the most important and urgent literacy-related challenge in Flanders consists in raising the expertise of school teams in Flemish compulsory education to detect children who are at risk of not developing sufficient literacy levels and support them in the most efficient ways.

Detecting Students at Risk

The fact that a substantial group of students with low literacy levels leave Flemish schools every year does not necessarily imply that Flemish schools fail to provide effective literacy education across the board. As a matter of fact, international comparative studies such as the international three-yearly PISA studies (OECD, 2004, 2007) have shown that the Flemish educational system ranks very high when it comes to developing literary skills. On the basis of the 2006 data, Flemish 15-year-olds shared the top position in reading skills with their Finnish peers. However, the difference between groups of high-performing and low-performing adolescents was nowhere as large as in Flanders. Flemish schools, then, seem to cater extraordinarily well to the needs of the highly achieving students but do not succeed in allowing a wide range of other students to profit from education to the same extent. This observation has incited a lot of heated debate in Flanders and inspired the former Minister of Education to launch a language policy plan that emphasizes that education should be "good for the strong students, and strong for the weak students" (Vandenbroucke, 2007).

From a "literacy for all" perspective, the extremely large gap between high and low achievers in the PISA studies raises the question who exactly these low achievers are. Being able to identify students at risk constitutes an important first step in stopping the influx of new low literates into Flemish adult society. The PISA study is particularly revealing in this respect. As it turns out, the results of the PISA analyses do not substantiate the hypotheses that have become common ground in the public educational debate in Flanders. In general, the media and the public audience believe that children who do not speak Dutch as their mother tongue (Dutch being the medium of instruction in Flemish compulsory education) score a lot worse on reading tests than children who have been raised in Dutch at home. In a similar vein, children who were raised in a local dialect rather than in a standard-like variety of Dutch are believed to score significantly lower on literacy tests. As the figures in Table 10.1 show, these notions are not fully borne out by the data.

Whereas the data clearly show that children with Turkish or Arabic as their mother tongue have a very low average score, this does not hold for mother tongue speakers of English and, to a lesser extent, French or other EU languages. These differences in the relation between reading score and home language suggest that home language background offers at best only a partial explanation of the variance in the students' reading comprehension results. What must be taken into account is that in Flanders, most students with English as their mother tongue have a relatively high socioeconomic background, in comparison to the average Flemish student. For students with Turkish and Arabic as their mother tongue, the opposite is true. So, the effect of mother tongue background needs to be interpreted in interaction with the students' socioeconomic background. In addition, Table 10.1 reveals that only a very limited number of mother tongue speakers of languages other than Dutch were included in the PISA sample. As a result, the wide variation in the reading comprehension scores in the Flemish sample cannot be caused by children with Turkish or Arabic as mother tongue alone.

Table 10.1 PISA Scores (Reading Comprehension) in Flanders Related to Pupils' Mother Tongue

Language at Home	Mean	N	SD
Standard Dutch	546	3,431	83.4
Flemish dialect	539	813	83.2
French	510	95	88.1
English	561	13	84.0
Other EU language	472	16	96.4
Eastern European language	458	7	113.7
Arabic	443	22	83.2
Turkish	409	70	98.4

A striking pattern in the PISA data that did not attract much attention in the public debate is the large difference in scores between the different types of schools that the PISA informants were recruited from. In Flanders, the educational system aims to offer comprehensive education until the end of the first grade of secondary education (when students have reached the age of 14[1]). From the third year of secondary education onward, children have to choose between general education (ASO), preparing students for higher education; technical education (TSO), enlisting students who want to build up a career as skilled technicians; or vocational education (BSO), preparing students for professions that require less sophisticated technical and academic skills.[2] Table 10.2 shows that there is a systematic variation in the students' average reading scores across these three types of school.

As Table 10.2 shows, students with very low literacy levels in the PISA study are vastly overrepresented in the vocational strand (BSO). The two other school types reach an average score well above the overall OECD average (set at 500). So, it is clear that, if we want to detect the children who run the risk of leaving compulsory education as adults with low literacy, we should focus on what goes on in BSO. It is quite remarkable that the public discussion about the effectiveness of education and the role that language plays in this matter by and large missed this crucial observation. If we keep in mind that the PISA data were collected at the end of comprehensive education, the results suggest that at the beginning of the second grade of secondary education (at the age of 14), very strong streaming tendencies occur, regrouping the vast majority of students for whom literacy education (in primary education and the first grade of secondary education) turned out to be unsuccessful, in BSO. Looking at the social profile of the students enrolled in the three strands, the streaming appears to be strongly socially biased. While, on the whole, about 20% of the Flemish 15-year-olds follow BSO, 34% of the subgroup with a socioeconomic (SES) background below the average of the school population are enrolled in this strand of secondary education. Of the students belonging to the group in the lower quarter of the OECD SES-index scale,

Table 10.2   PISA Scores (Reading Comprehension) in Flanders Related to Strands in Secondary Education

School Type	Reading Score	N
ASO	595 SD = 52	2229
TSO	526 SD = 57	1454
BSO	440 SD = 63	908

almost 50% are situated in BSO. Likewise, half of the students speaking Arabic or Turkish at home are enrolled in the BSO strand. Because this is not the main focus of this chapter, we will not further elaborate on the mechanisms behind the streaming. What matters here is that the analysis of the PISA data we present provides strong indications that the burden of preventing adolescents from leaving Flemish compulsory education with insufficient literacy skills primarily rests on the shoulders of school teams within the BSO strand.

ASSESSING BSO STUDENTS' GROWTH OF LITERACY SKILLS

In the wake of the discussion on the PISA results, and as a result of the general conclusion that language and home language background play an important role in educational success, the Flemish Minister of Education financed a literature study (Colpin et al., 2006) investigating whether the introduction of standardized language tests could have a potentially positive impact on the development of "strong education for the weak." In their conclusions, Colpin et al. emphasized the urgent need of screening students' literacy skills at the onset of BSO, in view of identifying pupils who are in danger of becoming members of the Level 1 and Level 2 literacy groups when leaving compulsory education. Detecting pupils at risk at the onset of the BSO track (when pupils are at the age of 14) may give BSO schools ample time to remedy the problem during the remainder of these pupils' compulsory educational career, which, in turn, may bring the growing influx of citizens in adult literacy courses to a halt.

For this purpose, a digital reading and writing test was developed by the Centre for Language and Education of the Katholieke Universiteit Leuven. The tests were constructed following the principles of task-based test design (Colpin & Gysen, 2006; Long & Norris, 2000). A number of reading and writing tasks, closely resembling authentic tasks, were designed and pretested. On the basis of the trial runs, a large calibration study was set up, in which 1,807 pupils in the first year of BSO (i.e., third year of secondary education) participated.

For the reading test, a scale ranking the items according to their difficulty level and ranking the subjects in terms of ability was constructed. The construction of this scale was based on an Item Response Theory model, more specifically a Rasch model. In this model, the probability of a correct response is modelled as a logistic function of the difference between the person and item parameter (i.e., ability and difficulty). Basically, the higher a person's ability relative to the difficulty of a specific item, the higher the probability of a correct response on that item will be. When a person's position on the latent trait scale is equal to the difficulty of the item, there is (by definition) a 0.5 probability of a correct response in the Rasch model. In this way, a scale was constructed with items that cover a broad spectrum of difficulty, ranging from very easy to very difficult. Subsequently, this scale was presented to a panel of experts who were asked to define the cut-off point between items that do and do not indicate risk of low literacy. Risk was defined as there being a larger than 50% chance that a pupil failing the item, and all the other items below this item in the scale, would leave compulsory education without possessing the literacy skills that are necessary to function adequately in society and in the labor market.

For the writing test, a scale was constructed on the basis of judgments of the quality of the texts that the subjects had written to accomplish each writing task. Subsequently, the panel of experts was presented with a range of students' products of different quality levels. Here again, a bookmark procedure was followed as the experts defined the cut-off point between products that did and did not indicate a great risk of ending up as low literates by the age of 18.

Both for reading and writing, two cut-off points were identified. Based on the cut-off point that was determined by the expert panels, the researchers deduced a second, lower cut-off point (relating to literacy Level 1 of the Bohnenn et al., 2004, scales) by subtracting one standard deviation from the expert panel's cut-off point. In this way, a further differentiation could be made within the group of students at risk. Both cut-off points were externally validated using test data from 514 students in the final year of the BSO strand (19- and 20-year-olds). The final year of BSO is an optional year that BSO students can follow after finishing compulsory education. If they succeed, they receive a secondary school diploma that allows them to attend most programs in higher education. This measure can be interpreted as an indication that students who succeed in this final year have developed literacy skills at Level 3; BSO students in the last year of compulsory education who are allowed to start the final year might be hypothesized to have developed literacy skills up to Level 2. Our test administrations from the final year students further substantiated the results from the expert panel's bookmark procedure.

In essence, the results of this study clearly corroborated the conclusion we had drawn earlier on the basis of the PISA study: The first year of BSO appears to attract a large proportion of the students who are in danger of becoming low-literate adults. The panel of experts estimated that, for writing, about 70% of the students and, for reading, 80% of the students scored below the cut-off point, identifying them as pupils at risk of becoming school-leavers with low literacy skills. For writing 31% of the students, and for reading 42% of the students were situated below the L1 cut-off point. Extrapolating these results to the population of students leaving compulsory school each year, and using the data in the PISA project as an indication of the composition of that population, we can see that, if no additional support is given to these students during the 4 years they are enrolled in BSO, 16% of all students will leave compulsory education with reading skills below Level 2 (i.e., 20% of all Flemish children are enrolled BSO and 80% of them score below L2 cut-off point) and 8% with reading skills below Level 1. For writing, the percentages are 14% and 6%. Taking into account that we have left special education and the part-time vocational strands out of this picture, these figures corroborate the earlier estimates of low literacy in Flanders rather well.

As for the relation between low literacy and home language background, the results of this study display a slightly different picture as compared to the PISA results. In our study, students were asked to indicate which language they use most often to speak with their mother. As Table 10.3 shows, literacy skills and home language background turned out to be strongly related.

Table 10.3   Reading Skills of Flemish BSO Students Related to Their Home Language Background

Home Language		Reading	Writing
Dutch	Mean	,94	-,2571
	N	1099	1312
	Std. Deviation	1,15	,92167
French	Mean	,51	-,3520
	N	65	96
	Std. Deviation	1,20	1,06280
Turkish/Kurdish	Mean	,22	-,7262
	N	41	70
	Std. Deviation	1,13	1,18035
Arabic/Berber	Mean	,42	-,6420
	N	115	146
	Std. Deviation	1,19	1,06943
Western European language	Mean	,76	-,3724
	N	16	29
	Std. Deviation	,94	,98014
Eastern European language	Mean	,20	-,8326
	N	18	32
	Std. Deviation	1,44	1,20153
other	Mean	,32	-,4687
	N	33	53
	Std. Deviation	1,20	,96624
Total	Mean	,83	-,3326
	N	1387	1738
	Std. Deviation	1,18	,97301

A one-way analysis of variance with a post hoc Scheffé test of difference between the various language groups revealed a significant difference between the mean scores of pupils with Dutch as their mother tongue on the one hand, and students with Turkish or Kurdish as mother tongue (p = .018 for reading and p = .015 for writing), and Arabic or Berber as mother tongue (p = .002 for reading and writing) on the other hand. A remarkable outcome, however, is that the effect we found in this study is much smaller than the impact of mother tongue in the PISA data. When the differences between the groups are expressed in proportions of the standard deviations, the differences in this study are systematically smaller than those in the PISA study.

Another striking difference between the two studies is that the PISA study registered fewer BSO pupils with a mother tongue other than Dutch than our study. Whereas PISA reports only 9% of their sample as having a mother tongue other than Dutch, the sample for this study included 21% of these pupils. This percentage corresponds more closely with the real proportion of non-Dutch-speaking students in the BSO. One of the problems with the PISA study is that 14% of the BSO pupils in their sample showed missing values with regard to the mother tongue variable. This, in fact, may threaten the validity of the conclusions that were drawn about the impact of mother tongue on reading comprehension in the PISA study.

Nevertheless, both studies agree in their claim that a large number of pupils in BSO have a low level of literacy skills at the age of 14 or 15. Pupils' poor performances at a literacy test at the beginning of BSO, or at the age of 15, does not mean, of course, that these pupils are bound to end up in the Level 1 or Level 2 groups for literacy upon leaving compulsory education. Most of those pupils still have a number of school years ahead, so they still have considerable chances to further develop their literacy skills. In this respect, we also administered the reading and writing test that we used in 3 BSO[3] to a random sample of students in 6 BSO. The sample in 6 BSO was drawn from the same schools as the sample of 3 BSO classes, in this way adding to the comparability of both samples. The results of both groups are presented in Table 10.4.

Table 10.4   Reading and Writing Scores of Flemish 6 BSO Students

Jaar		Reading	Writing
3,00	Mean	,83195	-,3326
	N	1387	1738
	Std. Deviation	1,179895	,97301
6,00	Mean	1,20974	-,0965
	N	373	476
	Std. Deviation	1,266806	,94666
Total	Mean	,91202	-,2818
	N	1760	2214
	Std. Deviation	1,208380	,97205

As Table 10.4 shows, the students in the sixth year had higher reading and writing scores than the students in the third year. However, the difference between the two groups is remarkably small. For reading comprehension, the difference is less than one third of a standard deviation, and for writing, the difference is even less than one quarter of a standard deviation. If we interpret the data of 6 BSO using the cut-off points that were determined for the test in 3 BSO, we find that 66% of the group fall short of the Level 2 cut-off point for reading and 43% for writing.

Moreover, we should take into account that the pupil population in the BSO strand in Flemish schools drastically changes between the third and the sixth year. Quite a number of students in the BSO strand fail to pass one or more grades during their school career. As a result, they reach the age of 18 (the age at which they are allowed to leave compulsory education) before they have started sixth grade of BSO. Many of these students drop out. Furthermore, the student population in BSO changes over the years as a result of the "cascade system" in Flemish secondary education: Many students first try to succeed in the general academic strand (ASO) or technical strand (TSO), but if they fail there, they will shift to the BSO strand. As a result, a number of students in 6 BSO were not enrolled in 3 BSO, which may give rise to higher average scores in 6 BSO, in view of the fact that the majority of these students must have developed a reasonable level of literacy to be allowed in ASO or TSO in the first place. In sum, considering the small difference in the scores between 3 BSO and 6 BSO, and the fact that changes in BSO population between the third and sixth year tend to raise the average level of literacy of the group, we tend to conclude that the BSO strand does not succeed in providing adequate stimuli to their students to allow them to make significant gains in terms of literacy development between the ages of 14 and 18. This study, then, can be interpreted as an alarm signal: Strong, concerted, and sustained actions to enhance the quality of literacy instruction in the vocational strand of Flemish education are direly needed.

DEVELOPING POLICY PLANS TO TAKE APPROPRIATE ACTION

In this section, we will discuss what actions can be taken to support the Flemish BSO schools in raising the quality of literacy instruction. We will first look at the policy plans that were developed by the Flemish government in the period before the previously mentioned assessment study in BSO was carried out; we will critically reflect on their strengths and weaknesses. Next, we will present the guiding principles of a recent action plan that specifically focuses on supporting BSO schools to offer their students richer opportunities to develop their literacy skills.

Actions Undertaken in the Past

During the past 20 years, the Flemish government has taken a number of initiatives to raise the quality of education in terms of maximizing opportunities for the development of key skills by all students, irrespective of their socioeconomic or home language background. The main initiatives that are relevant in this respect are listed as follows:

- From 1991 onward, the Flemish government launched its major "Educational Priority Policy" (EPP), which was redefined in 2002 into a "General Policy for Equity in Education." Basically, this policy is intended to support primary and secondary schools that enlist a relatively high percentage of socially deprived students and/or students speaking a mother tongue other than Dutch, by giving these schools additional grants and teaching staff. The grants are provisional, in that schools need to write a school policy plan and take appropriate actions to enhance educational effectiveness. The actions of the school should be linked up with two out of six content areas defined by the Flemish government. Language education is one of these six content areas. Reports show that about 40% of the Flemish EPP schools select language education as their primary target. The schools are granted additional means for a period of 3 years; they are assigned a pedagogical counselor who supports them in drawing up and implementing their action plan. At the end of the 3-year period, the Inspectorate assesses the quality of the school's policy-making efforts and the effects of the actions that were taken by the school team.
- Along with the launching of the EPP to enhance equity in education, a government-subsidized, university-based Centre for Language and Education (at the Katholieke Universiteit Leuven) was founded. Combining research activities with the development of educational tools and the organization of training programs, this center supports school teams (in primary, secondary, and adult education) in their efforts to raise the quality of their language education and language policy across the curriculum so as to cater for all students' learning needs.
- The curriculum of the vocational strand of Flemish secondary education consists of two major components: a professional training component (focusing on the teaching of skills, knowledge, and attitudes connected with a specific profession or professional domain) and a general education component. From the 1980s onward, the subdivision of this general education component into different subjects was given up in favor of an integrated course called "Project General Subjects" (In Dutch: PAV). The main goal of this integrated course is to support adolescents in building up the skills that are necessary to function well in modern society and in growing up as self-confident, socially able, assertive, and balanced individuals. Building up class-

room activities around topics and themes that are relevant to adolescents' lives, PAV aims to promote the development of key skills, among which are language proficiency and functional literacy. For this integrated course, the Flemish government has issued specific attainment targets.

- The former Minister of Education, Frank Vandenbroucke, has strongly emphasized the crucial role of language in the battle against inequity in Flemish education. In his "Language Policy Plan," Vandenbroucke (2007) calls upon all schools to develop a comprehensive school language policy across the curriculum. School teams are summoned to jointly design a school language policy plan, to adapt their teaching to the language learning needs of their students, to carefully monitor the students' language development, to remedy the students who are lagging behind, to pay sufficient attention to the complexity of the language of instruction in academic subjects, and to enhance professional development of all staff members with regard to language and literacy education.

- In 2005, the Flemish government launched a "Policy Plan for Enhancing Literacy" (In Dutch: "Plan Geletterdheid Verhogen"). This policy plan aims to decrease the number of individuals in Flemish society who are insufficiently able to use written information for personal or professional objectives, to use modern technology (such as multimedia), and to cope with numerical information. The plan mentions a wide variety of target actions, including the screening of individual literacy, sensitizing companies to enhance literacy among their employees, setting up community networks with libraries and the cultural sector, stimulating adults with low literacy to follow a language course or literacy course, funding research into literacy development, enhancing the quality of adult education, taking appropriate action for the support of literacy education in the vocational strand of secondary education, and issuing official attainment targets for information and communication technology skills.

As could be inferred from the analyses presented in the previous paragraphs, all these policy measures and action plans have, so far, been insufficiently effective in fighting low literacy, especially among low-SES, non-Dutch-speaking adolescents who follow secondary education in the vocational strand (BSO schools). Next, we will explore a number of possible explanations for these observations and explore potential directions for appropriate action in the future. As a point of reference, we will use some of the most recurrent and pressing recommendations that have come out of a number of recent, international reports on the enhancement of "literacy for all" (August & Shanahan, 2006; EFA Global Monitoring Report, 2006; Riley, 2001; Short & Fitzsimmons, 2007; Stahl, Dougherty, & McKenna, 2006; Thomas & Collier, 2002; Twist, Sainsbury, Woodthorpe, & Whetton, 2003).

1.   Lack of a Comprehensive, Tightly Focused Literacy Policy in (Secondary) Education

As the overview of initiatives taken by the Flemish government clearly shows, a comprehensive governmental policy specifically focusing on decreasing the number of students who leave compulsory education without possessing the literacy skills that are necessary to function well in society, on the work floor, and in higher education has been very slow to develop in Flanders. In most of the policies relating to this issue that were implemented by the Flemish government during the past 20 years, actions regarding literacy were just one of the many targets that schools could select. Both in the General Policy Plan aimed at enhancing equity in education and in the reorganization of the curriculum in the vocational strand (cf. PAV), the main policy targets of the Flemish government addressed the quality and organization of education in general, rather than tightly focusing on literacy as such. For school teams, this leaves open the option *not* to focus on literacy, but instead to select actions and topics that they deem more relevant, crucial, or feasible. Research into the actual use made by Equity Priority Schools of the additional financial means they are granted clearly shows that this is the case: The financial means are mostly used to decrease the sheer number of pupils in the classroom, to tackle general learning and disciplinary problems, and to remediate pupils with severe learning problems (Padmos & Van den Berghe, 2009; Van Petegem et al., 2004). Reports by the Flemish inspectorate (Ministerie van de Vlaamse Gemeenschap, 2006, 2007) stress that in many Equity Priority Schools, a coherent school language policy plan, in which a clear view on the enhancement of literacy is integrated, is lacking. Bearing this in mind, it is somewhat unfortunate that the recent literacy plan of the Flemish government has, so far, mainly focused on adult education and has not given rise to any action with regard to the enhancement of literacy in secondary education yet. Moreover, links between this literacy plan and a governmental policy plan aiming to raise the quality of literacy education in primary education are generally lacking. So, although action has been taken on different levels, the Flemish educational field still lacks a comprehensive policy plan on literacy development.

2.   Raising the Professional Expertise of Teachers with Regard to Literacy Education

Teachers play a crucial role in enhancing the quality of literacy education. Motivating students to engage in literacy-related activities, supporting students while they are performing these tasks, reflecting with the students on reading and writing strategies, and providing individualized support to children at risk are just some of the ways in which a teacher can make a difference for adolescents with low literacy. However, the teacher will only be able to do so if he or she has the expertise to offer high-quality literacy education and, particularly in the vocational strand of secondary education, to functionally integrate literacy education with the teaching of other competencies or with professional training. At present, many teachers in secondary education do not possess this expertise, nor do they regard the enhancement of literacy as crucial to the lives of the adolescents they are working with. Training programs organized by the Flemish Centre for Language and Education, aiming to raise teachers' literacy teaching skills, show only minor effects (Padmos & Van den Berghe, 2009; Van Petegem et al., 2004). In these training programs, teachers were supported to implement a task-based approach to literacy education, stressing the need to work with motivating, authentic, challenging tasks, adapted to the learning needs of the students, and giving rise to holistic learning activities in which functional reading and writing education are embedded. As a range of empirical studies into the implementation of task-based approaches to language and literacy education in Flanders show (for an overview, see Van den Branden, 2006), teachers, especially those teachers who have built up relatively low expectations of their students' learning potential, tend to chop up holistic literacy activities into smaller units (down to the level of teaching isolated, meaningless elements), tend to dominate and control classroom interaction, and/or tend to be reluctant to confront their students with tasks that are above their current level of proficiency.

All these observations emphasize the need for far more daring, intensive coaching and support programs that aim to (a) raise a general awareness of the need for literacy activities among teachers in the vocational strand of Flemish secondary education, and (b) enhance their pedagogical expertise to create powerful learning environments for literacy development. As research amply shows (Borg, 2006; Van den Branden, 2009), an intensive program of practice-oriented teacher training including job-embedded practice and reflection on personal experience on the work floor is necessary to stimulate fundamental change in teaching practice; so far, at the level of secondary education, such intensive teacher training programs have not yet been realized.

3. Connecting in-School and Out-of-School Literacies

Adolescents have a full and fascinating life outside school. In modern life of the 21st century, literacy-related activities abound in adolescents' out-of-school experiences. However, as far as literacy education is concerned, schools rarely exploit students' real-life skills or link up educational activities with youngsters' outside world experiences and needs. Literacy activities, if any, tend to be driven by the curriculum or the handbooks teachers use, rather than by the prior knowledge, real-life problems, worries, and questions that young people face in everyday life and society. Connecting literacy education to students' lives is one of the most systematically recurring recommendations in the international reports on literacy education.

For one, the Flemish educational system has only recently started to experiment with the concept of extended schools, which aim to create networks between the school and cultural/social institutes in the neighborhood. Literacy development, however, is not a key issue in the 16 experimental extended school projects that are currently running under the supervision of the Flemish Department of Education. Neither is any kind of systematic cooperation between secondary schools and public libraries being set up.

In fact, the outside world, in general, and the young students' home environments are not regarded as possible assets but rather as part of the educational problem that low-SES students are facing. In the minds of many Flemish teachers, students of a low SES who were raised in a mother tongue other than Dutch are underachieving in Flemish education *because* they have a low SES and because they have been raised in a mother tongue other than Dutch (Berben, Van den Branden, & Van Gorp, 2007; Padmos & Van den Berghe, 2009). This attitude is strongly reflected in Flemish teachers' attitudes toward multilingualism and toward the mother tongues of their low-SES, minority language speaking students. In a study that asked 360 Flemish student teachers, in-service teachers, and pedagogical counselors about their subjective beliefs concerning language teaching and language acquisition, Van Gorp and Van den Branden (2003) found that a large majority of the respondents thought parents of minority language speaking students should be encouraged to raise their children in the Dutch standard language, and that this in turn could improve these students' chances of educational success. In line with this, Berben, Van den Branden, and Van Gorp (2007) documented Flemish teachers' strong resistance against any use of minority languages in their classrooms.

These perceptions often go hand in hand with teachers' and headmasters' low expectations in general about the learning potential and the academic achievement of students in the BSO strand in general, and nonnative speakers of Dutch in particular. In fact, a number of classroom observations carried out in BSO and TSO schools by the Flemish Centre for Equity in Education (Padmos & Van den Berghe, 2009) provided clear indications that in the BSO strand, many school teams, for several reasons, devote primary attention to technical vocational skills, while reducing the attention and stimuli for the development of literacy to a minimum. The written word is systematically replaced with oral instructions and information and the many possibilities to work with functionally relevant texts (such as safety instructions on the work floor or instructions to work with particular machines or tools), and authentic texts that the students are confronted with in the outside world (advertisements, e-mails, papers and journals, Internet information, etc.) are barely exploited. Many of the syllabuses that the BSO teachers have to work with are of a low pedagogical quality (Wyns, 1999). For the earlier mentioned general course, there isn't even a syllabus available yet. Teachers who would like to optimize their language and literacy across the curriculum face the challenge of developing educational tasks and tools themselves. In sum, one of the main reasons why the 6 BSO students did not perform significantly better than the 3 BSO students was that in the classroom, they were hardly invited to perform tasks involving written language, let alone offered powerful reading and writing instruction.

SETTING UP AN ADEQUATE COACHING PROGRAM

Taking up the challenges mentioned in the previous paragraph, the Flemish government has recently started subsidizing an intensive coaching program specifically aiming to support school teams in raising the quality of literary education in the vocational (BSO) and technical (TSO) strands of Flemish secondary education. This program, which involves a close cooperation between a university-based expert center (Centre for Language and Education, K.U. Leuven), 10 schools, and their pedagogical counselors, was started up in 2009. In this section, we will describe the guiding principles behind the project, as we believe these may provide inspiration to anyone aiming to raise the effectiveness of literacy education in vocational strands of education.

An Intensive, Sustained Coaching Program Aiming for Joint Ownership

The number of schools involved in the coaching program was deliberately restricted to 10. This restriction must ensure that intensive coaching can be offered to all the teachers who want to be involved in the program. From the very beginning, the coaching program was conceived as a joint project between the school teams and the coaches. Aims, methods, and procedures were negotiated and constructed together, to make sure that the teachers and headmasters could build up a strong sense of ownership from the start, assign personal meaning to the innovation, and build up basic confidence that the coaching would improve their daily classroom practice for themselves and for their students. In line with the currently available research on the implementation of innovation in language education (for an overview, see Van den Branden, 2009), the coaches and pedagogical counselors support the teachers in practical, educational, and affective ways while the latter are learning about and trying out new approaches to literacy education. The training takes place in the schools, rather than at the in-service training institute, and utilizes different coaching formats, including classroom observations, workshops, stimulated recall sessions (based on classroom video recordings), material development sessions, theoretical sessions, and individual coach–teacher discussions. Throughout the whole process, the pupils' reactions to new activities and their literacy development is followed up, using a number of different assessment techniques and formats (e.g., reading and writing tests, observations on task performance, portfolio assessment, and peer assessment). The assessment continuously feeds back into the support program: Teachers and coaches together monitor and, where necessary, revise the decisions taken to enhance the quality of literacy education on the basis of the reactions and progress produced by the students.

Co-Constructing Powerful Learning Environments for Enhancing Literacy Development

During the first year the coaching program has been running, school teams and coaches have explored the field and pedagogical literature aiming to bring together the main ingredients of powerful learning environments for enhancing literacy development. Subsequently, teachers and coaches tried to discover and exploit all kinds of opportunities in daily classroom practice to put these principles into practice. Following are the main principles they listed.

1. Increase the frequency with which texts are used in the classroom.
   If teachers aim to enhance adolescents' reading and writing skills, the latter will have to perform a lot of reading and writing tasks. Students whose reading and writing skills are relatively poor should not be put on a literary diet, because this will raise the chances that their literacy skills will decrease rather than increase. Teachers should suppress their inclination to replace written text with oral instructions.

2. Work with texts across the curriculum.
   Across the curriculum, texts can be embedded in education. Not only during language or general subject courses but also during vocational training can reading and writing tasks be used and integrated in ongoing activities. Literacy training should be taken up by all teachers and instructors. All sorts of text genres can be used to promote students' subject- and literacy-related development: newspaper articles, interviews, Internet documents, advertisements, instructions, short notes, and letters.

3. Work with relevant and authentic texts.
   The focus of educational activity for the BSO students should be on performing functional reading and writing tasks rather than on phonics and orthography. Adolescents won't be motivated by the latter type of activity anymore. Interesting and relevant texts, accompanied by motivating tasks, should constitute the starting point for educational activity. Students should preferably work with texts that they will likely encounter on the shop floor and in society: safety instructions, instructions for handling certain machines, nonfiction texts about their profession, articles from journals and magazines, itiner-

aries, e-mail messages, Internet documents, job descriptions, and so forth. Using authentic texts will raise the chances that text selection will be fine-tuned to the students' learning needs and their interests. Allowing students to self-select the topic of discussion, or to negotiate about this with the teacher, and allowing students to introduce topics (and texts) that are connected to their personal lives (outside the school) may help to improve the match between texts, learning needs, and interests of the students.

4. Embed texts in relevant and challenging tasks.

   Reading and writing should preferably be embedded in functional tasks. People read texts with a purpose: to find out something, to gather information, to be able to carry out a certain action, and so forth. A simple rule of thumb states that students should be confronted with text comprehension questions *before* they are invited to read a text, rather than after reading. "Why should I read this text?" is a question that should be answered before students start performing a reading task. This may enhance the goal-orientedness of student activity in the classroom.

5. Do not oversimplify texts.

   Authentic texts may be complex, difficult, and way above the students' level of reading proficiency. In that case, many teachers tend to simplify the text. However, while doing so, they should make sure the text they produce still holds a challenge for the students. As a rule of thumb, the maximal size of the gap between students' reading skills and the reading demands of the text should be strongly related with the students' level of reading motivation.

6. Carefully edit text material.

   Sometimes teachers produce text material themselves, because they are not able to find authentic texts that suit their educational purposes. In that case, teachers are advised to pay sufficient heed to the following aspects:
   - Contents: Be aware of the fact that the reader is not an insider. Provide sufficient information to allow the student to build up new knowledge, establish links with his or her prior knowledge or experience, provide examples and illustrations, be explicit about the structure of the text, avoid excessive jargon, and be redundant (by presenting new information in different ways, by paraphrasing and repeating crucial information).
   - Language use: Always be aware of the complexity of metaphorical speech, implicit links between sentences, complex syntactic constructions, scientific terms, nominalizations, and passive constructions.

- Lay-out and presentation: Make sure the lay-out is clear and well-balanced, use subtitles, and interconnect different parts of the texts by using advance organizers and short summaries.

7. Support students' text comprehension and text production.
Text comprehension can be facilitated by embedding abstract information within descriptions of concrete situations, by using illustrations, visual cues, (photo)graphs, and tables, or by linking the contents of the text to actions, objects, and experiences in the real world. One of the most important ways in which teachers can enhance text comprehension is by discussing the text with the students. After all, conversation is the default form of communication and information processing (Clark, 1996). Communication through written texts is a derived form of communication that makes the process of joint meaning-making more difficult. Discussing difficult passages of a text with the students, and stimulating them to discuss text interpretation with their peers, may enable them to deal with texts that are objectively above their current level of reading proficiency. In a similar way, students will learn more from performing writing tasks if they are provided with personalized feedback on their (preliminary) text versions or if they discuss the topic or the effect of their texts with their teacher or peers. Especially weaker students may benefit from this individualized form of support.

8. Work with heterogeneous, cooperative learning groups.
By definition, all classes are of the "mixed ability" kind. Teachers should be made aware of the potential of working with heterogeneous groups. Heterogeneous groups offer much more opportunities for relevant forms of interaction (see Principle 7). More-competent readers can support the less-competent readers and, by doing so, further develop their own (productive) skills or gain more insight in reading strategies and effective ways to perform reading and writing tasks. Cooperative learning formats elicit intensive interaction among students, allowing the teacher to maximally focus on his or her supportive role.

9. Create a safe and positive learning environment.
Adolescents in the vocational strand may get a boost from receiving positive feedback and working in an encouraging environment, in which teachers have high expectations of the students' learning potential. These students will often need mental support in order to carry on with relatively challenging tasks. In this respect, the use of tests should be well-considered: Although reading and writing tests can be useful in helping the teacher to monitor the students' reading and writing development, their use often tends to divert the attention of both teacher and student away from the authentic reading and writing process toward more discrete elements or analytic aspects of the task (words, grammar,

orthography). The use of holistic, task-based tests may help to preserve the advantages tests can offer without sacrificing the functional perspective on literacy development.

10. Foster teamwork.
    Stimulating literacy should be taken up by the whole school team. All teachers, coordinating staff, and headmasters should deliberate together about appropriate measures and be involved in implementing the selected actions on the floor. Teachers should inform each other about the possibilities they have discovered or tried out, to raise the number of texts the students are invited to work with, raise the students' motivation and the quality of literacy education, and follow up on their students' progress. Teachers should be encouraged to team teach, prepare lessons together, observe each other in the classroom, and exchange ideas and tools.

CONCLUSIONS

In this chapter, we have shown that in Flanders there is a wide gap between the literacy skills of high-SES, Dutch-speaking adolescents and their low-SES and/or non-Dutch-speaking peers. As a result of a complex combination of several mechanisms, many of the students who face the risk of leaving compulsory education without having developed the literacy skills that modern-day life (in society, at the workplace, in higher education) demands are concentrated in the BSO schools (the vocational strand). Between the age of 14, when the students enroll in BSO with a relatively poor level of literacy skills and the age of 18, when they leave compulsory education, they seem to make hardly any progress in reading comprehension and functional writing skills. Concerted action and policy measures at the different levels of the educational system are needed to reverse this trend. A well-designed, forceful policy plan at the governmental level emphasizing the crucial importance of literacy development for all students, including those enrolled in BSO, should provide for a general framework that can incite and stimulate schools to pay more attention to reading and writing skills. Within the framework of this plan, syllabuses need to be designed, making use of functional, relevant, and authentic texts that can motivate students into devoting mental energy to the learning tasks at hand; teachers and vocational trainers need to be trained and supported to apply the basic principles of language and literacy across the curriculum to their classrooms and shop floor practices; and students need to be motivated and made aware what crucial impact literacy development may have on their future lives and careers. Crucially, if literacy is one of the key competencies that young citizens need to develop in order to function well in modern-day society, then all schools should be sensitized, and intensively supported, to stimulate the literacy development of every single student in compulsory education, irrespective of the educational strand he or she is enlisted in, the home language he or she speaks, and his or her socioeconomic and cultural background.

NOTES

1. At least, this is what the official policy stipulates. A number of mechanisms, however, give rise to a certain degree of streaming from the start of secondary school (age 12) onward.
2. Again, the official version of the profiles of the three strands of secondary education is slightly different from the one presented here. The official version primarily refers to students' motivation, rather than to the cognitive and technical requirements of education in the different strands. However, we have strong reasons to believe that the description we provided corresponds more closely to daily school practice (see also Nicaise & De Smedt, 2008). In fact, besides these three strands, Flemish secondary education also includes art education (KSO), part-time BSO (DBSO) and special education (BUSO). The latter two types also include a large number of graduates who can be situated in the low literacy group. But because they are not involved in the study reported here, we will not take them into further consideration.
3. With 3 BSO and 6 BSO, we refer to the third and sixth year of secondary education in the BSO strand, respectively.

REFERENCES

August, D., & Shanahan, T. (Eds.)(2006). Developing literacy in second-language learners. Report of the National Literacy Panel on language-minority children and youth. New York: Lawrence Erlbaum.

Berben, M., Van den Branden, K., & Van Gorp, K. (2007). "We'll see what happens." Tasks on paper and tasks in a multilingual classroom. In K. Van den Branden, K. Van Gorp, & M. Verhelst (Eds.), *Tasks in action. Task-based language education from a classroom-based perspective* (pp. 32–67). Cambridge: Cambridge Scholars Publishing.

Bohnenn, E., Ceulemans, C., van de Guchte, C., Kurvers, J., & Van Tendeloo, T. (2004). *Laaggeletterd in de lage landen. Hoge prioriteit voor beleid*. Den Haag: Nederlandse Taalunie.

Borg, S. (2006). *Teacher cognition and language education. Research and practice*. London: Continuum.

Clark, H. (1996). *Using language*. Cambridge: Cambridge University Press.

Colpin, M., & Gysen, S. (2006). Developing and introducing task-based tests. In K. Van den Branden (Ed.), *Task-based language education: From theory to practice* (pp. 151–174). Cambridge: Cambridge University Press.

Colpin, M., Gysen, S., Jaspaert, K., Heymans, R., Van den Branden, K., & Verhelst, M. (2006). *Studie naar de wenselijkheid en haalbaarheid van de invoering van centrale taaltoetsen in Vlaanderen in functie van gelijke onderwijskansen*. Leuven: Centrum voor Taal en Onderwijs.

EFA Global Monitoring Report Team. (2006). *Education for all. Literacy for life*. Paris: UNESCO.

Long, M. H., & Norris, J. M. (2000). Task-based teaching and assessment. In M. Byram (Ed.), *Encyclopedia of language teaching* (pp. 597–603). London: Routledge.

Ministerie van de Vlaamse Gemeenschap (2006). *Onderwijsspiegel 2006.* Brussel: Ministerie van de Vlaamse Gemeenschap, Departement Onderwijs.

Ministerie van de Vlaamse Gemeenschap. (2007). *De specificiteit van het Vlaamse onderwijs in het Brussels Hoofdstedelijk Gewest.* Brussel: Ministerie van de Vlaamse Gemeenschap, Departement Onderwijs.

Nicaise, I., & De Smedt, E. (Eds.). (2008). *Gelijke kansen op school: het kan!* Mechelen: Plantyn.

Organisation for Economic Co-operation and Development (OECD). (2004). *Learning for tomorrow's world. First results from PISA 2003.* Paris: Author.

Organisation for Economic Co-operation and Development (OECD). (2007). *PISA 2006 science competencies for tomorrow's world: Vol. 2. Data.* Paris: Author.

Padmos, T., & Van den Berghe, W. (2009). *Het verschil maken. Gelijke kansen in het beroeps—en technisch secundair onderwijs in Vlaanderen.* Leuven: Steunpunt Gelijke Onderwijskansen.

Riley, J. (2001). The National Literacy Strategy: Success with literacy for all? *Curriculum Journal, 12,* 12–58.

Short, D., & Fitzsimmons, S. (2007). *Double the work. Challenges and solutions to acquiring language and academic literacy for adolescent English language learners.* New York: Carnegie Foundation.

Stahl, K., Dougherty, E., & McKenna, M. (Eds.). (2006). *Reading research at work: Foundations of effective practice.* New York: Guilford Press.

Thomas, W. P., & Collier, V. P. (2002). *A national study of school effectiveness for language minority students' long-term academic achievement.* Santa Cruz, CA: Center for Research on Education, Diversity and Excellence, University of California-Santa Cruz.

Twist, L., Sainsbury, M., Woodthorpe, A., & Whetton, C. (2003). *Progress in International Reading Literacy Study (PIRLS): Research summary.* Slough: NFER.

Van Damme, D. (1997). *Hoe geletterd/gecijferd is Vlaanderen? Functionele taal—en rekenvaardigheden van Vlamingen in internationaal perspectief.* Leuven: Garant.

Van den Branden, K. (2006). Training teachers: Task-based as well? In K. Van den Branden (Ed.), *Task-based language education: From theory to practice* (pp. 217–248) Cambridge: Cambridge University Press.

Van den Branden, K. (2009). Diffusion and implementation of innovations. In M. Long & C. Doughty (Eds.), *The handbook of language teaching* (pp. 659–672). Oxford: Blackwell.

Vandenbroucke, F. (2007). *De lat hoog voor talen. Goed voor de sterken, sterk voor de zwakken.* Brussel: Departement Onderwijs van de Vlaamse Gemeenschap.

Van Gorp, K., & Van den Branden, K. (2003). Hoe vernieuwend denken studenten in de lerarenopleiding over taalonderwijs? Een onderzoek naar de percepties van eerstejaars—en derdejaarsstudenten kleuteronderwijs en lager onderwijs op het vlak van taalvaardigheidsonderwijs. In J. Verhaeghe & J. Van Damme (Eds.), *Naar meer gelijke kansen in en door onderwijs. Studiedag georganiseerd door het Vlaams Forum voor Onderwijsonderzoek (VFO)* [CD-ROM]. Leuven: Steunpunt Loopbanen.

Van Petegem, P., Verhoeven, J., Buvens, I., & Vanhoof, J. (2004). *Zelfevaluatie en beleidseffectiviteit in Vlaamse scholen. Het gelijke onderwijskansenbeleid als casus.* Antwerpen: Edubron.

Wyns, L. (1999). Methodes Nederlands voor de B-stroom van de eerste graad secundair onderwijs: huilen met de pet op! *Vonk, 28,* 58–67.

11 Caring Mothers and Teachers, Not Acting White, and Religiosity

What are the Success Factors of High-Achieving DiaspoRicans[1] and Moroccan Students in Belgium?

René Antrop-González, William Vélez, Tomás Garrett, and Dana-María Baldwin

INTRODUCTION

The purpose of this chapter is to describe and compare the schooling experiences of high-achieving Puerto Rican urban students with those of high-achieving Moroccan students schooled in Flanders, Belgium. We were inspired to conduct this line of inquiry because we could not help but notice a huge gap in the educational research regarding the schooling experiences of urban Latina/o youth. This gap consisted of an overemphasis regarding the underachievement of urban youth of color at the expense of describing the schooling experiences of high-achieving urban youth of color. In other words, stories of academic success were largely invisible. Hence, we began a quest to fill this notable gap in the research literature, which resulted in a number of publications that were paid considerable attention by some sectors of the research, teacher educator, and educational policy-making communities (Antrop-González, Vélez, & Garrett, 2004, 2005, 2007).

In addition to our passion for understanding the schooling experiences of these urban youth in the United States, it was about 3 years ago that the first author began his journey to connecting with his family in Belgium. Consequently, he also began to wonder what the schooling experiences of students of color, namely, Moroccans in Belgian schools might be like. Thanks to the first author's cousin, who is a trusted police officer among the Moroccan community in his Flanders hometown, he was able to meet young Moroccan men who were willing to share their experiences for this project. Thus, we decided to conduct this comparative study across international contexts. Our findings reveal that the Puerto Rican and Moroccan students we interviewed have much in common with regard to who they credit for their high academic achievement. In the next section, we provide a review of relevant literature that enables us to ground the framework for this study.

REVIEW OF RELEVANT LITERATURE

In this section we will first discuss educational research pertaining to the academic achievement of urban Latina/o Puerto Rican youth. Next we will move to the Flemish scene, discussing the educational research describing the variables that impact on the academic achievement of Moroccan young people in Belgium.

The U.S. Context

Scholars have recently produced research that serves to deconstruct, reconstruct, and transcend the scholarship on academic underachievement by examining factors that foment the high academic achievement of urban Latina/o Puerto Rican students. These factors include the importance of these students' families, especially the role of the mother and/or grandmother, as support systems (Díaz, 1998; Gándara, 1995; Hidalgo, 2000; Hine, 1992; Rolón, 2000), these students' acquisition of social capital and their participation in social networks, including churches and extracurricular activities with institutional agents (Flores-González, 1999, 2002; Hine, 1992; Reis & Díaz, 1999; Sikkink & Hernández, 2003; Stanton-Salazar, 2002), and the importance of caring teachers and culturally relevant curricula within schools (Ladson-Billings, 1995; Nieto, 1998; Valenzuela, 1999).

Hine (1992) interviewed 10 gifted Puerto Rican urban high school students and their families to understand factors that contributed to their high achievement. The students and their families revealed the importance of mothers and the support they offered their children. This support included monitoring their child's success in school by checking their schoolwork, offering help with their child's homework and/or finding someone who could help if they were not able to, and showing interest in topics being studied in school. The students also belonged to families that strongly encouraged their children to develop their linguistic skills in both Spanish and English, held their children to high academic expectations, and encouraged their children to use negative cultural stereotypes and low teacher expectations as a motivating tool. In other words, they encouraged their children to prove to others that Puerto Ricans can achieve academic success. Lastly, these families strongly encouraged their children to participate in extracurricular activities and socially bond with their classmates. Like Hine (1992), other researchers have recently revealed the powerful influence of mothers and/or grandmothers on the high academic achievement of Puerto Rican elementary school aged children and female urban high school students (Hidalgo, 2000; Rolón, 2000).

Hidalgo (2000) interviewed four working-class Puerto Rican mothers of kindergarten students in Boston whom teachers identified as high achievers. These mothers used a variety of strategies to start their children on the path to academic success: monitoring strategies, communication strategies, motivational strategies, and protective strategies. The monitoring strategies included checking children's schoolwork on a daily basis, checking their book bags daily, doing homework with them, and attending open house meetings at school. The communication strategies consisted of maintaining family bonds that nurtured the maintenance of Puerto Rican values, such as the use of Spanish at home and encouraging a strong sense of Puerto Rican ethnicity. This communication and transmission of cultural values between mother and child also included the establishment of behavioral parameters like counseling against drug use and other negative peer influences like gang membership. The motivational strategies these mothers provided for their children consisted of positive messages such as trying their best, working hard, and keep trying even if their child received low grades.

Rolón (2000) interviewed 10 high-achieving, Puerto Rican females who attended an urban high school. These students revealed three key elements that contributed to their school success. First, they all perceived their mothers to be their driving forces for their academic achievement, because they strongly encouraged them to succeed so they could better themselves economically. Second, they saw their school as being a second home, because they had female teachers who embraced their ethnic and linguistic realities. In fact, these students referred to these teachers as "second mothers." Third, they all aspired to earn a college education, so they could obtain a middle-class lifestyle and become role models for their families and communities. Whereas this scholarship specifically focuses on the influence of families on the high academic achievement of Puerto Rican students, educational researchers have also described the positive connections between these students' high academic achievement and school-related factors like participation in scholastic clubs and extracurricular activities (Flores-González, 1999, 2000, 2002; Reis & Díaz, 1999).

Flores-González (1999, 2002) used role identity theory to explain the multiple ways in which urban high schools structure inequitable opportunities for Puerto Rican students by influencing whether they adopt either a "school kid" or "street kid" identity. The high-achieving Puerto Rican students whom she interviewed and classified as having a "school kid" identity were more likely to be sheltered in safe social niches with other school kids and encouraged by school staff to actively participate in extracurricular activities like athletic teams, church-related activities, and academic-based school clubs. These extracurricular activities also enabled these students to set themselves apart from the "street kids." Moreover, these school kids were more likely to view postsecondary education as a way through which they could become a member of the middle class.

On the contrary, the low-achieving Puerto Rican students who adopted a "street kid" identity found it difficult to situate themselves within school-oriented peer social networks, and the school staff neither encouraged nor facilitated these students' participation in school-related activities. Hence, the self-concept that children and young adults develop reflects their images of their future and what they hope to become, and thus guides their actions in schools and other social institutions. Additionally, unlike the schooling experiences of high-achieving African American students in previous studies (Fordham & Ogbu, 1986), the high-achieving Puerto Rican students interviewed by Flores-González (1999, 2002) voiced a strong Puerto Rican ethnic identity, revealing that they neither perceived themselves nor were perceived by other school peers as "acting White." Finally, recent quantitative research has provided explanations regarding the connection between religiosity as a source of social capital and the high academic achievement of Latina/o and other youth of color (Jeynes, 2003; Muller & Ellison, 2001; Park, 2001; Sikkink & Hernández, 2003). Religiosity and active participation in church-related activities has been found to be an important source of social capital for two reasons. First, church membership provides mentoring relations between adults and youth that instill positive attitudes, values, and behaviors that promote school success and serve as protective measures against oppositional youth behaviors like gang membership, drug use, and truancy. Second, participating in church activities like retreats and conventions facilitates intergenerational closure (Carbonaro, 1998; Sikkink & Hernández, 2003). Intergenerational closure is valuable, because it helps these students, through the relationships they have with their friends and their friends' parents, gain access to important resources like advice, mentorship, and other positive help-seeking behaviors that encourage them to pursue and maintain their high academic achievement.

Although the previously mentioned scholarship is important, much work remains to be done because, with the exception of a few studies (Flores-González, 1999, 2002; Hine, 1992; Reis & Díaz, 1999; Rolón, 2000), very few scholars have attempted to describe and make sense of the experiences of Puerto Rican high achievers in urban high schools. Thus, the study reported herein is significant, because it continues to test and build upon these very few studies.

The Flemish Context

Very little research pertaining to the schooling experiences of high-achieving Moroccan youth has been undertaken in Belgium (Eldering, 1997; Gibson, 1997; Hermans, 2004). Moreover, the little research that has been conducted pertaining to the schooling experiences of these youth has been done through interviewing their parents rather than interviewing the Moroccan students themselves. For example, Hermans (2004) examines the schooling experiences of Moroccan youth in Belgium and the Netherlands, applying Ogbu's cultural-ecological theoretical framework. This perspective contends that the children/youth of voluntary immigrants (like Moroccans in Belgium) generally perform much higher academically than the children/youth of involuntary immigrants

(Hermans, 2004; Ogbu & Simons, 1998). According to Ogbu (1998, 2003), voluntary immigrants in the United States would consist of Jewish and Korean immigrants whereas involuntary immigrants/migrants would consist of African Americans, Mexicans, Native American Indians, and Puerto Ricans. Ogbu (1998, 2003) has nonetheless suggested that this typology could perhaps be applied to an international context. In this perspective, Hermans (2004) interviewed the parents of Moroccan youth schooled in Belgian urban, public schools and found that the children of these voluntary immigrant parents fared much more poorly than White Belgians, because several community forces collided with the cultural and linguistic realities of these families.

The first community force dealt with Moroccan families' frame of comparison to Belgians and Dutch. In other words, most Moroccans felt they were not being afforded the same good opportunities and access to schools and housing as their Belgian and Dutch counterparts. The second community force had to do with Moroccan's relationship to the dominant society as related to issues of identity and language. Thus, Moroccan parents spoke to the countless examples of what Angela Valenzuela (1999) would term *subtractive schooling*. That is, just like the Latina/o students in Valenzuela's study, Moroccan parents strongly felt that schools and other social institutions were working hard to divest their children and youth of their heritage language (Arabic), culture, and religious preference (Islam). The third community force that Hermans (2004) describes is that of the overall instrumental value of education in the eyes of Moroccan parents. Many of these parents felt that education was extremely important. However, they also felt that there was very little evidence to suggest that their educational performance would be rewarded through the attainment of good jobs and/or equal housing opportunities. Hermans (2004) concluded that Ogbu's United States–based typology pertaining to voluntary and involuntary immigrants did not readily apply to the lives and overall schooling experiences of second- and third-generation Moroccan students in Belgium and the Netherlands. Hence, he seriously questioned the applicability of such a framework to a European immigrant and first-generation context. Although Ogbu's research is important, it only takes into account the perspectives of parents and not the perspectives of the youth themselves.

Therefore, much more youth-driven research is needed in this area. In other words, although the aforementioned research studies regarding the schooling of Latina/o and Moroccan students are important, they mostly take into account the academic underachievement of these racial/ethnic/linguistic groups. We think much more research needs to be undertaken that examines these groups' stories of academic high achievement. Thus, although the aforementioned research strands have served to expand our thinking regarding the educational performance and attainment of these racial/ethnic groups in a U.S. urban context, much more needs to be done regarding comparing and contrasting the schooling success factors of urban youth of color in an international context.

RESEARCH METHODS

In this section we will describe the research methodology we adopted to fill part of the earlier mentioned gap in the current research base.

Participant Selection Criteria and Data Collection

This project's research methods were designed to discover, compare, and contrast the types of factors that working-class Puerto Rican urban, public high school students enrolled in Milwaukee, Wisconsin, and urban Moroccan youth in Flanders, Belgium, attributed to their high academic achievement. Hence, we interviewed 10 Puerto Rican youth in Brew City, Wisconsin, and 3 Moroccan youth in Flanders, Belgium.

The youth we spoke with for this study had to meet five criteria that we developed to recruit possible participants. First, the student had to self-identify herself or himself as Puerto Rican or Moroccan. Second, the Puerto Rican youth must have been enrolled at their high school for at least 1 year and either be in the 11th or 12th grade, as the majority of students of color in the United States drop out of school by the 10th grade (Nieto, 1998). In other words, we thought it was important to interview "miracle workers," or those students who had survived schooling beyond the pivotal 10th-grade year, because they were much more likely to complete high school. With regard to the Moroccan youth we recruited, we sought recent secondary school graduates who were enrolled in the university at the time they were interviewed.

Third, the students must have had a cumulative grade point average (GPA) of 3.0 on a 4.0 scale or its equivalent in Belgium, as we believe this GPA is indicative of a high-achieving student. GPA, in the U.S. context, is measured from the lowest of 0.0 to the highest of 4.0. In other words, a 0.0–0.9 GPA would indicate a failing or "F" average, a 1.0–1.9 indicates a poor or "D" average, a 2.0–2.9 indicates an average or "C" average, a 3.0–3.5 is indicative of a good to very good or "B" average, and a 3.6–4.0 GPA represents an "A" or the highest of academic performance. Fourth, the student must have been enrolled in at least one honors or advanced placement class. Fifth, the students must come from a working-class background, as indicated by their parent/s' or caregiver/s' occupation/s. Based on these five criteria, we were able to identify and recruit 10 Puerto Rican students and 3 Moroccan men.

Our main data collection tool consisted of structured interviews. Our interview questions were designed to elicit the voices of our participants around the following five areas of inquiry:

1. Are there similarities and/or differences between the kinds of social capital/networks that high-achieving Puerto Rican and Moroccan students use within their classrooms and homes/communities?
2. Are there similarities and/or differences between the types of roles that adults, such as parents, guidance counselors, teachers, community members, and administrative staff, assume in the personal and scholastic lives of these students?
3. What kinds of classes are these students taking, and to what extent do students feel these courses have prepared them for college-level work?
4. To what extent does these students' working-class background impact their post-graduation aspirations?
5. To what extent are there notable similarities and/or differences between the schooling experiences of these students across gender?

More specifically, the questions that we integrated in our structured interviews were intended to garner information regarding our participants' age, family background, previous and current schooling experiences, and neighborhoods. We felt these types of questions would best capture responses related to the aforementioned research questions. We interviewed each student participant one time, and each interview lasted approximately 1 hour. All the interviews were audiotaped and transcribed verbatim.

Data Analysis

The objective of the phenomenological data analysis process is to identify and examine recurring meaning units, which are the "the smallest segments of texts that are understandable by themselves" (Tesch, 1994, p. 148). Moreover, phenomenological researchers "do not establish categories, but aim at discovering the 'themes' in the data" (Tesch, 1994, p. 148). Thus, our data analysis consisted of the three study team members reading and analyzing all the interviews to discover meaningful recurring themes and the ways in which our participants linked them to their high academic achievement. When these recurring themes were discovered within the interview data, we proceeded to color code them and place them into distinct categories called "success factors."

Research Settings

This study was conducted in two distinct settings. The first setting was University High School (a pseudonym), a large comprehensive high school located in a large Midwestern city. This high school enrolls 1,500 students from grades 9 to 12 of which 55% fall below the federal poverty line. Approximately 70% of the high school's students are of color, with 15% of these students being Puerto Rican. This school is regarded as one of only two of the district's best high schools out of 20, because its curriculum offers many advanced placement and honors level courses, and because 70% of its graduates go on to pursue some sort of postsecondary education. As a result, this high school attracts many students of color from around the city because of its reputation as a college preparatory high school. Moreover, we selected this high school for the study because of this reputation. Our interviews with the Puerto Rican students took place in a private room at the high school in order to maintain confidentiality for each participant.

The second setting was a small, rural town in the Flemish area of Belgium. Like the Puerto Rican participants, the Moroccan participants we interviewed in Belgium were also selected because of their status as high-achieving students when they were enrolled at the high school level. At the time they were interviewed, these participants were newly enrolled university students in Flanders. These interviews took place at an outdoor café, and they were also asked to reflect upon their recent experiences as young Moroccan men who had been recently enrolled in high school in Belgium. The Moroccan participants were interviewed by the first author, who relied on a cousin who is a police officer in the town where the study took place, as he is highly trusted in the Moroccan community.

The Puerto Rican Participants

Of the 10 Puerto Rican high achievers who shared their experiences with us, 7 were female and 3 were male. All had a grade point average (GPA) of 3.0 or higher. Additionally, all of them were enrolled in advanced placement (AP) or honors classes, and they all considered themselves to be English-dominant bilinguals. Moreover, all of the students commented that their parents had either dropped out of high school or had not had a college experience. Although all the students we spoke with came from working-class backgrounds, their personal backgrounds varied in many ways, including the neighborhoods where they resided and how they described their families. In the following section, we provide a brief glimpse into their school, community, and family lives.

Lisa was an 11th grader who was born and raised in Brew City. She lived with her extended family, which was comprised of her mother, father, maternal grandmother, sister, and maternal uncle. She mentioned that she hoped to be the first in her family to attend college. Lisa was enrolled in Honors Chemistry and Pre-Calculus. Her mother was a bill collector and her father a construction worker; both were high school graduates. She described her neighborhood as a quiet one with residents who were of different racial/ethnic backgrounds. She chose to attend Brew City High School because her mother had studied there. Most of Lisa's social networks were largely African American and Latina/o. Her post-graduation aspiration was to become a social worker.

Erica was an 11th grader who moved to Brew City from Puerto Rico when she was 10 years old. Her family consisted of her mother, father, and several sisters and brothers. She described herself as a "second mother" to her siblings, because she took a central role in cooking, cleaning, and caring for them because her parents worked long hours. Her mother was employed as a custodial crew supervisor, and her father worked with an auto parts supplier. Neither of Erica's parents graduated from high school. As a result of her parents' long work hours, she also mentioned that her social life outside school and home was non-existent. Her closest friend, however, was another Puerto Rican girl who attended a Catholic high school. Erica's post–high school aspirations included finding her place in the world of work.

An 11th grader who was born and raised in Brew City, Cecilia lived with her parents, two brothers, and a sister in the city's east side. She quickly pointed out that her brother was an "outpost student." In other words, he had been expelled from Brew City High School and referred to an alternative high school. When asked to describe her neighborhood surroundings, she remarked that there was a very prominent drug culture and that prostitution was rampant. She mentioned that her father was a construction worker and her mother a licensed practical nurse. She chose Brew City High School because of its academic reputation and diverse student body. She was enrolled in various honors classes, such as English and Trigonometry. She was also very involved in school-sponsored extracurricular activities. For example, she played flute and was on the high school's varsity softball and basketball teams. She talked about how her grandparents, who lived in Brew City, facilitated her academic accomplishments, because they offered her continual mentorship in times of need. She also mentioned the influence of her "school kid" friends who helped her with homework. Cecilia's life aspirations included being a physical education teacher and having her own family of a husband and three children.

Ivelisse moved to Brew City from Puerto Rico when she was 8 years old. Her mother, who had 2 years of college, was employed with the Brew City public school district as a teacher's aide, and her father was a high school graduate and a farmer in Puerto Rico. She was enrolled in the school district's bilingual education program for 6 years. Ivelisse resided in the city's Latino south side, which she described as being a rough area because of the high crime rate and overt gang presence. Like many of her Puerto Rican peers we spoke with, she stated that she chose Brew City High School because of its reputation regarding a strong college prep curriculum. In 11th grade, she was taking advanced Spanish and English classes and saw herself as a mother and teacher in the future. In addition to her regular academic course load, Ivelisse held a part-time job and considered herself very active in her church.

Rachel was a senior who, like many Puerto Ricans, had experienced circulatory migration. Although she was born in Brew City and her first four years of her formal schooling experiences were in public schools in the United States, her family later moved to Puerto Rico, where she attended public schools from the fifth through eighth grades. Rachel described her family as working class, because her mother was a high school graduate and a factory worker. She had three sisters who lived at home and ranged in age from 16 to 23 years. Her father had an eighth-grade education, was disabled, and unable to work. Rachel resided in the east side of the city and chose to attend Brew City High School because it was close to her home. She was enrolled in various honors classes and hoped to become an elementary school teacher. Rachel remarked that a majority of her social networks at school were multiracial/ethnic. Like a number of the students we interviewed, she mentioned being active in church.

Alexia was born and raised in Brew City. She was a junior who alternated between living with her mother and her boyfriend. Her mother dropped out of high school in the 10th grade and was employed as a receptionist. Her father, who also did not finish high school, worked with a maintenance company. She described her neighborhood as a tough one, and she expressed the desire to leave it when she finished college. Although she was 6 months pregnant, she was determined to remain in school, go to college, and obtain a career in high school teaching. She was enrolled in honors classes in U.S. History and Chemistry, and was active in the Latino community, where she volunteered her time at various social agencies like the YMCA, the Salvation Army, the Latino Community Center, and the Christian Center.

Limari was a senior who arrived in Brew City from Puerto Rico when she was 11 years old. Neither of her parents completed high school. Her mother was a lunchroom worker with the local public school district, and her father worked in a shoe factory. Limari spoke of the many racist teachers she had encountered over the years. For Limari, these teachers did not believe in her potential to be a stellar student. Her academic load was demanding—she was enrolled in several honors classes—but she still found time to play on the high school's varsity softball team. On more than one occasion, she credited her church friends and her mother for encouraging her to realize her potential as a student. She credited this encouragement with her ability to obtain a full academic scholarship to a major private university.

Daniel was born in the United States and was raised in several places within the United States. He was a junior with a 3.8 GPA in spite of the fact he had attended five different high schools in the last 3 years, in Texas, Florida, and Wisconsin. He lived with his mother, who completed high school and held two jobs, as a waitress and as a receptionist with the state's division of motor vehicles. His father, who also completed high school, was a truck driver. Daniel described his neighborhood as one where there was a lot of crime. He said that he was tired of living in such a dangerous neighborhood and felt that pursuing a postsecondary education would be his key to leaving it. Academically speaking, he was enrolled in three advanced placement classes, English, Psychology, and Economics, and was also taking a Pre-Calculus honors class. Additionally, he was an athlete and a member of the high school's varsity football and weightlifting teams. His future aspirations were to pursue an MBA in international business and own a business.

Jordan was born and raised in Brew City. He was a junior with a 3.4 GPA and is the only student we interviewed who did not have an immediate desire to go to college. Instead, he chose to enlist in the military. Jordan lived with his parents, two younger sisters, and one older brother. Neither of his parents completed high school. His mother worked in a shoe factory, and his father was disabled and unemployed. He mentioned that seeing his parents struggle economically helped him to realize that having an education was important and that he would be the first person in his family to graduate from high school. Jordan stated that he was once involved in gang and drug activities when he lived near the high school. He mentioned, however, that becoming a father had forced him to rethink what he wanted out of life. Consequently, he moved with his parents to the north side of Brew City so he could escape his previous lifestyle, concentrate more on his studies, and work to support his daughter. Although he mentioned liking sports and taking challenging classes, he felt working 30 hours a week washing and detailing cars prevented him from becoming more actively involved with extracurricular activities and enrolling in honors classes in addition to the Calculus class he was already taking.

Angel was born in Puerto Rico where he attended public school from the first through fourth grades. He moved with his parents and two sisters to Brew City at the beginning of the fifth grade. Angel was a 19-year-old senior with a 3.6 GPA, whose high academic achievement was the result of a traumatic experience he had when he was in the ninth grade and involved in a Brew City gang. While involved with his gang, he was shot and became paralyzed. Now confined to a wheelchair, he was receiving services from the exceptional education program because of speech difficulties he acquired as a result of the shooting. He revealed that this traumatic experience was an important turning point in his life, because it caused him to become serious about his schoolwork. He stated that becoming a high achiever would enable him to go to college and make it much easier for him to provide his 5-year-old daughter a life in a safe neighborhood with the material things he never had. Neither of his parents had completed high school. His mother worked at a bar, and his father worked in an auto parts factory. Angel was enrolled in an honors English class and commented that he was not quite sure what career he wanted to pursue, but that he was going to enroll in a 2-year college and decide his career path in the near future.

It is interesting to note that while all the students we spoke with desired a middle-class lifestyle, we noticed there were gender differences concerning their career choices and other future aspirations. For instance, the female students voiced their desire for academic achievement around the idea of one day being able to raise families and/or become a teacher, whereas the male students voiced their desire to obtain a postsecondary education so they could either have their own business or join the military. Hence, it was evident that these students' career choices and future aspirations were reflective of traditional gender roles.

The Moroccan Participants

Rashid lived in a rural area in Morocco until he was 5 years old. He moved with his mother and father to Brussels in search of employment. Eventually, his father found work in the textile industry.

Zaki's father worked in the coal mines in Wallonia, the French ethnic/linguistic region located in southern Belgium. His father immigrated to Belgium from Morocco when he was 13 years old. Hence, Zaki was born and raised in Belgium.

Mustafa was born and raised in Belgium. He lived with his grandfather, parents, and nine siblings in the same household in Brussels until he was 6 years old. During our interview, he mentioned that he acquired French from his uncles as a result of spending much time with them. As Arabic was the language of his grandparents and parents, he was bilingual. Once he started primary school in Flanders, he explained that he had a difficult time, because he had not yet acquired Flemish, which is the primary language of this region in Belgium. As a result, he recounted that the director of the primary school approached his father and strongly encouraged him to encourage his son to acquire Flemish for school purposes. As Mustafa stated, "School was very difficult for me because I did not understand anything. My parents also did not understand Flemish. I remember that my teachers would always ask me to seek help with school assignments from my parents. But, my parents could not help me, because they did not understand Flemish. So my grades at school were not good."

STUDY LIMITATIONS

It is important for us to stress and note that our study has several limitations. First of all, we must stress that our total number of participants was small. Based on the schooling experiences of 10 Puerto Rican students and 3 Moroccan students, we cannot possibly draw general conclusions, as related to the schooling of *all* Puerto Rican schooled in the United States and/or *all* Moroccan students schooled in Belgium. To draw such generalizations would be disingenuous on our part. Nonetheless, we do feel comfortable noting that although we interviewed a small number of participants, their experiences are rich and can offer keen insights regarding the factors that greatly contributed to their high academic achievement.

Another study limitation that we must note concerns the matter of our positions as educational researchers. Hence, the interpretations that we have attached to our participants' experiences are limited by our subject positions as three Latino males born and schooled in a variety of schooling settings, particularly Puerto Rico and the United States. Moreover, we come from a variety of class positions; namely, working class and middle class as defined by our previous and present income levels. Finally, we identify ourselves as heterosexual and able-bodied.

RESULTS

In this section we will discuss the results of our study. We will cluster the insights springing from our interviews in a thematic way. This will allow us to highlight the main variables that appear to impact upon our respondents' academic success.

Religiosity as Source of Inspiration and Social Capital

Many of the students we interviewed voiced a connection between their high academic achievement and access to sources of social capital through their ties to a religious organization and/or other extracurricular activities. When asked which religious faith or church they professed or belonged to, our Puerto Rican participants stated that they were either Catholic or Pentecostal. The three Moroccan students who were interviewed in Belgium identified themselves as Muslim. Our Puerto Rican participants mentioned that the main benefit of participating in these activities consisted of targeted recreational activities for youth that steered them away from anti-school, oppositional youth culture like gang membership and truancy. These high degrees of social capital also facilitated their access to school-related resources like homework help and mentorship. Daniel commented:

> "Growing up my mom always took me and my sister to church and she always had us involved in youth groups as far as you know, Sunday school and we went on trips with our church groups and that always helped me keep on a straight path."

In addition to his church involvement, Daniel's participation on athletic teams also played a major role in his high school career, because it helped him gain much access to positive help-seeking resources like information regarding college, mentorship from his teammates' parents, and access to computers at his friends' homes. This intergenerational closure (Carbonaro, 1998), marked by social and informational networks comprised of Daniel's friends and their parents, proved to be valuable for Daniel, because he now is very confident that he has the information that he needs to become successful in college, get a job after graduation, and obtain a middle-class lifestyle. He commented:

"A lot of my friends who I play with on the teams are a lot better off than me. Like, David's parents live out in the suburbs and both his parents are college psychology professors and make a lot of money. They both have been a great influence on me because they've talked to me about what I need to get into college and be successful in college. They helped me make the decision on which university to apply to. I like their advice because I see that they have become successful. I want to follow their examples and also have a big house and nice cars like them one day."

As evidenced in recent studies (Flores-González, 1999, 2002; Hébert & Reis, 1999), several of our participants suggested that multicultural peer networks consisting of other high-achieving urban youth were valuable assets that influenced their academic achievement. Cecilia remarked that she valued her church involvement and its impact on her academic achievement because of the multicultural peer networks she belonged to. These networks were highly conducive to supportive relationships and to her strong sense of belonging. In fact, although the majority of the students were English-dominant bilinguals, they spoke about their multicultural approach in their school peer networks, as they expressed the importance of their friendships with Latinas/os and other friends of color like African Americans and Mexican Americans. This finding suggests that students seek friends who possess diverse cultural and linguistic backgrounds because they positively support their academic achievement.

"Ever since I was in the ninth grade, I have been going to church regularly. I also sing in the church choir. The people at church have always been friendly and supportive of me. I feel like I really belong. I have also met a lot of people at church. I have a lot of friends from different backgrounds. I have Hispanic, White, Asian, and Black friends. We all treat each other as friends and we keep each other in line. I really think going to church has helped me become a better student."

Estrella also talked about her involvement in a church and connected it with her high academic achievement. Like Cecilia, she was able to participate in church activities with peer networks consisting of other Latina/o youth. She also felt that these friendships and her participation in religious-based activities had a positive impact on her academic achievement. She remarked:

"I'm involved in church very much. I have lots of friends in church. We do lots of things together. We do retreats and we invite other youths to come. We also evangelize together. We want other youths to know God and Jesus. There are also lots of camps in the summer and conventions in the Midwest. There are lots of Latinos that get together for these conventions and we have lots of fun. I really think that these church things have helped me be a good student."

While Daniel, Cecilia, and Estrella talked about the importance of receiving mentorship and informational resources through their social networks at church, several students specifically mentioned the influence of spirituality in their scholastic lives. This particular finding is consistent with recent research (Cook, 2000; Jeynes, 2003), which shows that religious people are more likely to have an internal locus of control because they feel that the spirit of God resides within them and steers them to positive things like high academic achievement. Rachel commented:

"God has helped me become a good student. He has helped me keep focused. I know he helps me do the best I can in school."

Likewise, Limari also commented:

"God had helped me become a good student because He has been with me through all my struggles."

Whereas these participants credited their high academic achievement with their participation to church and school-related activities, other participants spoke about their involvement with community-based agencies and how it facilitated their engagement with school and meeting people from different walks of life. Alexia stated:

"I do all kinds of work with people in the community. I work with the Private Industry Council and help people get jobs. I also work with the Historical Society. These jobs keep me busy and focused on school and help me meet lots of interesting people."

Just like the recent research that shows religiosity (Jeynes, 2003; Muller & Ellison, 2001; Park, 2001; Sikkink & Hernández, 2003) and participation in extracurricular activities (Flores-González, 1999, 2002; Hébert & Reis, 1999) has a positive impact on academic achievement for students of color, our participants also suggested that involvement in church and other school and community-based extracurricular activities served an important dual function. First, church involvement served as a protective measure by discouraging them from participating in oppositional youth culture (i.e., gang life and truancy), because it impinges on their scholastic endeavors. Second, involvement in these kinds of activities also contributed to their high degrees of social capital through the intergenerational closure between these students, their friends, and their friends' parents (Carbonaro, 1998). This high degree of intergenerational closure was valuable, because it insured that these students gained access to important resources like good advice through adult mentorship and other positive help-seeking behaviors that encouraged them to pursue academic excellence and a school kid identity (Flores-González, 2002). Additionally, recent research (Carter, 2007; Suárez-Orozco, Suárez-Orozco, & Todorova, 2008) strongly suggests that high achievers of color including immigrant students are much more likely to feel comfortable crossing racial/ethnic, class, and linguistic borders. Furthermore, these high-achieving border crossers also actively seek membership in extracurricular activities, which suggests a high degree of bidirectionality between and among high academic performance and participation in these out of school activities (Carter 2007; Suárez-Orozco, Suarez-Orozco, & Todorova, 2008).

Finally, just like the Puerto Rican participants who discussed the impact that religiosity had on their academic achievement, Rashid, Zaki, and Mustafa mentioned the special importance that their Muslim faith had on their outlook regarding their roles in school. Zaki stated, "Learning is highly valued and stressed in Islam. In fact, the better you do in school, the more you please Allah." Mustafa reinforced Zaki's sentiments when he explained the significance of the word *Iqra* in the Arabic language. *Iqra* literally means "to learn" and is regarded as being the first word revealed in the Qur'an. Contrary to what many deficit theorists would argue, then, education for both the Puerto Rican and Moroccan participants and their families is highly valued and motivates and drives them to excel at scholastic endeavors.

Affirmation and Maintenance of Ethnic Identity

All the high-achieving students with whom we spoke were very clear about their respective ethnic identities. All of the participants in this study were very quick to note their Moroccan or Puerto Rican ethnicity. This particular finding challenges the belief held by other researchers (Fordham & Ogbu, 1986; Ogbu, 1978) that, for many students of color, being a good student is essentially tantamount to "acting White." Contrary to these beliefs, Flores-González (1999) documented that the high-achieving students she interviewed did not hide their Puerto Rican ethnicity. In fact, Hine (1992) found that the negative stereotypes held by teachers and peers served as a motivating tool for the Puerto Rican high achievers in her school to do well in school. Additionally, we also believe this phenomenon reflects the successful utilization of our participants' ethnic identities, because they were able to easily make the transition between their home and school worlds.

This finding compels us to believe that our participants' sense of school-based marginalization, rather than cause them to resist the idea of schooling, actually worked to motivate them to academically perform well. Thus, we have decided to name this finding the *marginalization as motivation concept*. This concept also works to support previous research (Flores-González, 1999, 2002) that challenges the commonly held belief that involuntary migrant group status, often associated with the sociopolitical reality of Puerto Ricans, is a strong and predictable indicator of low academic achievement (Ogbu, 1978). However, it is imperative that we state that although the students in this study noted that their teachers' and/or principals'/headmasters' low academic expectations had a positive, motivating effect on their academic performance, this phenomenon generally has the opposite, detrimental effect on urban students. In other words, our participants were rare exceptions to this rule, as low academic expectations usually have devastating effects on urban students' scholarly motivations, self-confidence, and academic achievements.

Similarly, Zaki remarked that education was very important to him, because Islam stressed the importance of acquiring knowledge to enrich the mind in addition to securing a secure economic future. However, he noted that he had the unfortunate experience of some of his Belgian teachers suggesting that in place of pursuing an academic track for university-level studies, he should instead pursue technical trades that would allow him to "work with his hands." Rashid echoed these sentiments when he disclosed that they had both studied very hard and get good grades in order to prove their teachers wrong. Currently, they are both enrolled in universities in Flanders. As Zaki stated:

> "Some of my high school teachers told me that I shouldn't work so hard, that I should just try to try to work with our hands. We were also told that we were not that intelligent. Being told this made us want to work harder to prove them wrong. So, when we received good grades and made it to the university, we told them and they said 'very nice, we did not think you were capable.' We have heard them say these kinds of things to many Moroccan students like us."

Similar to Zaki and Rashid, the majority of Puerto Rican students we spoke with also expressed their frustration about how Puerto Ricans were often negatively represented by their school peers and many of their teachers. In turn, they thought that their high academic achievement could have the potential of dispelling these negative stereotypical images. Jordan stated:

> "I'm proud to be Puerto Rican and bilingual. But, you know, White people stereotype Puerto Ricans and think that we're not serious about our education. I want to prove them wrong."

Jasmine also commented on the negative stereotypes that White students in her advanced placement classes held toward her by virtue of being the only minority student in the class. Therefore, she also felt compelled to use her high academic performance as a way to prove others wrong about the academic potential of Puerto Ricans.

"Sometimes in my AP [advanced placement] classes, like AP English and AP History, some of the White students make you feel really small because you're the only Latino student in the class. I remember one time when a boy asked me what I was doing in the class. He said that he didn't think that people like us could be in these kinds of classes. I told him that he shouldn't be so stereotypical and that we can be smart, too."

These students expressed pride in their Puerto Rican ethnicity. It became evident that many of the students used their education as a tool with which to prove to their peers they had the potential to be good students.

Maternal Influences on Students' Academic Achievement

Most of the students we spoke with mentioned the three distinct roles that their mothers played in their school and home lives. First, these mothers often took it upon themselves to help their daughter or son with schoolwork. When the mother felt she could not directly help with schoolwork, she actively sought out the necessary resources that would facilitate her child's learning process. Second, several of the students felt compelled to make their mothers proud of them by getting good grades. Third, several of the students commented that their mothers served as their friends or mentors in times of need or personal crisis. Rashid, Zaki, and Mustafa mentioned that in the Muslim faith, mothers were charged with providing their children with informal and formal education.

Like many youth who aspire to acquire material possessions, Rashid commented that he had desired to work in order to purchase a nice car, among other things. However, his mother did not approve of these plans and pushed him to study rather than seek work in order to satisfy his material desires. Mustafa also stated that his father, unlike his mother, stressed the importance of only completing high school, so that he could work and purchase homes and other material goods. However, he chose to follow his mother's advice and pursue a postsecondary education in order to acquire more knowledge in keeping with the Islamic notion of *Iqra*, or aspiring to find favor with Allah through the acquisition of knowledge through formal education.

Furthermore, Rashid shared another vivid memory regarding the way his mother had served as a staunch advocate for education. This memory involved his sister and her struggles to be held to high academic expectations at the secondary level in order to be well prepared for university studies in Belgium. Rashid stated:

"My mother found herself visiting my sister's school, because she was notified that my sister had not passed an exam. As a result, the teachers at the school wanted her to go to a lower academic level. But, my mother would not allow this. She told the teachers that she believed my sister could do the higher level work. But the teacher kept insisting that my sister should be lowered. My mother said no. So, they allowed my sister to remain at the higher level, and the next year she passed. So, my mother and sister were able to prove these teachers wrong."

It is highly evident that Rashid's mother served as her children's advocate, as she made it a mission to dispel teachers' negative beliefs regarding the academic potential of her children.

Similar to Rashid and Mustafa, several Puerto Rican participants in our study also commented on the special roles their mothers played in their academic achievement. For example, when asked to elaborate on her mother's role in her education, Lisa stated:

"Ever since I was in middle school, my mom has been sending me to pre-college programs and doing things like getting me stuff on the ACT and the kinds of questions they ask on that test. I also go to my mom for personal problems that come up. My mom is always coming down hard on me to do well in school. So if she can't help me with my school stuff she finds somebody who can."

Lisa's mother, like other mothers of students in this study, "went the extra mile" to counsel her daughter and seek informational resources that would aid in the college application and general learning processes. This finding supports the work of several scholars and their discussions pertaining to the influence of Latina/Puerto Rican mothers in the academic lives of their children (Hidalgo, 2000; Hine, 1992; Gándara, 1995; Reis & Díaz, 1999; Rolón, 2000), because our participants' mothers also held their children to high academic expectations and actively sought out human resources that could help their children (e.g., with homework) in the event that they were not able to.

Other students spoke about the power of their mother's influence and expressed the desire to do well in school to make their mothers proud of them. Daniel commented:

"My mom has been my inspiration to do well in school. I remember that I used to make bad grades in school and my mother would become sad. When I started to bring report cards home with As in them for the first time, I remember the happy look in my mother's eyes. When I saw that look in her eyes, I just felt that it was much more rewarding to get good grades. I also remember going to family picnics and my mother would be talking about my grades. The rest of the family would then start talking about me. They were all proud of me."

Daniel was driven to do well in school in order to make his mother happy. It was also important for him to be the pride of his family. He also mentioned that his school did not do much to help him select a college or to fill out financial aid or admissions forms. Although his mother was not a high school graduate and therefore had never been to college, she took up the role of helping him acquire and fill out the necessary forms he would need to go to college.

Erica was unique from the other participants in that she contrasted the roles that both her parents played in her school success. Whereas she perceived that her father played a limited role as an authority figure that demanded she follow the "rules of the house," she commented on the words of encouragement and friendship that were characteristic of her mother's role as a nurturing supporter.

> "My mother is the best. She supports me in everything I do. She is always willing to support me at whatever I do at school. She is always very excited about helping me with my work and she always talks to me more like a friend than a mom. My father is very different. He always comes across as the authority figure."

Cecilia also relied exclusively on her mother for her trust and support in times of personal need and remarked that teachers and friends could not be trusted for revealing or seeking support in times of crises. It was evident, then, that she was involved in a high-quality interpersonal relationship with her mother.

> "When I have a personal problem, I don't really trust my teachers or friends. I usually go to my mother who is always willing to be there for me because I know she won't go around spilling my personal life to everyone."

Rachel spoke about her mother encouraging her to do her best in school, so she would not be a high school dropout like her. Rachel's mother never had the experience of going to college; nonetheless, she knew the importance of after-school programs, tutoring services, and having access to college information, because these things would greatly facilitate her daughter's entry into college. Rachel commented:

> "My mom dropped out of high school in the 10th grade. So she doesn't want me to have the hard life that she has had. For her, it's a top priority that I stay in school and go to college. She has gotten me in after-school programs and found me jobs. She makes a lot of phone calls to people and asks about the kinds of programs that exist to get me help with schoolwork and information I need to get into college."

Based on these statements, it was clear that mothers felt much more obligated to take on substantial roles in the schooling lives of these high achievers and that fathers were not as willing to assume these types of

roles. However, we must note that the relative absence of our participants' fathers in no way is meant to suggest that these fathers were not
interested in their children's academic success. On the contrary, our participants strongly alluded to the fact that their fathers desired their children's academic success. However, their time was often compromised by
having to assume multiple responsibilities (e.g., multiple jobs). Nonetheless, although mothers also assumed multiple responsibilities, they went
above and beyond the extra mile to also take on the important responsibility of securing additional, community, and school-based academic
resources for their youth.

Moreover, we must note that this particular finding should not be interpreted to suggest that the mothers of underachieving youth of color are
inherently less caring and/or less supportive than the mothers of high achievers. We can only speculate that the mothers of the high-achieving youth in
this study were perhaps better connected to community and school-based
resources. Hence, the high achievers' mothers' social networks consisted
of individuals who had access to *high-stakes information networks* (Liou,
Antrop-González, & Cooper, 2009). Thus, these networks possessed
information that made it much easier for the high achievers' mothers to
navigate the complicated bureaucracies of community-based organizations
and schools. Additional, recent research further reveals and describes the
important extent to which working-class mothers of color utilize their *community cultural wealth* (Liou et al., 2009; Yosso, 2005). In the next section,
we highlight how students described good teachers and the potential they
could have on their high academic achievement.

The Role of Teachers and Other School Staff Members

All the participants in our study talked about the potential impact that caring teachers could have on their high academic achievement. The recurring
theme of caring was especially prevalent in their descriptions of good teachers. Our participants, like students in previous studies (Antrop-González,
2003; Nieto, 1998; Valenzuela, 1999), defined caring teachers as those
individuals who were interested in getting to know them on a personalized
basis, who could be trusted enough to talk about their personal problems
and seek advice, and who would hold them to high academic expectations.
Our participants also mentioned they felt it was important for students to
be able to rely on teachers, guidance counselors, and administrators for
obtaining information or assistance with important tasks like applying
for college, tutoring, or successfully securing part-time employment. Erica
defined a caring teacher in the following way:

> "A good teacher is one who knows you, cares about what you do,
> pushes students, and cares about the stuff going on in your life. A good
> teacher also wants you to absorb information and understand it."

Cecilia also defined a caring teacher as one who held students to high academic expectations and who constantly encouraged students to do high-quality schoolwork.

> "A good teacher is someone who cares enough not to accept low-quality work. I like being pushed and told that I can do better. Some of my better teachers are like this."

Zaki also described a caring teacher when he described an experience he had in high school. The high school Zaki attended in Flanders had a student body that he described as being "90 percent Moroccan, Tunisian, and French speaking." Most of the students felt the director of this school was racist, because he strongly encouraged students to leave the school. As Zaki stated:

> "Although many of us who were Moroccan or Tunisian felt the director of the school was racist, we had a White teacher who did everything in his power to help us. In fact, he once told us that he would never leave the school until the director left. This is the only memory I have of a teacher who cared."

Ironically, although these students had clear definitions of what it meant to be a caring teacher, only one Puerto Rican Spanish teacher, a Puerto Rican guidance counselor, and one White, Flemish teacher were viewed as being caring teachers or staff members. These students' other teachers, per se, were not described as caring. Consequently, our participants did not feel compelled to seek or maintain meaningful, interpersonal relationships, advice, or mentorship with the rest of their teachers.

IMPLICATIONS FOR RESEARCH AND EDUCATION

The Moroccan and Puerto Rican students who participated in this study attributed four success factors to their high academic achievement. Based on these success factors, we offer several suggestions for educators who work with students of color. First, teachers, guidance counselors, and school administrators/headmasters should encourage more Puerto Rican/Latino and Moroccan students to seek and/or maintain membership and participation in school-sponsored and community-based extracurricular activities. These activities can instill pro-school behaviors and facilitate the acquisition of social capital and intergenerational closure. These are enhanced when important college-related information and mentorship are shared between students, their friends, and their friends' parents. It must be kept in mind that restricting participation in extracurricular activities to Puerto Rican/Latino and Moroccan students with good grades only exacerbates the inequitable access to the social networks and subsequent information that these students need to be academically successful (Flores-González, 2000).

Second, school personnel should foster the development of their students' bicultural identities as assets that promote academic achievement. The high-achieving Puerto Rican and Moroccan students in this study did not find it necessary to "act White" or deny their ethnic and/or cultural identities in order to academically succeed. In fact, unlike the Moroccan parents in Hermans (2004), the Moroccan students in our study revealed that they viewed doing well in school as a key to obtaining good paying jobs and acquiring material wealth. On the contrary, they were more likely to affirm their respective ethnicities and use it as a way to prove to others that they have the potential to be academically successful in spite of the negative stereotypes and low academic expectations that some of their teachers and peers may hold.

Moreover, it is imperative that teachers and administrators/headmasters be willing to fully engage their students' and their families' lived realities (Raible & Irizarry, 2007). In other words, school agents must be willing to internalize dispositions, such as learning their students' primary language and understanding their primary culture. Furthermore, these dispositions also include living in or near their students' and their families' neighborhoods. In the event that these residential dispositions are not possible, teachers and administrators/headmasters at the very least should make genuine and intentional attempts to get to know where and how their students live. Consequently, school agents would be much more likely to intimately know their students' social milieu.

We also strongly encourage teachers, administrators/headmasters, and guidance counselors to facilitate and encourage higher enrollment in AP/honors classes for both underachieving and high-achieving Puerto Rican/Latina/o and Moroccan students. These classes must also infuse more sociopolitical and historical topics that are pertinent and of interest to these students. By conceptualizing classes that are culturally relevant (Ladson-Billings, 1995), students will be much more willing to form relationships with their teachers and learn from them. Moreover, these culturally relevant courses contribute to much more engaging and interesting school cultures. However, in order to conceptualize culturally relevant courses, teachers and administrators/headmasters must be willing to enable their students to have a voice and vote in terms of these courses' conceptualization (Freire, 1970). When students have a strong role to play in the construction of these courses, they are more likely to participate because they find them to be relevant to their lives.

In addition, it is of the utmost importance that teachers understand the important role families and mothers play in the lives of their children. The mothers of participating students played a crucial role in the lives of their children. Like the mothers highlighted in previous studies (Hine,

1992; Rolón, 2000), they spent time with their children, helped them with homework or found them homework help when they could not provide it, and offered encouragement and mentorship in times of personal crisis. Schools can benefit from relying more on the wisdom of these mothers and understanding that parents are indeed involved in their children's lives and care about their education. Therefore, it is essential for educators to think beyond traditional, middle-class conceptions of parental involvement by realizing that families have many ways of being involved in their children's education that involve home and community-based funds of knowledge (Moll, Amanti, Neff, & González, 1992). Schools can make additional efforts to make themselves inviting to Latina/o and Moroccan parents by hiring more bilingual/bicultural staff, including a Latina/o or Moroccan parent that serves as a liaison between the school and community so that school personnel can begin to explore, identify, and understand the funds of knowledge (Moll et al., 1992) that students and parents already bring to school.

Caring teachers have the potential to greatly impact the high academic achievement of Puerto Rican and Moroccan students. Caring teachers hold their students to high academic expectations, know their students on a personal basis, and work hard to make classes interesting, engaging, and culturally relevant to their students' lives (Ladson-Billings, 1999). Our participants' voices strongly suggest that high-achieving youth of color in Belgium and the United States experience high academic performance mainly due to factors outside of schools. Nonetheless, we have described several tangible methods that school agents can conceptualize and implement that have the potential to transform their places of learning from centers of student resistance to *schools as sanctuaries* (De Jesús & Antrop-González, 2006). Schools become sanctuaries when school agents are willing to engage their students and families in authentic relationships marked by culturally relevant pedagogy (Ladson-Billings, 1995) and high academic expectations, and recognize the community grounded resources that community-based organizations can bring to schools as partners.

Finally, parents/caregivers have much to share with their children in the learning and teaching process. In this study, our participants suggested that, contrary to deficit model educationists' weak conceptions of parental involvement, mothers played a very active role in their children's academic success. Hence, school agents would be wise to include parents/caregivers in the educational process as partners with voice and vote.

AUTHORS' NOTES

This research project was funded by generous grants from the University of Wisconsin–Milwaukee Institute for Excellence in Urban Education and the University of Wisconsin System Institute on Race and Ethnicity. Finally, the authors would like to sincerely thank the anonymous reviewers and the editors of this chapter and book for their generous and significant feedback on earlier drafts of this chapter.

NOTES

1. "DiaspoRican/s" is a term coined by the New York Rican poet Mariposa to denote Puerto Ricans whose identity primarily centers on their lived experiences in the United States. The United States has colonized Puerto Rico since 1898.

REFERENCES

Antrop-González, R. (2003). "This school is my sanctuary:" The Dr. Pedro Albizu Campos alternative high school. *Journal of the Center for Puerto Rican Studies, 15*(2), 232–255.

Antrop-González, R., Vélez, W., & Garrett, T. (2004). Challenging the academic (mis)categorization of urban youth: Building a case for Puerto Rican high achievers. *Multiple Voices, 7*(1), 16–32.

Antrop-González, R., Vélez, W., & Garrett, T. (2005). *¿Dónde están los estudiantes puertorriqueños académicamente exitosos* [Where are the academically successful Puerto Rican students]? Success factors of high achieving Puerto Rican high school students. *Journal of Latinos and Education, 4*(2), 74–95.

Antrop-González, R., Vélez, W., & Garrett, T. (2007). Religion and high academic achievement in Puerto Rican high school students. *Religion and Education, 34*(1), 63–75.

Carbonaro, W. J. (1998). A little help from my friend's parents: Intergenerational closure and educational outcomes. *Sociology of Education, 71*, 295–313.

Carter, P. (2007). *Keepin' it real: School success beyond Black and White*. New York: Oxford University Press.

Conchas, G. (2001). Structuring failure and success: Understanding the variability in Latino school engagement. *Harvard Educational Review, 71*(3), 475–504.

Cook, K. V. (2000). "You have to have somebody watching your back, and if that's God, then that's mighty big": The church's role in the resilience of inner-city youth. *Adolescence, 35*(140), 717–730.

Creswell, J. W. (1998). *Qualitative inquiry and research design: Choosing among five traditions*. Thousand Oaks, CA: Sage.

De Jesús, A., & Antrop-González, R. (2006). Instrumental relationships and high expectations: Exploring critical care in two Latino community-based schools. *Intercultural Education, 17*(3), 281–299.

Díaz, E. I. (1998). Perceived factors influencing the academic underachievement of talented students of Puerto Rican descent. *Gifted Child Quarterly, 42*(2), 105–122.

Eldering, L. (1997). Ethnic minority students in the Netherlands from a cultural-ecological perspective. *Anthropology and Education Quarterly, 28*(3), 318–329.

Flores-González, N. (1999). Puerto Rican high achievers: An example of ethnic and academic identity compatibility. *Anthropology and Education Quarterly, 30*(3), 343–362.

Flores-González, N. (2000). The structuring of extracurricular opportunities and Latino student retention. *Journal of Poverty, 4*(1/2), 85–108.

Flores-González, N. (2002). *School kids/street kids: Identity development in Latino students.* New York: Teachers College Press, Columbia University.

Fordham, S., & Ogbu, J. U. (1986). Black students' school success: Coping with the burden of "acting White." *Urban Review, 18*(3), 176–206.

Gándara, P. (1995). *Over the ivy walls: The educational mobility of low-income Chicanos.* New York: SUNY Press.

Gibson, M. (1988). *Accommodation without assimilation: Sikh immigrants in an American high school.* Ithaca, NY: Cornell University Press.

Hébert, T. P., & Reis, S. M. (1999). Culturally diverse high-achieving students in an urban high school. *Urban Education, 34*(4), 428–457.

Hermans, P. (2004). Applying Ogbu's theory of minority academic achievement to the situation of Moroccans in the low countries. *Intercultural Education, 15*(4), 431–439.

Hidalgo, N. M. (2000). Puerto Rican mothering strategies: The role of mothers and grandmothers in promoting school success. In S. Nieto (Ed.), *Puerto Rican students in U.S. schools* (pp. 167–196). Mahwah, NJ: Erlbaum.

Hine, C. Y. (1992). The home environment of gifted Puerto Rican children: Family factors which support high achievement. *Proceedings of the Third National Research Symposium on Limited English Proficient Student Issues: Focus on Middle and High School Issues* (pp. 1–20). Washington, DC: U.S. Department of Education.

Jeynes, W. H. (2003). The effects of Black and Hispanic 12th graders living in intact families and being religious on their academic achievement. *Urban Education, 38*(1), 35–57.

Ladson-Billings, G. (1995). Toward a theory of culturally relevant pedagogy. *American Educational Research Journal, 32*(3), 465–491.

Liou, D., Antrop-González, R., & Cooper, R. (2009). Unveiling the promise of community cultural wealth to sustaining Latina/o students' college-going information networks. *Educational Studies, 45*(6), 534–555.

Moll, L., Amanti, C., Neff, D., & González, N. (1992). Funds of knowledge for teaching: Using a qualitative approach to connect homes and classrooms. *Theory Into Practice, 21*(2), 132–141.

Muller, C. (2001). The role of caring in the teacher-student relationship for at-risk students. *Sociological Inquiry, 71*(2), 241–255.

Muller, C., & Ellison, C. G. (2001). Religious involvement, social capital, and adolescents' academic progress: Evidence from the national education longitudinal study of 1988. *Sociological Focus, 34*(2), 155–182.

Nieto, S. (1998). Fact and fiction: Stories of Puerto Ricans in U.S. schools. *Harvard Educational Review, 68*(2), 133–163.

Nieto, S. (2000). Puerto Rican students in U.S. schools: A brief history. In S. Nieto (Ed.), *Puerto Rican students in U.S. schools* (pp. 5–38). Mahwah, NJ: Erlbaum.

Ogbu, J. U. (1978). *Minority education and caste: The American system in cross-cultural perspective.* New York: Academic Press.

Ogbu, J. U., & Simons, H. (1998). Voluntary and involuntary minorities: A cultural-ecological theory of school performance with some implications for education. *Anthropology and Education Quarterly, 28*(3), 318–329.

Park, H. (2001). Religiousness as a predictor of academic performance among high school students. *Journal of Research on Christian Education, 10*(2), 361–378.

Raible, J., & Irrizarry, J. (2007). Transracialized selves and the emergence of post-White identities. *Race, Ethnicity and Education, 10*(2), 177–198.

Reis, S. M., & Díaz, E. (1999). Economically disadvantaged urban female students who achieve in schools. *Urban Review, 31*(1), 31–54.

Rolón, C. A. (2000). Puerto Rican female narratives about self, school, and success. In S. Nieto (Ed.), *Puerto Rican students in U.S. schools* (pp. 141–166). Mahwah, NJ: Erlbaum.

Seidman, I. (1998). *Interviewing as qualitative research: A guide for researchers in education and the social sciences* (2nd ed.). New York: Teachers College Press, Columbia University.

Sikkink, D., & Hernández, E. (2003). *Religion matters: Predicting schooling success among Latino youth.* Notre Dame, IN: University of Notre Dame, Institute for Latino Studies.

Solórzano, D., & Ornelas, A. (2002). A critical race analysis of advanced placement classes: A case of educational inequalities. *Journal of Latinos and Education, 1*(4), 215–229.

Spring, J. (1994). *Deculturalization and the struggle for equality: A brief history of the education of dominated cultures in the United States.* New York: McGraw-Hill.

Stanton-Salazar, R. D. (2001). *Manufacturing hope and despair: The school and kin support networks of U.S.-Mexican youth.* New York: Teachers College Press, Columbia University.

Strauss, A., & Corbin, J. (1998). *Basics of qualitative research: Techniques and procedures for developing grounded theory.* Thousand Oaks, CA: Sage.

Suárez-Orozco, C., Suárez-Orozco, M. M., & Todorova, I. (2008). *Learning a new land: Immigrant students in American society.* Cambridge, MA: Belknap Press of Harvard University Press.

Tesch, R. (1994). The contribution of a qualitative method: Phenomenological research. In M. Lagenbach, C. Vaughn, & L. Aagaard (Eds.), *An introduction to educational research* (pp. 143–157). Boston: Allyn & Bacon.

Valenzuela, A. (1999). *Subtractive schooling: U.S.-Mexican youth and the politics of caring.* Albany: SUNY Press.

Yosso, T. J. (2005). Whose culture has capital? A critical race theory discussion of cultural community wealth. *Race, Ethnicity and Education 8*(1), 69–92.

12 Full Service and Extended Schools
The Path to Equity?

Alan Dyson

INTRODUCTION

In the period between their first election victory in 1997 and their ultimate defeat in 2010, New Labour governments in England increasingly sought to develop a distinctive "outward-facing" role for schools. Rather than simply expecting schools to teach children well within the confines of the standard curriculum and normal school day, they also encouraged (and ultimately required) them to make available a range of additional activities and services for children, families, and members of local communities. Schools working in this way were given various labels—"extended schools" being the longest-lasting—but essentially they all offered a mixture of extracurricular activities, child care, child and family support, adult learning, and community use of school facilities (see, e.g., DCSF, s.d., 2002, 2003b, 2003c, 2005a; HM Government, 2007). In many ways, these schools were similar to the "full service" and "community" schools (again, the labels vary) that have sprung up in many administrations, particularly in the United States, over the past two decades (Dyson, 2010).

Most, if not all, developments of this kind tend to be predicated on some more or less explicit notion of educational and wider social equity. As we shall see, a common claim for full service and extended schools is that the services and activities they offer are capable of overcoming or significantly ameliorating the manifest disadvantages experienced by the children, families, and communities they serve. If such a claim could be substantiated, schools of this kind would have to be regarded as major contributors to educational and social equity and would have a claim to forming a major component of many countries' education policies.

In this chapter, I wish to examine this claim. In doing so, I shall draw upon a series of evaluations colleagues and I have undertaken of extended school initiatives in England (Cummings, Dyson, & Todd, 2004; Cummings et al., 2005, 2006, 2007a; Dyson, Millward, & Todd, 2002), supplemented by findings from other related studies in which we have been involved (Clark, Dyson, & Millward, 1999; Crowther, Cummings, Dyson, & Millward, 2003), and by the international research evidence. Reviewing this evidence leads me to conclude that the claims for full service and extended schools are undermined by three fundamental problems: the weakness of the evidence base, the limited scope of what such schools can do, and the highly problematic political relationships implied by many such schools. In each case, however, I wish to suggest that there are ways in which these problems might, in future, be overcome. Although, therefore, extending the role of schools is, by itself, unlikely to tackle the hitherto intractable problems of social and educational disadvantage, it is possible that what we have learned from full service and extended schools might point the way to more powerful strategies in the future.

EXCELLENCE AND EQUITY IN THE ENGLISH POLICY CONTEXT

The development of extended schools in England has to be seen in the context of the debates around excellence and equity that have informed English education policy in recent decades. As long ago as the late 1960s, there was a growing concern that the school system was sacrificing excellence of performance as a result, among other things, of an ideological commitment to comprehensive (i.e., nonselective) schooling and "progressive" teaching (see, e.g., Cox & Dyson, 1971). By the mid-1970s, even the prime minister of a left-of-center government could be heard worrying publicly about the quality of the school system, and whether a focus on individual development was preventing the system meeting the economic needs of the country (Callaghan, 1976). The policy response took some time to formulate, but when it came, it took the form of a reform package based on neoliberal principles (Gunter et al., 2010) of the kind now familiar in many Western democracies. In essence, this package involved establishing curricular control from central government, controlling school performance through various high-stakes accountability mechanisms, and creating an engine for "improvement" by introducing an education quasi-market in which schools compete for students.

When a center-left New Labour government was installed in 1997, there was surprisingly little change of direction. Prime Minister Tony Blair famously declared his three priorities to be "education, education, and education" (Blair, 1996), and once in office, he set about launching an "unprecedented crusade to raise standards" (Blair, 1999). The major elements of existing policies were all retained and, if anything, strengthened (Chapman & Gunter, 2009; Phillips & Harper-Jones, 2003). However, the established focus on overall standards of school and system performance was overlain by a second concern. Ministers began to talk not simply about excellence but about "excellence for the many, not just the few" (Blunkett, 1999). The issue that concerned them was essentially one of educational—and, ultimately, social—equity. Despite the radical reforms of the school system, some groups of students appeared to be getting left behind. In particular, there seemed to be an intractable link between disadvantaging factors in students' social background—as indicated in particular by low family income—and poor educational performance (see, e.g., DfES, 2005b; Kelly, 2005). This was seen by New Labour governments as a particular example of the wider phenomenon of "social exclusion," understood as

> what can happen when people or areas have a combination of problems, such as unemployment, discrimination, poor skills, low incomes, poor housing, high crime and family breakdown. These problems are linked and mutually reinforcing. Social exclusion is an extreme consequence of what happens when people do not get a fair deal throughout their lives and find themselves in difficult situations. This pattern of disadvantage can be transmitted from one generation to the next. (Social Exclusion Task Force, 2009)

The preferred response of governments to social exclusion in this sense was to direct targeted interventions at those "people or areas" experiencing the acutest problems. So, for instance, they initiated a child poverty strategy (HM Treasury, 2008) targeted at the poorest families and aimed at lifting their children above the poverty line. Likewise, they put in place a neighborhood renewal strategy (Social Exclusion Unit, 1998) aimed at tackling the interlinked problems of the poorest places in the country. In the school system, the equivalent was a wide range of strategies targeted at particular groups of low-attaining students, or at poorly performing schools, or at areas where educational standards were low (Antoniou, Dyson, & Raffo, 2008). Typically, these strategies made available extra resources and support, but in return expected a measurable improvement in performance. The overall aim was one of "narrowing the gap in outcomes" (DCSF, 2007) between the majority of students who were judged to be doing well in the (reformed) education system and those minorities of students who, for various reasons, were doing badly. Because educational success was regarded as an indispensible basis for generating good life chances, narrowing the gap in outcomes came in turn to be seen as a necessary step toward creating a more equitable education system and, ultimately, a more equitable society. As one Secretary of State for Education put it:

> I see my department as the department for life chances. And that is why I see it as my job to boost social mobility . . . Our task is to make sure that for everyone involved in learning, excellence and equity become and remain reality. (Kelly, 2005)

EQUITY AND EXTENDED SCHOOLS

It is in this context that New Labour governments began to pursue an interest in what have become known as "extended schools" or, latterly, "extended services in and around schools." There is a long history in England of schools of this kind, though interest had been somewhat dormant during the 1980s and 1990s when attention was focused on standards-based reforms (Cummings, Dyson, & Todd, in press). The first re-awakening came in the form of a proposal for the development of Schools Plus (DfEE, 1999a) as part of the National Strategy for Neighbourhood Renewal. Within this context, the additional services and activities offered by such schools were seen as part of an overall, multistrand strategy right across the public services for combating social exclusion in the areas they served. The assumption was that children and young people in these areas needed additional support in order to learn effectively, families needed support in order to maintain stability, and communities needed better access to learning and leisure facilities. Schools Plus, therefore, embodied

> a vision of these schools in the future as centres of excellence for community involvement with more services on site or co-located. Other agencies and bodies would provide integrated support for pupils and offer complementary learning activities. Budgets would be focused at school level, and schools would be resourced to offer flexible individual learning programmes and to have close links to other phases of education. Clear achievement and other targets would be set and monitored. (DfEE, 1999a, p. 6)

When School Plus gave way to extended schools, the essential rationale remained. As government guidance explained:

> Extended schools are a key vehicle for delivering the Government's objective of lifting children out of poverty and improving outcomes for them and their families . . . A key priority, and challenge, for schools is to reach the most disadvantaged families within a universal framework of providing mainstream services for all families. (HM Government, 2007, p. 2)

Schools working in this way add yet another strategy to governments' drive to "narrow the gap" and create greater educational equity. However, they offer the considerable bonus of being able to work with families and communities as well as with school students, which means that they can also make a direct contribution to the wider social inclusion agenda.

In this respect, the aims of extended schools in England are closely aligned with those of similar schools in many other countries. Some time ago, Joy Dryfoos, one of the pioneers of the full service movement in the United States, argued for the necessity of such schools in urban areas, on the grounds that

> schools are failing because they cannot meet the complex needs of today's students . . . The cumulative effects of poverty have created social environments that challenge educators, community leaders, and

practitioners of health, mental health, and social services to invent new kinds of institutional responses. (Dryfoos, 1994, p. xvii)

In a similar vein, the Children's Aid Society, which sponsors "community" schools in the United States, argues that in the context of "new realities in the lives of children and families and new challenges to our public schools," a community school approach can

> provid[e] students with extended learning opportunities, bringing together the key developmental influences in children's lives—families, communities and schools—and providing essential supports, protection, guidance and opportunities, community schools are designed to help all students develop into productive adults who are able to earn a decent living, become responsible family members, and contribute to the larger society through good citizenship. (Children's Aid Society, 2001, p. 27)

Viewed in this way, full service and extended schools can be seen as equity-oriented interventions in the lives of children. They target the most disadvantaged children (and, in most cases, families), who are seen as those most at risk of suffering from social and economic change, and least likely to be supported effectively by traditional public services. They reorient services around the needs of those children, with a view to tackling the multiple problems by which children and their families are beset. In this way, they remove the barriers that prevent children learning, enabling them to realize better educational outcomes, and, in the fullness of time, to develop into "productive adults." This is an ambitious and important agenda. If the aims of such schools could be realized, they would constitute an important step toward breaking the link between disadvantaged social background, poor educational outcomes, and limited life chances that bedevils both the English education system and, to varying degrees, education systems across the world (OECD, 2008).

THREE PROBLEMS FOR FULL SERVICE AND EXTENDED SCHOOLS

Unfortunately, however, there is no unequivocal evidence that these aims can be realized. There are three reasons for this: the problematic nature of the evidence base itself, the limited scope of school actions, and the nature of the politics implied by full service and extended schools. I wish now to address each of these in turn.

The Problem of Evidence

In many cases, extended schools in England and their equivalents elsewhere in the world have been developed through funded initiatives that have been accompanied by more-or-less substantial evaluations. This means that there is an evidence base that can tell us something about what such approaches can achieve (see, e.g., reviews by Dryfoos, 2000; Richardson, 2009). The findings of this evaluation effort are remarkably consistent and are very much in accord with what the evaluations of extended schools undertaken by myself and colleagues have found in England (see, particularly, Cummings et al., 2007a). The broad consensus is neatly encapsulated in a review of 20 "community school" initiatives in the United States by Blank, Melaville, and Shah (2003). They conclude that there is evidence for positive outcomes in four domains:

- *Student learning*: Community school students show significant and widely evident gains in academic achievement and in essential areas of non-academic development.
- *Family engagement*: Families of community school students show increased stability, communication with teachers, and school involvement. Parents demonstrate a greater sense of responsibility for their children's learning success.
- *School effectiveness*: Community schools enjoy stronger parent–teacher relationships, increased teacher satisfaction, a more positive school environment, and greater community support.
- *Community vitality*: Community schools promote better use of school buildings, and their neighborhoods enjoy increased security, heightened community pride, and better rapport among students and residents. (Blank et al., 2003, pp. 1–2, emphases in original)

This consensus, however, disguises some significant weaknesses in the evidence base. Despite a substantial literature in the field, there is "little systematic, rigorous evaluation of the concept and its implementation" (Wilkin, White, & Kinder, 2003, p. 5). There appear to be two sets of reasons for this. One is that many evaluations are simply underpowered; that is, they are too short-term, too narrowly focused, or simply too lacking in robustness to produce reliable evidence. As one review of the research evidence concludes:

> There is . . . not enough long-term research because of the limits of funding for such ambitious work. Many studies have small samples, while others depend on self-reports rather than independent verification. (Henderson & Mapp, 2002, p. 18)

The second set of reasons is, however, to do with the technical difficulty of evaluating initiatives of this kind. Most educational evaluation works on a simple intervention-outcome model. It assumes, in other words, that there is an identifiable input that will produce some equally clearly identifiable outcomes. So, for instance, a new mathematics program will produce higher scores on mathematics tests, or a new procedure for contacting the home will reduce student absences. Evaluation of this kind depends on two main conditions: that there is an intervention that is clearly present in one situation but not in another (e.g., in one school but not another, or in the same school at different times), so that the two can be compared; and that outcomes from the two situations can be measured, or assessed in some other reliable manner.

Unfortunately, it is often the case that neither of these conditions obtains in evaluations of full service and extended schools, where there tends to be a series of complicating factors (Dyson & Todd, 2010). Typically, it is difficult to specify what the "intervention" in this case is, because different schools offer different packages of services and activities. Similarly, the leaders of these schools are likely to have very different expectations of the aims their full service and extended provision will fulfill. They may aim at outcomes (such as "lifelong engagement with learning" or "a positive community culture") for which there are no good measures, or which are only likely to materialize many years after any evaluation has concluded. Even where outcomes are identifiable, it may be difficult to attribute them to full service and extended provision because the processes leading to those outcomes are extremely complex or multiple other developments are taking place in the school at the same time. Finally, it may be difficult to compare outcomes between schools with and without extended provision because many schools may have elements of such provision, whether or not they are designated as full service or extended schools.

The problem is compounded when evaluations—and, particularly, national school accountability systems—insist that the principal way to judge the worth of an intervention is in terms of its more or less immediate impact on attainment outcomes. As another review puts it:

> It seems intuitively obvious that creating a context that interweaves home, school, and community, and that makes students valued and contributing members should have a powerful effect on student learning. But attempts to connect community collaborations and student test scores have been few and contradictory. (Keyes & Gregg, 2001, p. 40)

This places full service and extended schools in a highly vulnerable position. On the face of it, they should be major contributors to educational and social equity, and there is indeed some indicative evidence that this might be the case. However, moving beyond indicative evidence to something robust has proved highly problematic. This leaves the nagging doubt that the problem may not, in fact, lie with the technical challenges of evaluation. As one group of skeptical researchers have put it:

> [I]t is perhaps more probable that the reason conventional evaluations fail to pick up evidence of changes in outcomes is because the changes have not happened. (Rees, Power, & Taylor, 2007, p. 267)

The Problem of Scope

There is an important point in which this skeptical position accords with such positive evaluation findings as we have available. In the evaluation of extended schools in England, colleagues and I have found that the most powerful impacts are identifiable in relation to a small (though not negligible) minority of highly disadvantaged students and families (Cummings et al., 2007a). Impacts on wider populations are much more difficult to identify. This is only partly explained by the difficulty of tracing these wider impacts. It also reflects accurately where extended schools tend to concentrate their efforts. By and large, they put considerable resource and energy into providing additional support for children and adults who are in difficulties—offering them mentors, counselors, and family support workers; giving them access to social care, health, and adult learning professionals; and giving them access to a whole range of schemes and placements. Not surprisingly, the results of these interventions were, we found, often dramatic at the individual level as young people's lives were put back on track, families were helped through crises, and disenchanted adults suddenly found new opportunities opening up out of the dead ends at which their lives seemed to have arrived.

Impressive as all this is, what it highlights is the difficulty schools have in making any impact beyond the level of individual children, adults, and families. Even as they develop full service and extended provision, schools are restricted to what can be provided on the school site, usually on the basis of little or no additional funding. This is often quite adequate to supporting individuals through crises or giving them some additional learning opportunities. However, dealing with the individual consequences of inequalities is quite a different matter from tackling their underlying causes. By and large, full service and extended schools have no way of, for instance, increasing the income levels of the families with which they work, or improving their housing conditions, or changing the opportunities available to local people. Similarly, although they may be able to do a little to change the attitudes and values of children and their families, they have, despite the ambitions that some of them hold, no effective way of changing the community and social class cultures out of which those attitudes and values arise. They have, moreover, no way of reversing the cognitive and social disadvantages that appear to accumulate in children's lives long before they enter the school system and that seem to result from a complex interplay of family dynamics and the social contexts in which families live (Goodman, Sibieta, & Elizabeth, 2009).

In view of this limited scope, critics of New Labour's approach to tackling disadvantage have pointed out the contradiction between trying to solve what is essentially a sociostructural problem through interventions that take place only at the local—community, neighborhood, or school—level. Such interventions, they argue, are based on the view that social and economic disadvantage is a "residual" category, which can therefore be defined in terms of remaining "pockets" of disadvantage in a wider context of increasing affluence. They do not acknowledge that, in reality, local disadvantage is a particular manifestation of the wider social inequalities which are endemic to societies such as the UK. Far from being an exceptional feature of British society, which can be tackled by special state initiatives . . . areas of social disadvantage are complex, but normal manifestations of the characteristic patterns of social differentiation and inequality in the UK (and elsewhere). (Rees et al., 2007, p. 271)

The message is clear. In an inherently unequal society, the way to tackle disadvantage is not by putting in place ameliorative interventions such as extended schools, but by tackling inequality itself at a whole-society level.

The Problem of Politics

For the most part, the literature on full service and extended schools is silent on matters of politics. However, such schools are intensely political in the sense that they constitute an intervention in the lives of children and families facing disadvantage by school-based professionals, who themselves live under quite different circumstances. The good intentions of these professionals are not in doubt. However, in practice, they often operate on the basis of strongly deficit-oriented views of the people they are trying to help. Overwhelmingly, teachers and other school personnel offer accounts of the children and adults they work with that are couched in terms of dysfunctional community cultures, ineffectual parenting, and low aspirations (Crowther et al., 2003; Cummings & Dyson, 2007; Cummings et al., 2007a, 2007b, 2010). Although the material conditions under which these people live are acknowledged, the focus of schools' interventions is very much on changing cultural factors—encouraging children to be more aspirational, helping families to support their children's learning more effectively, or promoting engagement with learning in local communities. As a result, children, families, and communities facing disadvantage are positioned as contributors to their own difficulties and as incapable of finding a way out of those difficulties without the support of well-meaning professionals.

This state of affairs has perverse consequences for efforts to "help" them. As Ebersöhn and Eloff (2006), writing about community development more generally, explain:

The dominant approach to development . . . has been needs driven. This approach starts out by focusing on the needs, deficiencies and problems of communities, and accordingly devises strategies to address these needs and problems. [However,] the needs-based approach creates mental maps of communities that encourage its members to think about themselves as fundamentally deficient and as powerless victims of their circumstances. (p. 462)

The consequence is that the people who are being "helped" in this way are in danger of becoming more dependent on the support provided for them by professionals (Crowson, 2001; Small, 2004). At the same time, the focus on what we might call the "soft" correlates of socioeconomic disadvantage—the cultural values and family practices—draws attention away from the "harder" material realities and makes it more difficult to develop the political will to tackle those realities. As one American scholar of school–community relations observes:

> [E]xperts and educators acting within the four walls of the school cannot solve the problems of urban schools and inner-city communities, because these problems are the result of fundamentally unequal power relationships in our society. We need an active and engaged citizenry to build the kinds of relationships and the type of power necessary both to transform education school by school *and* to address the broader structures of poverty and racism that trap our youth. (Warren, 2005, pp. 167–168)

In the absence of conscious efforts to build this "active and engaged citizenry," the problem with full service and extended schools' efforts to change the conditions of disadvantage under which people live is not simply that those efforts are limited in scope. It is that they do little to disturb the existing asymmetrical power relations which see people living in disadvantage encouraged to remain as clients of benevolent professionals but not enabled to take control of their own lives or to challenge the status quo on their own behalf.

MOVING BEYOND THE PROBLEMS

It seems to me that the three sets of problems I have outlined in the previous section are serious but are not necessarily fatal to the proposition that full service and extended schools can make a major contribution to social and educational equity. However, if those problems are to be left behind, there will need to be some fairly fundamental rethinking of what such schools are, what they are for, and how their work is to be judged. In the remainder of this chapter, therefore, I wish to outline briefly what such rethinking might look like and where it might lead us.

Toward Appropriate Evaluation and Judgment

The conclusion I draw from the weakness of the evidence base on full service and extended schools is not that such schools have no significant impacts, but that those impacts need to be identified using appropriate methods. This in turn means being clear about what kinds of outcomes it is reasonable to expect from these schools and how these outcomes might, in fact, be generated. The problem with most current evaluation and monitoring efforts is, as I suggested earlier, that they look for inappropriate outcomes—usually, school-level improvements in measured attainments—produced through an implausibly direct input–output process.

The solution to this problem which my colleagues and I have used in our evaluation of extended school initiatives in England is to deploy a "theory of change" approach (Anderson, 2005; Connell & Kubisch, 1998). Technical details of our work are available elsewhere (Cummings et al., 2005, 2006, 2007a; in press; Dyson & Todd, 2010). In brief, however, theory of change starts from the premise that purposeful human action is guided by a (sometimes implicit) theory in the form of a set of assumptions about how particular actions will produce intended outcomes in a given situation. Policy and practice initiatives (such as the development of full service provision) are also underpinned by theories of this kind. Evaluation, therefore, is always likely to miss the point if it does not start from these underpinning assumptions about how the initiative is intended to work and what it is expected to achieve. It follows that the job of evaluators is to engage in "a systematic and cumulative study of the links between activities, outcomes and context of the initiative" (Connell & Kubisch, 1998, p. 16). Once they have done this, it is possible to identify more clearly which long-term outcomes are important to the initiative and what kinds of intermediate changes the initiative expects to stimulate so that those outcomes can be realized.

The advantages of this approach in respect of an initiative such as the development of extended schools are many. Most obviously, evaluators start looking in the right direction for outcomes. They do not, for instance, start looking for short-term impacts on students' attainments if the leaders of the initiative are in fact aiming to support family stability or promote children's health. The evaluation is not stymied by the lack of appropriate outcome measures or (within reason) by the lack of time for outcomes to emerge. If schools are aiming at a long-term and hard-to-measure outcome, such as transforming community cultures, evaluators can seek for evidence of a chain of intermediate changes likely, in the longer term, to lead to such an ambitious outcome. If that evidence is forthcoming, then it is likely (to put it no more strongly) that the intended outcome will emerge in the longer term, even if the evaluators themselves cannot wait to see this happen or devise a way of measuring it when it does happen. Moreover, tracing and testing that chain makes the diversity of schools' approaches and the absence of "off-initiative" schools less of a problem. The point is not to compare outcomes from a group of schools that are unequivocally "extended" with a group that unequivocally are not. It is to trace the way in which each individual school's extended provision produces changes, and the links between those changes and any longer-term outcomes in that school.

There is, however, a more general point to be made. Theory of change evaluations are not simply alternative means of achieving the same ends as more traditional approaches to evaluation or to monitoring the school system. On the contrary, they assume that outcomes may be broader and more elusive than the usual measures of student attainment. They also assume that they are generated not by a direct response to a tightly focused intervention, but by more indirect means, through which multiple interventions interact to produce multiple outcomes, often over considerable periods of time. Applied to the work of schools, therefore, they imply a different model of what schools are for and how they achieve their results from that which has become familiar in educations systems such as that in England that have been driven in recent years by standards-based reforms. Put simply, changing the model of evaluation also means changing the model of schools.

Rethinking Scope

Even with the most appropriate of evaluation methods, however, it is not possible to find outcomes that are not actually there. In particular, if full service and extended schools are to move beyond limited individual impacts, what I have called the problem of scope has to be addressed. The solution, it seems to me, is twofold. First, it involves recognizing that, in the context of unequal societies, even limited, ameliorative impacts can be valuable. As Riddell and Tett (2004), reviewing apparently disappointing outcomes from the "New Community Schools" initiative in Scotland, argue,

> Even if a given initiative proves relatively powerless to bring about major social change, this does not mean that its contribution is worthless. In this case there were a number of achievements but they were not *transformative* in the sense that social exclusion was tackled or social justice enhanced. Nevertheless they were *sustaining* for the schools that participated in that they were able to implement a number of initiatives that led to modest improvements in the lives of staff, pupils and parents. (p. 227)

Moreover, acknowledging that full service and extended schools alone cannot tackle the sociostructural causes of disadvantage does not mean that they cannot form part of a more wide-ranging and strategic effort to do so. With this in mind, the American scholar of urban education, Jean Anyon (2005), invites us to rethink what "counts" as education policy:

> Policies such as minimum wage statutes that yield poverty wages, affordable housing and transportation policies that segregate low-income

workers of color in urban areas and industrial and other job development in far-flung suburbs where public transport does not reach, all
maintain poverty in city neighborhoods and therefore the schools. In
order to solve the systemic problems of urban education, then, we need
not only school reform but the reform of these public policies. If, as I
am suggesting, the macro-economy deeply affects the quality of urban
education, then perhaps we should rethink what "counts" as educational policy. Rules and regulations regarding teaching, curriculum,
and assessment certainly count; but, perhaps, policies that maintain
high levels of urban poverty and segregation should be part of the educational policy panoply as well. (pp. 2–3)

Although this may sound idealistic, developments in England over recent
years suggest that it is, in fact, possible to align the work of extended schools
with more wide-ranging policies to address disadvantage. As we have seen,
the development of these schools went hand in hand with a neighborhood
renewal strategy aimed at tackling the other problems of disadvantaged
areas. It also went alongside a child poverty strategy (HM Treasury, 2008)
and the development of multidisciplinary support centers for families in poor
areas (DfEE, 1999b). Perhaps most important, extended schools began to
be incorporated in a broader "Every Child Matters" agenda (DfES, 2003a),
which aimed at creating integrated child and family services capable of
pursuing shared aims in a coherent way.

None of these policies (and many others like them) is problem free. However, they have created in England a framework within which the work of
individual schools can be located and which does seem to have had some
(albeit limited) effect in reducing inequalities (Hills, Sefton, & Stewart,
2009; Hills et al., 2010). Moreover, at the local level we are now seeing
the emergence of area approaches in which extended schools form part
of a closely integrated network of family and community support, which
itself contributes to a strategy for economic regeneration (see, e.g., Barnsley
Metropolitan Borough Council, 2005; Knowsley Metropolitan Borough
Council, 2008). Again, these developments are far from problem free, but
they indicate, at the very least, that the model of the lone extended school,
limited to providing a few additional services to children and families and
incapable of tackling the wider causes of disadvantage, is not the only one
that is possible.

Rethinking Politics

In the same way, the politics of full service and extended schools are capable of being rethought. Earlier, I stressed the deficit-oriented views typical
of many school professionals and the perverse consequences of these views
in reinforcing the dependency of people facing disadvantage. However, the
reality is a little more complex than this might suggest. In the course of our

work, colleagues and I have also come across multiple examples of mutually respectful relationships between school-based professionals and the people they serve. Perhaps more important, we have found schools where there is a conscious effort to engage children and local people in decision making and to help them develop the capacity to solve their own problems and advocate on their own behalf (Cummings et al., 2007a, in press).

Such efforts, taken to their logical conclusion, lead to what is sometimes known as the assets-based approach to community development. This approach

> values the capacity, skills, knowledge, connections and potential in a community. It doesn't only see the problems that need fixing and the gaps that need filling. In an asset approach, the glass is half-full rather than half empty. (Foot & Hopkins, 2010, p. 7)

This in turn implies a reshaping of the politics around full service and extended schools from one in which powerful professionals offer services to helpless children, families, and communities, to one in which professionals and community members co-produce the solutions to problems. In this respect, some of the developments in the United States, where there are stronger traditions of community activism and community organizing, may be significant (Glickman & Scally, 2008; Mediratta, Shah, & McAlister, 2009; Shirley, 2001; Warren & Hong, 2009). If community members are able to organize themselves and advocate for their wishes and interests, school professionals are likely to find it more feasible (and, indeed, necessary) to engage with them on an equal footing. Moreover, as Warren (2005) has argued, full service and extended schools are one of a range of emerging relationships between schools and communities in which the combined power of professionals and community members to tackle disadvantage is greater than their power if they work separately.

BEYOND FULL SERVICE AND EXTENDED SCHOOLS

In the light of this discussion, the evident limitations of full service and extended schools—and of the evidence regarding their impacts—does not lead me to despair of their potential contribution to social and educational equity. It is certainly the case that, so long as such schools remain in their current form, their contribution is likely to be limited and ameliorative at best, and might even be responsible in part for maintaining and legitimizing the relatively powerless position of the very people these schools seek to help. It is also the case that, if they continue to be judged in terms of their short-term impacts on measured attainments, they are likely to be seen to be largely ineffective.

However, there is no reason *in principle* why this should continue to be the case. More sophisticated, sensitive, and appropriate ways of evaluating their achievements are available. It also seems likely that the limited scope of these schools can be overcome if their work is aligned with local strategic efforts to tackle disadvantage, and with progressive national policies. Finally, the disabling relationships of dependency that these schools have sometimes fostered are not inevitable. Relationships between school professionals and local people based on mutual respect and the co-production of solutions are possible and seem capable of correcting existing asymmetries of power.

There is, therefore, considerable potential for full service and extended schools to contribute to social and educational equity. Yet we should not fool ourselves that this potential will be fulfilled easily. What I am advocating here would involve, in the English context at least, some significant shifts—in models of what schools are, what they are for, and how they are to be judged; in the relationship between them and others in the community; in "what counts" as education policy and its place within public policy as a whole; and in deeply rooted cultural views of how school professionals should work with community members and of what the local democratic governance of schools implies. Such shifts would disturb long-held views and threaten well-established interests. In the English context, they would require that what, at the time of writing, is still a new government, should take the pursuit of equity as seriously as the pursuit of excellence. Whether it will, only time will tell.

REFERENCES

Anderson, A. (2005). An introduction to theory of change. *Evaluation Exchange*, *11*(2), 12–19.

Antoniou, L., Dyson, A., & Raffo, C. (2008). En Angleterre. Les nouvelles politiques prioritaires (1997–2007), entre incantation et fébrilité. In M. Demeuse, D. Frandji, D. Greger, & J.-Y. Rochex (Eds.), *Évolution des politiques d'éducation prioritaire en Europe: Conceptions, mises en œuvres, débats.* Lyon: INRP.

Anyon, J. (2005). *Radical possibilities: Public policy, urban education and a new social movement.* Abingdon: Routledge.

Barnsley Metropolitan Borough Council. (2005). *Remaking learning: Leading change for success.* Barnsley: Author.

Blair, T. (1996, December 16). [The twentieth anniversary lecture given by the Rt Hon Tony Blair]. London: *The Guardian.*

Blair, T. (1999, January 15). [Speech by the Prime Minister Tony Blair about Education Action Zones]. London: 10 Downing Street.

Blank, M., Melaville, A., & Shah, B. (2003). *Making the difference: Research and practice in community schools.* Washington DC: Coalition for Community Schools, Institute for Educational Leadership.

Blunkett, D. (1999, July 19). *Excellence for the many, not just the few: Raising standards and extending opportunities in our schools.* [CBI President's Reception Address by the Rt. Hon. David Blunkett MP]. London: DfEE.

Callaghan, J. (1976, October 18). Towards a national debate [Speech by Prime Minister James Callaghan, at a foundation stone-laying ceremony at Ruskin College, Oxford]. London: *The Guardian.*

Chapman, C., & Gunter, H. (2009). A decade of New Labour reform of education. In C. Chapman & H. Gunter (Eds.), *Radical reforms: Perspectives on an era of educational change*. London: Routledge.

Children's Aid Society. (2001). *Building a community school*. New York: Author.

Clark, J., Dyson, A., & Millward, A. (1999). *Housing and schooling: A case-study in joined-up problems*. York: YPS.

Connell, J. P., & Kubisch, A. C. (1998). Applying a theory of change approach to the evaluation of comprehensive community initiatives: Progress, prospects and problems. In K. Fulbright-Anderson, A. C. Kubisch, & J. P. Connell (Eds.), *New approaches to evaluating community initiatives: Vol. 2. Theory, measurement and analysis*. Queenstown: Aspen Institute.

Cox, C. B., & Dyson, A. E. (Eds.). (1971). *The Black Papers on Education (1969, 1970)*. London: Davis-Poynter.

Crowson, R. L. (2001). Community development and school reform: An overview. In R. L. Crowson (Ed.), *Community development and school reform* (pp. 1–18). London: JAI.

Crowther, D., Cummings, C., Dyson, A., & Millward, A. (2003). *Schools and area regeneration*. Bristol: Policy Press.

Cummings, C., & Dyson, A. (2007). The role of schools in area regeneration. *Research Papers in Education, 22*(1), 1–22.

Cummings, C., Dyson, A., Jones, L., Laing, K., Scott, K., & Todd, L. (2010). *Evaluation of extended services: Thematic review: Reaching disadvantaged groups and individuals*. London: DCSF.

Cummings, C., Dyson, A., Muijs, D., Papps, I., Pearson, D., Raffo, C., et al. (with Crowther, D.). (2007a). Evaluation of the Full Service Extended Schools Initiative: Final report. Research report RR852. London: DfES.

Cummings, C., Dyson, A., Papps, I., Pearson, D., Raffo, C., Tiplady, L., et al. (2006). *Evaluation of the Full Service Extended Schools Initiative, second year: Thematic papers*. London: DfES.

Cummings, C., Dyson, A., Papps, I., Pearson, D., Raffo, C. & Todd, L. (2005). *Evaluation of the Full Service Extended Schools Initiative: End of first year report*. London: DfES.

Cummings, C., Dyson, A., & Todd, L. (2007b). Towards extended schools? How education and other professionals understand community-oriented schooling. *Children & Society, 21*, 189–200.

Cummings, C., Dyson, A., & Todd, L. (in press). *Beyond the school gates: Can full service and extended schools overcome disadvantage?* London: Routledge.

Cummings, C., Dyson, A., Todd, L. (with the Education policy and Evaluation Unit, U.o.B.). (2004). *An evaluation of the Extended Schools Pathfinder projects* (Research Rep. No. 530). London, DfES.

Department for Children, Schools and Families, IDeA & LGA (DCSF, I.L.). (2007). *Narrowing the gap in outcomes*. London: LGA.

Department for Education and Employment (DfEE). (1999a). *Schools Plus: Building learning communities. Improving the educational chances of children and young people from disadvantaged areas* (A report from the Schools Plus Policy Action Team 11). London: Author.

DfEE. (1999b). *Sure Start: Making a difference for children and families*. London: Author.

Department for Education and Skills (DfES). (2002). *Extended schools: Providing opportunities and services for all*. London: Author.

DfES. (2003a). *Every Child Matters*. Cm. 5860. London: The Stationery Office.

DfES. (2003b). *Full service extended schools planning documents*. London: Author.

DfES. (2003c). *Full service extended schools: Requirements and specifications*. London: Author.

DfES. (2005a). *Extended schools: Access to opportunities and services for all. A prospectus.* London: Author.

DfES. (2005b). *Has the social class gap narrowed in primary schools? A background note to accompany the talk by the Rt Hon Ruth Kelly MP, Secretary of State for Education and Skills, 26 July 2005.* London: DfES.

DfES. (n.d.). *Extended schools detailed guidance.* London: Author.

Dryfoos, J. (1994). *Full-service schools.* San Francisco: Jossey-Bass.

Dryfoos, J. G. (2000). *Evaluation of community schools: Findings to date.* Washington, DC: Coalition for Community Schools.

Dyson, A. (in press). Community focused schools. In E. Baker, B. McGaw, & P. Peterson (Eds.), *International encyclopedia of education.* New York: Elsevier.

Dyson, A., Millward, A., & Todd, L. (2002). *A study of the extended schools demonstration projects* (Research Rep. No. 381). London: DfES.

Dyson, A., & Todd, L. (2010). Dealing with complexity: Theory of change evaluation and the full service extended schools initiative. *International Journal of Research & Method in Education, 33*(2), 119–134.

Ebersöhn, L., & Eloff, I. (2006). Identifying asset-based trends in sustainable programmes which support vulnerable children. *South African Journal of Education, 26*(3), 457–472.

Foot, J., & Hopkins, T. (2010). *A glass half-full: How an asset approach can improve community health and well-being.* London: IDeA.

Glickman, N. J., & Scally, C. P. (2008). Can community and education organizing improve inner-city schools? *Journal of Urban Affairs, 30*(5), 557–577.

Goodman, A., Sibieta, L., & Elizabeth, W. (2009). *Inequalities in educational outcomes among children aged 3 to 16: Final report for the National Equality Panel, September 2009.* London: Government Equalities Office, National Equalities Panel.

HM Government. (2007). *Extended schools: Building on experience.* London: DCSF.

HM Treasury. (2008). *Ending child poverty: Everybody's business.* London: Author.

Gunter, H., Raffo, C., Hall, D., Dyson, A., Jones, L., & Kalambouka, A. (2010). Policy and the policy process. In C. Raffo, A. Dyson, H. Gunter, D. Hall, L. Jones, & A. Kalambouka (Eds.), *Education and poverty in affluent countries* (pp. 163–176). London: Routledge.

Henderson, A. T., & Mapp, K. L. (2002). *A new wave of evidence: The impact of school, family, and community connections on student achievement: Annual synthesis 2002.* Austin, TX: Southwest Educational Development Laboratory.

Hills, J., Sefton, T., & Stewart, K. (2009). *Towards a more equal society? Poverty, inequality and policy since 1997.* Bristol: Policy Press.

Hills, J. C., Brewer, M., Jenkins, S., Lister, R., Lupton, R., Machin, S., et al. (2010). *An anatomy of economic inequality in the UK: Report of the National Equality Panel.* London: Government Equalities Office & Centre for Analysis of Social Exclusion.

Kelly, R. (2005, July 26). *Education and social progress.* London: DfES.

Keyes, M. C., & Gregg, S. (2001). *School-community connections: A literature review.* Charleston, WV: AEL.

Knowsley Metropolitan Borough Council. (2008). *Future schooling in Knowsley—A strategy for change 2008–2010.* Knowsley: Author.

Mediratta, K., Shah, S., & McAlister, S. (2009). *Community organizing for stronger schools: Strategies and successes.* Cambridge, MA: Harvard Education Press.

Organisation for Economic Co-operation and Development (OECD). (2008). *Ten steps to equity in education.* Paris: Author.

Phillips, R., & Harper-Jones, G. (2003). Whatever next? Education policy and New Labour: The first four years, 1997–2001. *British Educational Research Journal*, 29(1), 125–132.

Rees, G., Power, S., & Taylor, C. (2007). The governance of educational inequalities: The limits of area-based initiatives. *Journal of Comparative Policy Analysis*, 9(3), 261–274.

Richardson, J. W. (2009). *The full-service community schools movement: Lessons from the James Adams Community School*. Basingstoke: Palgrave Macmillan.

Riddell, S., & Tett, L. (2004). New community schools and inter-agency working: Assessing the effectiveness of social justice initiatives. *London Review of Education*, 2(3), 219–228.

Shirley, D. (2001). Linking community organizing and school reform: A comparative analysis. In R. L. Crowson (Ed.), *Community development and school reform* (pp. 139–169). Oxford: JAI.

Small, M. L. (2004). *Villa Victoria: The transformation of social capital in a Boston barrio*. London: University of Chicago Press.

Social Exclusion Task Force. (2009). *Context for social exclusion work*. London: Cabinet Office, Social Exclusion Task Force.

Social Exclusion Unit. (1998). *Bringing Britain together: A national strategy for neighbourhood renewal, Cm. 4045*. London: The Stationery Office.

Warren, M. R. (2005). Communities and schools: A new view of urban education reform. *Harvard Educational Review*, 75(2), 133–173.

Warren, M. R., & Hong, S. (2009). More than services: Community organising and community schools. In R. Deslandes (Ed.), *International perspectives on contexts, communities and evaluated innovative practices: Family-school-community partnerships*. London: Routledge.

Wilkin, A., White, R., & Kinder, K. (2003). *Towards extended schools: A literature review*. London: DfES.

Contributors

René Antrop-González, Department of Curriculum and Instruction, University of Wisconsin–Milwaukee, United States

Inga Arffman, Finnish Institute for Educational Research, University of Jyväskylä

Dana-María Baldwin, University of Wisconsin–Madison, United States

Marie Duru-Bellat, Sociology of Education, Sciences-Po Paris, France

Alan Dyson, Centre for Equity in Education, School of Education, University of Manchester, United Kingdom

Becky Francis, School of Education, University of Roehampton, United Kingdom

Ofelia García, Urban Education, Graduate Center, City University of New York, United States

Tomás Garrett, University of Wisconsin–Milwaukee, United States

Miyako Ikeda, Directorate for Education, Organisation for Economic Co-operation and Development (OECD).

Koen Jaspaert, Faculty of Arts, Centre for Language and Education, Katholieke Universiteit Leuven, Belgium

JoAnne Kleifgen, Teachers College, Columbia University, United States

Pirjo Linnakylä, Finnish Institute for Educational Research, University of Jyväskylä

Elke Lüdemann, Institute for Economic Research, University of Munich, Germany

Alain Mingat, IREDU-CNRS, Université de Bourgogne, France

Christine Skelton, School of Education, University of Birmingham, United Kingdom

Peter Stevens, Department of Sociology, Ghent University, Belgium

Jouni Välijärvi, Finnish Institute for Educational Research, University of Jyväskylä

Piet Van Avermaet, Centre for Diversity and Learning, Ghent University, Belgium

Kris Van den Branden, Centre for Language and Education, Katholieke Universiteit Leuven, Belgium

Michel Vandenbroeck, Department of Social Welfare Studies, Ghent University, Belgium

Mieke Van Houtte, Department of Sociology, Ghent University, Belgium

William Vélez, Department of Sociology, University of Wisconsin–Milwaukee, United States

Karin Zimmer, Deutsches Institut für Internationale Pädagogische Forschung DIPF, Germany

Index